INDIGENOUS RIGHTS AND DEVELOPMENT

THE ARAKMBUT OF AMAZONIAN PERU
Andrew Gray

The Arakmbut are an indigenous people who live in the Madre de Dios region of the southeastern Peruvian rainforest. Since their first encounters with missionaries in the 1950s, they have shown resilience and a determination to affirm their identity in the face of difficulty. During the last fifteen years, the Arakmbut have been under threat from a gold rush that has attracted hundreds of colonists onto their territories. This trilogy traces the ways in which the Arakmbut overcome the dangers that surround them: their mythology and cultural strength, their social flexibility, and their capacity to incorporate non-indigenous concepts and activities into their defence strategies. Each area is punctuated by the constant presence of the invisible spirit world, which provides a seamless theme connecting the books to each other.

Volume 1
The Arakmbut: Mythology, Spirituality, and History

Volume 2
The Last Shaman: Change in an Amazonian Community

Volume 3
Indigenous Rights and Development: Self-Determination in an Amazonian Community

INDIGENOUS RIGHTS AND DEVELOPMENT

Self-Determination in an Amazonian Community

Andrew Gray

Berghahn Books
Providence • Oxford

First published in 1997 by

Berghahn Books

© Andrew Gray 1997

All rights reserved.
No part of this publication may be reproduced
in any form or by any means
without the written permission of Berghahn Books.

Library of Congress Cataloging-in-Publication Data

```
Gray, Andrew, 1955-
   Indigenous rights and development : self-determination in an
Amazonian community / Andrew Gray.
       p.    cm. -- (The Arakmbut of Amazonian Peru ; v. 3)
   Includes bibliographical references and index.
   ISBN 1-57181-875-8 (alk. paper).
   1. Mashco Indians--Ethnic identity. 2. Mashco mythology.
3. Mashco Indians--Land tenure. 4. Rural development--Peru--San
José del Karene. 5. Self-determination, National--Peru--San José
del Karene. 6. Autonomy (Psychology)--Peru--San José del Karene.
7. San José del Karene (Peru)--Social conditions. 8. San José del
Karene (Peru)--Ethnic relations.   I. Title. II. Series: Gray,
Andrew, 1955-    Arakmbut of Amazonian Peru ; v. 3.
F3430.1.M38G75    1996 vol. 3
306'.089'983--DC21                                     96-53649
                                                          CIP
                                                          r97
```

British Library Cataloguing in Publication Data

A catalogue record for this book is available from the
British Library.

Printed in the United States on acid-free paper.

CONTENTS

Series Preface	viii
Preface	xiv
Introduction	1
Chapter 1 Indigenous Rights from Patio to Palais	21
Chapter 2 State and Community in the Peruvian Amazon	54
Chapter 3 Losing Control: Arakmbut Territories and Resources	90
Chapter 4 Peoples, Persons, and Plurals	127
Chapter 5 Knowing Your Place: Cultural Heritage	162
Chapter 6 Arakmbut Governance	199
Chapter 7 Self-development: An Alternative to the Impasse	236
Chapter 8 Self-determination and Arakmbut Decolonisation	274
Conclusion	310
Orthography	323
Glossary	325
Bibliography	328
Index	343

TABLES

Table 3.1	Arakmbut communities and their territories	100
Table 3.2	Colonists on the territory of San José	123
Table 4.1	Examples of relational pronouns	147
Table 4.2	Names of maloca groups associated with each community	149
Table 4.3	Distinctions between flexible and fixed social criteria	151
Table 6.1	Arakmbut government	218
Table 6.2	Indigenous Communities in the Madre de Dios	231
Table 7.1	Difference between Colonists and Indigenous Views of Development	265
Table 9.1	Comparison of Indigenous and Non-indigenous views of rights	317

MAPS

Map 1	The indigenous peoples of Peru	3
Map 2	Harakmbut communities in the Madre de Dios	4
Map 3	Indigenous communities in the Madre de Dios	6
Map 4	Resource use in San José	113
Map 5	Planned road through San José	248

SERIES PREFACE

The Arakmbut are an indigenous people who live in the Madre de Dios region of the southeastern Peruvian rainforest. They are one of seven Harakmbut peoples all of which belong to the same linguistic family and which number in total about two thousand people. Despite having been known as Mashco and Amarakaeri during their forty years of contact with Peruvian national society, the people of the community of San José del Karene, with whom I have lived periodically since 1980, request that they be known as 'Arakmbut'.

Since their first encounters with missionaries in the 1950s, the Arakmbut have shown resilience and determination to affirm their identity in the face of difficulty. For the last fifteen years, the Arakmbut have been under threat from a gold rush that has attracted hundreds of colonists onto their territories.

This trilogy traces the ways in which the Arakmbut strive to overcome the dangers that surround them: They use their mythology to reinforce cultural strength; they demonstrate social flexibility in the face of alien peoples; and they show a discriminating capacity to incorporate positive non-indigenous concepts and activities into their defence strategies. Each of these factors reflects the constant presence of the invisible spirit world, which provides a theme connecting these books to each other.

The mythology of the Arakmbut is extremely important to them and to the way in which they perceive the world. On my departure from the community of San José del Karene after two years in 1981, I was told by several elders that I should write up my material around the three central myths. The first volume of this trilogy looks at each of these myths in order to introduce different facets of Arakmbut life.

The first myth, 'Wanamey', tells of the origins of the Arakmbut, the visible world and their social and cultural existence. It provides the impetus for a discussion of Arakmbut social organisation, which is based on various overlapping principles such as gender, age, residence, patrilineal descent and marriage exchange.

The second myth, 'Marinke', tells of the relationship between human beings, animal species, and the invisible spirit world. The visible and invisible worlds interconnect in ways that parallel social relations within the community, and this accounts for the constant presence of spirits and soul-matter in Arakmbut daily life.

The third myth, 'Aiwe', describes the abduction of an Arakmbut child by white people (Papa) who threaten his people with destruction, yet provide the means for their survival. It looks at the history of Arakmbut contact with outsiders, and charts the effects of the rubber boom and the period that the Arakmbut spent in the mission of Shintuya. After their dramatic escape in 1969, the Arakmbut founded their present communities.

The book ends with a discussion about the relationship between myth and history, showing how the Arakmbut recreate their myths at dramatic moments in their history. The conclusion reflects on power relations, the significance of the spirit world, and the relevance of the political concept of self-determination. Furthermore, embedded within Arakmbut myths are strategies for defence against colonisation. By looking at Arakmbut social organisation, cultural diversity, and historical experience, the first volume shows how myth provides a bridge linking the visible and the invisible worlds.

The second volume looks at the changes that have taken place in the community of San José del Karene between 1980 and 1992 in order to establish the two main dynamic factors involved in social, political, and cultural change – shamanism and politics. The book begins at the outset of the gold rush, with the death of the last great shamanic dreamer in the community. It continues by investigating the invisible world and the different techniques used by the Arakmbut to make contact with the spirits in order to promote the wellbeing of the people. Food production and curing are used to illustrate the complicated web of communication linking animals, spirit, and human beings to ensure Arakmbut growth and health. In both cases, a profound knowledge of Arakmbut biodiversity is necessary to enable a shaman to influence spirits.

Arakmbut politics is based on an understanding of the relativity of the social world, linking together the contrasting dynamics of desire and generosity. Through numerous daily encounters, the Arakmbut build up opinions, make decisions, solve disputes and acknowledge skilled persons through titles reflecting their prestige.

Arakmbut politics is in constant flux, shifting its emphasis from one social principle to another.

The period from 1980 to 1992 witnessed a marked change of social organisation within the Arakmbut community of San José del Karene, from a comparatively hierarchical to a more egalitarian pattern of life. The book offers multiple explanations for the changes, including the influence of the gold rush, the cumulative effect of the domestic cycle within the community, and the presence of the spirit world.

The book demonstrates that Amazonian communities are not fossilised settlements but that they are, and have always been, highly dynamic. The patterns of change over the last fifteen years in San José reflect shifts that have taken place throughout its history. The generating factor for this change comes from the invisible world, which enters both political and shamanic fields of activity. The conclusion explains why the death of the shaman provides a key to understanding the changes that have taken place and continue to take place in the community.

The third volume looks at the Arakmbut's growing awareness of their rights as indigenous peoples to their territories and resources. This awareness has risen concurrently with the growing development of indigenous rights internationally. The book takes the concepts of territory, people, cultural identity, government, development, and self-determination and looks at their emergence in a non-indigenous framework, juxtaposing them with their relevance in an Arakmbut context. The result is a mapping between indigenous and non-indigenous perspectives. Fundamental concepts such as 'territory' and 'peoples' broadly cohere, whereas concepts such as 'development' or 'self-determination' are present in practice but not expressed verbally.

While there is no necessary matching between human-rights concepts and indigenous perspectives, the Arakmbut quickly grasp the meanings of the terms as they become relevant to their practical conditions. With the violation of their rights, the Arakmbut are beginning to use the concepts of human rights as a means for defending their lives. The conclusion is that whereas non-indigenous human rights legislation receives its legitimacy by judicial means, the Arakmbut find their legal system legitimised through the spirit world. Whether through access to resources, expression of cultural identity, potential for development and the assertion of self-determination, the spiritual features of Arakmbut life are a constant presence. For non-indigenous observers, the invisibility of the spirit world makes it appear non-existent; however, overlooking its importance prevents outsiders from understanding and appreciating its significance in the Arakmbut struggle for survival.

The perspective adopted here is one of an outsider who has been invited into the periphery of Arakmbut social and cultural life in order to explain the complexities and depths of their views of the world to others. The discrimination that the Arakmbut suffer is based on ignorance and lack of respect on the part of non-indigenous people, who consider their territories and existence as a people to be fair game for predatory colonial expansion. These books are not meant to explain away the Arakmbut into tidy packages, but to use the non-indigenous imagery of structures and processes to understand the importance of their survival in the future as a people and to express solidarity with their struggle against adversity. The conclusions here are not timeless truths, but the particular views of a person on the margins of their world.

Each of the three main Arakmbut myths is divided into three parts corresponding to the head word, the centre word, and the whole word. Although each section is independent, it also fits into a series. As with the internal structure of the myths, so with the relationship between the myths themselves: each one looks at a different aspect of Arakmbut life from within a similar framework. The theme which links them together is the blending or separation of the human, animal, and spirit worlds in the face of the constant threat of outside forces – harmful spirits and non-indigenous peoples.

A trilogy is thus an appropriate structure for writing about the Arakmbut, and these three volumes fit together within the framework of their mythology. Each book takes a theme that relates to the three Arakmbut myths analysed in the first volume: creation and organisation of social and cultural life; growth and change in the relationship with the animal and spirit world; and the relationship with non-indigenous peoples, the threats they introduce, and the ways in which the Arakmbut can combat or avoid the dangerous consequences of invasion. However the relationship between the volumes like so much of Arakmbut life, involves the superimposition of layers of meaning covering different aspects of the triadic relationship.

The first aspect is the narrative form which starts from one situation and draws the listener through a variety of experiences to a new set of conditions at the end. Both artistically and ceremonially, a triadic narrative structure is common to many cultures. The famous anthropological example consists of rites of transition marked by three phases: separation, liminality, and reincorporation. The directional nature of these triadic rituals makes them as linear as the triadic narrative convention found so frequently in Victorian novels. The meaning comes from the sequence.

A different view of triadic structures comes from a more spatial perspective, which places less importance on the sequence. Arakmbut myths are 'cubist', in that any section or theme can be taken out of the main structure and transformed into a new story, showing the original narrative from another angle, or complementing the theme. This cubist or sculpturesque point of view is illustrated in Lambert's observation about Eric Satie:

> Satie's habit of writing his pieces in groups of three was not just a mannerism. It took the place in his art of dramatic development, and was part of his peculiarly sculpturesque views on music ... . It does not matter which way you walk round a statue and it does not matter in which order you play the three Gymnopedies' (Constant Lambert, *Music Ho!* 1948:92).

Another aspect of the triadic structure of Arakmbut myth is the way in which each part 'eavesdrops' on the others, picking up themes and characters who reappear in different guises, drawing our attention to various facets of the stories. In this way the myth becomes a triptych in which each 'panel' makes sense in term of its similarities to and differences from the other two parts. John Russell points out that the painter Francis Bacon has frequently painted in groups of three (1985:127): 'Bacon in his triptychs plays over and over again with the idea of the eavesdropper – the figure who looks across to the central panel and directs our attention to it.' Arakmbut myths demonstrate this element through thematic cross-currents, which appear as the shifting of meaning within a framework of imagery such as birth/death, growth or cooking.

Each Arakmbut myth combines narrative, multiple perspectives, and thematic cross-currents, all of which take the listener into different domains, looking at the world from a variety of angles. The three volumes here also share the three aspects of Arakmbut triadic relationships within their mythology. From one perspective, the three volumes constitute a narrative moving from the first volume's description of the difference between mythical structure and historical process, to the second volume's account of the process itself and the third volume's demonstration of the struggle as to who controls history.

The three books can be seen as cubist in that there is a common element in each volume that is investigated from three different angles. This is the position of the spirit world, which is a constant articulating presence for the Arakmbut in their everyday life, as guarantor of mythical knowledge, as cause of the generative process of change and as the legitimiser, arbitrator and guardian of acceptable behaviour.

The final triadic aspect of Arakmbut mythology that connects these three volumes is the constant movement from one aspect of the triptych to another. In each of these three volumes there is information that adds, reflects and comments on the material contained in the others. The creation myth of Wanamey reappears regularly through the pages, pointing to the main crises of Arakmbut existence; the constant relativity operating between human beings, animal species, and spirits appears in different guises throughout the visible and invisible worlds according to contexts such as the myth of Marinke, in curing rituals or when hunting; and the invasions arising from the gold rush have mythological connotations in the story of Aiwe and appear as a trigger for change with the emerging consciousness of indigenous identity.

In this way, these three volumes fit together as a trilogy, providing an interpretation of Arakmbut experience from a peripheral perspective and trying as far as possible to reflect the aims of Arakmbut mythology – to draw attention to the importance of the invisible spirit world in the present struggle for survival.

PREFACE

Unwary visitors to Geneva during late July are likely to encounter an extraordinary aspect of the international political scene if they decide to enter the Palais des Nations, the European centre of the United Nations. While wandering through the gloomily majestic mock-Egyptian corridors, usually inhabited by strutting UN bureaucrats, self-important government delegations, and well-lunched panels of experts, the uninformed could well wonder if they are on some surreal stage-set as they catch sight of feathered crowns, painted bodies, or exotic robes. They are, in fact, catching a glimpse of participants at the annual UN Working Group on Indigenous Populations (WGIP), which has been meeting since 1982 to discuss and analyse the problems facing indigenous peoples and to draft international standards of their rights.

The Working Group has become one of the largest UN meetings, where indigenous peoples mingle with smooth government representatives, sleek lawyers, intense academics, and support groupies. A huge meeting room houses the forum with a semi-circular seating plan symbolic of the whole UN structure – governments to the front and indigenous representatives to the rear. At the Working Group, several hundred indigenous people from all over the world present statements to five legal experts; they explain their specific problems and make suggestions for the international recognition of their rights.

In 1993, the Working Group, after meeting for eleven years, completed a draft of the Declaration on the Rights of Indigenous Peoples, which broadly reflects the desires of indigenous peoples and the opinions of human rights experts. In the following year, the draft was sent on to the Working Group's parent body, the Subcommission on the Prevention of Discrimination and the Protection of Minorities. The twenty-six experts of the Subcommission unanimously passed the draft and sent it up to the Commission on Human Rights, which is composed exclusively of government representatives. With governments now working on the draft at the UN Commission on Human Rights, however, indigenous peoples fear that amendments could seriously weaken the text. The current fate of the Declaration lies in the debate between governments and indigenous peoples as to what these rights should consist of and how they should be defined. This book contributes to that debate by analysing different interpretations of indigenous rights within the context of a particular set of problems facing the Harakmbut peoples of the Peruvian Amazon.

In 1991, 1992, and 1993, Harakmbut representatives from the Peruvian Amazon participated at the UN Working Group. They were university students from the Asociación de Estudiantes Indígenas de Madre de Dios (ADEIMAD) and came to Geneva with representatives from their indigenous organisation, the Federación Nativa de Madre de Dios y sus Afluentes (FENAMAD). In these years representatives from these organisations came to Geneva as part of a collaborative research project with the International Work Group for Indigenous Affairs (IWGIA), based in Copenhagen, on indigenous rights and self-determination in practice.

Entitled 'Development, Identity and Self-Determination', and funded by the Danish government's development agency, DANIDA, the IWGIA project focused on indigenous peoples in Alaska, Brazil and Peru, and investigated the factors inhibiting their full control over their lives, resources, and cultures. The research looked into indigenous peoples' rights and development by analysing the practical implications of fundamental concepts such as territory, cultural identity, and self-determination.

This book is based on my contribution to the project, which consisted of one year's field-research in the Madre de Dios region of the Peruvian Amazon. During this period I was affiliated with the Universidad Católica in Lima and FENAMAD. Most of the period between August 1991 and July 1992 was spent with the Arakmbut – one of the seven Harakmbut peoples of the Peruvian Amazon. They were earlier known as Amarakaeri, but, as will be explained in chapter four, some of the elders of the community specifically requested the change.

This period provided me, my partner Sheila Aikman, and our son Robbie, with the chance to revisit the Arakmbut community of San José del Karene after five years' absence. The community consists of about 150 indigenous people who dedicate their lives to hunting, gathering, fishing, horticulture, and gold panning. San José lies on the forest-clad banks of the red, gold-bearing river Karene, upstream from the Boca Colorado trading post. The Arakmbut appear inscrutable to a newcomer; after forty years of missionary contact, colonisation, and exploitation, they are understandably sceptical of outsiders. This scepticism penetrates their philosophy of life, their political system, and their daily activities. It is not a cynical scepticism, but one that gives credence only to ideas and practices which make sense in the light of experience.

I worked informally in the Arakmbut community, joining discussions and sharing in activities. I conducted few interviews because the Arakmbut do not like formal information gathering. Myths, songs, and curing chants came predominantly, but by no means exclusively, from the elder, Ireyo; and I received much help from young men and students, particularly Elias Kentehuari and Tomás Arike, who are from San José. During December and January 1993-4, I returned to the Madre de Dios to present my findings to FENAMAD and the Arakmbut in the form of a written report. As a result of the discussions arising from these conclusions, the Arakmbut of five communities established the basis for a 'Plan Arakmbut' proposal which is summarised in chapter seven. This was further discussed in a brief visit to most of the Arakmbut communities in August 1995.

The Arakmbut currently face the greatest threat to their survival since the decimation of their communities during the 1950s. A gold rush, which has plagued them for fifteen years, has attracted colonists who consistently encroach onto their territories and take their resources. The effect of colonisation on the Arakmbut has been a severe drop in their gold production and a fear that they will no longer be able to lead their lives according to their needs and desires. The situation is being made worse by a series of national legislative measures on land ownership and gold production which have been passed over the last few years by the neoliberal Peruvian government of Alberto Fujimori.

This book documents the problems facing the Arakmbut, describes how they perceive these threats, and looks at the measures they have taken to defend themselves. My previous work on the Arakmbut has concentrated on various aspects of their way of living and views of the world. When I first visited them in 1980, they recommended that I should begin my work by looking at three myths which embrace the main concerns of their existence: Wanamey, which tells of the creation of the Arakmbut; Marinke, which concerns growth and the continuity of life; and Aiwe, which details the Arakmbut's relationships with outsiders.

Preface

My work on these myths traces the connections between myth and history, emphasising the socio-cultural organisation and its relationship with the invisible world of the spirits (see Volume 1 of this series). The subsequent volume looks at the dynamics of Arakmbut social life and illustrates the way in which politics and shamanic activities mark changes in a community; it focuses on the connections between non-indigenous, internal, and spirit-influenced aspects of change.

These writings on the Arakmbut are attempts to understand aspects of their thought and behaviour, so that non-Arakmbut people can begin to appreciate the complexities of their life. I have emphasised regularly in these books that there is no-one version of the Arakmbut world and so universal agreement among the Arakmbut and outsiders on any particular interpretation is impossible. The information which I present, therefore, has the status of a hypothesis from the perspective of a person who is marginal to the community, but who has received the good-will and support of many Arakmbut in trying to grasp the complexities of their social and spiritual life.

This is not, however, to say that descriptions of the Arakmbut are a free-for-all, where anything can be written. The Arakmbut and the researchers who have lived with them share a range of perspectives within a common framework. This is largely because anthropological fieldwork is cumulative; each researcher reacts to the experiences and conclusions of previous workers. Meanwhile, the Arakmbut themselves make known and become aware of those aspects of their lives which are of interest and which they wish to promote. The result is neither incontestable fact nor imaginary fiction.

This was demonstrated recently when a book on shamanism was published in Spain which claimed to have been written about the Harakmbut, but which appeared to be plagiarised from J-P Chaumeil's writings on the Yagua of northern Peru. In spite of the different approaches of writers on the Harakmbut, their writings shared a family resemblance which was clearly discrepant with the book on shamanism. This, coupled with the unsubstantiated appearance of Yagua material in an Harakmbut context, led an inquiry by the the European Association of Social Anthropologists to find in favour of Chaumeil (European Association of Social Anthropologists 1995). I spoke to several Arakmbut about the case during my 1995 visit to their territory; they were unanimous that whereas they could accept genuine mistakes from sensitive writers, they objected strongly to misrepresentation because they had very limited means of response.

Whereas this book makes no claim to speak for the Harakmbut, it does trace a connection between ethnographic material and the political implications of indigenous rights. This volume is slightly different in orientation from the previous two in the series because, instead of trying to come to grips with Arakmbut concepts and to understand them from a non-indigenous perspective, it takes non-indigenous concepts of rights and investigates how they relate to the Arakmbut. The starting-point of the study is an analysis of the principal concepts used in the international standard-setting procedures of the United Nations. They are then related to the perceptions and conceptualisations of the indigenous Arakmbut people. In order to do this, a distinct perspective of Arakmbut life emerges, which connects understanding to practical activities and traces its commensurability with non-indigenous rights systems.

This book tries to place the Arakmbut firmly in the context of the indigenous movement which has taken hold within the field of human rights over the last twenty years. Representatives of the indigenous movement have, through lobbying and a successful presence at international bodies such as the United Nations and (to a far more limited extent) the International Labour Organisation, secured the recognition of a series of fundamental concepts which are crucial for the defence of the rights of indigenous peoples. By linking these concepts to the threats which the Arakmbut face, it is possible to see a growing awareness among the Arakmbut as they become active participants in the global movement for indigenous rights.

Throughout this text a theme recurs which provides continuity with the conclusions of my previous works about the Arakmbut. This is the importance of the invisible spirit world, which is a constant factor affecting everything from socio-cultural change to the thoughts and feelings of each person. When looking at rights among the Arakmbut, it is important to note that whereas for non-indigenous peoples, juridical principles provide legitimacy for activities and practices, for indigenous peoples such as the Arakmbut, the spirit world is the basis of legitimacy over questions as varied as territorial rights, the expression of social, cultural, and political identity, and as indicators of the potential for self-development and self-determination.

This volume is not designed to treat the spirit world as a 'God of the Gaps', to provide some determining explanation for an analysis. It is rather a reflection of how the Arakmbut see existence. The invisible world reappears regularly throughout this book because it is a constant presence for the Arakmbut. Although many myopic non-indigenous observers consider an invisible world to lack existence because it cannot be seen, to ignore its significance removes an element crucial to an understanding of the Arakmbut and their struggle for survival.

Preface

Each chapter of this work takes a concept which is prominent in indigenous affairs and looks at its basis in non-indigenous thought. The concepts are then placed in applied contexts through a series of illustrations of incidents in Arakmbut experience which illustrate their relevance to daily life. The book begins with an introduction looking at human rights, the indigenous movement, and the practical application of the terms. It is followed by a chapter which compares the Arakmbut and Peruvian government views on indigenous rights and the epistemological basis for these positions. Chapter two focuses on the Peruvian state, its legal provisions for indigenous peoples and how these affect the Arakmbut. The subsequent chapters look at the terms territory, peoples, culture, and governance, analysing what they mean in an Arakmbut context. The two last chapters take on the topics of self-development and self-determination and place these concepts together in a scheme which connects the relationship between development and indigenous rights through practical action.

The conclusion considers the importance of the invisible spirit world for the Arakmbut and how it acts as a constant presence, providing them with the orientation as to what constitutes appropriate behaviour, the means for their awareness and the assertion of their rights. The aim of the book is to outline the marked diversity of ways in which indigenous peoples put self-determination into practice and how these give rise to multifaceted possibilities for self-development in indigenous communities. The argument looks at contexts where indigenous community development can benefit from close research collaboration in the field and well-planned political and financial support. But above all lies the basic right of indigenous peoples to exercise control over their resources, customs, and knowledge and to ensure that any external interference takes place with their full and informed consent.

Acknowledgements and Intellectual Property Concerns

To thank the Arakmbut seems somewhat lame, as without them this book could not have been written. Their patience, encouragement, influence, and friendship not only affected me while I was with them but have taught me the importance of the indigenous struggle throughout the world. I feel an immense gratitude to them which will always draw us together. I received wonderful hospitality and kindness from the communities of Villa Santiago, Boca Ishiriwe, Boca Inambari, Barranco Chico, Shintuya, and Puerto Luz. In particular I should single out San José del Karene. where I spent most of my time. Everyone in the community co-operated and helped me but I would like especially to thank Tomás Quique and Mariaflor Bolivar, whose household we joined.

Similarly, to thank Sheila Aikman and our son Robbie for their support does not express how much of them is in these pages. Whether in the field or in Europe they have provided the inspiration for this work.

In Peru there are countless people who have helped me in my work: Thomas Moore, Lizzie Wahl, Klaus Rummenhöller, Heinrich Helberg, Didier Lacaze, Robert Tripp, and Padres Adolfo Torralba and Mixtel Fernandez have all provided me with essential insights. The Universidad Pontificia Católica del Perú provided me with an affiliation between 1991-2. I would like to thank Teofilo Altamirano and also Juan Ossio for their encouragement.

Indigenous organisations such as the Asociación Interétnica del Desarrollo de la Selva Peruana (AIDESEP), the Federación Nativa de Madre de Dios y sus Afluentes (FENAMAD), and the Asociación de Estudiantes Indígenas de Madre de Dios (ADEIMAD) have been of great assistance. In 1991 and 1992 I was affiliated with FENAMAD after approval by their full Congress, which provided me with much moral and political support. Furthermore, members of ADEIMAD Tomás Arike, Elias Kentehuari, Hector Sueyo, Fernando and Javier Tijé, Guillermo Omnia, and Visitación Irey have been of invaluable help in discussions of the ideas in this text. Other people whose help has been of great value are the staff at the Centro Eori, Puerto Maldonado, and the organisation of health consultants, Seri, from Cusco.

In Oxford I have also been an Associate Researcher at Queen Elizabeth House which kindly invited me to present some of the ideas in this report in a research seminar. I would like to thank Dr. Peter Rivière for the guidance he provided throughout my doctoral work on the Arakmbut, the influence of which is present throughout this text. Kaj Århem from the department of anthropology at the University of Gothenburg has kindly given me the opportunity to try out some of these ideas at seminars and I must thank Dan Rosengren for many helpful conversations. I would also like to thank Elvira Belaúnde and Howard Berman who provided crucial comments, which I hope are sufficiently reflected in the text.

Special thanks, above all, must go to all at The International Work Group for Indigenous Affairs in Copenhagen (IWGIA), which provided me with the financial and institutional resources to carry out this research as a part of the project 'Development, Identity and Self-determination'. I would like to thank Jorge Monrás from IWGIA who provided all the maps and diagrams. IWGIA is currently working on a programme of support for the Arakmbut and regularly publishes material on their current situation. IWGIA can be contacted at: Fiolstraede 10, 1171 Copenhagen K, Denmark.

I am very grateful for the initiative, inspiration, and encouragement of Jens Dahl, without whom this project would never have materialised. I have also appreciated discussions on aspects of this report with Teresa Aparicio, Gordon Puller, and Kathy Ideus and have greatly benefitted from their insights, specifically in the symposia held in Copenhagen in July 1991 and 1992.

I would also like to thank Georg Henriksen and my colleagues from the Bergen research programme 'Social Organisation, Systems of Knowledge and Resource Management' who in 1989, with grant 550.88/013 from the Norwegian Research Council, funded my initial research work on environment and development prior to the IWGIA programme. Finally I would like to express my gratitude to the Danish government development agency DANIDA which, through the IWGIA research programme, has provided me with financial support for this three year research project and whose interest in indigenous peoples, particularly those of the Peruvian Amazon, has made an important contribution to the recognition of their rights.

The Arakmbut of San José have provided most of the information contained in this book and its perspective predominantly shares their orientation. Nevertheless, members of other Arakmbut communities have checked some of the information, and although there are discrepancies in detail, the main results are broadly similar. For this reason the information here, outside of its interpretation, is part of the Arakmbut cultural heritage.

Because Arakmbut is a collective tradition it would be inappropriate to attribute each piece of evidence personally. The only exception has been the acknowledgement of Ireyo, the myth teller, who is known and respected for his knowledge. On the basis of my discussions with the community, I am aware of no information in this text that has been told to me in confidence. After extensive talks with members of San José, other Arakmbut communities, and FENAMAD, I have received broad support for publishing this book. This in no way obliges those groups to agree with my particular interpretation.

* * *

This book is dedicated to the memory of my first Arakmbut friend, José Quique Cameno, shot by colonists, Rio Pukiri, 15 March, 1987.

"How can we make any progress in the understanding of cultures, ancient or modern, if we persist in dividing what people join and in joining what they keep apart?"

Hocart, The Life-Giving Myth

INTRODUCTION

'What is self-determination?' asked the young Arakmbut man.
'Why do you ask?' I said.
'I have heard the word used by indigenous leaders in the town and have read it. My father and the old men do not know what it is and so I am asking you.'
'Self-determination is about the right of indigenous peoples to control their lives without unwanted outside interference.'
'Oh, so that's what it is.'

This conversation took place in the indigenous Arakmbut community of San José del Karene at the end of December 1991. The young man was an indigenous secondary school student at the rainforest town of Puerto Maldonado, two days down river from the community. He was passing his vacation with his family and had visited me for a talk. This brief encounter encapsulates the purpose of my visit to the Arakmbut and my research into the meaning of indigenous rights in an Amazonian community.

The young Arakmbut man had encountered the notion of self-determination for indigenous peoples, but he was not aware of its precise meaning. When I provided an orientation as to how the term could be used in an indigenous context, his response was immediate recognition. He understood what self-determination meant without any further explanation. Although the word came from outside his vocabulary, its meaning did not come from outside his experience; it referred to his everyday life and the difficulties which he and his community constantly face. Indigenous peoples such as the Arakmbut recognise self-determination because they are self-determining. This book traces the process whereby, as indigenous peoples' capacity to be self-determining becomes increasingly under threat from colonisation, they become increasingly aware of their rights.

The Arakmbut people provides a useful starting point for looking at this question because they combine many of the features which outsiders often use to categorise indigenous peoples. They are neither completely integrated into the Peruvian state, nor are they completely isolated from the indigenous movement. They retain a substantial amount of distinct cultural thinking and social practices, while at the same time any visitor to an Arakmbut community will see the influence of national Peruvian culture in styles of dress, the presence of radios, and an awareness of the non-indigenous world around them. They are proud of their Arakmbut heritage, and their language (a defining feature for them) is strong; yet they face social, cultural, and even physical threats from the process of colonisation which is taking place on their lands.

Rather than see the Arakmbut as an isolated case, this book considers them as illustrative of the sorts of problems with which indigenous peoples are confronted all over the world. By grasping the difficulties which they face, it should become possible to see the importance of interpreting indigenous rights in ways which will provide them with the moral andpolitical support necessary to defend their lives, territories, and heritage.

The Arakmbut

The Arakmbut are one of seven Harakmbut-speaking peoples in the Madre de Dios rainforest of southeastern Peru. The Madre de Dios is the most culturally diverse part of the Peruvian Amazon; there are nineteen ethno-linguistic groups in the area, belonging to four language families: Arawak, Panoan, Tacanan, and Harakmbut (d'Ans 1973). The Tacana languages are spoken mainly downriver from Puerto Maldonado by the Ese'eja and possibly a group of Iñaparis. Arawak languages are spoken in the upper Madre de Dios by the Matsigenka and Piro. To the northeast, on the opposite side of the Madre de Dios river from Puerto Maldonado, are the main concentrations of Panoan speakers such as Amahuaca and Yaminahua (see Map 1). Apart from these peoples there are Shipibo, Asháninka, Santarosino, Huitoto, and Cocama, who were brought down from the central and northern Peruvian rainforest during the rubber boom as slaves and whose descendants have re-established their communities not far from Puerto Maldonado.

The Harakmbut number about two thousand people and are divided into the Arakmbut (also known as Amarakaeri), Wachipaeri,

Introduction

Arasaeri, Sapiteri, Pukirieri, Kisambaeri (also known as Amaiweri), and Toyeri (see Map 2). They have a unique language which appears to have no direct relationship with that of any other indigenous peoples of the Amazon (Ribeiro & Wise 1978:203).

Map 1: The indigenous peoples of Peru

- Towns
- ~ Rivers

Introduction

The Harakmbut, as a whole, have had connections with other peoples throughout their history (Gray 1987b:308). Archaeological and historical evidence shows that the Incas regularly visited the region and traded with peoples living in the headwaters of the Madre de Dios (Nordenskjöld 1902; Mensoza Marsano 1974; Aikman 1982; Wahl 1987:66). This contact is borne out by Arakmbut myths which refer to the Master of the Forest as Manco (an Inca name) – also known as *mbegnko* (the woodpecker) – who brought fire to human beings.

Map 2: Harakmbut communities in the Madre de Dios

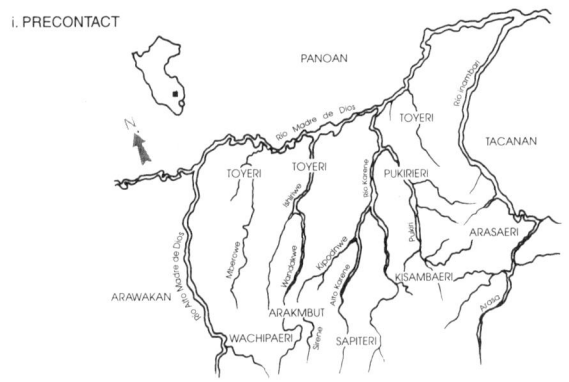

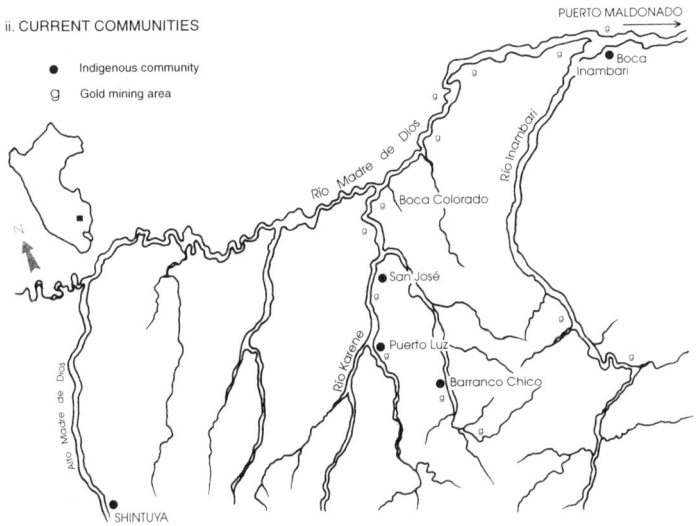

During the colonial period, the Madre de Dios was used as a source of coca, and plantations sprang up immediately after the Spanish invasion in or near Wachipaeri territory (Fuentes 1982:8). Even though there was a decline in production in the eighteenth century, there were still three hundred plantations in the area by the time of Peruvian independence in 1821 (Bovo de Revello 1848; Raimondi 1879; Lyon nd.). Nevertheless, in spite of these activities at the fringes of Harakmbut territory, there were few concerted efforts to penetrate the area until the nineteenth century. Expeditions came and went, but the first really devastating attack on the Harakmbut came in the 1890s.

During this period the infamous rubber boom was at its height and rubber barons such as Carlos Fermin Fitzcarrald and Nicolás Suárez were fighting for control of the lucrative trade route to Iquitos. In August 1893, Fitzcarrald opened the way from the Ucayali to the Madre de Dios river with the isthmus which takes his name, and this sounded the death knell for the Toyeri, thousands of whom were killed or forced into slavery (Reyna 1942; Rummenhöller 1985; Pennano 1988:158). The Arasaeri were similarly devastated by the rubber boom with incursions coming from Bolivia under the rubber baron Suárez (Rummenhöller 1984).

The initial encounter between the indigenous peoples of the Madre de Dios and the Peruvian state has taken place either through invasion by colonists or through the Church. In 1902 the Dominican missions entered the Madre de Dios. They worked initially with the Matsigenka and subsequently with the Ese'eja. The first Harakmbut people to be contacted by the Dominicans were the Wachipaeri who live in the headwaters of the Madre de Dios. They already had contact with the coca farms in the Cosnipata area but the main threat to their lives came from illness rather than murder or slavery. Regularly, the Wachipaeri suffered from waves of smallpox epidemics which continued until the 1940s. During that same period, the Dominicans made contact with the Sapiteri and Pukirieri, and ten years later entered the territory of the Arakmbut and Kisambaeri.

The last Harakmbut people to be contacted by the Church were the Arakmbut who, apart from a brief sighting in 1940, were met by the missionary Padre José Alvarez in 1950. The process of bringing the Arakmbut to the mission of Shintuya in 1956 was aided by a devastating epidemic of yellow fever which raged through the communal houses. By 1960 the Harakmbut had been 'reduced' into the missions of El Pilar in the lower Madre de Dios and Shintuya, in the upper Madre de Dios. However, tensions within Shintuya led most of

Introduction

the Arakmbut to escape between 1969 and 1974 and during this period they formed native communities downriver on traditional Harakmbut territory (Torralba 1979). The details of this process of contact, decimation, and proselytisation is described in the first volume of this series.

The five Arakmbut communities (Shintuya, Puerto Luz, San José del Karene, Barranco Chico, and Boca Inambari) have territories recognised by the Peruvian Law of Native Communities (22175), but each suffers from land invasions by colonists looking for gold or

Map 3: Indigenous communities in the Madre de Dios

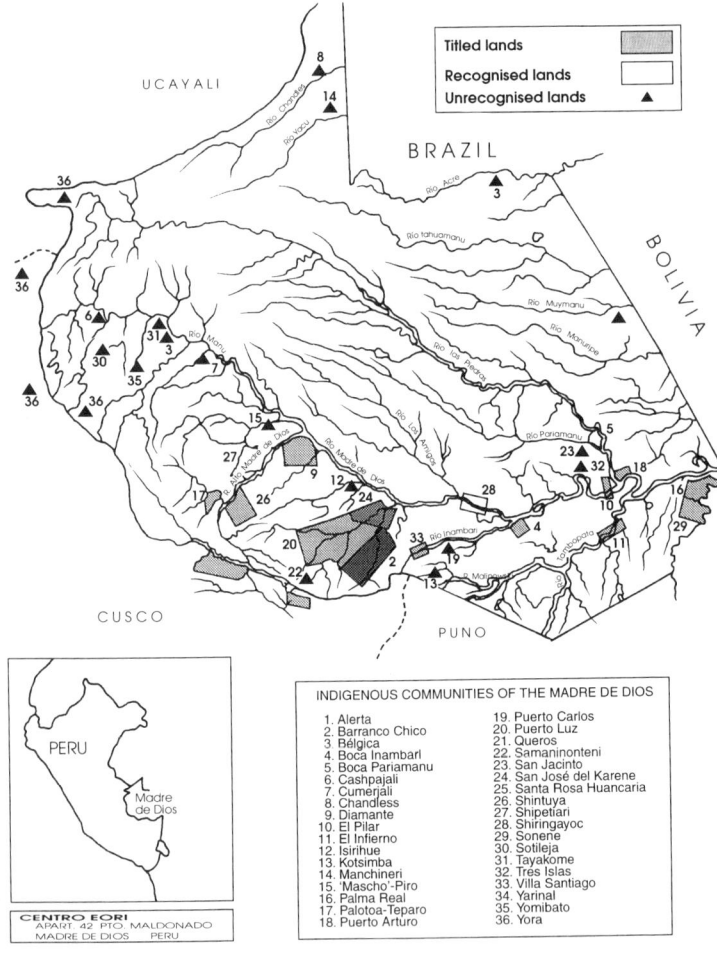

other resources (Gray 1986). Arakmbut political economy is based on hunting, fishing, gathering, horticultural work in the gardens *(chacras)*, and extraction activities, such as gold panning or timber extraction.

Every community has a school, with teachers provided either by the state or the missionary educational network, RESSOP. A few students study in Puerto Maldonado with grants from the Inka region (with its capital in Cusco). Four of these students are currently completing their higher education in Lima with grants from international agencies. Occasionally health workers are posted to a community, but with the exception of Shintuya, which lies on a road to Cusco, there is a high staff turnover and no resources. Transportation is time-consuming and expensive by river and so the communities further away from urban centres (Puerto Luz, San José and Barranco Chico) seem comparatively remote.[1]

Organisation from Community to International Level

Each community participates every three years in the Congress of the Federación Nativa de Madre de Dios y sus Afluentes (FENAMAD), which was founded in 1982 and tries, with practically no resources, to represent the concerns of the communities to local and national authorities. Furthermore, through FENAMAD, the indigenous communities of the Madre de Dios gain access to the wider indigenous movement.

FENAMAD is a member of the Asociación Interétnica de Desarrollo de la Selva Peruana (AIDESEP), which was established in 1980 and has its centre in Lima. It represents about thirty federations, similar to FENAMAD, from throughout Peru. AIDESEP carries out territorial defence, health, and education projects while campaigning on indigenous rights to the central government. Local offices in each region of Amazonian Peru are designed to secure efficient communication between the centre and local federations.

AIDESEP itself is part of a broader coordinating body of national Amazonian indigenous organisations called COICA (Coordinadora Indígena de la Cuenca Amazónica), which links organisations from Colombia, Venezuela, the Guianas, Brazil, Bolivia, Ecuador, and Peru. COICA operates internationally as a member of the Interna-

1. In Volumes 1 and 2 of this series, I provide a perspective of Arakmbut socio-cultural life. However, there are other accounts, such as Califano 1989a, 1989b, 1982; Rummenhöller 1985, 1987; Wahl 1987; Moore nd; and a forthcoming text by Helberg; all provide important insights into the Arakmbut people.

tional Alliance of the Indigenous Tribal Peoples of the Tropical Rainforest, which brings regional organisations together from the Americas, Africa, and Asia into an international network which has its secretariat in London.

In this way, the Arakmbut are connected from their community organisation through FENAMAD, AIDESEP, and COICA to the International Alliance. This should not be seen as a hierarchical set of Chinese boxes, but rather as spheres of influence moving out from the community. The ripples of problems which occur on a community level can, with the right information management, give rise to international representation. This, however, clearly depends on the efficacy of each organisation. In practice local communities and federations utilise whatever contacts they have to promote their cause locally, nationally, and internationally.

Before 1980, the Arakmbut defended their rights as members of their community and their people. As there were so many distinct peoples in the Madre de Dios of different sizes and speaking different languages, they helped to establish FENAMAD as a representative organisation at the community level to embrace the spectrum of ethnic diversity. However, the Harakmbut, who are the largest indigenous grouping in the Madre de Dios, became concerned that FENAMAD, operating on an organisational basis which transcended ethnic boundaries, was not reflecting the needs of the Harakmbut as peoples. In 1993, a Consejo Harakmbut (COHAR) was formed as an ethnic body within FENAMAD. COHAR reflects the fact that the indigenous movement is ultimately one of peoples which utilise the framework of organisations to advance their concerns and claims.

Indigenous Peoples

'Indigenous', according to the dictionary, refers to someone who is in-born or native to a land or region which is under the control of outsiders. It broadly refers to a people as a whole, as well as to the quality of a person, which relates collective identity to a particular area. It also distinguishes a people from other, 'alien' peoples who have subsequently settled the territory. This permanent settlement without the consent of the indigenous peoples is the basis of colonisation. Incorporated into this notion of indigenous is the sense of being disadvantaged and discriminated against. Indigenous peoples consider that the only way of overcoming these obstacles is to secure their right of self-determination – to control their lives and resources.

Introduction

This book is an attempt to build up an idea as to what self-determination means for indigenous peoples in practice.

Indigenous peoples frequently resent efforts to define them from the outside, as is clear from the statements to the UN Working Group on Indigenous Populations over the years. However, one definition from the UN which, although convoluted, has much general support comes from José Martinez Cobo (1986: paras 378-80). This provides a general orientation to the area under study here.

> Indigenous communities, peoples and nations are those which, having a historical continuity with pre-invasion and pre-colonial societies that developed on their territories, consider themselves distinct from other sectors of the societies now prevailing in those territories, or parts of them. They form at present non-dominant sectors of society and are determined to preserve, develop and transmit to future generations their ancestral territories, and their ethnic identity; as the basis of their continued existence as peoples, in accordance with their own cultural patterns, social institutions and legal systems.
>
> This historical continuity may consist of the continuation, for an extended period reaching into the present, of one or more of the following factors:
>
> (a) Occupation of ancestral lands, or at least of part of them;
> (b) Common ancestry with the original occupants of these lands;
> (c) Culture in general, or in specific manifestations (such as religion, living under a tribal system, membership of an indigenous community, dress, means of livelihood, life-style, etc,);
> (d) Language (whether used as the only language, as mother tongue, as the habitual means of communication at home or in the family, or as the main, preferred, habitual, general or normal language);
> (e) Residence in certain parts of the country, or in certain regions of the world;
> (f) Other relevant factors.

Five features mark this definition: self-definition (also included in ILO Convention 169, Article 1[2]), non-dominance, historical continuity, ancestral territories, and ethnic identity (Kingsbury 1995:26).[2] It shows that any orientation to the term indigenous has to embrace polythetic criteria.

The Rise of the Indigenous Movement

The indigenous movement is a wave of politically active peoples who have, with marked success, asserted their rights over the last

---

2. This definition also gives ground for concern in some quarters. Kingsbury (1995:29) comments that its stress on historical continuity might exclude some indigenous peoples in Asia who should otherwise be included.

thirty years. As noted in the Madre de Dios, some indigenous peoples represent themselves as peoples, while some use the form of representative organisations to claim their rights. Indigenous organisations have existed throughout the world for many years but their recent proliferation is marked.

At the turn of the century, for example, there was an indigenous organisation among West Coast peoples of Canada (Frideres 1983:233 ff.) while in the United States, the Alaskan Native Brotherhood and the Society for American Indians arose in the 1920s (Olsen & Wilson 1984: 92-3). However, during the 1960s a florescence of indigenous organisations took place. In 1973, for example, there were forty-eight indigenous organisations in Canada, a four-fold increase from ten years previously (National Indian Brotherhood 1973:6). At the same time similar increases in the numbers of indigenous organisations were happening in the United Sates, Australia, and Scandinavia.

Throughout the 1970s the indigenous movement spread throughout Central and South America. The foundations of the Shuar Federation in Ecuador and the Aguaruna Huambisa Council in Peru demonstrated that mobilisation was increasing on a local level with particular indigenous peoples. By the end of the 1970s, national indigenous organisations had sprung up in most countries in Central and South America.

Meanwhile, international initiatives were underway. The International Indian Treaty Council was established in 1974 in the United States and the World Council of Indigenous Peoples in 1975 in Canada. These bodies were instrumental in initiating the 1977 NGO conference in Geneva which effectively established the indigenous movement as an international body. The consolidation of the indigenous organisations and peoples throughout the Americas in the 1970s and early 1980s was paralleled by an upsurge of interest in Asia.

The Philippines has always had strong indigenous politicisation and during the 1980s the movement spread throughout Asia. East Timor, West Papua, Burma, and the Chittagong Hill Tracts of Bangladesh all expressed their interest in participating in the initiatives. India formed its first Tribal and Indigenous Council in 1986, and in 1992 the Asian Indigenous Peoples Pact was formed, representing indigenous peoples from as far apart as Nagaland, Burma, Thailand, Malaysia, Taiwan, and Japan.

During the 1980s the Pacific peoples became more involved in indigenous affairs. The native Hawaiians, West Papuans, and those who joined in the Free and Independent Pacific Movement, particularly the Kanaky and Tahitians, all participated at different fora, expressing indigenous perspectives on their problems. More recently, the people of Bougainville have been particularly strong, reclaiming their rights in their conflict with Papua New Guinea. In 1990, the indigenous peoples in the north of the then Soviet Union formed their own indigenous organisation (IWGIA 1990). This organisation has been developing over the last three years and regularly attends the UN Working Group in Geneva. The indigenous peoples of Africa, in the form of East African pastoralists and the Twa (Pygmies), began to assert their rights as indigenous in the late 1980s. Since then, Kwe (Bushmen), pastoralists, and Twa, in particular, have become active participants in the indigenous movement. A conference organised by IWGIA in Copenhagen during June 1993, with indigenous peoples from Africa, demonstrated the growing influence of the indigenous movement through the continent.

The Structure of the Indigenous Movement

The decolonisation of the European empires (particularly British, French and Dutch) between the 1940s and 1960s provided a context for indigenous peoples in the United States, Canada, and Australia to seek their own liberation from state colonisation. At the same time, a consequence of decolonisation was an increase in the number of states from under fifty members of the UN in 1948 to a current number of over 180. The indigenous peoples within these states also wanted their rights recognised.

The 1960s was the also time when, influenced by the civil rights and anti-racist movements, the idea of 'Red Power' in North America and the 'Black Power' of Aboriginal peoples in Australia took root. Connected with the rise in human rights movements was a growth in literacy and accessibility to the media which made indigenous struggles more apparent to the general public. Furthermore, funding organisations from both private and public sources provided material support for the establishment of indigenous organisations.

Out of these events in the 1960s, the indigenous movement emerged with a growing awareness of a common struggle. This mobilisation of indigenous peoples relates to a view discussed by Eyreman and Jameson (1991), who see movements as processes of collective creation that take place within a political historical context. The knowledge (termed by them 'cognitive practice') provided by the movement constitutes a new way of looking at the state from within. In an indigenous context this has been a challenge to the interpretation of colonisation as a process referring exclusively to overseas empires, but it can also take place within the boundaries of a state. Furthermore, the worldview of indigenous peoples, based on collective rights to territory and cultural respect, presents a challenge to the status quo of human rights which has been used to dealing with individual rights within the territorial integrity of states.[3]

The indigenous movement has features which lead to several problems of consistency for indigenous peoples. Alberoni (1984), for example, describes the 'nascent state' of a movement that consists of a discontinuity from life as it is seen by those outside of the movement. The indigenous critique of the state is relevant in this context, as is the common feeling that indigenous peoples are different from other peoples in the world. This aspect of the indigenous movement manifests the fervour and charisma of those who are changing the system.

On the other hand, aspects of the indigenous movement have also become institutionalised ('routinised' in a Weberian sense). For example, some indigenous peoples, particularly state-sponsored organisations, can become assimilated to government priorities and separate from their constituent organisations. These organisations can sometimes be effective as institutions but risk being compromised into taking positions which do not necessarily reflect the needs and desires of those directly affected by colonisation.[4]

3. The indigenous movement has not been alone in gaining strength over the last thirty years. Other social movements have emerged through the same period, particularly the women's movement, the anti-nuclear movement, and the environmental movement. Touraine (1978:29) sees social movements as 'the expression of the collective will' constituting opposition within a 'post-industrialist' society where a more fragmentary notion of social movement is replacing strict class struggle. To some extent the indigenous struggle blends in with this perspective, although the indigenous movement appears to be also an aspect of a larger processes of fragmentation which is taking place on a global level. Friedman (nd: 12-13) says, 'The crisis of identity in the center is expressive of a more general global crisis ... This crisis consists in the weakening of former national identities and the emergence of new identities ... based on "primordial loyalties", ethnicity, "race" local community, language and other culturally concrete forms ... The tendency to cultural fragmentation is ... a question of real economic fragmentation ... the beginning of a major shift in hegemony in the world system.
4. A difficulty for indigenous leaders is that they frequently need to be familiar with the national society to work more effectively. However, as they become more proficient, they can lose touch with their roots by using western concepts uncritically (Ramos 1994:160). Whereas this is a genuine concern for many indigenous peoples, it is important that the argument is not taken to extremes. Indigenous peoples are not isolated from the non-indigenous world, even in their communities, but are involved economically and politically in broader systems (Asad 1973; Nash 1975).

Alberoni argues that there is a general development from nascent state to institutionalisation; however, the indigenous movement contains both elements simultaneously because each organisation reacts to these aspects of movement in distinct ways and at different rates. The indigenous movement is thus a prime example of unity and diversity operating together, sometimes more in harmony than at others. For example within the unity of asserting rights, differences emerge not only in the type of organisation but also in strategy, which lead to distinctions between 'principled' and 'pragmatic' approaches to asserting and claiming rights.

The more 'principled' approach holds firmly to notions of sovereignty and self-determination, territorial rights and cultural expression. On the other hand, the more 'pragmatic' sectors of the movement consider that, in spite of agreeing with the goals in principle, in practice it is worth seeking a compromise with state bodies now to provide a basis for achieving long-term goals. The difference here is between indigenous peoples who assert rights which they already have, but seek recognition from states, and those who consider that they are claiming those rights from the state. This books aims to show that by using indigenous peoples' daily activities to understand the concepts embraced by the 'principled' view, a flexible, practical, and constructive approach can override the weaknesses of 'pragmatism'.

The UN on Indigenous Peoples

Until the last fifteen years, indigenous peoples were excluded from the international system. Whereas the pre-Second World War League of Nations Covenant, Article 23 (b), required that members undertook to secure 'just treatment of native inhabitants of territories under their control', in practice there was little evidence of any compliance. Furthermore, when in the 1920s the Maori leader Ratner

---

As indigenous peoples form organisations, or become trained to represent their peoples, they often need to mix many different aspects of history, culture, and political life in explaining their rights to other people. Friedman (1992) is concerned that the discussion of indigenous history does not become one of academics making judgements on indigenous authenticity: 'Constructing the past is an act of self-identification and must be interpreted in its authenticity, that is, in terms of the existential relation between subjects and the constitution of a meaningful world' (ibid.:856).

and the Six Nations Confederacy Chief Deskaheh tried to petition the League, they were rejected.

The first international instrument dealing with indigenous peoples was passed by the International Labour Organisation in 1957. Convention 107 'Concerning the Protection and Integration of Indigenous and Other Tribal and Semi-Tribal Populations in Independent Countries' was drafted without any indigenous participation. The Convention regulated state policy as a preparatory measure for the eventual development of indigenous peoples by promoting their integration into states as citizens (Bennett 1978; Berman 1993; Thornberry 1993:334-68). Between 1986 and 1989, the ILO revised the Convention to replace the integrative element with an emphasis on participation.

Participation was in short supply during the revision process, although representatives from indigenous peoples made a few strong presentations arguing for the inclusions of their rights within the limited framework provided. The revised ILO Convention 169 advocated a perspective of state policy regulation expressing indigenous rights in terms of participation and consultation, rather than that indigenous peoples' own rights should form the basis of the Convention, with the state relationship based on consent and control over their resources.

In many respects, the same topics and arguments which were aired at the ILO have now become the main areas of contention at the United Nations: the concepts of self-determination, territories, peoples, respect for indigenous institutions, control over resources, and consent for development initiatives on their lands are all pushed by indigenous representatives and a few governments, while the rest seek compromises or are directly hostile. (For a detailed account of the ILO debates see Gray 1987a, 1988, & 1989.)

The response by states and indigenous peoples to the ILO initiative has been muted. Falkowski considers that this has occurred because, 'It is unclear how it [the revised ILO Convention 169] removes the absorption or incorporation of indigenous peoples since it only recognizes the rights of indigenous peoples within the framework of the States in which they live and places numerous restrictions on their right to own land and be self-governing.' Even so, in spite of its draw backs, some indigenous peoples find ILO 169 useful. (1992:55).

The process whereby the United Nations took on the task of looking at indigenous rights stretches back to the 1970s UN Decade to Combat Racism. A UN study on racism addressed indigenous peoples, and in 1971 the Economic and Social Council commissioned the Martinez Cobo report on indigenous populations (which was substantially written by Agusto Willemsen Díaz, a Guatemalan indigenous rights expert).

As this report was under preparation, the 1977 NGO Conference on Discrimination against Indigenous Peoples of the Americas took place in Geneva. This was initiated and dominated by hundreds of indigenous representatives who entered the United Nations for the first time. The impetus from this meeting, and another NGO meeting in 1981 concerning land, led to the establishment of the Working Group on Indigenous Populations in 1982. The task of the Working Group was to review developments for the promotion and protection of human rights and fundamental freedoms of indigenous peoples and to look at the evolution of standards concerning their rights. During discussions, the Working Group has distinguished rights which are universal and rights which are specific to indigenous peoples such as to land and resources, culture, self-government, and self-determination (Eide 1985:204-5).

This process resulted in the Subcommission's approval of the WGIP's indigenous draft Declarations in 1994 and the current discussion of the text at the government-dominated Working Group of the Commission on Human Rights, which takes place in November. The debate taking place at the Working Group reproduces in many ways the frustrations surrounding the revision of ILO Convention 107 between hardline governments (such as India, Bangladesh, and Japan) who are reluctant to recognise indigenous peoples at all, those governments which advocate the integration of indigenous peoples into the nation state (Brazil, Peru, Canada, and the U.S.A.), those which recognise a limited form of indigenous rights as peoples (Philippines, New Zealand, and Sweden), and those which recognise the rights of indigenous peoples to self-determination and control over their own lives and futures (other Scandinavian countries, Australia, Colombia, and several countries in Central America).

How the outcome of the Working Group's deliberations fares depends on whether the governments which make up the United Nations are prepared to take the Declaration further along the road away from integration towards a genuine decolonisation. However, the drafting of the Declaration up until now has shown cultural sensitivity and a recognition of the aspirations of indigenous peoples. For this reason, although not an indigenous document, the draft Declaration is the clearest reflection to date of the demands of indigenous peoples for the recognition of their rights.

Introduction

Indigenous Rights

This book raises several issues concerning indigenous rights, not specifically from a legal framework (although that is certainly relevant), but more from that of an 'anthropological philosophy' which looks at a particular moral vision of human potential and institutions for realising that vision (Donnelly 1985:31). The purpose of approaching rights in this fashion is to try to analyse the political rhetoric of indigenous peoples and governments and then to look further into these visions with all their fears and hopes.

The discussion of indigenous rights within the United Nations rests on a framework of debate which has taken place over the last five hundred years, and many of the aspects of the discussion are still relevant today. Rights are entitlements to a moral space in which human beings can live in dignity (Lomasky 1984:45; Donnelly 1989:11). They can take negative and positive forms; negative rights protect people against coercive interference in their affairs by others, while positive rights are claims on others to provide basic necessities (Brown 1986:92). The objective of the negative right is liberty and social freedom, while that of the positive right is ensuring human life and social welfare. Furthermore, rights are both political and moral, both of which relate to indigenous peoples.

> 'Legal rights ground legal claims on the political system to protect already established legal entitlements. Human rights ground moral claims on the political system to strengthen or add to existing legal entitlements' (Donnelly 1989:15).

Indigenous rights, as discussed in the United Nations, are aspects of the human rights regime because their 'principal aim is to challenge or change existing institutions, practices, or norms' (Donnelly op.cit.:14). However, on a national level, particularly in Peru, where there already exist laws relating to indigenous peoples, indigenous rights can also take the form of legal entitlements.

Indigenous rights are about the claims of peoples with ways of life that are socio-culturally distinct from those of nation states. This provides a challenge for the recognition of cultural diversity within universal human rights instruments. A universal approach to rights assumes an equality of human nature (Hobbes 1985 [1651]:182) which enables all people to be treated as equal beneficiaries. During the Enlightenment, universal rights were considered 'natural rights' and were based on features common to humanity, such as reason or human needs. Grotius and Locke, for example, posited a universal 'state of nature' which provided a positive inspiration for a series of fundamental civil rights. Indeed, Locke is thought by some to be the precursor of current international standard-setting (Cranston 1966:77-78). More recently, philosophers have included other factors such as human action (Nozick, in Brown 1986) and interaction (Gerwith 1984).

When these common features encounter obstacles, human beings lose their dignity as human. Rights provide a moral framework for the entitlements of people in overcoming these obstacles and restoring human dignity. For writers such as R.J. Vincent (1988), human rights are inherent in all people, and notwithstanding cultural differences, they are implicit everywhere as defining features of being human (Steinzor 1992:10).[5]

A more relativist approach considers that human rights are historically contingent. The political scientist A. Vincent (1987:105) explains this as follows:

> The notion of rights is in fact comparatively recent. The concept *jus* is not really translatable from Roman law as a modern right, rather *jus* implies something which is right or correct in a given situation. It was closer in fact to our modern usage of justice.'

According to this view, human rights appeared in the seventeenth century and have been exported throughout the world since then. Along with imperialism and Coca Cola, human rights are, from this perspective, an example of the hegemony of the North over the

5. One of the obstacles to the universality of indigenous rights is that some countries (such as India, Bangladesh, and China) see the process as a form of disguised hegemony. According to this view, the United Nations human rights system has been formulated by a narrow group of like-minded, western-oriented states which operate ethnocentrically. Universal rights, from this perspective, means western interests.

In a recent Anti-Slavery International Newsletter (1993) the following concern appears in the editorial: 'Many countries in Latin America and Asia reject the principle of universality which they claim is a western concept. Some Asian countries claim that legitimate concerns about cultural attitudes are not always acknowledged by western governments and NGOs, while many Latin American and Caribbean countries, argue, for their part, that the concept of universality leads to an unacceptable level of foreign interference in their domestic affairs.'

These criticisms on the part of governments can be seen as an attempt to curtail the effective implementation of human rights and are exposed in an indigenous context because they do not seek to challenge 'western' notions of human rights from an indigenous perspective. Indigenous peoples are not opposed to human rights; they want the scope of human rights broadened to a culturally sensitive standpoint which seeks to ensure the application of human rights to the needs of discriminated peoples throughout the world.

South. This culturally relativist critique denies any common basis of human rights and opposes any absolute morality for human behaviour (Rorty 1993:116).

The process of describing indigenous rights relates to this discussion because one of the main aspects of the entitlement is the protection of the cultural uniqueness of indigenous peoples within a framework of international human rights instruments. Cultural relativity and universality need not be opposed, but cultural context should provide the framework of interpretation for international standards (Barnett 1988:22). This book looks at the context of the Arakmbut to demonstrate the implications of using certain concepts for international standards as opposed to others.

Indigenous rights are distinct for two reasons. The first is that they are a means whereby indigenous peoples try to deal with the colonial situation which threatens them. Indigenous peoples argue that they are self-determining peoples and that their rights are not only individual, but collective.[6] Collectivity in this context means ownership of territory, control over resources, decision-making through indigenous political institutions and shared self-identification within a distinct socio-cultural organisation (Falk 1988:27 ff.; Thornberry 1992:333; Dodson 1994:24). Indigenous rights are thus about decolonisation in the sense of freedom from unwanted interference.

The second aspect concerns indigenous legal systems and political institutions that provide the framework for acceptable and prescribed forms of socio-cultural behaviour and outline duties and obligations by which the social formation operates. Although these systems (sometimes referred to as 'customary law') are not always recognised by national or international legislation, they constitute an important, but frequently ignored, area of indigenous rights.[7] This is

---

6. The current demands of indigenous peoples resemble those of the 'rights of man' which took place in the eighteenth century (Dodson 1994:22). However, the context then was the growing emancipation of individuals in the face of unaccountable dictatorship whereas the threat now is colonisation. Nevertheless, some writers, such as Thomas Paine, understood the importance of collective rights and at the time of the French Revolution argued that the right to choose and control one's own government does not exist ... 'in this or that person, or in this or in that description of persons, but that it exists in the *whole*, that it is a right resident in the nation'(1797 [1987]:217). This statement could well come from a contemporary indigenous representative at the United Nations, referring to his peoples' right to exist as a self-determining people or nation.
7. Burke (1729-97), in contrast to Paine, thought that the 'rights of man' were morally false 'political metaphysics' (Parkin 1966:122; Held 1983:82). He considered that there were, on the contrary, natural rights based on common

because indigenous legal systems are embedded in the daily practices and knowledge of a people, consisting of the duties and obligations that are necessary for social life to continue. Without respect for indigenous peoples' inherent rights and collective freedom from colonisation, it is impossible for a people, such as the Arakmbut, to carry out their daily activities and mutual obligations. This dual aspect of indigenous rights is the subject of the next chapter.[8]

If all human rights apply equally to everyone in the world, how can there be a specific category of indigenous rights? Yet if all human rights are culturally relative how can there be any coherent body of human rights at all? Indigenous rights demonstrate that these positions are too extreme. Indigenous rights lie between universalism and cultural relativism. They are not universal for all human beings because the rights are about indigenous collectivities as well as individuals. However they are not discriminatory because they are designed to support peoples who are vulnerable to threats from colonising powers of the state.

The Scottish enlightenment philosopher David Hume considered that rights were derived from human practice:

> 'Those rules, by which properties, rights, and obligations are determined, have in them no marks of a natural origin, but many of artifice and contrivance. They are too numerous to have proceeded from nature; they are changeable by human laws; and have all of them a direct and evident tendency to public good, and the support of civil society' (Hume 1740 [1972]: 255-6).

For Hume, rights arise through practice and become recognised in so far as members of a civil society need them to regulate human self-interest. Rights can change over time, according to how people experience justice; they are thus created and recognised by human beings. This perspective sees human rights as historical phenomena which take different guises according to the political and legal experience of the time.

The indigenous movement is a process by which indigenous peoples' historical experiences of injustice have been transformed into a

---

features of human beings, such as feelings, habits, traditions and custom. Although this argument was conservative in the context of the nation-state, it reflects the importance of indigenous legal systems in a contemporary context because of the respect for real, living, concrete, local ways of life (Lukes 1993:28).

8. I am not referring here to the rights, duties, and obligations which arise as a result of the benefits of citizenship. These are distinct issues which are dealt with in chapter four.

process of international standard-setting, particularly in the context of the United Nations Working Group on Indigenous Populations. In this way cultural relativism becomes universalised through a historical process. The next chapter looks at the clash of perspectives taking place within this process between indigenous peoples and governments, and reviews the historical, ethnographic, and epistemological bases of their respective positions.

Chapter 1

INDIGENOUS RIGHTS FROM PATIO TO PALAIS

In July 1992, an indigenous delegation from the Madre de Dios, consisting of Angel Jipa (Shipibo) and Elias Kentehuari (Arakmbut), arrived in Geneva to raise the problems facing the communities of the area at the United Nations.[1] They participated for two weeks at the UN Working Group on Indigenous Populations. In the second week, under the agenda item on indigenous developments during the year, they signed up on the list of speakers and made their presentations on the Thursday morning.

The two representatives were called to speak by the indomitable chair Erica Daes, who has ruled the Working Group with a firm hand since 1984. Angel Jipa explained the general concerns of the constituent communities of FENAMAD, while Elias Kentehuari made a presentation that was drafted after discussions with the Arakmbut in his community, San José del Karene. This presentation makes a fitting case-study reflecting the theme of this book because it juxtaposes concrete human rights violations in the community where I carried out most of my fieldwork during this period with a discussion of international standards.

1. In 1991 the first indigenous delegation from the Madre de Dios came to Europe as a part of the IWGIA research programme, consisting of Miguel Pesha (Ese'eja) and Hector Sueyo (Arakmbut). They evaluated and observed the process but did not make presentations. The year after Angel Jipa and Elias Kentehuari attended, two Arasaeri from the community of Villa Santiago participated (Marcia Tijé for FENAMAD and Fernando Tijé for ADEIMAD).

Arakmbut Statement to the UN Working Group on Indigenous Populations

'My name is Elias Kentehuari. I am a member of the Arakmbut people who live in the Madre de Dios region in southern Peru. I am here representing my community, San José del Karene, and also the Asociación de Estudiantes Indígenas de Madre de Dios (ADEIMAD).

'The Madre de Dios of Peru is the area most forgotten by the national authorities. In our area there are more than five hundred colonists, including peon-workers, who are invading our lands, the lands of San José del Karene. Two-thirds of the beaches in that area have gold resources, but the gold is being illegally extracted by the invaders. My community has had repeatedly denounced this problem to the Peruvian authorities, meanwhile, the colonists threaten us with fire-arms. Six years ago a member of our community who had defended our territory and denounced the invasions was killed by colonists. The murderer is still free.

'Even though the national Law of Native Communities guarantees that our territories are inalienable, the mining law allows the Ministry of Energy and Mines to sell concessions to anyone at a very high price, which we indigenous peoples are not in a position to buy. This is because each concession costs about a kilo of gold. It is impossible for my community to raise this sum. Nevertheless, the big patrons and mining companies have sufficient capital to buy concessions for gold extraction in our territory. This legalised theft of our natural resources, in this case gold, deeply concerns my community. For this reason I request that the Peruvian government annul this law which does not favour us, and also relaxes its strict conditions on gold production in native communities.

'Peruvian national legislation should guarantee and protect our new Arakmbut Communal Reserve which unites our ancestral territories, yet non-indigenous hunters illegally enter our hunting grounds to kill and sell animals in the markets. This is another example of how we are illegally deprived of our natural resources while the Peruvian authorities provide no support for our legitimate claims.

'The Peruvian authorities are not taking into account the opposition of my community to the opening of a road which will pass through our territories. Madame Chair, the construction of this road will allow and facilitate the illegal entry of more colonists onto our territories, and consequently more invasion and plundering of our natural resources. The construction of the road will also lead to extraction of wood, brazil nuts, and other resources which we have reserved for the future, for our future generations. I urge the Government of Peru to intervene as quickly as possible to prevent the construction of the road which will have disastrous consequences for my community.

'Thank you' Madame Chair, for your attention.'

At first reading, this is a clear statement by an indigenous representative of the problems facing his community. He expresses some of the principal fears of the Arakmbut in San José in the face of threats such as invasions by gold colonists, hunting in indigenous areas, and a proposed road which will slice the community in two. Concerns such as these are shared by indigenous peoples throughout the world, who experience similar problems of territorial invasion and the plundering of resources. They come to Geneva to seek a forum within the international political system of the United Nations to denounce the violations of their rights.

However, on another level, the statement also uses the vocabulary of indigenous rights to stake out certain political claims. These concepts concern the basic principles behind the discussions which take place at the United Nations and which are analysed throughout this book. By looking at these concepts in the context of an indigenous UN statement, the connections between the themes in this book become clearer.

The statement begins with an identification of the speaker by name, as a member of the Arakmbut people and as representative of the community of San José. These sets of ethnic co-ordinates identify the speaker as a person belonging to a people ('*pueblo*' in Spanish) from a particular area in southeastern Peru. The reference to a 'people' is particularly significant at the UN because in international law all peoples have the right to self-determination. However, some states (including Peru) consider that recognition of this right will weaken their power and control over what they consider to be 'their' population (see chapter four).

Elias Kentehuari's presentation also provides some orientation as to what the term 'indigenous' means to peoples such as the Arakmbut. Although the term '*nativo*' is used officially in Amazonian Peru, the meaning of the term 'indigenous' becomes clear in the phrase 'non-indigenous' when referring to colonists ('*colonos*' in Spanish). The Arakmbut consider themselves indigenous in relation to outsiders who move onto their territories and exploit their resources. 'Indigenousness' arises at the moment when a people senses the injustices of colonisation.

The question of lands and resources is a crucial theme in the Arakmbut statement. The speaker expresses this as 'ancestral territories' over which the community has control recognised by the state. The complaint of the Arakmbut is that colonists, coming from outside of community lands, are illegally entering their territories and extracting resources, particularly gold.

In 1992, when the presentation was made, the Arakmbut had some protection through the inalienable right to their territories embedded in the Peruvian Law of Native Communities and the National Constitution. Since then, however, the Peruvian government has unilaterally removed the inalienability protection from the Constitution and opened up state lands to the free market. This has taken place prior to completing the process of demarcation and titling the indigenous communities of the Amazon.

Apart from the national problem over the de facto use of territorial resources, indigenous peoples find that the concept of territories is not popular among governments internationally. States such as Peru argue at the UN that territoriality is their right and that indigenous peoples only have limited rights over the surface resources of 'lands'. These positions reflect a long history of discussion over the notion of territoriality, which is currently still highly topical (see chapter three).

The Peruvian state appears at two points in the statement, both clearly marking the ambivalence which the Arakmbut, and indigenous peoples as a whole, feel towards governments. Whereas the benign and protective arms of the state appear in the national *Ley de las Comunidades Nativas* (Law of Native Communities), which has legally defended indigenous rights to their land until the constitutional revision in 1993, at the same time, the Ministry of Energy and Mines has produced an extremely complicated Mining Law which favours big business at the expense of small producers (see chapter two).

States are seen as both protectors and colonisers depending on the context, and the framework of the United Nations standard-setting exercise reflects this ambivalence. The states of the UN are responsible for approving a Declaration on the Rights of Indigenous Peoples as a protection against colonisation; yet at the same time, those very states making up the UN are either incapable of preventing or are actually encouraging the very threats which the draft Declaration is trying to remove.

The Arakmbut are extremely concerned that a local entrepreneur will succeed in carving a road through the community territory of San José del Karene and the neighbouring community of Barranco Chico. Those colonists who support the road do so in the name of development and progress, and have threatened Arakmbut opponents with death; yet the community does not have the power to stop the project. The Arakmbut find, on the contrary, that development decisions are foisted onto them by the local municipality of Boca Colorado without their consent (see chapter seven).

The Arakmbut statement emphasises the importance of indigenous control of territory and resources as a means of promoting the Arakmbut's own self-development. The reference to protecting ancestral territories in one paragraph is complemented by the reference to the protection of natural resources which are 'reserved for the future, for our future generations'. This connection between ancestors and descendants is extremely important for the survival of the Arakmbut as a people and their continuing cultural identity. These topics also relate to questions of governance and cultural expression and will be discussed in chapters five and six.

The points raised in this indigenous statement introduce the main themes in this book. The Arakmbut are striving to control their territories and to develop their resources through their own political decision-making institutions according to their own socio-cultural principles. This totality relates to Arakmbut multifaceted identities as a people and consequently to the comprehensive notion of self-determination (reviewed in chapter eight).

The Arakmbut and Rights

The Arakmbut do not have a word which covers all of the meanings of 'rights', but they have a clear concept of what is appropriate or inappropriate behaviour and frequently discuss claims and obligations between people. A person's behaviour can be categorised in many ways, but the general terms *ndak* (good) and *ndakwe* (bad) are the most useful orientation to judgements of actions. However, these are not concepts based on an absolute morality stemming from external sources, as is the case in the Christian missions, where priests act as one-way intermediaries of God, defining, rewarding, and chastising good or bad behaviour (Wahl 1987:200 ff.).

The Arakmbut do not come to an understanding of morality through religious dogma, but through the identification of a problem, manifested as illness (a problem with a spirit) or hatred (a problem with another member of the community). The problem is solved by diagnosing the cause and solving the difficulty through a process of negotiation. This takes a political form with other Arakmbut, while with spirits, it occurs through visionary understanding and shamanic interpretation. Morality is thus a dynamic process for solving problems and establishing order in a recalcitrant world (see Volume 2, chapter five).

The Arakmbut customary legal system consists of rights and obligations which are bound up in three areas: the socio-cultural organisation of the community, the invisible world of the spirits, and the unpredictable and highly volatile sets of relationships with non-Arakmbut people known to the Arakmbut as 'white people'. These three areas are the focus of the three main myths in the Arakmbut canon: Wanamey, the tree of salvation; Marinke, the culture hero; and Aiwe, the orphan who escapes from the non-indigenous Papa. (For detailed accounts of these myths see Volume 1, chapters, one, five and nine.) Whereas the myths do not consist of commandments for behaviour, they establish focal points where it is possible to see rights and duties operating in practice.

Socio-cultural views on rights

The story of Wanamey tells of the creation of the world. In the face of a boiling flood the Harakmbut peoples save themselves by climbing into the giant tree Wanamey. After the flood dies down, the people descend from the tree and, with fire and water, create their culture and social organisation. This myth focuses on Arakmbut socio-cultural formation and its imagery centres around the consequences of appropriate and inappropriate sexual relations and culinary practices. Sexual relations and social organisation constitute one area where the Arakmbut have sets of personal duties and claims, while cooking is a key moment in the process of production which stakes claims on property.[2]

Arakmbut social organisation is based on several overlapping principles of gender, age, residence, descent, and marriage exchange. The relationship terminology is one of symmetric prescription with categorical equations implying the exchange of opposite-sex siblings (sometimes conceptualised as 'sister exchange'). Although this form of marriage does not take place very often between biological siblings, each marital union fits categorically into the system. The Arakmbut have seven patrilineal clans: Yaromba, Idnsikambo, Wandigpana, Singperi, Masenawa, Saweron, and Embieri. The Arakmbut also have an alliance-arranging category called the *wambet*, which has a cognatic aspect arising from the inclusion of the relatives of both parents.

In daily life these socio-cultural principles appear in the practical activities of production and reproduction and from where it is possible to see the moral principles from which customary rights flow. All of the main Arakmbut production activities – hunting, fishing, gath-

---

2. This distinction has some connection to the legal relationship between personal rights *(jus in personam)* and rights in things *(jus in rem)* (Radcliffe-Brown:1970:11-12). However, as Leach notes (1961:107-8), rights come in 'bundles', which blur the person/thing distinction. Furthermore, the Arakmbut take jural notions of rights beyond the visible world; thus the importance of the soul *(nokiren)* in both things and persons makes this a distinction of degree rather than of kind.

ering, horticulture, and gold mining – are organised on co-operation based on the above principles. Social organisation is, in this way, not expressed through abstract categories but through practice.

Claims to property are made through investing labour in an object *(e'ka / e'mba'a)*. Thus, a manufactured artifact, dead animal or cleared area for gardens or gold-mining are all claimed by the person or household responsible for the work involved. These claims are not accepted without some obligation to share the benefits to the rest of the community, particularly if the commodity is not available to all. Meat sharing between related households and drinking parties with alcohol bought from the gold are the main forms of distribution. Rights thus consist of claims through labour and obligations to share.[3]

If a man goes hunting *(e'machunka)* with his son, his action expresses something about gender, age, clan membership, and the relationship terminology. This is because every man is in the same clan as his son and to hunt together is a sign that the boy has become a youth and is learning techniques he will need as a future husband. In contrast, when women go in small work groups to the chacras they express something about gender, residence and wambet relations. Women who marry into the community do not have their gardens associated with their name until they have an independent household, whereas women who have always lived in the community are always seen as owners of their gardens. Women working with relatives from neighbouring households will often be allied together through the wambet which links people together through the father's and mother's relations, and later in life, through children's relations.

Relations between these different groups and categories are based on different forms of reciprocity. Between husband and wife, for example, the man brings meat into the household, which is then distributed to other clan and wambet members. The wife ensures that the gardens produce enough crops to provide a constant supply of food and firewood and through her knowledge of cooking transforms the dangerous flesh from living creatures into meat for eating.

The marriage couple is thus the foundation of a household and provides the means for reproducing the clan line. Marriage *(e'toepak)* involves considerable negotiation between households involving discussions of personal capacities and histories of genealogical relationships. The classificatory relationship terminology implies a balanced

---

3. Helberg, forthcoming, refers to the Arakmbut term *wayawaya* (balanced exchange) as an important aspect of this reciprocity, covering goods, services, and people.

exchange over time between households (see Volume 1, chapter four), but the larger number of men than women means that this cannot usually be carried out. However, a period of uxorilocal residence, during which the husband lives and works with his in-laws for a few years, until they are more independent economically, provides services which tie the households together with mutual obligations involving the couple.

The rights described here are based on claims and duties between members of a community and they are inherent to Arakmbut social life. The behaviour described above is based on practice and thus, over time, on the customary legal system. However, should anyone fail to respect these customs, the Arakmbut have an informal process of negotiation to ascertain the problem and seek solutions. Inappropriate behaviour might consist of stealing crops from a garden, not distributing meat, not sharing a gold-bearing beach with neighbours and relatives, or eloping with a young woman from the community. The common element in all of this is selfishness *(senopo)*, which refers to someone holding things for him or herself, and is not only a form of activity but a state of the soul *(nokiren)*.

Each Arakmbut person consists of a body *(waso)*, soul (nokiren), and name *(wandik)*. The relationship between these three elements constitutes the state of being of each person in relation to the rest of the community (see Volume 1, Chapter six). A person who is selfish has strong emotions which can lead to hatred of others *(ochinosik)*. This can cause harm to other people's souls and is considered by the Arakmbut as sorcery. Claims and obligations are thus bound up with a person's being, and involve not just the material world but also the state of the soul.

Solutions to conflicts over claims and obligations take place through negotiations on a political level. Decisions and negotiations usually emerge through informal discussions in the house, work groups, and casual talks in the evening; from these encounters, the Arakmbut seek consensus agreements. Wrongdoing is censured verbally and through avoidance, but solutions rather than punishments are sought. On failing agreement, fights break out at the drinking fiestas and, if the conflict is serious, one party may leave the community.

The invisible spirit world

The second main Arakmbut myth, Marinke, tells of a woman who is seduced soon after her marriage and taken to a distant community where she becomes pregnant. While trying to return home she is killed by jaguars and her foetus thrown into a river. Protected by fish, the foetus becomes a child, Marinke, who is the Arakmbut culture hero. When he grows he passes through the periods of initiation and on reaching adulthood kills the jaguars. Fearing their revenge, he escapes to the sky.

The myth of Marinke is about the relationship between humans and spirits and uses the imagery of animals, fish, and birds to express the connections (Califano 1978b). In mythological times, humans and animals were interchangeable in visible forms, but after conflicts between the species the two orders of being separated. Communication can take place through the intermediary activities of spirits, which can be contacted in the heightened consciousness of dreams, visions, and hallucinations *(wayorok)*.

Spirituality is based on the life-giving matter in all animate beings, which for human beings is called nokiren (soul). Soul-matter which is not tied to bodies is free and constitutes several orders of spirits. The most dangerous are known as *toto* and they are attracted by sorcery, lack of respect for the invisible world, and through accidental encounters. Toto are usually portrayed as concentrated soul-matter but a less dangerous dispersed form *(wamawere)* floats through the air as a breeze and can also cause sickness.

Dispersed beneficial spirits *(ndakyorokeri)* appear in dreams as beautiful people and give advice to those with shamanic skills, while the more concentrated beneficial spirits, such as the *wachipai* and *chongpai*, appear during ayahuasca sessions are either otiose or appear to human beings only for brief periods.

The invisible world can harm human beings who transgress the boundaries of morally acceptable behaviour. This is not based so much on principles of good and evil as on the dangers of concentrated soul-matter or the influence of beneficial or dangerous forces. There are three contexts in which the invisible world exerts dangers: sorcery, spirit attack, and accident.

Sorcery *(chindign)* is a harmful activity carried out by human beings using harmful spirits as intermediaries. This varies from now obsolete attacks by young girls *(chiwembet)* to the current use of tobacco and chants by those with shamanic knowledge (Califano 1978a). Sorcery means that the soul of a person has become spiritually harmful, yet this activity has its relative aspects because a person using spirit powers to defend a community will appear as a sorcerer from the perspective of the enemy. Sorcery is difficult to cure, as it involves a serious transgression of spiritual codes.

People are vulnerable to spirit attack if they have violated prescribed sexual relations. These forbid sex within the patrilineal clan or among parallel cousins. Incestuous behaviour leads to contamination from the physical and spiritual meeting together. The moral action is condemned, but the sickness is a direct effect of the action, rather than a punishment.

Arakmbut who transgress social and spiritual behaviour expectations open themselves up to spirit attack. A particular danger comes from overhunting animals or fish because this means ignoring the advice of the ndakyorokeri. It demonstrates greed and selfishness (senopo) relating to the spirit world, and illness is almost always the result. If someone is ill, the sickness is not so much a moral judgement on that person's behaviour as the effect of a direct causal relationship. For the hunter who has killed too many animals, the symptoms will take on the charactersitics of the species who have been offended at this behaviour.

The spirit world is beyond space and time, and its inhabitants know the past, the present, and the future. Shamanic skills consist of tapping this information and using it for the benefit of other Arakmbut. Invisible soul-matter is a fundamental aspect of the Arakmbut philosophy of life and death. Spirits are bound up with notions of causality, potentiality, legitimacy, and dynamic change, while the soul-matter of each person provides the contact between the Arakmbut and the spiritual dimension – invisibility. Curing is an extremely important aspect of Arakmbut life and the shamanic skills involve direct contact with the spirit world through chants, visions, and dreams.

The curing process consists of the shaman negotiating a solution to an illness with the spirits involved. Sorcery is the most difficult; animal spirits can respond to chants; accidental encounters with harmful spirits in the forest are unpredictable. The shaman resolves the problems of illness in the same way that political processes solve community problems. The question of rights and obligations apear here because the spirits are the guardians of what constitutes appropriate behaviour and act as an invisible legislative judiciary with which shamans can negotiate in their dreams and visions (see Volume 2, chapters one to five).

The importance of the spirit world is that it legitimises customary Arakmbut legal systems. The spirit world monitors behaviour and in the form of causality, which links invisible to the visible, marks out transgression. The shaman and the beneficial spirits try to ensure the establishment of order out of the threats and chaos which surround the community. Thus the animating spirit brings to life the rights which are embedded in customary law. The implications of this in terms of territorial rights are discussed in chapter three.

In this way, the question of rights within the Arakmbut communities are based on a customary legal system which is at once sociocultural and spiritual. The Arakmbut are self-determining because they carry out these activities politically on the basis of their own decision-making capacity. In this sense, it is possible to say that these rights are 'inherent' because they are invested in the people as a whole, although the extent of their articulation varies. The flexibility and negotiated approach to morality takes place because the constant presence of the spirit world provides stability and this ensures that there is a regular replenishment of meat, humans and soul-matter. However, a third aspect of Arakmbut rights is a challenge to all of this.

Interference by outsiders

Aiwe, the third myth in the Arakmbut canon, tells of a young boy who was stolen from his community by the Papa, white cannibal monsters who are described in similar terms to rubber barons. The boy undergoes several adventures with the Papa and manages to escape from them with the help of the bones of a dead Papa chief. On returning to his community he grinds the bones into a drink to gain the power of the Papa, but after ingesting too much he dies.

This myth has several versions, in which the Papa variously appear as rubber barons, Incas, and Spanish conquistadors. It tells of the great dangers that these powerful non-indigenous people pose to the Arakmbut, yet refers also to positive effects if contact is controlled. The story explains that the Arakmbut do not live in a closed, safe world but are surrounded by dangers which threaten their very existence. Unlike sorcery and illness, which harm specific persons, the dangers from these beings are more permanent; they threaten the future of the Arakmbut as a people. This was brought home to me strongly in San José del Karene, where a respected elder once dreamt that the community as a whole faced annihilation from the white colonists. The Arakmbut were very afraid when they heard about this dream and still refer to it when they are threatened by outsiders.

The threat of destruction encompasses the whole inherent system of rights and obligations which operates within the social and cultural organisation of the Arakmbut. Life continues because the spirit world secures continuity by providing resources for production and reproduction. When resources disappear, this means that the spirits have gone, reproduction becomes impossible, and life is no longer self-sustaining. Thus the potentiality inherent in the world with the all-knowing spirits seeing into the future and past is lost.

The concern in Elias Kentehuari's presentation about the increased number of gold colonists, the proposed road, and the entry of non-indigenous hunters into the communal reserve is precisely about this depletion of resources. With support of the spirits all resources should be renewable, but with the onslaught of colonisation, gold, animals, and the forest begin to go forever. When the Arakmbut lose their territory, they lose their capacity to survive sustainably – for this reason they are afraid of the future.

However, the Aiwe myth offers hope to the Arakmbut because it demonstrates that they can defend themselves against white people by 'drinking' a little of their ways to use in defence. However, if they take too much they will die. This crucial message opens up the possibility for the Arakmbut to decide what outside influences are beneficial. To take on too much white influence will destroy Arakmbut identity. Knowledge of production and shamanic techniques can only continue if the relationship between elder and youth is positive and constructive. Elias Kentehuari mentions this in his view of the present Arakmbut connecting their ancestors to their as yet unborn descendants. But to take on too much outside influence, whether through education, medicine, or religion, leads to several dangers for the Arakmbut.

One particular threat is the loss of relativity. Each Arakmbut species sees the world from its own perspective. For example, fish appear as crops to the *waweri* river sprits, and tapirs *(keme)* appear as human to each other. This relativity avoids classifying the world into absolute immutable categories, and facilitates the link between behaviour and the consequences of one's actions. According to their moral relativity, through understanding and negotiation, the Arakmbut seek solutions to their problems by grasping other peoples' points of view. Once strict absolute moral criteria become influential, all Arakmbut indigenous morality which is inherent to their sociocultural organisation can be criticised and questioned. The Arakmbut have two defences here.

Whereas the absolute morality of Christianity had some effect on the Arakmbut during their period in the mission of Shintuya, they consider that the Christian God (with his medicine and education) is the appropriate approach to deal with 'white' problems. For this reason, the Arakmbut try to keep western education, medicine and religion compartmentalised within their way of life. Furthermore, as the colonising frontier affects the communities, the Arakmbut have turned to the language of rights as a means of encircling the relative morality of their inherent customary rights and obligations with an absolute moral and legal framework to defend their territory and their identity from the external threats which they face.

Even the form of political structure and decision-making has been affected by this change. As a part of their self-defence, the Arakmbut have complied with the Peruvian Law of Native Communities which demands, for external purposes, that each community has an elected political organisation. This runs parallel to its internal political system. Whereas the informal consensus decisions still take place, for matters dealing with affairs outside the community, formal meetings take place and decisions are made publicly.

This book will look in detail at how this use of indigenous rights has come about, and the cultural and political processes by which they are becoming increasingly important. The change of focus from inherent rights to clearly defined indigenous rights is something which has emerged at the interface between the colonising frontier and the world of the Arakmbut. This is not to say that the Arakmbut are totally separate from an 'outside world', but rather that there is a flexible distinction which they recognise and use in their daily lives.

Embedded within the three myths is the Arakmbut sense of identity as a people connected to a territory, which has become more bounded as it has been threatened by invasion. Whereas the Arakmbut have always been self-determining, in the face of threats to their existence they are becoming aware of indigenous rights as a form of defence.

In contrast to the Arakmbut perspective, the government of Peru has a distinct view on indigenous rights which is based on its own needs and desires. Whereas the Arakmbut notion of rights is centred on a pragmatic relation between myth and history, the government interprets moral issues through philosophical thought and political ideologies which have shifted and reformulated over the last five hundred years.

The Peruvian government speaks to the UN Commission on Human Rights

In a statement made in November 1995 to the Working Group of the Commission on Human Rights, the Peruvian government made several general comments on the draft declaration. This position is by no means indelibly fixed, but it provides a parallel perspective on indigenous rights to the position of the Arakmbut, from the point of view of a state:

'Mr. Chairman: The draft Declaration which we have in our hands is a good basis for the work of our Group. We believe that the most interesting aspect of the draft is that it systematically covers a wide range of themes and concepts which are indispensable for incorporation in the future Declaration on Indigenous Populations.

'Nevertheless, my delegation considers that there are several problems of definition and scope in the articles of the draft.

'The delegation of Peru, at the level of the Working Group of the Subcommission, in the Subcommission itself, and in the Commission on Human Rights, has expressed the need to make this Declaration a realistic document, politically viable and applicable, and juridically congruent with the body of international instruments on human rights; only in this way will we reach universality and consequently international support for the draft Declaration.

'Therefore, taking into consideration the mandate of the Commission on Human Rights, this group meeting here is authorised to elaborate a draft Declaration in an exercise that will take the draft Declaration elaborated by the Subcommission as the main document, and which will deal systematically with the question of indigenous populations in its broadest sense. We believe that it will also be of great use and be obligatory for our work to look at Chapter 26 of Agenda 21, and Convention 169 of the International Labour Organisation.

'Mr. Chairman, in relation to the nature of the participation of the delegates present in this meeting, we believe that to be consequent with the spirit of the draft, the broadest participation should be authorised for indigenous delegations represented here, with the aim of establishing efficient mechanisms of consultation and dialogue.

'Mr. Chairman, we have heard some delegations who have shown their interest in starting with the prior exercise of defining 'indigenous populations'. The delegation of Peru considers that this would be a positive initial approach for this work. There exist important precedents, such as the definition of UN expert Martinez Cobo, ILO Convention 169 and the document on application of criteria on the concept of 'indigenous peoples' elaborated by the expert Erica Daes.

'In relation to the objective of the Declaration, the Peruvian delegation considers that it ought to ensure that states secure the enjoyment and exercise of the rights of indigenous populations as citizens of a state. This is, for my delegation, the central meaning of what ought to be in the Declaration.

'The contrary, to establish a series of 'erga omnes' rights when what is being dealt with here are aspirations, would be politically impractical, incompatible with international law and with Peruvian national law.

'In this sense, it will be necessary to ensure that fundamental concepts contained in the draft, above all in the first part, such as 'peoples', 'self-determination', 'territory', and 'nationality', are eventually drafted in a precise manner in both their scope and nature.

'On the other hand, the many references to criteria, aims, and scope of the participation of indigenous populations in issues which directly concern them, ought to be carefully examined, taking into consideration the framework of sovereignty, independence, and authority, which states hold for managing those affairs which affect their citizens. This involves seeking space for adequate participation to address the immediate needs and desires of indigenous populations without weakening the established constitutional order.

'Finally, Mr. Chairman, in relation to the mechanism we should follow over the next few days, we consider that as this is the beginning of a difficult process of negotiation at the level of states, it would be beneficial to begin with a reading of the draft Declaration article by article. It is clear that there exist themes and articles which are clearer and less contentious than others. Nevertheless, we should not lose sight of the Declaration as a whole. An ordered reading of the draft would allow all delegations to determine openly which articles or themes are more accessible than others. Thank you, Mr. Chairman.'

The Peruvian government's statement lacks the descriptive element of the Arakmbut presentation, which is embedded in a practical situation and cites specific events to express the importance of indigenous rights. The Peruvian government, on the other hand, addresses indigenous rights from the more abstract perspective of the draft Declaration itself, and, in a coded and diplomatic way, the representative shows his disquiet. Several aspects of the statement illustrate this concern, in marked contrast to the Arakmbut position.[4]

The distinction between indigenous 'peoples' and indigenous 'populations' is fundamental. A people is a collective body with the right to self-determination (according to the Human Rights Covenants), whereas indigenous people (with no 's') or populations are terms based on the assumption that collectivities are made up of individuals whose rights are endowed in a personal capacity. The draft Declaration refers consistently to 'indigenous peoples' and recognises in Article 3 the right of indigenous peoples to self-determination. The Peruvian government, therefore, by using the term 'populations' declares its opposition to the fundamental concept of 'peoples'.

Later in the text, Peru explains that the 'central meaning of what ought to be in the Declaration' is that indigenous people are citizens of the Peruvian state. This has important implications for the identity

4. This statement was disappointing for the indigenous peoples present at the meeting. It placed Peru in the position of one of the less progressive governments. This attitude has been reflected in national policy with the amendment of the 1979 Constitution which protected indigenous rights to their territories. However, there are some indications that Peru is contemplating a more positive approach in 1996, particularly because the Peruvian chair of the Commission Working Group was received very positively by the indigenous representatives in 1995 as a fair and constructive arbitrator of the discussion.

question which Elias Kentehuari discussed in the Arakmbut presentation. He saw himself first as being Arakmbut, part of an indigenous people, and only then as a citizen of the state.

Whereas for the Peruvian government indigenous rights are about participation in the state and integration into its framework, for the Arakmbut they are about control of the colonisation process and the establishment of a self-determined relationship within the framework of the state. This has repercussions for the meaning of the word 'indigenous'. The Peruvian government's position sees 'indigenous' as a category of citizen, but for the Arakmbut, the term 'indigenous' refers to a people whose territories are being invaded.

Clearly the government's paper indicates that it is not comfortable with this and proposes a discussion on definition in its statement. Even though the government mentions several constructive definitions, such as the Martinez Cobo definition (see Introduction) which has been used throughout the deliberations of the Subcommission Working Group drawing up the draft Declaration, the Peruvian government still wants further discussion. This definitional question is seen by indigenous peoples as problematic because it has been advanced by several Asian governments (particularly Bangladesh and India), which are trying to ensure that the term indigenous does not become applicable in their countries.

The Peruvian government considers that several terms need to be 'drafted in a precise manner'. Concepts such as 'self-determination', 'nationality', 'territory', and 'indigenous peoples' are given as examples of 'controversial' terms. Two of them, peoples and territory, appear in prominent positions in the Arakmbut statement and constitute an important aspect of Peruvian indigenous peoples' assertion of their rights.

The references which the government makes to Chapter 26 of Agenda 21 (the United Nations Programme of Action from the Earth Summit at Rio) and ILO Convention 169 are relevant here because they both make use of a weaker vocabulary on indigenous questions than the draft Declaration. Agenda 21 consistently uses 'lands' and 'indigenous people', recognising neither the notion of territorial control nor the collectivity of indigenous peoples. Although ILO 169 uses the terms 'peoples' and 'territories', both words are weakened by qualification. Within the context of discussions on the draft Declaration, therefore, this means that Peru does not favour the pro-indigenous vocabulary set out by the Arakmbut.

At the root of the Peruvian government's argument is a positivistic reliance on the precedents of international law, the national constitution, and Peruvian legislation on indigenous questions. This is justified by adjectives such as 'realistic', 'politically viable', and 'juridically congruent'. When the Peruvian government statement refers to the goal of 'universality', this means that 'universal rights' must coincide with international human rights standards. In this way, rights are based on the lowest common denominator with which all states feel comfortable.

This 'positivist' approach, based on precedent, reflects the power structure and preoccupations of states more than those of indigenous peoples; it considers that legal developments should be based on an existing framework whereby activities are legitimised juridically through the state. This contrasts with the 'normative' Arakmbut presentation, which is based on a moral argument stemming from the experience of injustice and which looks at rights as a means to solve problems, rather than as a reflection of the world as it currently is.

The principles of state power described in the Peruvian government presentation consist of a 'framework of sovereignty, independence and authority which states hold for managing those affairs which affect their citizens'. According to this view, states hold power to manage a citizen's affairs; this leads to serious repercussions for indigenous peoples, who, in contrast, see themselves as 'self-governing' through their own political institutions. The Peruvian government thus sees indigenous individuals living within national boundaries as under the control of the state; the Arakmbut would see this as an aspect of state colonisation.

The consequence of this is pertinent in questions as to who owns resources and who controls development. For the Arakmbut, these should rest in the hands of indigenous peoples and not the colonists; however, the Peruvian government position is primarily concerned with the fact that everything is ultimately managed according to state dictates. In Peru, this is clearly manifest when considering the two major changes of indigenous legislation in recent years which have involved neither consultation nor participation with those indigenous peoples affected.

The Peruvian government statement addresses, both directly and indirectly, all of the terms raised in the Arakmbut statement. Indigenous peoples, territory, indigenous political institutions, self-development (control over resources and consent prior to activities taking place on indigenous lands), and self-determination are all seen as problems. The result is two sets of opinions, one from the state and one from a people. While they use the same words, the meaning which they place on them is very different. The result is a struggle over semantics, one of which is based on legal precedent, the other on practical experience.

The Grounds for State Claims over Indigenous Rights

The difference of perspective between the Arakmbut and the Peruvian government is reflected throughout the world, although there are distinct historical circumstances and national legislations which make governments appear more or less progressive. The negotiations currently taking place in the UN reflect a history of attitudes by governments, missionaries, and lawyers regarding indigenous peoples which places many of the current political positions in the context of a debate stretching back to the sixteenth century.

This debate consists of moral principle in conflict with political expediency and its main protagonists are philosophers, jurists, politicians, theologians, and historians. Until the upsurge of the indigenous movement over the last thirty years, the indigenous voice was muffled and usually silent on these matters. The following outline of the debate sketches the discussion about indigenous peoples from a South American focus, yet, as will be seen, the primary orientation for the discussion of rights stemmed from Europe. This is a marked contrast to the mythological and practical basis for Arakmbut rights.

With the current emphasis on the drafting of international standards for indigenous peoples' rights, there is a temptation to reduce all human rights to the formulation and interpretation of the law. However, the law is fundamentally about the exercise of the power of states. An appropriate illustration of this appears in the discussions about the rights of the indigenous peoples of the Americas which took place at the time of the Spanish invasion.

The Spanish Invasion

Only six months after Columbus reached America there was a dispute between Spain and Portugal as to which country controlled the newfound lands. The Borgia Pope, Alejandro VI, was asked to arbitrate. In his Bull Inter Caetera of May 3rd, 1493 (also known as the Bull of Donation), he split the lands between Spain and Portugal. Furthermore he says in the text addressed to the King and Queen of Spain:

> 'By the authority of Almighty God ... we ... give, grant and assign forever to you and your heirs and successors, kings of Castile and León, all and singular the aforesaid countries and islands thus unknown and hith-

erto discovered by your envoys and to be discovered hereafter, provided however they at no time have been in the actual temporal possession of any Christian owner, together with all their dominions, cities, camps, places and villages and rights, jurisdictions and appurtenances of the same' (Falkowski 1992:9).

The Spanish, during the time of conquest, used a legalised justification of war called the Requerimiento or 'Call to Conversion' which was made mandatory by the King in 1513. If the people did not recognise the Pope and the Spanish Crown as their lords, it said, 'We shall forcibly enter into your country and ... shall subject you to the yoke and obedience of the Church and of their Highnesses; we shall take you and your wives and your children and shall make slaves of them, and as such shall sell and dispose of them as their Highnesses may command; and we shall take away your goods, and shall do all the harm and damage that we can, as to vassals who do not obey ... and we protest that the deaths and losses which shall accrue from this are your fault.' (Falkowski op.cit.:12)

If, after having read this document, the indigenous people did not surrender immediately, they were attacked by the Spaniards in the manner of a Christian version of the Islamic jihad or Holy War (Barry 1992:12). The Inter Caetera and the Requirimiento between them laid the foundations of colonisation and genocide in the Americas. The root of the Spanish claim in the early years of the conquest was the Bull of Alejandro VI and the right to conquer 'infidels' (Stavenhagen 1988:15) which assumed the territorial jurisdiction of the Pope and the Crown of Spain, the right of discovery, and the right to convert unbelievers.

On the whole, the juridical scholars and government representatives favoured seeing the indigenous peoples of the Americas as being in a state of servitude (Ots Capdequi 1940:65). The concept of natural slavery, arising from Aristotelian classification, was frequently used to argue that indigenous peoples were 'barbarians' whose reasons were ruled by their passions (Pagden 1986:42). The colonisers used 'natural slavery' to justify controlling labour and resources through practices such as the notorious *encomienda* which tied indigenous peoples to lands to serve the Spanish. Jurists such as Juan de Solórzano Pereira, for example, said that lands and resources in the Americas should be treated as *regalias* or goods belonging to the King (Ots Capdequi op.cit.).

However, there were opponents of this doctrine. Condemnation of the abuses of indigenous peoples by colonists were first raised, in

1511, by the Dominican priest Antonio de Montesinos (Pagden 1986:30). During the following year, the 'Burgos Laws' established limited protections for the Indians from slavery, but servitude was still enshrined in Spanish law.

From the 1520s, the School of Salamanca provided the strongest theological defence of indigenous rights. The Dominican Francisco de Vitoria (1502-1575) approached the question from the perspective of '*ius naturae*' (natural law), which supposedly had its origins in antediluvian times. He argued that the affairs of the Indies were the domain of the theologian and wrote in *De Indis et de Iure Belli Reflectionis* that the Indians of the Americas were fully human with 'true dominion in both public and private matters' (Bennett 1978:29). He disputed the power of the Pope to authorise colonisation and stated that the Indians of the Americas were owners of their territory and that the Spanish had no right to occupy their lands (Lindley 1926:12; Grisel 1976).

However, Vitoria did not consider indigenous peoples equals of the Spanish but as grown children who need guardianship and education. He argued that 'the government of aboriginal communities by nations "of more mature intelligence must be subject to the limitation that any such interposition be for the welfare and in the interests of the Indians and not merely for the Spaniards". He went on to say that the relationship between invaded and invader was that of a ward to his or her guardian. This doctrine of guardianship is one of the key concepts for the understanding of the status of aboriginal rights in international law' (Heinz 1988:49).

On the basis of Vitoria's writings, Pope Paul III issued a Bull Sublimis Deus in 1537, five years after Pizarro reached Peru in 1532, which countered the previous Inter Caetera Bull of Alejandro VI and stated that Indians should not be deprived of their liberty or property. In 1542, a move to improve the treatment of indigenous peoples secured the passing of the 'New Laws' which would have abolished the encomiendas, but protests from the colonists led to their becoming a dead letter (Stavenhagen 1988: 21).

King Ferdinand and Queen Isabella of Spain held regular *juntas* or 'consultations' at which theological, civil, and canon law were debated; these events became the fora for discussions on the rights of the indigenous peoples of the Americas. They took the form of debates between 'colonistas' and 'indigenistas' (Friede 1974:28) and one well-publicised hearing took place in 1550 between Bartholomé de Las Casas and Juan Ginés de Sepúlveda before Charles V of Spain.

Sepúlveda argued that indigenous peoples were natural slaves and that they could neither own land nor form governments (Falkowski

1992.:27). Las Casas opposed this position. He argued in his '*Apologetica Historia*' that all indigenous peoples were human and that the pre-conquest Indians fulfilled the requirements of Aristotle's civil society. Using the examples of the Incas and Aztecs, he argued that indigenous peoples were capable of creating more complicated forms of self-government than in Europe. Furthermore he asserted indigenous sovereignty over their territories and opposed vehemently the notion of a just war against them (Falkowski ibid.: 28-9).

The most influential Spanish writer of the time on the indigenous peoples of the Americas was José de Acosta, the historian, who wrote *Historia natural y moral de las Indias*. Like Las Casas and the Salamancan school, he accepted that human beings shared a fundamental identity and explained cultural difference through historical change (Pagden 1982:146). Acosta lived in Peru and had direct experience of indigenous peoples. He proposed the recognition of a diversity of peoples and social systems in the Americas which could be explained as a mixture of migration and development.

Even though writers such as Vitoria, Las Casas, and Acosta opposed the mistreatment of indigenous peoples, they did not question the right of the Spanish to be in the Americas. Ultimately, their justification was that the Spanish could instruct the indigenous peoples in Christianity and educate them into 'civilised' ways while respecting their natural rights. In contrast, while the jurists and hardliners also justified their presence as civilising influence, for writers such as Sepúlveda, the labour and resources which the indigenous peoples provided were a just return. The Spanish Crown noted these different positions and took a pragmatic approach to colonisation.

The justification of colonisation on religious grounds fits in with the overall view of 'the Other' in the Renaissance period, when indigenous peoples were identified primarily on the basis of their being pagan (McGrane 1989). However this was not just a view of the 'Other', but also a call for destruction, either physically or through 'civilising'.

Stavenhagen (1988:14) says, 'the negation of the "other", that is to say, the Indian, of his culture and humanity was characteristic of Columbus and of many who followed him; this negation of the Other constituted the basis of Spanish dominion, of the oppression and exploitation of the indigenous peoples. The negation of the other is the first and most fundamental violation of human rights.' This process is also called 'othercide' by the Argentinean writer Galeano (1992:3).

The Peruvian government statement lacks both the theological and genocidal features of the Spanish discussions which took place five hundred years ago. Nevertheless, certain ideas remain contemporary. Like Las Casas, the government respects that indigenous peoples have rights and through a secular form of 'civilisation' (citizenship) they can become integrated into the state. However the government is still, after five hundred years, unwilling to share Las Casas' conviction that indigenous peoples, as peoples, have rights to their territories.

The Enlightenment

The history and philosophy of the Spanish theologians were influential during the Enlightenment. Acosta, for example, was widely read and became a major source of South American history throughout the seventeenth and eighteenth centuries, particularly in northern Europe (Huddleston 1967). Furthermore, the writings of Vitoria and later of the Jesuit Francisco Suárez on the notion of natural law were taken up in other guises through the work of Grotius and Locke.

Hugo Grotius (1583-1645), the Dutch jurist and diplomat, postulated reason as the basis for a common human nature governed by a law. Grotius saw this 'law of nature' as founded on the rational nature of human beings (Starke 1984:21). Although Grotius' views on international law were based on the relationships between states, he made several comments on the rights of indigenous peoples of the Americas. He, along with other jurists of the time, considered 'that wherever a country is inhabited by people who are connected by some political organisation, however primitive and crude, such a country is not to be regarded as *territorium nullius* and open to acquisition of occupation' (Lindley 1926:17). By not acknowledging rights of discovery and recognising indigenous claims to land, Grotius' perspective on the indigenous peoples of the Americas was influential in subsequent generations (Kingsbury and Roberts 1995:45).

Even though the theoretical ideas of the Spanish theologians were influential, their relatively progressive approach to the treatment of the indigenous peoples of the Spanish Empire was not upheld by other writers. Two particularly influential writers of the time were the French encyclopedist, Buffon, who argued in the mid-eighteenth century that the animal species and indigenous peoples of the Americas were inferior to those of Europe, and De Pauw, the Prussian philosopher, who reworked the image of Aristotle's 'natural slave' from Sepúlveda and argued that the natives of the Americas were 'ignoble savages' (Gerbi 1973:55). In this way the renaissance debate between those who saw nobility in the indigenous peoples and those who saw savagery continued. This discussion influenced the book, *History of the Americas*, by the Scottish Enlightenment historian, William Robertson, who, in 1777, incorporated the qualitative differences between Europe and the Americas, established by Buffon and de Pauw, (ibid.165) into the framework of Acosta's comparative history. The result was a history of progressive stages, which reflected the general developmentalist philosophy of the Enlightenment (Pagden 1994:39).

However, the new philosophy of the seventeenth and eighteenth centuries, particularly that of Descartes, although influenced by Spanish theologians, was not well received in Spain, where writers largely continued to demonstrate the rational principles underlying the Christian message. Particularly objectionable to Spanish theologians were the notions of scepticism and the primacy of self which directly challenged their more rigid Aristotelian world view based on Christian theology (Pagden 1994). However, this philosophical climate transformed the discussion of human rights, which proved critical in the revolutionary turmoil of the eighteenth century.

The emergence of a notion of individual rights took root among European philosophers of the seventeenth and eighteenth centuries. This period is also considered by some to be the nascent period of the subject of anthropology, when philosophers began to seek features which were common to all of humanity. These features were said to be 'natural' to all human beings regardless of place or time, and the indigenous nations of the Americas provided the inspiration for these theories of the state of nature. Locke was influenced by accounts from New England, others 'drew their picture of man in a state of nature from what had been published about the Indians of the St. Lawrence [and] Rousseau's portrait of natural man was largely drawn from what was known of the Caribs of South America' (Evans-Pritchard 1951:26).

Out of this 'human nature' arose the basis for universal rights. For example, in his book *Leviathan*, Thomas Hobbes says: 'The Right of Nature, which Writers commonly call *Jus Naturale*, is the Liberty each man hath to use his own power, as he will himselfe, for the preservation of his own Nature' (Hobbes 1985 (1651):189). For Hobbes, natural rights consisted of a power within each individual human, generated from the passions. They were natural aspects of individuals which, in order to avoid a state of endless conflict between competing individuals, have to be transferred or renounced when people form governments.

This theory of possessive individualism (Macpherson 1962:17) was taken up from a different direction by John Locke (1632-1704), who saw rights and government as a means to protect the individual from the excesses of political authority (Lloyd Thomas 1995:95). He developed these ideas from an initial attack on Robert Filmer (a thinker who took an extreme Hobbesian position) into the notion of the 'Natural Rights of Man' – life, liberty, and property – which are common to all people. In order to preserve these rights, human beings form civil society (Locke 1681 (1993)). Thus, rather than rights disappearing with the presence of government, as Hobbes argued, for Locke the object of civil society is to protect natural rights. However for Locke, membership of civil society, citizenship, was not opened to universal franchise, with the consequences which Macpherson (1962:262) notes: 'The greatness of seventeenth-century liberalism was its assertion of the free rational individual as the criterion of the good society; its tragedy was that this very assertion was necessarily a denial of individualism to half the nation'.

Nowhere was this more apparent than in Peru. The liberator of South America, Simón Bolivar, was influenced by European Enlightenment thinkers, particularly Locke (Trend 1946:129). After the victory of Peru over Spain, Bolivar established a new 'enlightened' regime. In his 1826 Peruvian constitution, Bolivar defined an electoral branch for Peru, restricting the franchise to literate men of Peruvian nationality, of twenty-five years or more, who practised a profession. This effectively excluded all indigenous peoples in the country.

Furthermore, in Locke's references to the indigenous peoples of the Americas, he justifies colonial exploitation by giving preference to the more hard-working colonists over the wasteful Indians (Chapter Five of the Second Treatise – 'Of Property'). According to Goldie (1993:xl), the two Treatises were subsequently used in American courtrooms to support arguments against native rights. This becomes particularly pertinent in Peru during the struggle for independence, because the Lockean notion of limiting individual rights to those with the franchise was compounded by the property laws of a few years earlier. In 1824, Bolivar decreed that Indians were now individual owners of the lands which they occupied and could sell them if they so wished. This replaced the Spanish colonial reservation of lands to communities (Dobyns and Doughty 1976:147), had the effect of opening up indigenous lands to the highest bidder, and established the basis for the inequalities of the semi-feudal hacienda system during the nineteenth century.

Bolivar was also highly influenced by the writings of Jean-Jacques Rousseau. 'Like Rousseau, Bolivar underlined the importance of educating as many of the inhabitants of the country as possible so that they might become fitted for democracy' (Trend 1946:141). However, in spite of the prominent position of the 'noble savage' in Rousseau's work (1984:103), education for the disadvantaged was not promoted in Peru, and the possibility of indigenous peoples benefitting from the independence struggle became increasingly remote.

The period of the Enlightenment thus eventually became bound up with the liberation experience in the Americas. The concepts of natural law (from Vitoria), notions of progress (from Acosta's history), and the debate between positive and negative imagery of the indigenous peoples of the Americas provides a continuity with the colonial period. However a marked difference arose later in the Enlightenment, particularly in the works of Locke, which looked at individual rights and property as a criteria for state membership, and of Rousseau, which emphasised the importance of education. These ideas were exported to the Americas with the struggle for independence. During this period, a shift took place: the features which separated indigenous from non-indigenous peoples were not so much distinctions between Christianity and paganism, but increasingly between a civilisation based on knowledge and ignorance (McGrane 1989:69ff.).

The importance of these ideas are still relevant today. The Peruvian government's statement of concern about the notion of territories and collective rights reflects the notion of individual rights based on citizenship and the franchise. The new Peruvian Land Law and the attempt to break into the inalienable land holdings of the indigenous peoples of the country reflect attempts to weaken collective territorial ownership in favour of more individualistic attitudes to property.

Nineteenth Century – Positivism

To some extent the shift which took place between the eighteenth and nineteenth centuries relates to what Foucault (1970) calls the break in 'episteme' from the classical to the modern era. According to his thesis, during the eighteenth century, classical notions of order, classification and representation underwent a change marked by a new preoccupation with change, development, and analysis of structure. This has been expressed by Kamenka (cited in Steinzor 1992:23):

> 'The demand for rights in the seventeenth and eighteenth centuries was a demand against the existing State and authorities, against despotism, arbitrariness and the political disenfranchisement of those who held different opinions. The demand for rights in the nineteenth and twentieth

centuries becomes increasingly a claim upon the State, a demand that it provide and guarantee the means for achieving the individual's happiness and well-being' (Kamenka 1988).

Debates, similar to those of Spanish colonial times and the Enlightenment, continued in the early nineteenth century when information from the Americas was used to further a discussion which took place in Germany. Humboldt had travelled extensively in South America and was strongly opposed to the ideas of de Pauw that there were higher and lower races. Hegel (1770-1831), on the other hand, portrayed America in his *Philosophy of History* as immature and impotent (Gerbi 1973:417). Indeed, according to Hegel, 'only in the state does man have a rational existence' (Held 1983:94). The way to protect a person's rights is through the state responding to people's needs (Plant 1972: 215). Those people who live outside of the state, according to this Hegelian view, would not have rights.

During the first half of the nineteenth century the indigenous communities of South America struggled to maintain control of their collective lands. From 1826 all indigenous people in the country had to pay a head tax called a *contribución* and many had to mortgage their lands to pay it (Dobyns and Doughty 1976:166). Head tax was abolished in 1856, only to be restored again in 1862, and with the expansion of the colonising frontier and capitalism (Vayussière 1988:83), indigenous peoples not only in the highlands but in the lowlands increasingly came into conflict with the growth of the nation state. External colonialism had turned in on itself (Favre 1988:114). 'The dominant ideology, based on liberalism and positivism, considered that the Indian or indigenous element had no place in the new national cultures which were being constructed' (Stavenhagen 1988:29), and increasingly a new concept of state nationality arose emphasising the notion of *mestisaje* (mixed race).

An early advocate of this positivist thinking was the Venezuelan Andrés Bello (1781-1865), who lived in London for eighteen years and knew the utilitarian philosophers J.S. Mill and Jeremy Bentham. The utilitarians placed much emphasis on the importance of statute law, interpreted and controlled by the State (Harrison 1983:238). Bello placed this into the context of the newly independent South American states and, when he eventually moved to Chile, he argued that to civilise a people it was necessary to legislate for them.

This reflected the jurisprudence of John Austin, who followed Bentham's ideas by emphasising the importance of a 'positive law' under the command of the sovereign state (Eastwood 1916:37).

Austin asserted state precedence over aboriginal rights arguing that customs can only become law when judges enforce them (Brown 1906:325). J.S. Mill, who was a student of Austin, similarly saw rights as closely associated with the law. He divided rights into legal rights, which are recognised by law, and moral rights, which the law ought to respect (Mill 1991:182). The lack of recognition of customary law among the utilitarian positivists is something which is very apparent with the emphasis on Roman law in contemporary Latin America (Stavenhagen 1988:96).

Other South American social philosophers followed this utilitarian line. The Argentineans were influential here. Juan Bautista Alberdi (1810-1884) and José Victoriano Lastarria (1817-1888) both followed Bentham. These thinkers saw Europe providing standards for the march of progress. Estebán Echeverría (1805-1851) saw that independence was the route to freedom while too many citizens were slaves to old ideas; he advocated education to change the situation. This reference to progress became more intense with the influence of Auguste Comte.

Comte was the main European proponent of positivism among social philosophers and produced a system which seemed very appropriate to those states involved in nation-building. He argued that society based on theology was dying and that a new scientific society was emerging, replacing priests with industrialists (Aron 1965:65). The scientific organisation of the industrial order, based on empirically understood laws, would ensure historical progress. The influence of Comte reached its height when independent Brazil placed his slogan 'Progress is the development of Order' on its national flag. Writers such as Lastarria and Echeverría saw in positivism a philosophical doctrine of salvation (Stavenhagen 1988:34).

Another influential European in the nineteenth century was Herbert Spencer, who, like Comte, was a sociologist. Spencer reinforced the racial element of nineteenth century thought in South America; he considered that cultural distinctions between 'savage' and civilised' persons emerged over time through the inheritance of acquired characteristics which 'could be arranged in hierarchical racial terms that provided what seemed an assured framework for the continuing belief in both intellectual and moral progress' (Stocking 1987:141).

Domingo Faustino Sarmiento (1811-1888) was the most vociferous advocate of European, particularly Anglo-Saxon, immigration to improve the blood of the nation-state. In his later writings, such as *'Conflict and Harmony of Races in America'* (1883), he was highly influenced by Spencer (Crawford 1961:50) and expressed himself in racial terms: 'What is it that distinguishes Spanish colonisation? The fact that it made a monopoly of its own race, that when it migrated to America it did not leave the Middle Ages, and that it absorbed into its own blood, a prehistorical and servile race'(Sarmiento 1883 II:415).

The nineteenth century brought together the positivism of social theory and jurisprudence with the strengthening of the nation-state and empires. This conglomeration of ideas was reinforced by racism. International law during this period reinforced racist assumptions by denying indigenous peoples their sovereignty. Lindley, writing in 1926, expresses this as follows: 'in comparatively modern times, a different doctrine has been contended ... which denies that International Law recognises any rights in primitive peoples to the territory they inhabit' (p.20). While the Monroe doctrine of 1823 guaranteed that there would be no more acquisition of territory on the American continent by European powers without their consent, this did not apply to indigenous peoples. International lawyers, such as Lorimer, (1883:157) Lawrence (1895:143), and Westlake (1904:89-9), agreed with the precedent set by US Judge Marshall who, in 1823, recognised the de facto rights of discoverers and conquerors over indigenous territories. Indigenous peoples had no rights because they technically did not exist as separate entities within the state.

These state-centred imperialist views of the second half of the nineteenth century combined positivism with an evolutionary framework both in jurisprudence and in the social sciences. Anthropology of the same period reflected this view in the work of such people as Maine (1861) and Morgan (1877), who placed states, peoples, and territories on a higher level than indigenous 'natives'. Although human beings were united as members of the same species, natives were of a markedly lower development category than the state citizens. The distinctions between savagery, barbarism, and civilisation, which had been used to differentiate ability but not capacity, had now taken on a racial hue.

Although the work of the nineteenth century anthropologists and English-speaking jurists were not directly influential in Latin America during the period, the whole racial and imperialistic frame of thinking was incorporated into state-thinking through influential European writers such as Comte and Spencer. This was particularly apparent in Peru during the time of the rubber boom from 1880 to 1920. At the turn of the century the demand in the USA and Europe for rubber gave rise to a massive increase in the extraction throughout the western Amazon. The violations of indigenous rights by J.C. Arana's

Peruvian Amazon Company led to an international campaign and subsequent scandal (Gray 1990b). Throughout this period, however, the Peruvian government was more concerned about securing its international boundaries than with the welfare of the Amazonian peoples, who were devastated by killings, disease, and slavery.

The nineteenth century constituted a shift in thinking on indigenous questions and in the place of the previous criteria of paganism and ignorance, the dominant discourse was centred around race and natural difference marked by a progress through time from 'primitive' to 'civilised' (McGrane 1989:89). Nevertheless the nineteenth century did not consist exclusively of people who opposed indigenous rights. In Peru, Manuel González Prada (1848-1918) was particularly important. He was the first thinker to raise the question of indigenous peoples in a constructive manner. He argued that there were no inferior races, only good and bad people, and vigorously opposed those who wanted to 'modify' race. In his book, *Horas de Lucha*, González Prada argued strongly against the exploitation of the indigenous peoples of Peru through tax and forced labour. His influence was the leading light in the formation of the *indigenismo* movement which took hold in the twentieth century.

Nevertheless, the influence of nineteenth century positivism is perhaps the strongest trait in the statement of the Peruvian government to the United Nations. Based on strong positivist legal principles, all indigenous rights are subject to control of the state, its legislation, and its constitution. The government can change legislation when and how it likes, and indigenous peoples have no option other than to accept this.

The Twentieth Century: From indigenism to indigenists to indigenous

Indigenism was a movement in Peru at the turn of the century which championed indigenous peoples. Inspired by González Prada, a group of intellectuals participated in the 'indigenismo' movement. The first institutional manifestation of this was the Asociación Pro-Indígena which was founded by Dora Mayer and her husband Pedro Zulen in 1909. The work of Mayer as both writer and lobbyist established the movement in Peru and provided an impetus which was to last eighty years (Cárdenas 1988:141). Whereas Mayer still adhered to the evolutionary positivism of the nineteenth century, but within a humanist approach, the socio-economic writings of her contemporary, José Carlos Mariátegui, reinterpreted indigenism through the work of Karl Marx, approaching indigenous questions from a class position.

From about 1910 onwards, an indigenist movement in literature which used features such as magical realism, lyrical intensification, emphasis on indigenous themes, and indigenous styles was taken up by writers such as Enrique López Albújar, Ciro Alegría, and José María Arguedas (Escajadillo 1994:55ff.). This aspect of indigenism in Peru is significant because it drew the value of indigenous culture to the attention of the reading public.

The struggle of indigenous peoples had been increasingly supported by the indigenists, and by the 1920s the movement had influenced the government of Leguía to approve a Constitution which recognised, after a hundred years, the collective rights of Peruvian indigenous peoples to their communities (García 1995:20).

At the same period, the indigenismo movement was gaining ground in other countries. In Brazil the Serviço de Proteção aos Indios (SPI) was founded in 1910. Its dominant philosophy was the idea of integration, assimilation, or civilisation of the Indians (Stavenhagen 1988:105). A similar development took place in Mexico after the 1910 revolution. A key writer in this area was Andrés Molina Enriquez, who argued that indigenous peoples suffered because of their position in the national social structure. He argued that the solution was to integrate indigenous peoples into the nation-state (Marzal 1986:404). The idea of integration was to prove fundamental to the indigenist movement when it went international.

The first Interamerican Indigenist Congress took place in Mexico in 1940, after which indigenist institutes began to spring up throughout the Americas as arms of government. Peru's Indigenous Institute was established in 1946 under the directorship of Luis Valcarcel, an anthropologist who campaigned actively for indigenous rights. However, during the same period, the integrationist aspect of indigenism became increasingly problematic for indigenous peoples.

In 1957 the International Labour Organisation adopted Convention 107 *Concerning the Protection and Integration of Indigenous and Other Tribal and Semi-Tribal Populations in Independent Countries.* The Convention, which is still in effect for those signatories who have not ratified the revised Convention 169, follows the indigenist line in that its primary aim is to integrate indigenous peoples into the State using protection as a preparation (Bennett op.cit.:18). Integration is not defined in detail in the Convention but it involves a hierarchy of rights:

> 'Under the convention ... the right of tribal populations to self-government by their own institutions is subordinate to "the national legal system or the objectives of the integration programmes". In return for the loss of the tribal populations' collective right of self-government, the convention

substitutes the development of individual rights and equal citizenship' (Falkowski 1992:54).

Indigenism became incorporated quickly into governmental thinking because it provided a way of strengthening state control over indigenous peoples through integration while opposing violations of their rights. Nevertheless, while indigenism sought to reduce the socio-economic disadvantages facing indigenous peoples, its effect was to tie them more securely into the national identity. As McBane (1989:113) points out, in the twentieth century, culture has become a more important feature of the discourse about indigenous peoples.

The reaction to indigenism started in the late 1960s and received its first shift in the Declaration of Barbados, in which the integrationist approach of the indigenists was criticised. The changes in indigenism entered the Interamerican Indigenist Institute in the 1970s. From 1972, indigenous peoples began to participate in the conferences (Stavenhagen 1988:113) and cultural respect and support for indigenous organisations became increasingly apparent. In 1986 the ILO decided to revise its Convention 107 to move from its integrationist perspective to one in keeping with indigenous peoples' desires and needs. This shift was designed to be from an 'indigenist' to an 'indigenous' perspective (Gray 1986:73).

The indigenist paradigm thus broke away from the racial categorisation of indigenous peoples and concentrated on socio-economic and cultural factors. The defining factor of indigenous peoples had been their isolation or marginalisation, and states proposed to solve this by integrating them into national society. This argument broke down with the increasingly vociferous rise of the indigenous movement, which no longer wanted to be addressed by advocates but which wanted to take its own future into its hands and speak for itself.

The Peruvian government position shares an indigenist position to the extent that it advocates the integration of 'indigenous populations' into the state, through citizenship. Thus, while respecting rights, it takes away the capacity to be self-determining. This was the approach of the indigenist movement in the 1940s, and it is currently alive and well.

This section has looked at four periods in the history of indigenous-state relations with particular focus on Latin America. The conclusions parallel the classification made by McGrane (1989) as to the categorisation of 'the Other'. It shows that during the last five hundred years different aspects of indigenous affairs have been emphasised. During the Spanish colonisation of the fifteenth century the debate centred around whether indigenous peoples were pagan and whether as such they had rights to their territories; during the period of independence from Spain, the influence of Enlightenment philosophy emphasised individual rights to land and citizenship with a franchise and ownership based on education, which labelled indigenous peoples as ignorant; during the nineteenth century, positivism and state-centred approaches to progress and development excluded indigenous peoples on the basis of their racial (natural) differences; in the twentieth century, cultural and socio-economic differences have come to the fore and these are seen as based on marginalisation, leading to the argument that indigenous peoples need to be integrated into the state to solve their problems.

This explains to some extent the sources from which arises the Peruvian government's position. If we review the points which were made in its analysis, it is possible to see that features from throughout the last five hundred years co-exist in their position:

a) Although the government does not attack the indigenous peoples of Peru as being pagan or barbarian, its refusal to recognise rights to indigenous territories and resources reflects the debate which took place in the sixteenth century. The government seems to be on the side of the Spanish colonists, not with the advocates of indigenous natural rights.
b) The Peruvian government advances the case of individual rights, so prominent in the Enlightenment period, with its emphasis on citizenship.
c) The government's emphasis on state control in governance and its positivistic interpretation of the law comes straight from the nineteenth century.
d) The refusal to recognise 'indigenous' as a colonial relationship, and the emphasis on recognising rights within the framework of citizenship, is a clear reference to the integrationist aims of the indigenists.

The grounds of the position of nation states rests on the de facto power of states, coupled with a legal positivist notion of human rights. However, this does not mean that the positions of nation states are always negative. As has been noted in this review of the conceptualisation of the rights of indigenous peoples, in each period there have been relatively pro-indigenous perspectives in the discussions. Vitoria and de las Casas, for example, recognised the importance of indigenous peoples' rights to their territories; in the Enlightenment, the indigenous peoples were at least theoretically accredited with rights (particularly in the writings of Rousseau), in some cases collectively and on the basis of their customary institutions; in the nineteenth century, organisations lobbied to prevent the destruction of indigenous peoples (such as the Aborigines Protection Society and countless missionaries); while in the twentieth century, indigenists and pro-indigenous advocates have increasingly recognised the rights to self-determination, territory, political recognition, and cultural freedom, which Elias Kentehuari mentions in his statement to the United Nations.

This chapter has juxtaposed the presentation of an Arakmbut with that of the Peruvian government to the United Nations. Embedded within both texts are elements of the epistemological and ontological basis for approaching indigenous rights. The indigenous approach rests on the interface between an internal relativistic morality based on social relationships in which solutions can be found within a socio-cultural and spiritual framework and external threats from the national society, which risk the destruction of that very socio-cultural framework and the moral principles on which it rests.

The government position, on the other hand, reverberates with a history of legal, political, and philosophical discussion about colonisation. A common thread is that, with the state in power, the indigenous peoples have to accommodate themselves to the prevailing situation. This positivistic approach combines what governments refer to as 'realistic' goals with political power.

Both indigenous and non-indigenous representatives use a rhetoric based on morality and political power. However, it is clear that the armaments of indigenous peoples come predominantly from a moral sense of justice and a description of the facts of human rights violations. For the state, on the other hand, the approach is biased to legal positivism combined with political expediency. For the Arakmbut, myths explain experience, while for the government, ideology sets out a mythological framework for experience.

Having established the outlines of difference between indigenous peoples and the state government, subsequent chapters will refine these distinctions and look for over-lapping areas. Government and indigenous peoples need not be pitted in an eternal conflict, but strategies based on mutual understanding might possibly lead to a political space where genuine dialogue can take place.

Chapter 2

STATE AND COMMUNITY IN THE PERUVIAN AMAZON

'When someone comes into the community and says *"todos somos Peruanos"* (we are all Peruvians), watch out, he is trying to screw you.'

This comment was made by a young Arakmbut man in June 1992, expressing the tension between Peruvian and indigenous identity. When colonists or state officials use the appeal to common nationality in order to persuade a sceptical Arakmbut community into making a particular decision, the division between indigenous *paisano* and alien *colono* takes precedence over common national identity and frequently leads to a clash of interests and identities.

This clash between indigenous peoples of the Amazon and colonists who wave the flag of Peruvian national identity reflects a broader phenomenon – the ambivalent and contradictory relationship between indigenous peoples and the Peruvian state. While 'native communities' of lowland Peru are legally recognised with demarcated titles to their territories under the juridical protection of the state, national policies threaten these indigenous peoples with devastation from colonisation and the plundering of their resources.

This chapter traces the complexities of this relationship, looking at the incoherent aspects of state identity, the limitations of state control, the inconsistencies between state and government, and the tension between legitimacy and force. In spite of the common assumption that indigenous peoples will inevitably become integrated into the state, the Arakmbut show that this option is far from straightforward. The power of state rulers is never sufficient to gain absolute control over all aspects of resources and persons. Therefore, the state consists of gaps and areas where its power is weaker than others. Within these political spaces indigenous peoples such as the Arakmbut, who have lived in the area since before the state was formed, provide a challenge to state authority.

Throughout this chapter there is a constant shift of vision between the Peruvian state and the national or local government. Government officials like to think of themselves as representatives of the state; however, this relationship is not simply a hegemonic self-definition by those in power. Indigenous peoples may perceive government and state as a single entity which they can ignore or embrace, but they can also separate the two entities and assert their claims in the intervening political space through the popular movement in civil society.

The most immediate relationship between the Arakmbut and the state takes place between communities and the local municipality. In the case of San José del Karene, contact takes place regularly with the thousand or so colonist population of the trading post, Boca Colorado, one-and-a-half hours downriver from the community. The Arakmbut usually visit the settlement every few weeks to sell some gold, buy provisions and catch up on news. During these contacts friendships are struck up and agreements made.

An example of apparent goodwill took place in 1989, when the then-mayor of Boca Colorado agreed, as a part of his electoral campaign strategy, to provide new schools for San José and the neighbouring Arakmbut community upriver, Puerto Luz. The initial positive relationship gradually turned sour, however, as inactivity on the part of the municipality led to resentment among the Arakmbut, which came to a head in March 1992.

The Storming of Boca Colorado[1]

The meeting between San José and Puerto Luz was planned for 20 March and I had been asked along as an observer. But the trip nearly had to be postponed because several of the young men from San José returned late from gold work that day and were tired; the rain in the headwaters meant that the river would be high and maybe there was no petrol available. Several Arakmbut lay in their houses, no one making the move to go; then, at the last moment, someone

---

1. A shorter version of this case study was published in Gray 1992. The account of the meetings are taken from verbatim notes made at the time.

shouted for those who wanted to go to hurry up. In less than five minutes we were all in the boat going upriver.

On reaching Puerto Luz, we waded through the mud, climbed the steep red sandstone cliff and slowly dawdled along the river bank to the main community. The San José group then sat on a bench outside the main patio, while the Arakmbut of Puerto Luz finished a game of football. Some women passed and greeted the visitors. The game finished and the San José Arakmbut waited to be formally invited in. Eventually some elders came out and welcomed visitors who went forward and shook hands with their relatives, using the appropriate relationship term. This entry was reminiscent of the descriptions of formal entries of visitors to communal houses before the missionaries first came to the Arakmbut on the Wandakwe river in 1950.

The meeting began an hour later at *baysik* when the sun began to set and the soft light played gently on the clusters of Arakmbut seated outside their houses. The discussions covered various problems, but the most immediate concern was the municipality. There were no long speeches. Ernesto, a young Arakmbut leader from FENAMAD summarised the situation: For more than three years, since Boca Colorado became a municipality, the non-indigenous authorities of the settlement had promised materials for the two communities to construct new schools. In November 1991, corrugated iron, paint and nails had been stored in the warehouses of Boca Colorado ready for use as building materials. Several members of the community had been shown them. However, officials refused to hand them over and reports said that the school materials were about to be sold to the highest bidder. After the presentation of the problem there was a long discussion as the elders picked over the details and reached agreement.

However this was not the only problem. The rainy season of 1991-92 had been particularly intense. The rivers had burst their banks and many of San José's gardens, which were planted close to the river bank had been flooded or washed away. Boca Colorado had also been flooded several times and so the local authorities contacted the regional and central governments in Cusco and Lima to seek support. In response, emergency food and medicines had been provided by the state for all the inhabitants of the area. However, the medicines and food had never been distributed because the civil defence committee, which controlled the supplies, said that the native communities were not eligible to receive support.

The meeting continued, and with all the elders talking at once, the decision emerged. The elders suggested that the Arakmbut go to

Boca Colorado and get the materials for themselves. San José and Puerto Luz set the deadline for ten days later, 30 March 1992. If the authorities would not move by then, the Arakmbut would handle the matter in their way.

Men and women from both communities co-ordinated their plans over the following week and informed the municipality at Boca Colorado of their intentions. In the early morning of 30 March, two boats from San José and three from Puerto Luz sailed down the Karene river to Boca Colorado. In all, about seventy-five Arakmbut landed at the trading settlement at 10am. A meeting was called in the school. The mayor was not present, as he was in Puerto Maldonado, but several members of the council attended, as well as the state-appointed governor, responsible for law and order, and the judge (a juridical appointment).

After introductions, Eziquiel from Puerto Luz said: 'We have come to collect the materials for the community schools and the distributions for the flood victims. You have not distributed anything. Our gardens have been destroyed by the floods, but the *wahaipi* [highlanders] are getting all the help.'

Then Tomás from San José said: 'Donations from all over the world come for the poor to Peru, but here it is the opposite. Those who have more, they are the ones who receive hand-outs. In the shops people sell materials and medicines which should go the indigenous communities. The Law of the Native Communities says that state functionaries are obliged to give priority to native communities.'

The community representatives were told by the council members that the mayor was in Puerto Maldonado and could not be contacted. They were not authorised to hand out materials to the Arakmbut. The judge said that they would have to wait until the matter was settled. No one knew about the Law of Native Communities.

Then Andrés said, 'The communities have nothing. The authorities are sleeping. Maybe you people share the pickings, but not with us.'

'The problem is the mayor,' said one of the council. 'We can do nothing until he arrives. We will try to contact him by radio and get his permission for you to take the things.' The judge and the council said that the mayor was a problem but that nothing could be done without advice from Puerto Maldonado.

The governor then said: 'I will contact the Prefect of Maldonado who is responsible for law and order and say that there is an emergency and that the community will take power if the mayor does not come.'

As the voices got louder some Arakmbut were saying, 'Let's just get it now with an axe'.

'The mayor is looking for an arrow up his arse,' said an elder.

After waiting for a while, it was agreed that the governor of Boca Colorado would try to contact the Prefectura, saying that he must give his approval for the removal of the materials or else violence might erupt. In spite of the emergency call by radio which all could hear, there was no response. ('The Brazilians could have invaded by now,' said one Arakmbut wit.)

The Arakmbut agreed to wait overnight to give the authorities twelve hours to change their minds. They considered that when the authorities had wanted to sell off their materials, access had not been a problem, but now, no one was responding. The Arakmbut slept the night at Boca Colorado and some, who had gold money, began drinking and singing traditional songs in the bars. The settlers seemed uneasy with fifty discontented Arakmbut wandering through the settlement with a grudge against the authorities.

At dawn, a boat-load of free handouts from the Ministry of Health arrived at the trading post on its way to the illegal colonists' settlements of Bajo Pukiri and Alto Pukiri. Over fifty sacks and barrels of cooking oil and milk-fat stopped at Boca Colorado. The Arakmbut became angry when they saw this, and went to the health post to complain to the doctor who was responsible for distribution. The doctor had previously refused to grant food to the communities, but with stern insistence from the Arakmbut, he eventually agreed to donate five sacks of powder and three tins of oil for each community.

At 11am, the Arakmbut from San José and Puerto Luz went to the council offices and demanded that they open the door to release the materials. Tempers flared, but the officials backed off. The Arakmbut then found a massive log and smashed the lock on the door of the storeroom. Organised and orderly, the Arakmbut then removed a hundred sheets of corrugated iron, nails, and some paint. Several items for construction had already disappeared, particularly cement for the school floors. After writing down carefully everything which had been taken, the Arakmbut carried away the materials to their canoes.

A bemused and surprisingly sympathetic local population watched the proceedings, mentioning that in the end this was the only way to deal with the authorities. The Governor wrote an Act of Agreement which was signed by the communities as a receipt.

As the final materials were placed in the boats, a group rounded on the medical doctor and the chairman of the support committee for victims of the flood. While they were in control of the situation, the two representatives from San José and Puerto Luz who were responsible for health went with the officials to the civil defence office and insisted that the communities receive the medicines due to them. After twenty minutes' negotiation, the Arakmbut received five boxes of medicines for the two communities.

But the Arakmbut had to act fast. The authorities had radioed to the police and rumours were beginning to run wild that armed guards were flying up from Puerto Maldonado by helicopter. Eventually, with canoes laden, the Arakmbut made their way up-river, tense and nervous. At the moment when they passed the boundary of San José's territory, however, a cry of joyful triumph went up. The stoic faces broke into smiles and tension fell away. In the evening they distributed the food to all the households and put the materials in the old school. They had won a victory.

At first sight, this account of a series of events which occurred in 1992 describes the problems which can arise when local authorities, with the backing of the state, fall out with indigenous peoples. Indigenous peoples such as the Arakmbut need the state and want support in the form of facilities and services (in this case materials for school and flood relief). However, when the state, in the guise of local authorities, does not fulfil its obligations, the indigenous communities, providing that they are united and motivated, use direct action to achieve their goal.

According to the view of those in power, the state is a unified entity bounded by its territorial integrity. Indigenous peoples live within this framework, as other citizens, but with limited autonomy. However they cannot escape the market mechanism of the state, and sooner or later they will be integrated through their needs, regardless of whether this is desirable or not. Exponents of this view of the state (typified by the Peruvian government statement in the last chapter) argue that indigenous peoples are already integrated into the mainstream of national society. Those who try to avoid the state retain a romantic primitivism and should be helped to integrate with as much understanding as possible.

This chapter questions these assumptions. Embedded in the description above are references which show that the relationship between the state and indigenous peoples is complicated and contradictory. The state is not necessarily as straightforward as we might initially suppose. The case study brings together several aspects of state relations with the Arakmbut which raise questions of coherence, integrity, and government legitimacy. Each of these dimensions is a commentary on the nature of the state itself.

Homogeneity and disaggregation

The description above illustrates the point that, rather than a coherent institution, the state is a 'fluid and disconnected set of arenas' (Hoffman 1995:23).[2] On the one hand, homogeneous symbols of Peruvian identity, citizenship, and national symbols are meant to be shared by the people living within the boundaries of the country. Yet, from the perspective of the Arakmbut, who in many cases lack national electoral cards and are frequently pitted against the authorities, any sense of Peruvian identity is far more complicated.

The first people with whom the representatives of the communities met in the school on their visit to Boca Colorado demonstrated the complexity of state relations with the Arakmbut. The mayor was not present, but the council (elected representatives of the municipality) realised that they could not defend the mayor and kept a largely neutral position.[3] The judge (an appointment by the judiciary) used delaying tactics throughout the meeting, advocating waiting for advice. The governor (a Presidential appointee under the Prefectura and responsible for law and order) was, in contrast, more amenable and tried to seek ways of solving the problem. In fact, the governor's careful handling of the situation ensured that the Arakmbut victory had only limited consequences (see chapter four).

To some extent, the personalities of the participants at the discussion explains these different perspectives; however, the three ways of appointment are significant. The governor is an outsider and, as a relatively new person to the district, saw the justice of the indigenous claim, but was reluctant to break completely with the other officials. The judge was chosen from Boca Colorado and shared the

2. Other writers on the state reiterate this point. Andrew Vincent, for example, says: 'When dealing with the state we must be aware that it is the most problematic concept in politics ... Despite its apparent solidity (try not paying taxes or leaving the country without a passport) it is none the less difficult to identify – an idea or cluster of concepts, values, and ideas about social existence' (1987:3-4). Similar views on the complexity of the state can be found in Claessen and Skalnik (1978) and Held (1983:1).

3. The municipal district of Madre de Dios (not to be confused with the larger subregion which will be discussed later) covers about 10,000 square kilometres with a population of about seven thousand (of whom a tenth are indigenous). At the previous election in 1990, the then mayor was elected on the basis of seventeen votes out of a total of under fifty. The reason for such a low vote is that electors in Peru vote where their electoral cards were issued. Nearly all the colonists come from the highlands or Puerto Maldonado and cannot vote in the district. The indigenous people, on the other hand, are mainly disenfranchised because they have not had the means to obtain electoral cards until recently.

colonists' perspectives. His ignorance of the Law of Native Communities was perhaps one of the features which brought the conflict to a head. The council members broadly shared the judge's opinion. They were aware that elections were due in a few months and wanted the mayor to lose face so that they could disassociate themselves from his unpopularity and put themselves forward as candidates. Indeed this took place, and within the year one of the council became mayor.

The first distinction which the case study indicates is the lack of homogeneity among the state functionaries. However, these divisions, from an indigenous perspective, depend on the extent to which their political interests converge or diverge with the Arakmbut. Even though the authorities disagreed with each other, they all showed ignorance of the Law of Native Communities and were reluctant to fulfil the state's obligation to the indigenous peoples of the area. As we shall see, this law is the state's key legitimising factor in Arakmbut eyes; when the officials all expressed their ignorance of indigenous rights, the local government appeared united against the Arakmbut, and the storming of Boca Colorado went ahead.

Whereas local government should not be confused with the state, from the perspective of the Arakmbut the authorities at Boca Colorado in the context of this conflict were a manifestation of the state. The irony in the case study, however, is that even though the state authorities in Boca Colorado all disagreed with each other, what eventually drew them together was common cause against the Arakmbut – they were all opposed to the communities receiving their school materials. This led eventually to the Arakmbut reacting as outsiders to the local governmental representatives of a homogenous state. Thus with the local government identified with the state, the Arakmbut challenged not only local government but also the state.

Integration and separation

A second distinction reflected in the case study is between appointed and elected officials. The chances of an Arakmbut person being appointed to an official governmental position in the municipality is practically non-existent.[4] However, indigenous people in several parts of Peru have been elected as mayors of districts, and even of

---

4. Some Arakmbut have been appointed 'lieutenant governors' of their communities. This is an honourary position which means that the state recognises that they are responsible for 'law and order' in the community, but it has limited meaning for the Arakmbut themselves, and minimal effect outside of the community.

provinces (the next largest administrative unit). This possibility arises in areas where indigenous peoples are the majority population of an area; the District of Madre de Dios is one of these. Elections provide the indigenous peoples of Peru with a framework for participation, even if gaining an official position is extremely difficult.

This opens out the extent to which the Arakmbut are prepared to relate to the state and use its framework to bring to fruition their aims and desires. Although the official Peruvian position is that indigenous peoples are automatically integrated into the state, the case study questions this assumption. Migdal (1994:25-6) argues that the state is constantly defining relations with social forces. The two most common relationships are either that the state draws existing social forces into its orbit (integration) or that social forces draw the state into their own local framework (incorporation). This option occurs throughout the state, but is particularly noticeable among indigenous peoples such as the Arakmbut.

By breaking away from the focus on the dominance of state power, an indigenous perspective converts the periphery to the centre. The integrity of the state is dependent on the extent to which officials are in control of the area. In the case study, whereas the authorities refused to allow the Arakmbut to take their materials from the warehouse, they were powerless to stop them sacking the municipal store. The governor certainly appeared to have the upper hand, in that he was assumed to be the only person capable of mobilising the police force *(Guardia Civil)* and the only moment when the Arakmbut nearly lost their nerve was when they thought (erroneously) that the Governor had double-crossed them and sent for the armed police.

For the duration of one day, the Arakmbut effectively took over Boca Colorado. They dictated the terms of agreement and asserted their claim. It is very difficult to describe this assertion of indigenous rights as 'integration' into the state. The Arakmbut were connected to the state in that they were prepared to accept its facilities and services, yet when the mayor reneged on his promises, they challenged not only the authority of the mayor, but asserted their claim over the opinion of the council, the judge, and the governor. The point is that the Arakmbut are neither integrated nor isolated from the state, but rather the relationship varies according to the context.

This presents a second view of the relationship between state and government. The Arakmbut felt that the authorities had double-crossed them and ignored their rights under state law. By taking over Boca Colorado and subsequently looking at the possibility of entering local government through elections, the Arakmbut recognised that the government officials could be challenged and forced to comply with state commitments; in this context, government and state appeared distinct.

Legitimacy and force

The third aspect raised in the case study is a contradiction which goes straight to the root of Arakmbut relations with the state and, indeed, constitutes one of the main inconsistencies lurking around state formations; the contradiction between legitimacy and force (Hoffman 1995:86).[5] The legitimacy of government comes from a claim over the state which is backed up by the potential use of force. Should the government step over the line of what is perceived to be just, it loses its legitimacy. This is what occured in Boca Colorado.

When the Arakmbut arrived at Boca Colorado, they asserted their claims through recourse to the Law of Native Communities 22175. This law is the major protection for indigenous peoples of Peru, guaranteeing them their rights to their territories and recognition of their juridical status. Their appeal to this law is an important claim for justice, and is their principal expression of their acceptance of the legitimacy of the Peruvian state and its respective government. Yet the governor, judge, and council all claimed ignorance of its provisions.

The Law of Native Communities was originally drawn up by a paternalistic state, but, from an indigenous perspective, although not perfect, it is sufficiently beneficial to provide an incentive for forging a constructive relationship with the state. A state that consists exclusively of oppressive institutions is not an advertisement for a constructive relationship, but one which respects indigenous rights

5. Force and legitimacy have been prominent in discussions of government since the sixteenth and seventeenth centuries. Whereas in the sixteenth century, writers such as Hobbes and Bodin saw monarchy as the best way of organising a state, by the seventeenth century, Locke and Montesquieu held a more constitutional view, where the rights, obligations, and duties of the subjects became more important (Held 1985:44).

The notion of the state as protector or oppressor concerned philosophers of the eighteenth and nineteenth century. Rousseau believed in the state as an expression of the sovereign will of the people (1968:61-2), yet citizens were 'in chains' and their liberty constrained within the stricture of the state. In the nineteenth century, writers such as Hegel thought that liberty could be found within this constraint (Plant 1985:122) whereas Bentham and Mill saw the state as a threat to individual liberty, which could only be overcome by accountability of government and the protection of citizens' democratic rights enshrined in the law (Mill 1991:207).

attracts indigenous participation in a full and democratic sense, rather than through processes of forced integration.

In contrast to the Law of Native Communities, which stipulates the obligations of functionaries in dealing with problems faced by indigenous peoples, the Arakmbut also fear state oppression. They rushed to leave Boca Colorado when the rumour was spread that the armed police were on their way from Puerto Maldonado to arrest them. They know that officials of the Peruvian state can be oppressive: shootings, arbitrary imprisonment, and torture are all familiar to the indigenous peoples of the Madre de Dios. No one was prepared to wait around to see whether the rumour was true.

Protection and aggression of the state are the two contradictory poles which frame the relationship between the Arakmbut and the Peruvian authorities. The contradiction between force and legitimacy explains the suspicions which the Arakmbut have of the state. They see it as the apotheosis of oppression, yet it is also a means of protection against oppression.[6] The case study shows that the state authorities were incapable either of applying the law or of asserting the state's authority through force, which questions the very capacity of the state to control its boundaries. Thus, paradoxically, the Arakmbut were motivated to storm Boca Colorado by a sense of injustice reinforced by their knowledge of the law and left in haste in fear of state oppression, both of which were outside the vision of the state officials.

Thus, from an Arakmbut perspective, government and state can appear as the same oppressive force, in which case the Arakmbut respond by asserting their rights and retreating. However, in another context, corrupt officials can be distinguished from the state structure,

6. Whereas general criteria can be used to identify the modern state, this does not necessarily mean that states constitute an ahistorical political category (Giddens 1985). There have been many different types of state in world history: the Inca, Aztec, Egyptian, or Mesopotamian organisations bear only a passing resemblance to modern states, while the Greek states, based on notions of territory, citizenship, and the rule of law for the purpose of securing the common good and the submersion of the individual within the collective, contained features found in most indigenous communities (Aristotle 1992:59).

The word 'state' comes from the Latin *status* meaning 'established' or 'recognised'. Between Roman and medieval times the meaning shifted from referring to the personal condition of a ruler to political rule itself (Vincent, A. 1987:16-17). Influenced by Machiavelli's ideas of a state as the structure of public institutionalised power, the modern idea of the state arose in the 16th century (D'Entrèves 1967:29; Held 1985:2). However, the ideology of modern state sovereignty is associated with the French Revolution.

and by incorporating the state into their way of life, the Arakmbut can stake a claim to its benefits. Thus the more a particular government is distinguished from the state apparatus, and the more indigenous peoples such as the Arakmbut have the political space to control the contexts in which they deal with the state, the more room there is for seeking constructive agreement and peaceful co-existence.

Indigenous Peoples and the State

The case study has raised the paradoxical and contradictory features of the state, juxtaposing homogeneity and disaggregation, integration and incorporation with force and legitimacy. Bringing these features together can make one question the extent to which the state exists as a coherent category.

No legal definition of state exists in international law, even though states are the main protagonists of the formation of international legal standards for other sectors (Howard Berman pers. comm.). Three approaches can provide some orientation to the notion of state. Some writers consider that a definition of the state is impossible and that a more general term, such as 'political system', is adequate (Easton 1971). However, this does not really illuminate the Arakmbut situation, in which distinct forms of political system are in conflict.

Other writers take a Weberian view (Migdal 1988:19; Hoffman 1995:48), according to which a state consists of various authorities (bureaucratic, executive and legislative, for example) which claim a monopoly on the legitimate use of force within a given territory. This claim is something unique to the state, which other forms of government, particularly indigenous ones, do not have (Hoffman op.cit:42). Whereas this approach connects government and state, it does not, on its own, grasp the social interests which control the state.

According to the third view, the Peruvian state is part of a political system controlled by *blancos* (whites). This is, in fact, an ethnic version of Marx' view that states are reflections of class divisions. In the *Communist Manifesto* he says: 'The executive of the modern state is but a committee for managing the common affairs of the whole bourgeoisie' (1977:223). In this way government is linked to socioeconomic interests and is an instrument of class oppression (see also Lenin in *The State and Revolution*, 1971:280).

Each of these approaches is relevant to the Arakmbut. The state is a social system made up of political interests; however, it also exists as a constant presence for the Arakmbut, in Weber's terms, as a public power of interests, which claim control over a territory and persons through potential use of force.

The conclusion here is that states cannot be separated from the social processes which operate in a country, whether nationally or locally (Migdal 1988: 9). What is of interest in Peru is that the official view of the state as a strong set of institutions governing social interests relies on national ideology as promoted by the current government. This 'lay-man's' view of the state appears in many national and international fora, particularly at the UN Working Group on Indigenous Populations. It pervades the statement reproduced in the previous chapter and is frequently accepted without much thought. However, as noted above, government in its generic sense is a part of state, but any one government which makes the claim that it is the state soon encounters a multitude of limiting factors.[7]

The Peruvian State

A general description of Peru, based on information from reference volumes such as the Statesman's Year-Book (Paxton 1987:982 ff.), presents Peru as a country of 496,093 square miles, geographically divided between coastal desert, highlands, and tropical forest. The majority of its twenty million citizens are indigenous peasant farmers from the highland areas although Peru contains over sixty different indigenous peoples, the majority of which reside in the Amazon.

Peru was the land of several pre-Columbian civilisations, the most famous of which were the Inca. They were invaded by the Spaniard Francisco Pizarro in 1532 and, in spite of many years of resistance, from 1542 the country came under the direct rule of Spain through a viceregal system. The dreadful treatment of the indigenous people of Peru, who died from disease, slavery, and murder, was an international scandal. In spite of several revolts the Spanish remained in control until Bolivar's general, San Martín, declared independence on 28 July 1821. The Peruvian state began on that date, establishing its existence on the defeat of the Spanish (De Jasay 1985:15).

For the first fifteen years of independence the commanders of the liberation struggle fought each other to control the country. The first

---

7. Carrithers (1989:189) would call this a 'pop' view of the state. He uses the term to refer to the reinforcing of a collective representation in our civilisation. 'Such reconfirmations are perceived to be weighty, and therefore achieve popularity, just in so far as they have moral consequences. The reconfirmation is of a moral vision, a view of what human beings are in the light of what they ought to be.'

period of stability, between 1845 and 1862, came under President Ramón Castilla, who carried out various reforms, including the abolition of slavery, installing the first liberal constitution in 1860. Dictatorship and war with Spain (1865-6) and with Chile (1879-83), during which Peru was occupied for a period, marked a collapse in the economy, which became increasingly dependent on Europe and North America. The history of Peru this century has consisted of shifts between elected democratic Presidents and military dictatorships.

Indigenous peoples of the Amazon have been most directly affected by the state since the regime of General Juan Velasco (1968-75) when the progressive indigenous laws were drafted, although they were weakened by General Francisco Morales Bermúdez (1975-1980). After the restoration of democracy in 1980, Fernando Belaúnde Terry, Alan García, and Alberto Fujimori were elected Presidents. In 1992, Fujimori, with military support, unilaterally closed the Congress, established a new assembly providing him with political backing, and re-wrote the Constitution for the fourth time this century. The authoritarian rule of Fujimori (called a *'dictablanda'* rather than *dictadura*) has gained public support because during this period two great inconveniences for Peruvians have been reduced – hyper-inflation and the guerilla movement, Sendero Luminoso. Fujimori was elected for a second term of office in 1995.

With a Gross National Product of about $980 per capita, Peru is a republic operating with a President and a Legislative Assembly. The fifteen ministers of the Cabinet lead the bureaucratic administrative machinery of government and the Supreme Court is the highest level of the judiciary. The state is responsible for energy and natural resources, communications, and the economy. Peru is organised on several administrative levels: the capital in Lima is the main focus of state government and political decision-making; in 1988, however, Peru was decentralised into regions each of which has some autonomy over its internal affairs. At a local level, municipalities are run by elected mayors and councils.

Peruvian 'civil society' (Gramsci 1988:306) consists of private organisms such as churches, trades unions, political parties, and cultural associations which are 'distinct from the process of production and from the public appurtenances of the state' (Simon 1991:70). The civil society relates to the state in different ways according to the government and the institution. Whereas the state structure itself does not depend on any one aspect of the civil society, it needs its citizens.

This general view of the state relates the idea of a coherent and consistent state to each individual. State and civil society coincide within each person by means of two elements which are more powerful than all the other aspects of state discussed above: national symbols and citizenship. The flag and national anthem are displayed every day at school and on Sunday public parades. To some extent a successful President can become a national icon. For example, a recent cover of *Newsweek* (10 May 1993) compared Fujimori favourably with other South American Presidents because of his 'anti-politics'. The article portrays him as a 'cultural phenomenon' in the line of Inca autocracy and a member of the civilian society taking on corrupt political parties. By identification with imagery such as the flag, national anthem and in this case, the President, the state can by-pass de facto chaos and reach out to the individual. The effect of national symbols is to blur, albeit temporarily, the gap between the individual citizen and the state.

Apart from the symbolic conjunction of state and individual through national symbols, the most enduring example of a person's relationship to the state comes through citizenship. All citizens in Peru have to possess a voting card. Men can only receive this if they have served or been exempted from military service. Women need not do national service. The electoral card is not just for voting but is the main basis of individual control by the state. At check-posts, river, sea, and air terminals, or at any entry into official buildings, the electoral card has to be shown.

This general 'establishment' view of the Peruvian state reflects the official view of the country as represented by the government in international bodies such as the United Nations. However in the case of Peru, there are several factors which question such a description when we look in more detail at the influence of the state.

Inconsistency in the Peruvian State

The Peruvian state is not a consistent or coherent phenomenon. One of the reasons for this is that each government tries to redraw the state in its own image. The result is a continual shift of organisation and power. The state is constantly buffeted by different social interests and throughout history leadership, class, administration, the law and the constitution have regularly changed. The effect is a constant attempt by whoever is in power to install order where they see chaos, but none has succeeded in institutionalising the limited control they achieve (Stefan 1978).

Migdal (1988:36-7) explains this phenomenon as the inability of the state to get a strong society to do as it wants. This is particularly apparent in countries where 'web-like societies host a melange of fairly autonomous social organisations'. Peru, according to this view, is a 'diffused structure consisting of a strong society and a weak state.' Hammergren (1977:449) agrees:

> 'It is true that constitutions and legislation often accord enormous powers of control to central government, but the question remains as to whether this control is actually exercised or exists only on paper. The limited success of Latin American governments in enforcing their own legislation suggests that the extent of this control is not great'. (See also Migdal 1988:7.)

The leadership structure of the Peruvian state is illustrative here, in particular, in terms of who runs the country. Peru is headed by a President, but his powers are kept in check by two sources: the military and the Congress. Under the military dictatorships which chequer Peru's history, the army controlled most of the state apparatus. When the Congress is in power, influence shifts to the political party system and the state administration is filled by party patronage, through the President.

Although the Peruvian state can be defined by its Constitution, even this is not consistent. This century alone, constitutions have been drafted in 1920, 1933, 1979, and 1993. In April 1992, Fujimori dissolved Congress, suspended the Constitution and formed a 'Democratic Constitutional Assembly' (which was neither democratic nor constitutional); this was boycotted by the mainstream political parties (Peru Support Group nda:15). The Assembly then drafted a new constitution which was 'approved' by a national referendum, the results of which have not been made public. Unofficial sources say that it was approved by 51 percent of the electorate and it was subsequently described by opponents as 'legal but not legitimate'. The danger of the 1993 Constitution is that it considerably weakens the territorial rights of indigenous peoples.

As with the Constitution, there is little or no continuity in the administrative bureaucracy of the state, most senior positions are appointments from patronage. However, at the same time, the size of the state bureaucracy rises and falls according to historical circumstances. New offices are created and dissolved according to the priorities of the regime. According to the testimonies of people working in ministries such as Agriculture, in 1985 the Peruvian state was an employer of millions, but ten years later, an estimated 80 percent of permanent employees have been dismissed. Those that remain have their contracts renewed on average every three months. In this way the state not only changes in terms of its constitution, government, and interest groups, but in the size and structure of its administration.

The Peruvian state is also controlled by class interests. Power and influence rest on certain interests groups, in particular the army, parliamentarians, business interests, the church, and a small group of wealthy families. Whichever group is in power, one or more of these will benefit. In this way, certain elements of the civil society are drawn into the state apparatus according to the government. Those who are excluded will be opponents of the system. Under Fujimori, for example, the army and business are supportive. Parliamentarians, the aristocracy, and the church, however, are critical of the current regime as they had more influence under the previous presidents García and Belaúnde.

Those elements of the civil society which are not usually drawn into the state are known in Peru as the 'popular movement'. The relationship between the state and the popular movement in Peru varies under different governments. Part of the flux within the Peruvian state is that governments have the potential to change the political shape of the state; at the same time, however, governments are not powerful enough to ensure that these changes endure. In order to illustrate the range of differences we can compare the state under General Velasco (1968-1975) and the current President Alberto Fujimori (1990-).

Velasco and the military in 1968 saw a problem in the lack of integration between Peruvian civil society and the state. The regime therefore proceeded to construct an elaborate corporatist system. A corporatist system here refers to state-chartered associations which provide the link between the civil society and the state (Stefan 1978:46ff). A state body, SINAMOS (National System to Support Social Mobilisation) was involved in the organisation of these social sectors during the rule of Velasco. SINAMOS worked successfully with urban migrants, and to some extent with peasant and native communities (Skar,H. 1988:59). It had less success with workers who were already organised into syndicalist associations. The strategy of the military regime was to integrate civil society into the state in order to avoid social conflict.

In contrast, Fujimori seeks to cut loose civil society from the state and leave its organisation to the forces of the free market. In this way he aims to reduce state expenditure while raising more revenue through taxation to pay the external debt. At the same time, without the support or protection of the state, the associations of the popular movement become weaker and less able to challenge its authority. In this way although the state is reduced, its power remains through revenue and the support from the military. In spite of the free market, control is used to ensure that the free system does not create the conditions for alternative power sectors (Poole & Rénique 1992:132ff.).

These examples demonstrate that it is hard to define in detail where the state in Peru begins or ends. Markedly different criteria can be used to define the state according to the regime, but what is clear is that the Peruvian state is constantly under revision. However, rather than argue that the state in Peru is weak and society strong, it would perhaps be more pertinent from an indigenous perspective to say that the state is unpredictable in its actions and arbitrary as to where its powerful groups and institutions will manifest their strength.

Territorial Integrity and the Alternative Civil Society

Perhaps the most distinctive feature of Peru is the fact that state control does not reach the borders of the country. There are several areas where the country is beyond state economic and political influence. On an international level, debt crisis is a major problem. Although the crises of 1825, 1875, 1930, and 1958 had no lasting effects, the current debt grew astronomically in the 1970s and 1980s. The current Peruvian annual debt repayment (1993) is $22,200 million owed to international financial institutions such as the World Bank and the Inter-American Development Bank, to the Paris Club (bilateral debts) and the commercial banks (Peru Support Group ndb: 8-9). The dramatic curb on inflation and negotiations for debt repayment have strengthened the economy since 1994, but this has occurred at the expense of increased poverty and unemployment and devastating cuts in public services. Furthermore, the effect has been to weaken state control over the informal economy.

a. The Informal Sector

In Lima alone, there are now an estimated one million street sellers *(ambulantes)* (Peru Support Group ndb:12). Passing through the city, one is accosted by people selling everything from kitchen sinks to puppies. None of these people is registered for sales or tax purposes. They constitute the main part of the 'informal sector' or 'underemployed' people in the country. However, the informal sector includes not only street sellers, but also transport drivers and a whole system of 'special services'. The labyrinth of Peruvian bureaucracy makes everything from buying a house to registering a car a massive undertaking. By utilising the informal sector for a small price, it is possible for the public to bypass the state bureaucracy and to complete official procedures in a far shorter period of time.

The informal sector consists of an aspect of Peruvian society which operates in parallel to the state. Unofficially, some say that the informal sector constitutes up to 90 percent of Peru's daily economic activity. Government figures for 1993 say that there are 12.7 percent employed, 9.9 percent unemployed, and 77.4 percent underemployed (informal sector). Although the most famous exponent of the informal sector, Hernando de Soto (1987), does not fix a percentage, he considers that its influence is substantial.

There are several interpretations of the informal sector. Some consider it to be Peru's *lumpenproletariat* while others consider it to be a manifestation of the strength of market forces. However one places it politically, the informal sector is outside of the state structure for two main reasons. Since the neo-liberal reforms of Fujimori, the taxation office, SUNAT, has actively sought state revenue, but the informal sector is, on the whole, beyond its clutches. Secondly, the informal sector is dislocated from the state apparatus and largely operates on the basis of a subsistence economy arising from the poor sectors of the country. Thus, it could be argued that the strength of the informal sector is a sign of the increasing strength of social forces at the expense of the state.

b. Narco-Dollars

The figure of 90 percent of Peru's economy as unofficial does not seem so high if we include the illegal sale of coca within the 'informal' sector. Peru produces between sixty and seventy percent of the world's coca leaves (Poole & Rénique 1992:21). Production has increased with the Fujimori-led recession in Peru to 300,000 hectares (Rumrill 1992:6). Whereas Peru generates just short of $3 billion in legal exports, coca exportation brings in between $1.3 and $2.8 billion (Poole & Rénique ibid.). All of this is technically illegal, yet the narcotics trade provides the largest means of foreign currency in the economy.

The main beneficiaries of the drug trade have been the guerilla movements operating in the Huallaga Valley of Peru. When the military successfully cut off this revenue in 1992, the state was able to take advantage of the benefits of controlling coca production (Simpson 1994). This placed the unofficial economy in an even stronger position. The state was now actually participating in a clandestine manner in the unofficial economy in order to take financial advantage of the drug market. However, at the end of 1995, a dramatic drop in the price of coca and the arrest of eleven army officers (including two generals) may have changed the situation. The state is currently balancing the advantages of the benefits of following the US government's Drug Enforcement Agency and perhaps ameliorating the worse excesses of the debt or taking advantage of the illegal benefits of coca trafficking. In both cases, the state is caught between forces outside of its control.

c. The Guerilla Movements

Until 1992, the largest guerilla force in Peru was Sendero Luminoso. Since 1980, this Maoist group waged a war against the Peruvian state. After an estimated twenty-five thousand deaths caused both by the guerillas and the armed forces, large areas of the Peruvian highlands and lowlands were left in a 'state of emergency'. In the last few years Sendero has held areas in the Huallaga Valley, Junin and Puno, as well as other regions. At the same time, the smaller Movimiento Revolucionario Tupac Amaru (MRTA) also held areas in the Huallaga. These two organisations vied with the military to make money out of the coca trade.

In the triangle formed by the Pichis Valley, the Ucayali, and Tambo rivers (about 100 square kilometres in the Central Rainforest), the indigenous Asháninka took up arms in 1989 when the MRTA killed their leader, Manuel Calderón. Since then, they have successfully kept both the army and guerillas at bay with their 'Asháninka army'. This is effectively a de facto control of a sizeable part of the rainforest where the indigenous peoples of the area – independent from government and guerila – hold sway.

The decrease in guerilla activity has not ameliorated the situation in the highlands and lowlands. As soon as the military tension had calmed somewhat, the government passed what has become known as the Land Law *(Ley de Tierras)* 26055. This opens up all state land in the country for 'privatisation' and selling off to the highest bidder (García 1995). Thus, having lost control of a third of the country during the period of the guerila violence, the state is prepared to lose control of its economic resources in order to satisfy its international creditors.

d. Citizenship

The fundamental link between the people and the state arises from citizenship. Officially recognised citizenship is not universal in Peru.

The procedure for obtaining an electoral card is complicated and can be expensive, but without a card, a person is outside of the state and has his or her rights in the society severely curtailed.

Regardless of the regime, the bureaucracy and the extent of territorial or political control by the state apparatus, the electoral card is a sign of citizenship and legitimacy. For this reason, the people who do not have cards run the risk of being seen as enemies of the state. If they are found and provide no reason for their lack of a card, they are usually investigated and taken to detention centres and sometimes even disappear.

Estimating how many people in Peru are without a card is difficult, but one estimate puts the number at two million – 10 percent of the state population (Sarah Skar pers. comm.). The fourth chapter looks at the dilemma citizenship poses for indigenous peoples in Peru.

This section has tried to illustrate how the Peruvian state is not a monolithic entity but consists of several elements: a series of social relationships of power which are frequently changing, an administration which waxes and wanes with the fate of government, a territory which it does not completely control, an economy which operates largely outside of the legal sphere and a relationship with the civil society which fluctuates between coherence and conflict with the state. All of this takes place within a strong relationship of dependency on the international economy.

From a *de jure* position, the Peruvian state is coherent with its people. Citizens choose governments from which stem legitimacy. However, *de facto*, the state is a small subset of society which tries as much as it is able to impose order. The lack of institutionalisation of any government for more than a few years means that the state ebbs and flows with the meanderings of power. Rather than the centre being in control, as is usually assumed, the power of the state is conditioned by the international world outside and the social forces within.

The Peruvian Amazon and its Native Communities

Of the three regions of Peru – coast, highlands, and rainforest – the Amazon rainforest is the most removed from state influence. At the turn of the century, it was quicker to travel from Iquitos to London by steamer (three weeks) than by land to Lima (six weeks). Nowadays, to travel by land from Puerto Maldonado to Lima takes no less than a week – assuming that there are no problems with the condition of the roads or guerillas, in which case the trip can be considerably longer.

The Peruvian Amazon covers just under 60 percent of the country (775,650 km^2) consisting of humid tropical and subtropical rainforest (Caufield & Pino Zambrano 1985:91). In spite of the apparent fertility of the area, the soils are fragile and any potential for sustainable production, whether extractive, agricultural, or animal rearing, is low (Rumrill 1982:11-13). The population of the Peruvian Amazon is difficult to ascertain but the total is between two and three million people, of whom at least 500,000 are indigenous. The figures of indigenous peoples are constantly growing as more long-term inhabitants of the Amazon reveal themselves to be indigenous peoples.[8]

The destruction of the rainforest is particularly problematic in Peru. According to Dourojeanni (1990: 81), nearly eight million hectares of the Peruvian rainforest have been deforested (about one tenth of the total) at the rate of about 340,000 hectares per year, and this is increasing. From the point of outsiders, the resources of the rainforest has been its greatest attraction. The main interests have been the Peruvian state, independent colonists, and foreign companies.

Resource exploitation

Exploitation of the resources in the Amazon take two main forms. The first consists of the extraction of resources which follows the familiar 'boom and bust' cycle of Amazonian enclave economies. Whether rubber, barbasco, oil, or gold, the pattern of extraction consists of a response to international demands. The largest and most destructive boom was that of rubber at the end of the last century. During a period of approximately forty years (1880 to 1920) individual companies, usually with foreign financial backing, extracted rubber using largely indigenous labour, primarily for export.

The current gold rush in the Madre de Dios or the coca boom in the Huallaga follows largely the same pattern. The state tries to latch onto the profits wherever possible, but the market and production remain largely outside of the control of Peruvian official institutions. (Where the state intervenes, as in the militarisation of the coca, this is strictly unofficial.)

8. This is a global phenomenon which accounts for the marked rise in indigenous peoples all over the world. In Argentina, for example, there are officially 350,000 indigenous peoples, although unofficially there are over 1.5 million in the northern provinces alone (IWGIA 1988:78).

However, over the last fifty years the Peruvian state has encouraged a second form of development in the Amazon. A recent article (Barclay 1991) discusses the role of the state in the incorporation of Amazonia into the national economy. Barclay argues that the state has three interests in the Amazon: securing frontiers, extracting wealth and establishing political control.

The colonisation process largely consists of the conflicts of these three interests. The first concerns extractors, traders and explorers who identify areas in which there are indigenous peoples. Missionaries of different Christian denominations – Catholics such as Dominicans, Jesuits, Franciscans, and various Protestant sects – gradually make contact with the indigenous peoples of the rainforest and constitutes the buffer between them and the state as a whole. Then gradually the colonisation, encouraged by the state, moves into the lowland towns and into the forest.

The weakness of state boundaries in the Amazon has involved conflicts with Bolivia, Colombia, and Ecuador over the last century. Peruvian companies worked with the government during the rubber boom to secure Peruvian frontiers with Bolivia and Colombia which were targets during the rubber boom. Since 1940, however, Ecuador and Brazil have been focuses of national security. The government has taken a 'living frontiers' approach; this consists of encouraging poor people from the highlands to colonise the rainforest. The effect is to promote extraction, populate an area, and, by establishing municipal government, extend state control into the region.

Since the 1940s, the Peruvian state has regularly seen the Amazon as an outlet for migration from the highlands. The lowlands of Peru comprise 57 percent of the country's area, with 11 percent of the total population (Dobyns & Doughty 1976:20). Governments, particularly those of Manuel Prado and Belaúnde, encouraged a population movement from the highlands to provide the impetus for a 'colonisation'. The hope was that the rainforest would generate development and incorporate the area into the country as a whole.

Governments have invested in administrative apparatus in the Amazon and ways of communication such as roads and air transport. Furthermore, at various times, the state provided grants to colonists so that they could begin to cultivate export crops such as coffee, tea, and barbasco. However, these initiatives largely took for granted the myth of the 'vast emptiness' of the Amazon (Smith 1982), forgetting that there are peoples belonging to sixty different language groups living in several thousand settlements comprising at least half a million people. The argument of the 'vast emptiness' is nothing less than the reappearance of the doctrine of *terra nullius* which was used to justify indigenous colonisation all over the world in the nineteenth century.

Indigenous Rights in Peru

Since Bolivar's 1824 Decree allowing for the individual parcelisation of lands, the territories of indigenous peoples in Peru have been under constant threat. In 1845 Ramón Castilla offered lowland lands to anyone who cared to colonise the area, and this was supported by further laws in 1893 and 1889, and by the General Law of Montaña Lands in 1909 (Law 1220), which remained in force until 1974. This declared all lands to belong to the state and leased them to colonists with their inhabitants. No indigenous communities were recognised.

Indigenous rights for the Amazon were overshadowed by the rights of the indigenous peoples of the Andes, which were gradually established through the first three decades of this century. The 1920 Constitution recognised indigenous communities, while the 1933 Constitution recognised the inalienability of community lands. Subsequent laws recognised citizenship and the prohibition of bureaucratic intervention in community affairs were guaranteed. In 1938 a procedure of registration for communities was established (Isbell 1978:28-9). These rights were assumed to be appropriate in the highland areas (García 1995:34).

This changed during the period of the Velasco regime. In line with his other reforms he looked for corporatist solutions to the problem. The result was the 1974 Law of Native Communities (DL 20653). Before the Velasco regime passed the law, there were no 'native communities' in Amazonian Peru. The indigenous peoples of the Amazon lived in concentrated or dispersed patterns of settlement, exercising their dominion over their ancestral territories. According to the Native Community law (which was revised by Velasco's successor, Morales Bermúdez, in 1978 as DL 22175), the Amazonian indigenous peoples were to have all their lands demarcated and recognised as their inalienable territory. The protections from the 1933 Constitution were now applicable throughout the country.

Through the law, native communities were encouraged to take out loans and produce cattle and crops. Furthermore they were not liable for tax. The titling process divides indigenous territories into protected areas such as river banks, areas for agrarian use and lands for forest exploitation. The forest lands are technically state land held in trust by the indigenous community. In spite of this zoning, all community land is recognised *de facto* as belonging to the indigenous peoples in whose name the title was issued. This law was the most advanced recognition of indigenous rights in Latin America at the time. Since then, however, there has been a gradual weakening of the law.

The process of titling was developed out of the Law of Native Communities. It is a highly bureaucratic procedure, involving up to twenty-six stages and, not surprisingly, titling has been slow in Peru. An initial spree by SINAMOS in the time of Velasco slowed down under Morales Bermúdez and stopped entirely during the presidency of Belaúnde (1980-5), who was an open advocate of colonisation. However, during the time of Alan García, titling started up again and is still, though with difficulty, taking place under the increasingly negative gaze of Alberto Fujimori, whose so-called democratic system has unilaterally removed the inalienable protection clauses from the Constitution.

However, the law is not perfect and the process of titling contains various features which illustrate the ambiguous position of indigenous communities in Peru. On the one hand, the legislation has been drawn up by the state and has several features of integration. Prior to the legislation, each people lived as it had done customarily in accordance with its own socio-political system. The Law of Native Communities arbitrarily divides each people into communities, many of which are not contiguous. The consequence of this is that islands of indigenous communities appear throughout the rainforest which do not reflect the territory of any people as a whole.

A second problem is that each community, according to the Law of Native Communities, is structured according to a non-indigenous system of President, Secretary, and Treasurer, who are elected every few years. This has had the effect of superimposing a western representative democratic system on top of the customary direct democratic system in which decisions were taken by consensus. In fact, most communities have adapted the law to fit in with their own customs and the two systems co-exist, but not without tensions.

The Law of Native Communities was not an indigenous initiative, and this is reflected in its application. It is a form of 'treaty' whereby indigenous peoples recognise the Peruvian state and in return have their lands and territories recognised. Nevertheless, the protection is ultimately in the hands of the constitutional provision which recognises the rights of indigenous peoples of Peru but which the government considers itself competent to amend unilaterally. Unfortunately, the indigenous peoples themselves have no means to insist that the constitution reflects their rights. Since the 1993 shift in policy of the Fujimori government, it is possible to hear members of the Ministry of Agriculture referring to the legal provisions for the rights of indigenous peoples as 'outdated' or 'socialistic'.

The indigenous peoples of the Peruvian Amazon Peru have been able to utilise the law as it exists to ensure that they are, in many cases, in control of their ancestral territories. Titling projects nowadays try to follow the law strictly to ensure that each community receives recognition of the full extent of its territory, bordering wherever possible with neighbouring communities.

A large-scale titling project in the central rainforest where the International Work Group for Indigenous Affairs has been working with the national Peruvian indigenous Amazonian organisation AIDESEP (Inter-ethnic Association for the Development of the Peruvian Rainforest) has tried to ameliorate some of these problems. The result has led to a titling strategy consisting of a patchwork of communities which together constitute a territory. For those areas which the communities rarely use but need for the replenishment of hunting stocks, the Forestry Law allows for the establishment of 'communal reserves' which are protected areas within indigenous ancestral territory. As yet, only one communal reserve exists among the Yanesha, although several are in preparation. Should the Native Community and Forestry laws be used in conjunction, the result could be a substantial legal recognition of the ancestral dominion of the rainforest peoples of Peru.

The Law of Native Communities was remarkably far-sighted in many of its provisions. The effect of the law has been to establish in many parts of the Amazon inalienable community territories in which indigenous peoples have the legal right to control their own development. Unfortunately, all of this faced a major setback in the drafting of the recent 1993 Constitution, which addressed the three provisions of the 1933 Constitution. These are that indigenous territories are inalienable (cannot be sold), unmortgageable (cannot be placed as security for a loan), and imprescribable (cannot be claimed by any other party). The 1993 Constitution removed the inalienable and unmortgageable provisions and stated that any lands which the state considered to be 'abandoned' could be claimed by third parties and bought from the state.

These were enshrined on 18 July 1995 in Law 26505 (Law of Private Investment in the Development of Economic Activities in the Lands of National Territory and of Peasant and Native Communities – the 'Land Law'). The law was passed with no public debate, but appeared after a letter of intention to the International Monetary Fund promised to look into ways of raising money out of the agrarian sector (García 1966:86). The aim of the law is to make all state land available for sale.

Indigenous territories can be sold, providing two thirds of the community are in agreement (although this was present in the 1979 Constitution). The most worrying aspect, however, is the use of community land as security for loans. This means that any debtor can take land in lieu of money from an indigenous defaulter. Already, in the summer of 1995, government agencies were travelling through the Madre de Dios offering loans to the communities. Although the Land Law does not directly destroy the Law of Native Communities, it weakens protection and makes despoliation of indigenous lands and resources much more straightforward.

The law of indigenous peoples in Peru has moved from positive initiatives such as the Constitution of 1933 and the 1974 Law of Native Communities to the 1993 Constitution and the current Land Law, which unilaterally impose deregulation of lands and neo-liberal attitudes to national resources over and above national and international obligations, such as ILO Convention 169, which Peru signed on the same day as the 1993 Constitution.

Indigenous Organisation

The Law of Native Communities, as with other corporatist arrangements from the Peruvian state, does not allow for representation above the basic level of the community. The effect is to accommodate only individual villages, and leave indigenous peoples as a whole without any representation. For this reason, since the 1970s, the Amazonian peoples of Peru have established their own organisations in the form of federations which represent the local native communities at a larger level. In some cases these federations are supported by untitled communities in order to provide the political pressure to ensure recognition of their territorial rights.

Indigenous communities of the Peruvian Amazon have joined up with the international indigenous movement which has grown quickly over the last thirty years. They have formed federations which constitute a part of the 'people's movement' (*movimiento popular*), opereateing as an intermediary form of lobbying group between Peruvian society and the state. These are non-governmental organisations. In Peru the non-governmental organisations are divided into technical institutions and representative organisations. The indigenous peoples' organisations belong to the latter type. They are independent and make political alliances on their own terms.

The Inter-ethnic Association for the Development of the Peruvian Rainforest (AIDESEP) was established in 1980 by Aguaruna, Yanesha and Shipibo representatives. Since then it has grown to an organisation representing over thirty indigenous federations. Whereas in the 1980s the government respected AIDESEP and the two bodies carried out several joint programmes in health, education, and land titling, the current government is less enthusiastic. The Peruvian Indigenist Institute has been adopting a strategy of bypassing indigenous organisations and trying to deal 'directly' with native communities. This has had the effect of weakening the indigenous movement, because the national indigenous leadership is increasingly ignored as unilateral government policy becomes predominant.

The alternating government policies of supporting and then rejecting indigenous rights closely reflects the relationship between indigenous organisations and the state. When legislation is progressive and supportive, the federations are positive and work more closely with the government. On the other hand, in periods such as the present, the federations are increasingly ignored by the government, which simultaneously passes unilateral legislation threatening the integrity of native communities. As can be seen in the case of the Madre de Dios, this has the effect of separating indigenous peoples from the state and distancing them from any sense of national identity.

The Madre de Dios and the Gold Economy

In 1989 the Peruvian government, under President Alan García, completed the process of regionalisation of the country and on 19 January the Inka Region was formed. Comprising 175,282 km^2, the Inka Region was made up of the previous Departments of Apurimac, Cusco, and Madre de Dios. Because it was the only Amazonian part of the region, Madre de Dios was made into a sub-region.

The original department of Madre de Dios was formed in 1912 and consists of 73,402 km^2. The three provinces of Tambopata, Manu, and Tahuamanu are divided into municipal districts. Madre de Dios has always been precariously connected to the highland and coastal areas of Peru. State presence in the Madre de Dios has been centred in Puerto Maldonado throughout most of its history. Contact with the indigenous peoples of the region has been largely mediated by the priests, who still have an influential stake in the control of regional welfare amenities such as health and education. However, the priests made several questionable alliances with the rubber barons during this century in order to gain the financial resources to establish their missions. This has always placed the Church in an ambiguous position regarding the indigenous peoples of the Madre de Dios (Fuentes 1982; Rummenhöller 1985; Wahl 1987).

Apart from a brief rubber and gold booms in the 1900s and 1940s, the Madre de Dios remained on the periphery of the state perspective of national life. Colonists moved into the area gradually, but communications have always been difficult. The main road to Cusco was only completed in the mid-1960s, and attempts to establish air communication within the forest have been short-lived.

The increase in gold prices in 1973 changed the nature of the Madre de Dios rapidly. The economy of the Madre de Dios is primarily extractive, with brazil nuts, rubber, lumber, and gold as the main products (Paredes Pando 1990:9). However, of all the activities in the Madre de Dios, gold extraction is the main source of income. Including the temporary colonists along with those permanent residents and indigenous peoples who mine gold, over 50 percent of the workforce is dedicated to mining production. About 20,000 km^2 are used for gold mining, particularly areas on the banks of the rivers where the deposits are left by the waters running down from the Andes. Much of the gold area lies within the boundaries of the indigenous communities, which leads to serious conflicts between the gold colonists and the indigenous peoples of the region, many of whom work gold themselves. The negative impact of the gold rush on indigenous peoples of the Madre de Dios has been considerable (Moore 1985a; Gray 1986) and will be discussed in more detail in later chapters.

The population of Madre de Dios has increased sharply since 1978, when the gold rush came to a head, from fifteen to forty thousand people (CAAAP 1992:4-8). The indigenous population of the area is about ten thousand, a quarter of the total.[9] However this proportion diminishes rapidly when we take into consideration the forty

9. Ten thousand is considerably higher than the figure of four thousand which appears in Gray (1986:55). The reason for this is twofold. On the one hand the mobilisation of indigenous peoples, particularly those closer to Puerto Maldonado, has meant that far more people now recognise themselves as indigenous. Secondly, the census material on which the previous figure was based is now over ten years old and the figure here is based on projections as to what the population ought to be now.

thousand colonists and gold workers who live temporarily in the area as part of the rush to extract gold from the rivers. The figure of forty thousand, although an estimate, is double that of 1985 (Gray 1986:55), which indicates that mining has been increasing, in spite of the fall in value of gold. However, in certain areas, gold is waning and people can now see the first signs of a 'bust' period taking over from the 'boom'.

According to Pacuri and Moore (1992:31), Madre de Dios produces on average 8,000 kilos of gold annually, 91 percent of which comes from small artisan miners. One eighth comes from the indigenous mining communities. This information is based on estimates rather than official figures because from 1989 gold no longer had to be sold to the state through the Banco Minero but has been open for sale on the free market.

The most exploited workers in the Madre de Dios are the peons who work for the rich patrons. Sometimes working in gangs of fifty or more, their plight has been the cause of international concern (CODEH-PA 1983; Whittaker, 1985; Guillen-Marroquin, 1990; Rädda Barnen, 1991). Migrants are forced or cheated by debt into working for patrons and spend periods of ninety days working gold, suffering from disease, overwork, and poor living conditions. The slave-like existence of these people extends to children as young as twelve or thirteen years old, who can be seen on the banks of the rivers washing gold for their patrons.

The gold economy of the Madre de Dios takes place mainly outside of the control of the state, even though the state lays claim to all sub-surface resources. Labour rights are ignored, human rights violations are a daily occurrence, and even where the indigenous peoples have their territories recognised according to the law, colonists refuse to respect them. The lack of state presence throughout the area is very marked. This has been exacerbated by the government deregulation of the national gold market.

The trajectory of legislation on gold has affected the Madre de Dios, and in particular, the indigenous communities. The gold rush developed on the back of the 1978 Law of Gold-mining Promotion (Law 22178) which opened up the area for concessions throughout the 1980s. This law was revised in 1981, but at all times, the official buyer of gold from mining concessions was the state Banco Minero. All of this changed with Legislative Decree 708 in 1991, when President Fujimori liberalised and privatised mining activities. This law opened up the possibility of mining concessions in protected areas, including indigenous communities, and centralised all the administration of concessions. Conditions were also established whereby all mining concessions could only be renewed on the basis of a proven production level of $100 per hectare annually, a tax of $1 per hectare, and payments for claiming a concession totalling about $1,000.

Pacuri and Moore's conclusion on the cause and effect of LD 708 parallels García's analysis of the Land Law: 'LD 708 was passed by the government of President Fujimori in response to the demands of the IMF; it means that about 90 percent of small-scale miners and indigenous communities will not be able to seek concessions or will lose those which they currently own because of the impossibility of complying with the "legal requirements".' The law plays into the hands of large mining companies at the expense of miners of the Madre de Dios.

Since 1978, Puerto Maldonado has grown in size and the local state corporation has carried out some development support in the area; even so, access to these resources depended on party affiliation and personal contacts. The state's presence in Maldonado is apparent through the military, the prefectura, the church, and the administrative functionaries in Puerto Maldonado. Most of these officials are not from the area but are sent there from other parts of Peru, although, in recent years, public opinion has been able to influence the appointment of sub-regional functionaries.

During the period when the Inka regional assembly functioned, the people of the Madre de Dios had representatives who were able to influence the Region's decisions more than they had been able to with the central government. However, Fujimori's constitutional reforms dissolved the democratically elected Regional Assemblies in 1993, leaving a regional bureaucracy in its place. Apart from its capital, the Madre de Dios is divided into provinces and districts, such as Boca Colorado, discussed in the study at the beginning of this chapter.

The further away from Puerto Maldonado one travels, the more the state is co-opted by local interests. The provinces and districts are run by elected mayors and councils who organise state provisions according to the Municipal Law. In fact these are usually traders and patrons who monopolise state grants which are channelled through the municipality. The colonists thus utilise the financial support for themselves and those small miners or indigenous communities who are prepared to back them in the elections. The districts do not carry out a state policy, but improvise on the basis of the mayor and the council's immediate interests.

The lack of state accountability and the shortage of resources in the Madre de Dios means that the popular movement has become very important. The popular movement is essentially a political pressure block made up of representative organisations to push for their interests from the state. In some parts of Peru each element in the popular movement caters for its own interests whether peasants, workers or indigenous peoples. In the Madre de Dios, however, an interesting alliance has built up over the last five years between FENAMAD and other sectors of the popular movement.

FENAMAD was established in January 1982 after several years of mobilisation by the indigenous peoples of the Madre de Dios. The organisation consists of representatives from forty-one native communities in the Madre de Dios, who make policy decisions at its congress which is held every year or two. The leadership is elected at the congress and based at an office in Puerto Maldonado. There they deal with the daily problems facing communities and indigenous peoples in general according to the guidelines established in the Congress.

Over the last ten years, FENAMAD has established its position in the Madre de Dios as part of the popular movement. The alliances which it has formed have furthered the influx of indigenous peoples' points of view into state organs and among the general public. FENAMAD has not allied much with the small-scale miners because they see the indigenous peoples of the Madre de Dios as competitors for the gold resources. At the same time, the miners are not sufficiently organised to link together in associations to defend themselves from other interest groups. These rise and fall according to the ebb and flow of colonists from the highlands. The indigenous and agrarian federations are two of the most stable pressure groups and are able to follow up their political interests in a relatively consistent and coherent manner.

The main organisations with which FENAMAD works are the representatives of the settlements on the outskirts of Puerto Maldonado, environmental groups, and the Agrarian Federation of the Madre de Dios (FADEMAD). FADEMAD is a body representing peasant farmers who have come from the highlands and have individual properties in the Madre de Dios. Although over the years there have been problems between the agricultural colonists and indigenous peoples as they compete for resources, they have discovered that they are united over two important questions. Firstly, they both need to influence the regional state authorities to provide them with facilities. Secondly, both indigenous peoples and agriculturalists are in a struggle to defend their lands from the invasions of gold miners.

This popular mobilisation of indigenous peoples has arisen because of the lack of state interest in the rainforest and its inability to enforce the Law of Native Communities. Since the counter-regionalisation policy of Fujimori, Peru has become more centralised and the state is even more removed from the Amazon. This means that at any moment the arbitrary arm of the state could suddenly move in to take full advantage of the resources there. Thus the lack of state presence is not reliably permanent, but the calm before the storm.

The Arakmbut and their Relationship to the State

The 'native community' is largely a construction of Peru's state corporate policy of the late 1960s and early 1970s. The community is defined legally as a socio-political unit, but this does not mean that each people automatically controls its resources in practice because the process of state-encouraged colonisation limits indigenous self-determination. This is particularly noticeable in the Madre de Dios which is dominated by the gold rush and where land invasions are widespread.

Most native communities in the Peruvian Amazon, in spite of their formal 'official' leadership (President, Secretary, and Treasurer), have their own internal political system which can be extremely varied.[10] The relationship between the native community as a legal institution imposed by the state and the internal political system belonging to each indigenous people is a direct reflection of the relationship between the people and the state as a whole. Thus, while all communities are connected to the state at the *de jure* level, this is not always the case in practice.

Another difference in perspective between the state and the community is marginality. From the state perspective, native communities are at the margins of national society, but from the perspective of the indigenous communities the picture is quite different: the state is marginal to the indigenous perspective. Furthermore, any representative of the state who visits the community is automatically assumed to be of low status and of little importance.

To a superficial visitor, the community of San José del Karene appears to be integrated into Peruvian society. The Arakmbut have

10. Rosengren (1987) provides a detailed comparison between formal leadership in a Matsigenka community as constituted by the Law of Native Communities and the more flexible traditional leadership system. He notes that the official leadership system is not popular and sometimes it is hard to find candidates. The same phenomenon can sometimes be seen among the Arakmbut.

been in contact with Dominican priests for over forty years and the current school is run by lay missionaries. The people in the community wear western clothes, work gold, buy beer, and, in some cases, employ highland workers as gold diggers. There are several men in the community who run shops. Several members of the community have completed secondary education and one is studying at university in Lima. This student has also participated at the UN Working Group in Geneva (see chapter one).

However this apparent 'integration' into Peruvian society is merely superficial. The actual relationship is far more complicated. In the first place, the Arakmbut survive on the basis of self-sufficiency of resources. Their needs can only be met from their immediate environment. Meat and crops provide the much of their food, while the gold which lies on their territory is the source of all their market commodities. The line between participating in a capitalist money economy and product exchange is unclear, because all trade with the external society is made with gold as the medium of exchange. The gold has an exact value, but it is not earned, it is gathered.

Secondly, the Arakmbut do not save gold or money in the same way as the outside system. The Arakmbut economy operates on a 'potlatch' system where prestige and respect comes from generosity. After people have bought capital goods necessary for production and basic commodities for the house, the rest is spent on beer parties for households and in-laws which regularly take place. In this way the principles of the market are inverted to cohere with the indigenous political economy. The Arakmbut relate to the national economy in terms of exchanges, but this does not alter their independent stance and control over their production. The outside economy is adapted to suit the indigenous economic system rather than vice versa.

The Arakmbut are neither isolated nor integrated from the national society of Peru; they remain independent but connected. This is the basis of the paradoxical relationship outlined in this chapter. The state has two faces to the Arakmbut, the positive side of the Law of Native Communities and the negative side of armed forces and colonisation. The role of government is ambiguous, sometimes supporting one side, sometimes the other. The problem which the Arakmbut face in the first case is an absence of the state to protect the legal provisions, in the second case the problem is the presence of the state through its unilateral means of threatening indigenous survival.

Thus whereas at a national and regional level the state of Peru is legally obliged to defend the rights of the indigenous peoples of the Amazon, on a local level the mining colonists, and in other areas lumber extractors or oil companies, are in alliance with the state apparatus. This makes it more difficult for the indigenous peoples of Peru to exercise their rights. Four options face the indigenous peoples of the area, all of which they have tried to use, according to the situation.

1. The state recognises indigenous rights to their territory and provides limited support for their continuing capacity to defend themselves and develop their communities as they see fit. This is rare.
2. When the state and the local oppression is vicious, indigenous communities try to keep as far a distance as possible. They emphasise their independence in terms of social organisation, economy, political decision-making, and control over which elements of the outside world they wish to accept into their communities. When sufficiently outraged, they resort to direct action.
3. When the state does not wish to support indigenous peoples, and they on their own are not powerful enough to defend themselves, the indigenous peoples use their own organisations and forge alliances with other sectors of the popular movement to influence the state at higher regional, national, or international levels. The alliances, such as that between FENAMAD and FADEMAD, are examples where indigenous peoples can surpass the state/colonist alliance at a local level and try to exert pressure at a regional, national, or even international level.
4. Indigenous communities try to incorporate the institutions of the state into their political field. They do this by accepting Peruvian citizenship and taking over the local councils and become mayors. This has been successful in other parts of Peru among the Aguaruna, Asháninka, and Shipibo. The Arakmbut could achieve this in Boca Colorado, but the problem has been trying to find candidates.

In spite of the victory at Boca Colorado in April 1992, the Arakmbut are finding that their defences are becoming increasingly weak. The state is more frequently taking the side of those colonising indigenous territories; the legislation under the current regime is undermining the Law of Native Communities on which in their eyes rests the very legitimacy of the state; indigenous self-sufficiency is becoming more difficult as the gold rush dwindles and colonists turn to exploiting timber, while the Arakmbut cannot produce enough gold to keep themselves economically independent; the alliance with the popular movement is fragile and the ethnic alliance on which FENAMAD is based is constantly under pressure through lack of resources and administrative experience; finally, the colonists are determined to remain in the area, thereby challenging Arakmbut attempts to create political space within the municipality.

The result is a tension between two co-existing systems in Boca Colorado. On the one hand is the weak state, on the other the strong indigenous communities. Both recognise each other's legitimacy but distrust each other. In between lies Peruvian society, which is made up of opponents (usually from the colonist interests and local government) and allies (usually others in the popular movement). Those who argue that indigenous peoples will inevitably integrate into the national society look at the situation from a state-centralised perspective. What is common to all the above options is that, from the perspective of the community, the state has to be incorporated into indigenous political life to solve these problems.

The paradox is that when the state imposes its ideology on indigenous peoples, the response is resistance or retreat. When indigenous rights are recognised (as occurred for brief periods in the 1970s and mid-1980s), relations between the state and indigenous peoples are positive and constructive. Currently, with the neo-liberal approach of the present government they are negative and give rise to considerable distress and unrest.

The Peruvian state is not in control of itself because of two main factors: its international economic dependency and its internal incapacity to appear legitimate to its constituent peoples. Government in Peru has consisted of a balancing act when during periods of hostility to international dependency (particularly during the regimes of Velasco and García) indigenous rights were more respected, while in periods of governmental emphasis on international debt obligations (Morales Bermúdez, Belaúnde, and Fujimori) indigenous rights have been weakened, ignored, or extinguished. Part of the solution is for the international community to recognise its own responsibilities in the treatment of indigenous peoples, which is tied in with the global system and for the state to go 'beyond itself' and appreciate its international and local responsibilities (Hoffman 1995).

Indigenous peoples of the Peruvian Amazon, in spite of colonisation and discrimination, know that to survive they must hold on to the basis of their power and identity – territory. As long as their ancestral territories are recognised legally and they can control the extent to which national life encroaches upon their own, they can survive as an indigenous people. This is the topic of the next chapter.

❖ Chapter 3 ❖

LOSING CONTROL

Arakmbut Territories and Resources

'Our homeland is the place where our ancestors lived and were buried. It is our Arakmbut territory and is sacred.' Arakmbut leader from San José

In December 1991 a commission from the indigenous federation FENAMAD visited San José del Karene to investigate the allegations of land invasions and death threats from gold colonists. At the meeting, the discussion moved to the establishment of a communal reserve for all the Arakmbut on their homeland. The Arakmbut and the federation worked for six months to justify the claim. At the moment when it was due to be signed, Mobil, the oil company, took out a concession in the area and is starting explorations on Arakmbut ancestral lands. Since then no final approval has been forthcoming for the communal reserve. The government is eager to encourage foreign currency into Peru, through resource extraction; the Arakmbut want their territories intact. This chapter looks at the roots of these conflicts of interest.

The International Indigenous Perspective

Throughout the discussions on indigenous rights at the International Labour Organisation and the United Nations Working Group on Indigenous Populations, a question is consistently raised: do indigenous peoples have territories or not? The question may seem strange considering that anthropologists have more or less accepted territoriality as a fundamental feature of indigenous social organisation since the 1940s, yet the debate regarding territories contains significant practical consequences.

The ILO revision of Convention 107 took place in Geneva between 1986 and 1989. During these meetings the debate over territory became intense. In 1986:

> 'The main point made by the indigenous representatives and NGOs was that land is too restrictive a term and that "territories of the earth" would be preferable. This is because indigenous resources include not just land, but water, air, coastal waters, and sea ice as well as sub-surface rights. Indigenous peoples see themselves as custodians of their territories for their future generations and so these resources cannot be "owned" in the same sense as in industrial societies' (Gray 1987:82).

A similar position was presented at the 1988 meeting (Gray 1989:172) and in 1989 where it was debated with vigour (Gray 1990:184-5). Whereas the indigenous representatives wanted territories to be used as a generic term to cover all lands and resources, the hard-line governments (particularly India, Venezuela, and Canada) 'would have no truck with the word territories which, they claimed, threatened the national integrity of the state' (ibid.:185).

The argument continued at the United Nations where, in 1990, Argentina and Brazil argued against the incorporation of the term territories in the draft Declaration on the Rights of Indigenous Peoples (Gray & Dahl 1991:169-170).

The current draft declaration of the UN Working Group on Indigenous Populations has largely taken on board the concerns of indigenous peoples. Particularly significant are Articles 25, which looks at the philosophy of territorial relations, and 26, which asserts indigenous ownership. Although these articles are a substantial improvement on the ILO Convention, the resources protection provision is still too weak as it is limited by the ambiguous term 'traditional':

Article 25
Indigenous peoples have the right to maintain and strengthen their distinctive spiritual and material relationship with the lands, territories, waters and coastal seas and other resources which they have traditionally owned or otherwise occupied or used, and to uphold their responsibilities to future generations in this regard.

Article 26
Indigenous peoples have the right to own, develop, control and use the lands and territories, including the total environment of the lands, air, waters, coastal seas, sea-ice, flora and fauna and other resources which

they have traditionally owned or otherwise occupied or used. This includes the right to the full recognition of their laws, traditions and customs, land-tenure systems and institutions for the development and management of resources, and the right to effective measures by States to prevent any interference with, alienation of or encroachment upon these rights.

The discussion as to whether indigenous territories should be recognised brings to the fore the initial problem with the politicisation of descriptive terms such as territory. Those governments which argue that the recognition of indigenous peoples' territories threatens the national integrity of states reiterate a particularly entrenched position stretching back over a century.

The theoretical position which denies that indigenous peoples have territories stems from the early anthropological lawyers Maine and Morgan. These scholars argued that there were two forms of government, one based on kinship and the other on territory. In 1861 Maine wrote:

> 'The history of political ideas begins, in fact, with the assumption that kinship in blood is the sole possible ground of community in political functions; nor is there any of those subversions of feeling, which we term emphatically revolutions, so startling and so complete as the change which is accompanied when some other principle – such as that, for instance, of *local contiguity* – establishes itself for the first time as the basis of common political action' (Maine 1912 (1861):137).

In 1877, Lewis Henry Morgan made this point even more clearly:

> 'It may be here premised that all forms of government are reducible to two general plans ... The first, in the order of time, is founded upon persons, and upon relations purely personal, and may be distinguished as a society *(societas)* ... The second is founded upon territory and upon property, and may be distinguished as a state (civitas)' (1877:6).[1]

Both of these writers share the nineteenth century preoccupation with social evolution, which placed peoples on a hierarchy defined by western imperial ideas of progress. According to evolutionary writers, those who did not live according to a state social organisa-

---

1. According to Godelier, 1973, 1871 Morgan wrote in *Systems of Consanguinity and Affinity of the Human Family*: 'Each tribe is individualised by a name, by a separate dialect, by a supreme government and by the possession of some territory which it occupies and defends as its very own.' However, Morgan's later 1877 position is more well known and was the approach taken up by Engels: 'In contrast to the old gentile organization, the state is distinguished firstly by the grouping of its members on a *territorial basis*' (1973:229).

tion belonged to a lower, more primitive, level of evolution. Thus there are two classes of political organisation, societies based on kinship and states based on territories. This fitted in with the positivistic colonial legal approach of the late nineteenth century (such as Westlake and Lorimer, referred to in chapter one) which considered colonial states with their territories as the subjects of international law.

Several contemporary government representatives at the ILO and the UN continue to adhere to this doctrine in the context of indigenous peoples living within the boundaries of the nation state. This approach is clearly discriminatory and ignores subsequent developments in the understanding of the concept of territory, particularly by anthropologists.

The reaction against evolutionary ideas came during the 1920s. Lowie (1920:378-9) argued that the Australian Aborigines clearly had territorial systems while ten years later Radcliffe-Brown (Radcliffe-Brown 1977:161) considered that 'the strong local solidarity which is the most important thing in the social life of the Australians, is correlated with a very strong bond between the local group and its territory'. By 1940 he considered that

> 'Every human society has some sort of territorial structure ... To try to distinguish, as Maine and Morgan did, between societies based on kinship ... and societies based on occupation of a common territory or locality, and to regard the former as more "primitive" than the latter, leads only to confusion' (Radcliffe-Brown 1940:xiv).

Over the next twenty years, anthropological writings included the notion of territory as a basic prerequisite for an understanding of political systems. The breadth of territorial practices expressed by Fortes & Evans-Pritchard (1940) were followed up by more detailed studies of territory such as Schapera's work in South Africa (1956). In 1962, Lucy Mair summarised these findings by using the idea of 'government without the state'. The fact that states have legislative, executive and judicial functions and authority extended over a fixed territory does not mean that they have a monopoly over government (p.11). On the contrary, 'the political community, then, has its own territory whether or not it is organised in the form of a state.' (ibid.:16)

The concept of territory was, by 1960, accepted as an uncontroversial aspect of non-state political systems. This theoretical movement took place, not only in the shift from evolutionary ideas of the nineteenth century to the structural functionalism of the early twentieth, but also within the framework of colonisation and empire to that of decolonisation. The parallel with indigenous peoples today is marked, because in response to the nineteenth century-style arguments of governments who oppose the notion of territory, indigenous peoples use the argument of decolonisation, which is reflected in the anthropological writings of the mid-twentieth century.

The theme of what constitutes a territory and why it is particularly important for the Arakmbut can be illustrated by the history of colonisation on the Río Pukiri. This river passes into the Karene and constitutes about one third of the gold-bearing beaches on San José's territory.

The Pukiri: Life and Death of a River

The river Pukiri is a picturesque clear water river running past long pebbled beaches and sandy river banks through the Arakmbut community territories of San José and Barranco Chico. According to Arakmbut mythology, the river bed was gouged by a giant isula ant *(tagnpi)* and the water was deposited by a dragonfly *(toku)* during the period of creation, when the giant tree, Wanamey, saved the Harakmbut from a fiery flood (see Volume 1, chapter one).

After the effects of the cataclysmic flood had abated, the Harakmbut went downriver and founded settlements on the banks of the rivers. The headwaters are the ancestral territory of the Pukirieri Harakmbut, who took their name from the river. The homeland of the Harakmbut covered the area between the Tambopata and the upper Madre de Dios. Within this 'national territory' the Harakmbut peoples moved during their history. The Pukirieri were missionised in San Miguel de Kaichihue in 1940s and many died of disease. However, a community of their descendants still live in Kotsimba on the river Malinowski. Their lands in the upper Pukiri were taken over by the Kotsimberi Arakmbut who fled Shintuya to found Barranco Chico in 1975. They still use the peach palm groves and barbasco chacras of their Pukirieri relatives (see maps 2 and 3).

Prior to the first incursion by a Peruvian scientific expedition in 1940, the Sapiteri moved from the Nawene river at the headwaters of the Karene and lived on the lower parts of the Pukiri. Several households still have their settlements in this area where they share territory with San José. The Arakmbut of San José joined the Sapiteri in 1969, when they fled from sorcery and exploitation at the mission of Shintuya. In this way, the Pukiri has had a continuity of Harakmbut communities since the beginning of remembered time.

The escape from Shintuya took place on the instigation of a shaman *(wayorokeri)*, who dreamt that the Arakmbut would find the site of their community by ascending the third river on the right bank of the Madre de Dios and travelling up this river (the Karene) until they met the mouth of the Pukiri. San José was thus first founded at its mouth in 1969. Two or three colonists had moved into the area a few years before and were living near the Sapiteri; initially relations were friendly and the Arakmbut co-existed with the colonists.

The Arakmbut knew that they were on ancestral territory, but as the small number of colonists did not affect them particularly, there were no disagreements with the highland people. The first difficulties in the Pukiri came with the discovery of gold deposits on the beaches and river banks. A gold rush took off in 1978. The few colonists who had been living in the area in 1969 suddenly expanded their influence and brought large numbers of workers down from the highlands. Gradually, from being small-scale miners, the old colonists started to employ dozens of workers and became wealthy patrons, becoming more negative in their attitude to the Arakmbut. Gradually more small-scale miners entered the area.

When the Arakmbut communities were mapped in 1979, both old and new colonists resisted. The whole area was considered Harakmbut territory but the patrons objected. The refusal of the government of Belaúnde to title any community lands meant that from 1980 to 1985 there was no protection for the communities of San José and Barranco Chico. As the Arakmbut found gold in the Pukiri, several households moved there to mine gold from placers on or near the beaches. Initially relations were not hostile because the Arakmbut had several camps on the Pukiri where they washed gold during the week and returned to the community at week-ends (a trip of about one hour by boat or two by forest track).

In 1985 tensions rose because of the conflict between San José and a patron, Jaime Sumalave, over a mining area off the Karene river. In November of that year, during a two month stay at San José del Karene, I visited the river Pukiri at the boundary of community lands. The indigenous camp I visited was situated by a notice which said 'Welcome to the Territory of San José del Karene'. The Arakmbut slept in small huts, and during the day they hunted, fished, tended a few crops, and worked gold. There were signs of patrons. The old colonist 'Pinto' threatened the Arakmbut occasionally and once forced a group off the beach at gun-point. However, on the whole, the patrons and Arakmbut kept apart.

During 1986 all this was to change. In the first place, the community titles of San José were approved. Patrons were given the option of accepting the existence of the community and living within the area with the permission of the Arakmbut, or leaving. The patrons stayed and continued to rule the area as if it was their domain. During the year several lucrative gold finds were made and some Arakmbut hired small numbers of highland workers (several of whom had escaped from the patrons). The potential wealth was considered problematic. 'We do not want to be capitalists' was a frequent phrase heard before and after that date. They distributed the wealth in the Arakmbut manner of conspicuous consumption and drinking parties.

However, the lure of gold was too strong for the families of the patrons. One day, at the onset of the rainy season in 1986, a flotilla of boats made their way to the Pukiri. These were the seven adult children of 'Pinto' who established armed settlements from the boundary of San José almost to the mouth of the Pukiri. This family now controls about 80 percent of the river. When the Arakmbut complained, death threats were sent to the community, and then one Sunday, late in 1986, José Quique was shot by a colonist after a fight on the beaches. This event stunned the community and from that time onwards, the Pukiri became practically a no-go area for the Arakmbut of San José.

When I returned in 1991 to the same boundary post that I had visited in 1985, the situation was quite different. Few Arakmbut had been willing to go upriver into the Pukiri. They said that they were not welcome. Pinto had died, but his children lived in their well-defended houses and were illegally clearing the lands. Eventually two young Arakmbut and a friendly gold worker agreed to take me so that we could map the river and assess the numbers of colonists in the area.

We passed down the Karene and entered the Pukiri; the 'lunar' landscape produced by intensive gold work, which had in 1985 been visible at the mouth of the river, had now extended further inland. Stopping at the house of the last remaining Sapiteri in the area, we were told us how he was being constantly threatened by the children of 'old man Pinto' who wanted his house and land. Carlos, the Sapiteri, agreed to accompany us upriver.

We passed the settlements occupied by the children of Pinto and could see up to six gold mining placers operating on a beach. Young boys of twelve or thirteen years were working in the teams. As we approached the boundaries of the community we saw the place where we had stayed six years previously. There was no longer a sign of welcome to the territory of San José. Now the notice said 'Welcome to the Rural Settlement of Bajo Pukiri'. The area which had been settled by the indigenous miners had now been taken over and become a colonist village. Twenty-seven huts, some mere shacks, others of two stories, showed that the place was a mining settlement. At the time of our arrival women were distributing food aid from the United States for the poor of Peru to the mining colonists through their Mother's Club. As we left, the Sapiteri saw a chicken of his which had been stolen a few weeks before.

We returned to San José. A few days later some of the community leaders came to talk. They said that they were concerned for our safety. I had been seen travelling up the Pukiri with members of San José, and colonists accused us of mobilising the community against them. The patrons said that if I knew what was good for me and the family, we should leave immediately. The community were concerned this time. There had been threats in 1985 but these had been dismissed as jokes. This was serious. We had previously planned to leave the community for a few weeks around that time and when we eventually left, someone from San José was present at every moment until we were safely on the boat from Boca Colorado to Puerto Maldonado. By the time we had returned one month later, we learned that the death threat had passed from us because we were only interested in 'native culture'. The threats had moved to some traders.

The threat which we received was similar to that regularly received by the leaders of the community. Whenever any member of the community asserts their rights to their territory, it is only a matter of time before the threat arrives, usually passed by word of mouth via traders at Boca Colorado. The Pukiri was effectively closed by the colonists so that the Arakmbut could only pass if they were not stopping or wanted to sell or buy something.

In 1995, the intense mining by companies in the Huaypetue, an affluent of the upper Pukiri, had lowered the gold production in the Pukiri substantially. A visit by a Welsh film crew at this time reported four hundred placers in the lower Huaypetue over a distance of twenty-five square miles with pits to the depth of 20-30 metres (Russell Isaacs and Dilwyn Jenkins, pers. comm.). In August, the colonists were already discussing transferring their extraction activities to timber, rather than gold. The river, at that time of year, should have been either completely clear or with a rich red silt colour; instead the Pukiri was a sickly yellow colour.

The Arakmbut are very concerned about the river; the few households who risked a fishing expedition in the dry season found nothing. On the visit in August 1995, we reached the mouth of the Pukiri: 'The river is sick', said a young Arakmbut man, as we passed the confluence. 'It is dying.'

This case study of a river and its people demonstrates the importance of territory for the Arakmbut. The multifaceted meaning of territory for indigenous peoples is one significant feature of the description, while another is the devastating effect of untrammelled colonisation. As with the case study in the last chapter, this example shows how ethnographic descriptions originate in events and practical activities. This is particularly apparent when looking at Arakmbut notions of territory.

Territoriality

The history of the Pukiri is broadly the same as any river on which the Harakmbut peoples have lived for the last thousand years or more. The case study shows that there were movements of the different Harakmbut peoples over the centuries, but all of this took place within their homeland. All Arakmbut claims to territory are based initially on the mythological creation of the world.

The Pukiri demonstrates the change which took place between the time when the Arakmbut joined the Sapiteri of the area in 1969, when colonists were living in relative harmony with the indigenous peoples, and the present. In 1969 some colonists even began to learn Harakmbut and establish co-operative relations. However, by 1985, tensions were increasing.

When the Arakmbut first encountered non-indigenous peoples in 1950, they lived in the headwaters of the Karene and Ishiriwe rivers, which are affluents of the Eori (Madre de Dios) river. The Arakmbut were divided into Kipodneri, who lived in five communal houses or malocas *(hak)* along the Kipodnwe river in the headwaters of the Karene, and the Wandakweri, who lived in seven hak in the headwaters of the Ishiriwe. Each communal house and its residents were named after some environmental feature in the vicinity. For example, crops such as sugar cane *(apik)* and coca *(kuka)* gave rise to the Apikmbote and Kukambote. The people who lived there were referred to by the name of the house with the suffix *'-eri'*. Thus the Apikmbote communal house contained the Apikmboteri.

The world for the Arakmbut was defined by the term *wandari*. The Harakmbut language does not distinguish between singular and plural nouns, which means that there could be one or several wandari depending on the context. The wandari of the Arakmbut encompassed all the malocas and the area they controlled, whereas the wandari of a maloca depended on the extent to which the people living there controlled the surrounds. Each maloca was a self-determining and largely self-sufficient community, blending horticulture with hunting, gathering and fishing. Relations between the different houses waxed and waned according to exchanges. Mutual invitations to feasts and ceremonies provided the opportunities for young men and women to become acquainted and marriage alliances were frequent. At other times hostilities between malocas could result in periods of feuding.[2]

The boundaries between the malocas and between the Arakmbut and other neighbouring peoples were thus flexible and more social than physical. Friends could come close to the community with impunity while enemies were attacked. The word 'wandari' was therefore relative to the person using the term. It could refer to the world as a whole or to the area around a maloca. Kaplan (Overing) finds a similar notion of territory among the Piaroa (1975:57):

> 'The word *Itso'fha* can be glossed as 'a land', 'a Territory'; but it does not denote a land that is circumscribed once and for all. The boundaries of an Itso'fha fluctuate from year to year as its members re-position themselves both physically and politically.'

The sense of territoriality has undergone two changes over the last forty years. The first occurred during the period when all the Arakmbut lived in Shintuya between 1956 and 1969. Here communal houses and gardens were replaced by what the priests considered more 'civilised' houses and gardens allotted for each group that ate together, or extended family. The maloca groups in Shintuya continued to live together in different parts of the mission. After the maloca groups dispersed from the mission of Shintuya in between 1969 and 1975, the five Arakmbut communities were established and quickly created reformulations of the maloca groups. The communities still spatially resemble the rooms within a maloca and operate to all intents and purposes as independent communal houses.

The second change, after 1978, occurred when the increase in colonists, mentioned in the history of the Pukiri above, began to make the Arakmbut aware of a pressure on their resources. Unlike in pre-mission times, outsiders did not come and go. The patrons of the Pukiri and Karene remained stubbornly tied to the same areas. Land was becoming bounded. In 1979 the Peruvian government rein-

---

2. The evidence for this reconstruction of the period of the malocas comes from discussions with the old people from all the Arakmbut communities, and an analysis of the stories of fighting with the non-Arakmbut Taka which have been discussed in Volume 1, chapter ten.

forced this process by mapping out the Arakmbut communities with a view to titling indigenous territories. The first title was awarded to Shintuya in the name of the mission. However, the other communities pursued their titling procedures and with the support of FENAMAD and the Centro Eori in Puerto Maldonado the other four communities eventually received their titles in 1986:

Table 3.1 Arakmbut communities and their territories
1. Shintuya; titled (with an extension) 23/5/1985; 8,651 hectares;
2. San José del Karene; titled 6/3/86; 23,604 hectares;
3. Puerto Luz; titled 6/3/86; 56,873 hectares;
4. Boca del Inambari; titled 5/9/86; 6,731 hectares;
5. Barranco Chico; titled 23/1/88; 3,363 hectares.

Territorial demarcation has, for the first time, established a fixed boundary of the Arakmbut wandari. When talking to the Arakmbut now it is clear that when they refer to the wandari of the community they mean the titled area. The reason for this is that, unlike the period before contact with the missions, when the enemies came and went and the political situation fluctuated, the mining colonisation became a permanent fixture. The Arakmbut no longer suffer raids from indigenous peoples living at a distance who come to steal women or crops, but from colonists who reside in permanent settlements on Arakmbut land and take resources and women. Underneath the veneer of friendship, the Arakmbut and colonists are deadly competitors for the resources of the indigenous communities.

The relativistic relationship with outsiders which existed before contact has become a more absolute relationship to the colonising frontier.[3] The legalisation of the community boundaries has added a rigidity to the wandari of each community. However, beyond each community the territory is still wandari belonging to the Arakmbut themselves. All the area which was inhabited by their ancestors in the past is still considered to be their homeland and has been demar-

3. By colonising frontier, I refer to Henley (1982:156), who develops Ribeiro's notion of 'fronts of national expansion' (Ribeiro 1970) as follows: 'a "front" can be defined as any group of members of the national society who share a common interest, economic or otherwise, in establishing themselves in a region inhabited by indigenous groups'. The Amazon is not the only example where territorial rights have become more fixed as a result of colonisation. Schapera noted in Africa: 'In general it is only within the past century and a half, and largely owing to the spread of European domination, that tribal territories have become fairly stable and precisely defined. But much of what was formerly tribal land has been appropriated for European settlement' (Schapera 1956:14).

cated as a communal reserve for the Arakmbut. FENAMAD carried out the mapping and investigation process in 1992 and presented the material to the government. The Minister of Agriculture, four years later, has still not approved the reserve because he is simultaneously negotiating rights to oil exploration in the area with Mobil.

Multifaceted Notions of Territoriality

The case study of the Pukiri drew together several different aspects of Arakmbut relations with their territories. As the process of colonisation has increased, the notion of wandari has become bounded and is used to translate the Spanish word *'territorio'* (Chirif, García & Smith 1991:27-28). However, in addition to this meaning, the Arakmbut have several other connotations which arise when they say 'wandari'.

1. The World and the Earth

The Pukiri, as all rivers, has a mythological origin and provides an entry into the underwater spirit world, Seronwe. Communication with spirits takes place through dreams (wayorok) and this accounts for the significance of the founding of San José through a shamanic dream (see Volume 2, chapter four). The spirituality of the Arakmbut is crucial for understanding their attachment to territories and their sense of responsibility over how the forest and river should be treated.

All phenomena are animated through soul-matter which ranges from the souls of humans (nokiren) to the free spirits of the invisible world. The Pukiri lives because it reflects the state of the *waweri* river spirits who inhabit its depths. When the river dies, the spirits disappear and it becomes lifeless; nothing can exist in its waters. This spiritual aspect of territory can be seen in the Arakmbut term wandari.

Wandari refers to different worlds or realms. *Kurudn* is the sky. This is an otiose domain above the flight of birds. The sky is the place where the culture hero Marinke fled from the jaguars. The people who went with him are called *kurudneri* (people of the sky) and they rarely have contact with human beings. Below the river and forest are underworlds. The river underworld (Seronwe) is a largely beneficial place to which people who have died a good death go. The forest underworld (Totoyo or Takayo) lies under mysterious lakes deep into the interior. Arakmbut whose souls are captured on death are taken there in the afterlife. There are several stories about the world under the river, and how people have accidently found themselves in this other world. When people enter the underworld the landscape appears the same as above – there is sky, river, forests and houses.

The sky and underworld are wandari but belong to the beings of the invisible spirit world. Invisible spirits can move from one world to another, but human beings with bodies live in the wandari of our visible world, which could be called 'the Earth'.[4] Everything living in the visible world is animated by soul-matter which pervades life in different intensities. Human beings and larger animals have most soul-matter which gives rise to consciousness in the form of an animating 'soul' (nokiren). Stones and trees have less soul-matter, while small creatures are in between. Arakmbut spirituality or religion consists of an attempt to influence and control soul-matter.

The way in which the Earth is treated affects the health and welfare of human beings. For example, if a hunter overkills, he lays himself open to attack from the spirits associated with the creatures he has killed. If someone treats the forest or river without respect, such as clearing areas considered too large, making too much noise, or laughing loudly, this will attract the spirits and lay them and their close relatives open to attack. The Arakmbut see the Earth as the vehicle for invisible spiritual activity which is a constant uneasy balance between different forces. Arakmbut shamanic activities are centred on restoring order in a world of spiritual danger and chaos.

2. Lands

When the Arakmbut talked of the Pukiri, they referred to it as the source of fish, animals, and gold. The territory is not only controlled

4. Anthropologists looking at spirituality in connection with territory often use the term 'Earth'. Fortes (1940:254) refers to the 'cult of the Earth' in his study of the Tallensi, and Evans-Pritchard similarly refers to 'spirits of the earth' in his study of Nuer religion (1956:63). More recently Ortiz (1969:21) refers to 'Earth mother' in Mexico and Nash (1979:121-20) to Pachamama as the 'ancient space/time imminent in the earth' in the Andes. Earth denotes the spiritual dimension of territory, as can be seen in the following statement to the ILO by Hayden Burgess of the World Council of Indigenous Peoples:

> 'For indigenous peoples, life and earth are synonymous. The earth is our foundation, the source of our spirituality, the fountain from which our cultures and language flourish. The earth is the keeper of events and the bones of our forefathers, the substantial evidence of our peoples' existence before memory. The earth is our historian, our educator, the provider of food, medicine, clothing, and protection. She is the mother of our races' (Burgess 1987:133).

(Although by no means universal, the concept of 'mother earth' has entered the indigenous movement's vocabulary to express the spiritual relationship between indigenous peoples and their territories.)

by humans and spirits, but contains the very resources which are necessary to enable life to continue.[5]

Wandari is a term used by the Arakmbut to refer to any extended area which includes the ground, water, and sky. This area contains all the resources which the Arakmbut need to live. All resources are found in the wandari. Thus birds in the air, fish in the water, and animals or tuber crops on or under the ground are also dwellers in the wandari. I specifically asked the Arakmbut about gold mining, because according to Peruvian law, all subsurface resources belong to the state. The Arakmbut argued that gold is found in the sand under the river and in the forest and belongs to them in the same way as any other subsurface resource: whether fish, tuber crops, armadillo, or even soil.

The Arakmbut wandari is divided into three different domains which are horizontal, as opposed to the three vertical worlds of the sky, earth, and underworld:

(a) *Ndumba* means the forest. Forest is one of the two main divisions of the non-human world and mythologically considered to be under the control of a spirit called Mano (associated with the woodpecker *mbegkno* and the sun). The forest contains animals and birds which are connected to the *ndumberi* (forest spirits). It also contains dangerous spirits which are associated with carnivorous animals and people who died unexpectedly. The forest is primarily a male domain and is fraught with dangers – particularly snakes which are the arrows of hostile spirits (toto). Men only learn to penetrate the depths of the forest with experience. Usually no one will spend much time alone in the forest until they are adults with enough spiritual strength to resist the invisible dangers and enough practical experience to avoid getting lost.

(b) *Wawe* means river and is the second main division of the non-human world. The river is mythologically under the charge of

---

5. With the increased influence of Marxist thought on the social sciences in the late 1960s, anthropologists shifted their emphasis from notions of territory to the political economy of land and resources. Marxism emphasised that economic relations dealing with land were relations between people. With the influence of capitalism, land (means of production) becomes transformed from an object of labour, to which all have access, to a commodity under the ownership of a landlord. The consequent form of exploitation through land expropriation was taken up by social analysts and was very relevant to indigenous peoples' concern with invasions of their territories. This factor may explain why the term 'land rights' frequently covers both access to resources and territorial control in the indigenous movement. The Marxian approach therefore looked at territory from a political economic perspective.

a male spirit, *pugn*, who is the moon from the underworld. The river is more beneficial than the forest, although it also contains its dangers. The waweri water spirits are the source of fish for the Arakmbut, which in the invisible world appear as plants. River spirits are particularly dangerous for children and old people who are attracted to the depths of the water. Women are more associated with the river than men and there are a considerable number of connotations linking women's bags, the main material artifact which they make, with the river. Among the Wachipaeri, Fernandez Distel (1976:17) notes a further connection: women sing to the crops as if they were fish.

(c) The third domain of wandari concerns human beings and it is dominated by the hak and *tamba* (gardens). Whether maloca or community, this settlement always lies between the river and the forest. In the past the maloca had two entrances, one for the river and one for the forest. Although the paths to and from the community are now more numerous, the same orientation can be seen nowadays. The gardens are also areas where the forest has been transformed. There are two forms of garden: *oteyo* are on the high banks away from the river, while *wendari* are on flooded land down by the river itself. In this way the hak and the tamba themselves provide a microcosm of the wandari including the forest and river as the extremes of a flexible duality surrounding the human world of the settlement in the centre.

The Arakmbut use their territories for their economic activities. They hunt, fish, and gather from the forest and rivers. Each household has its gardens in which crops such as yuca, plantains, sweet potatoes and fruits are grown. All of the money the Arakmbut have is acquired in exchange for the gold which is found on their territory. They do not work for other people but mine the gold and use it directly in exchange for non-indigenous commodities and money. Thus economically they are largely independent, apart from those who have debts to local traders. However, wandari also refers to the effect of human and spiritual activity on the environment and this is the third aspect of the term which is relevant to their notion of territory.

3. Landscape

Wandari consists of elements and features. The elements constitute the fabric of the territory. For example, *wae* is the word for water, *kurudn* for air, and *sorok* for soil. Sorok does not refer to anything under the soil, nor does it have anything growing above it. The word *barak* is used to refer to ground, in the sense of something which has objects on the surface – whether plants or stones. Other elements which the Arakmbut use are *kuwadn* (sand) and *widn* (stones). The resources which the Arakmbut use to subsist are found in or around these elements: animals on the barak, fish in wae, gold in the kuwadn, plants in the sorok.

Each of these elements is a constituent aspect of wandari rather than a substitute. Whereas we could say that wandari refers to territory, land, or the earth, we cannot say that wandari refers to sorok. Thus to say that a people have rights to land in the sense of soil (sorok) is meaningless. I have asked Arakmbut whether the term *'tierra'* (land) should be translated by wandari or sorok. The answer is unequivocal. Sorok refers to soil and is on its own useless. In order to survive, the Arakmbut need all that exists on the wandari. Sorok is not sufficient.

Features of the landscape constitute the character of wandari.[6] There are some features which have mythological origins and some which are human and others which are unknown. Riverbanks *(wakumbogn)*, for example, were formed with rivers by the isula ant and dragonfly. Undulating ground *(wakupa)* was formed by the woodpecker (mbegnko), who, after providing human beings with fire, flew away in a manner which follows the shape of the landscape.

Some features of the landscape have unknown origins but they serve animals. For example the *sorokmbayo* are salt licks which attract animals. These are discovered by humans and are often named after the person who found them. Their locations are highly prized knowledge, as they provide a central point for hunters to look for game. Other animal-related features of the landscape are *kotsimbayo* (aguajales) or watery areas where the aguaje palm grows. These are favoured by many animals but particularly the white-lipped peccary *(akudnui)*.

Human activity on the landscape can be seen primarily in old gardens *(anenda tamba)*. These are particularly used for peach palm trees

6. For many indigenous peoples, including the Arakmbut, time and space are intimately related. By analysing landscape it is possible to see the past in the present layout of the world. Landscape has become important in anthropology as a way of looking at the process by which human beings create their environment (Bender 1993:1) and how people perceive and act on their surroundings (Hirsch and O'Hanlon 1995). Posey (1995:3) argues that human-modified landscapes have important implications for ownership, and consequently for Intellectual Property Rights.

(ho), which remain for many decades after a garden has finished. Furthermore, in the Pukiri and on the Ishiriwe it is possible to see the remains of gardens from pre-contact times. In these areas, people nowadays also use the barbasco *(kumo)* from the old gardens. Of all the Arakmbut crops the most long-lasting, peach palm and barbasco, are considered to have spiritual properties.

On all rivers there are the old settlements of the Harakmbut malocas. In the Wandakwe, the Arakmbut know the places where their houses were situated so well that they serve as relative markers for historical periods: they refer to the period when they were at the malocas of Apikmbote to refer to the period between 1940 and 1950 and Kotsimbote to refer to the period between 1952 and 1956. The landscape thus reflects mythology, animal behaviour, and the history of Harakmbut settlements, all within the notion of wandari.

Wandari is a broad term which, when unwrapped, covers the contexts in English of world, earth, territory, land, and landscape. The spiritual, political, economic, and geographic aspects of the environment are all blended together into one word with a multifaceted series of connotations. Rather than see the terms territory, land, earth, and landscape as alternatives, we should see them as a way of building up a polythetic definition (Needham 1975) of the relationship between human beings and the environment. Territory thus refers to the political control over an area, the land to the resources contained in that area, the earth to the spirituality connected with the area, and the landscape to its historico-semantic meaning. These are not discrete entities but different ways of looking at the same relationship. Dividing the spiritual from the territorial, or resources from the meaning of activities carried out on an area, is an artificial compartmentalisation which is temporarily useful for an analysis but useless in establishing legal provisions that reflect indigenous perspectives.

This reinforces the conclusion reached earlier that all these different ways of relating to the environment were, for indigenous peoples, practically and logically connected. To separate the political from the economic or the spiritual, as happens in the non-indigenous world, is an artificial construct which divides the indivisible.[7]

7. The Arakmbut experience is relevant to the discussions on indigenous rights at the ILO and UN, in which governments seek to compartmentalise phenomena which, for indigenous peoples, are aspects of a holistic perspective. An example of the consequences of unnecessary compartmentalisation arose with a conflict over the terms 'lands' and 'territories' in revising ILO Convention 169. The final compromise was to use the term 'land' as if it were 'territory', thereby

Use, Possession, and Ownership

The three concepts heading this section cover different ways in which people relate to things. Amazonian studies tend to divide the items of production into two: an individual's own tools and objects, and gardens, which belong to households and are held in usufruct. The territory as a whole is not considered. For example, Henley says of the Panare (1982: 64-66):

> 'After the sexual division of labour, the most important principle underlying the social organisation of production is the absence of property rights over natural resources. The Panare have a strong sense of private property in so far as items of personal use are concerned ... A man can cut a garden ... but this right is no more than a right of usufruct.'

In a similar vein, Jackson says of the Colombian Tukanoans:

> 'Tukanoans have implicit usufruct rights to resources in these areas, but the concepts of "tribal lands", "inalienable rights" or "title" are foreign ones ... Individual property seen as inalienably owned by the individual is confined to items of almost daily use' (Jackson 1983:62-3).

These authors are correct to avoid imposing western notions of property onto indigenous peoples. However, for the Arakmbut, the difficulty with the question of use, possession, and ownership is that the concepts exist but in a distinct manner from non-indigenous claims to commodities. For these authors, property is primarily something held by individuals, while rights to lands are usufruct and secondary. Usufruct actually means land which is owned by a person, but used by another. Presumably, in an indigenous context, this refers to individual families using an area which is considered to be held by the community. However, the relationship between indigenous peoples and their lands is rarely approached by outsiders in terms of the collective ownership of land or territories.

Among the Arakmbut the relationship between people, tools, and territory cannot be categorised so easily into personal ownership and collective use. Here are some examples which illustrate the difficulties such a classification encounters.

Kumamin is a favourite trickster character among the Arakmbut. There are many different stories about him. Frequently he

---

depoliticising the control of indigenous peoples over their territories (Plant, R. 1991:60). However, this shows that one cannot escape from the implications of the term 'territory' merely by changing the word into 'land'.

tells lies, but his main trait is to steal *(e'mbere)* from the gardens. Here is a typical story:

Kumamin had found out where there were chacras to steal from and he knew what grew there. When Kumamin left with his arrows the people said: 'Ah ha! Where is Kumamin going? Kumamin! Kumamin! Kumamin!' they called. 'Where are you going?'
When Kumamin went with his arrows, a woman said: 'I have my chacra in that direction. My plantains are hidden in a hole in the ground to mature. Watch you don't take them!'
Kumamin replied, 'I am going on my own elsewhere.' He denied her accusation. 'I am not going by your chacra. I am going this way. I am not going to take your plantains. But where did you say they were? In which chacra?' asked Kumamin.
Kumamin went a long way round to steal the plantains and reached the chacra and took the plantains. First he ate two *makoy* (bunches) of plantains and took one other to his house.
'Let's see', said the woman. 'Perhaps he is going to my chacra. I am going to look.'
She arrived at her chacra, looking where they had been buried, she found nothing. Everything had been taken. She reached the house and asked Kumamin, 'Who has taken my plantains from my chacra?' Kumamin denied everything.

This story shows that a person who has cleared the ground for a garden owns the produce from the plot. Stealing from the gardens was a concern of the households in San José. This is not necessarily because crops were valuable in themselves, but because they involve much personal investment and hard work to produce. Whereas people have the right to pass through another's chacra, they do not have the right to take the produce. Furthermore they do not have the right to plant their own crops in someone else's garden.
In the past when the Arakmbut made collective circular gardens, each person working had their own plot or plots within its radius. Stealing from a garden was always considered a serious offence. I was told an apocryphal story of two brothers in the Wandakwe before contact:

'They continually robbed the chacras of others. They were told by the elders that if they did not stop robbing and plant their own crops they would be in trouble. Three times they were told. Then the people said something should be done. They were invited to go fishing and eagerly they went to the river. At the river's edge, the men bound them up and sliced the hair of their head around with an axe blade so that the blood flowed. They didn't die immediately but soon maggots came and infected the wounds so that they both died.'

There has never been a shortage of land and so an Arakmbut can more or less pick a plot where he or she wants. Yet this story and the concern expressed in the Kumamin story demonstrate the seriousness which the Arakmbut treat the produce of gardens. Gardens are cleared at the beginning of the dry season by the men and after a few months drying out are burnt to increase the nutrients in the soil. Planting, weeding, and harvesting are the responsibility of women, although men also participate or do their own work if they are single.

Land is not a commodity, but it is not simply usufruct either. Gardens are usually associated with people and take their name (wandik). Usually the name of the woman who tends them is given as the owner although single men and men who have recently married women from different communities will find their name associated with the clearing. Furthermore, to name a garden after the man or woman responsible for producing the crops for the household invests part of that person into the area both in terms of responsibility for the production and in terms of possessing or holding that area.

Gardening is considered the hardest work there is. It shares with gold work the verb *e'mba'a* which means 'labour with hands'. The value of the garden is undoubtedly in the labour invested in the clearing and tending the crops. The crops themselves also belong to the owner of the garden. The juxtaposition of a person's name with a garden is extremely important. It constitutes a claim over the whole area which has been cleared and its produce for as long as the garden provides for the household. This can in fact take place over a person's lifetime, because, peach palm and barbasco, as well as other fruit trees, can last for ten years or more. Indeed the fewer crops there are in the garden, the less of a hold a person has over the area, yet even then people should not go into a used garden and take the fruit if the person who originally cleared it is still living. In any case, as used soil, it is of limited use apart from the few trees left standing. In this way the borderline between usufruct and household property is very vague. To categorise gardens as held by usufruct right involves a misinterpretation. It separates the value of work and produce from the meaning of land itself. The value of the land lies in the fact that it has been cleared by labour and the products that arise from this belong to those who cleared it.

Further proof of the personal or household ownership of gardens arises when we look at personal property. In the literature on Amazonia, the only personal property which people recognise are the means of production – tools and capital goods. This holds for the Arakmbut too. Each person has tools and goods. Some of these, such as bows and arrows for men or string bags for women, have been made personally with great skill. Men make canoes in the forest and also houses. Other goods, such as pots, pans, clothes, or capital goods, such as shotguns or mining materials, can be bought with gold, but these are also personal property. All of these goods belong to individuals and no one should steal them. A thief who is caught will find himself physically attacked at the next drinking party unless he or she returns the property.

Property is destroyed when a person dies. The pots, pans, material artifacts, and domestic animals, as well as certain capital goods, are destroyed in a massive fire. However, the house is also destroyed and in certain circumstances, the crops in a garden are also destroyed and the land abandoned. This demonstrates that the chacras are, in Arakmbut eyes, as much a part of the personal property of the dead person. However in contrast to a bow and arrow or an axe for chopping wood, the house and gardens are the responsibility of the person who built them and those who look after them, such as a married couple. Rather than looking at use, possession, and ownership as discrete types of property relations, a more productive approach among the Arakmbut is to look at the multi-levelled relationship between persons and things. This arises from three simultaneous factors:

1. e'ka / e'mba'a – to make, do or work

These two words contain a difference in intensity of activity rather than something qualitatively distinct. They refer to making an object such as a bow and arrow or a string bag, and also to its use. In the same way, a garden is worked when it is cleared and used to produce goods. Thus the usufruct aspect of gardens refers to the personal labour invested in its preparation, planting, tending, and harvesting.

2. e'tae – to have

This means to have on one's person or to 'possess'. The item is therefore in a contiguous relationship to a person. For example, a bow and arrow made or presented to someone is accepted as his because it is held by that person, rather than another. A garden can therefore belong to a household and not to people from the other side of the village. This is a contiguity which arises through constant use or having something stored or kept in a person's house.

3. *e'e – to be*

This is the relationship which arises after long periods of contiguity or association between a person and the object. After a while the inanimate object begins to become related to the personality of a person. The bow and arrow become recognisable as belonging to that person. The chacra has certain characteristics when cleared, which, after a time, reflect the men who cleared it. We could perhaps call this 'presence'. The Arakmbut explain this as a part of the Being or nokiren of a person which 'leaks' and surrounds the object. This spiritual connection is the nearest the Arakmbut come to the idea of ownership. For this reason, when someone dies these objects have to be destroyed because part of the dead person's soul is present around the inanimate object and could cause harm.

The distinctions between use, possession, and ownership are aspects of the relationship between the maker or user and the object. They are not different types of relationship as in our heavily classified notions of private property, but attributes or qualities pertaining to a relationship. Furthermore they are expressed in the form of verbs rather than nouns, thereby demonstrating the dynamic element in the relationship between people and things.

Houses, gardens, and the goods or produce within them all demonstrate different aspects of ownership operating simultaneously. Each of these can be associated with one person or with several. However, collective ownership among the Arakmbut is not invested (even symbolically) in one person, as occurs with the Piaroa (Kaplan (Overing) 1975:26).

In San José del Karene in December 1991, a community leader met with a commission from the Ministry of Agriculture, Centro Eori and the Native Federation (FENAMAD), to discuss the establishment of a communal reserve throughout traditional Arakmbut territory. He gave several arguments as to why the community wanted the area around the Wandakwe and Ishiriwe reserved:

> 'The people from this community still go to the Ishiriwe to hunt animals. We do not want colonisation to take place in the area nor do we want outsiders taking our resources. The Wandakwe is the homeland of the Arakmbut people; my ancestors were born and died there and should not be disturbed.'

These arguments parallel the use, possession, and ownership elements of title, but they were presented from a community based perspective:

1. Territory as used

The first aspect of the relationship between the Arakmbut and their territory is use, and this can be seen most clearly by means of Map 4. As mentioned above, the Arakmbut now have a more fixed notion of wandari than they did fifty years ago. However the utilisation of territory outside of the community has not changed dramatically. The easiest way of looking at the utilisation of community resources is through a series of concentric circles radiating from the community at the centre. At the centre of the map is the community itself with its houses, school, shops, and river harbour. Wherever anyone is within community territory, San José del Karene is the base. Even for those who live further upstream or spend time in the gold camps, the village school provides a focus for formal meetings and education, while the shops provide the beer for drinking parties and supplementary subsistence foods.

In the first 'circle' around the village are the gardens. These are either placed on high ground where the soils are lower in fertility but where pineapples, barbasco, yuca, and rice can be grown without difficulty, or on the lower flooded ground where bananas, papaya, yuca, and other crops are grown. The gardens are as near to the community as possible and are rarely more than twenty minutes to half an hour's walk because carrying the produce can be burdensome. The river banks, however, have gardens further away because the women can punt in their canoes to collect the produce and pole them back to the community.

The next 'circle' shows the gold mining operations. On the whole these are more than half-an-hour's walk and begin at the point when the gardens finish. Partly this is because of the effect of fifteen years' gold working – the more lucrative inland placers are further afield from the community. Some households will occasionally work on beaches closer to the main village, but this is usually a temporary measure. As the gold placers are so far away from the main community, workers and their close relatives will often live in small camps during the week and return to the community on a Sunday to catch up on the news and buy provisions. Other Arakmbut employ workers who live in camps far from the village and work gold, while the Arakmbut visit from time to time and remain in the main community.

The gold mining placers are primarily based on the main rivers (Karene and Pukiri) and on the banks of the smaller streams (Mboraiwe and Kiraswe) which meander into the interior of community

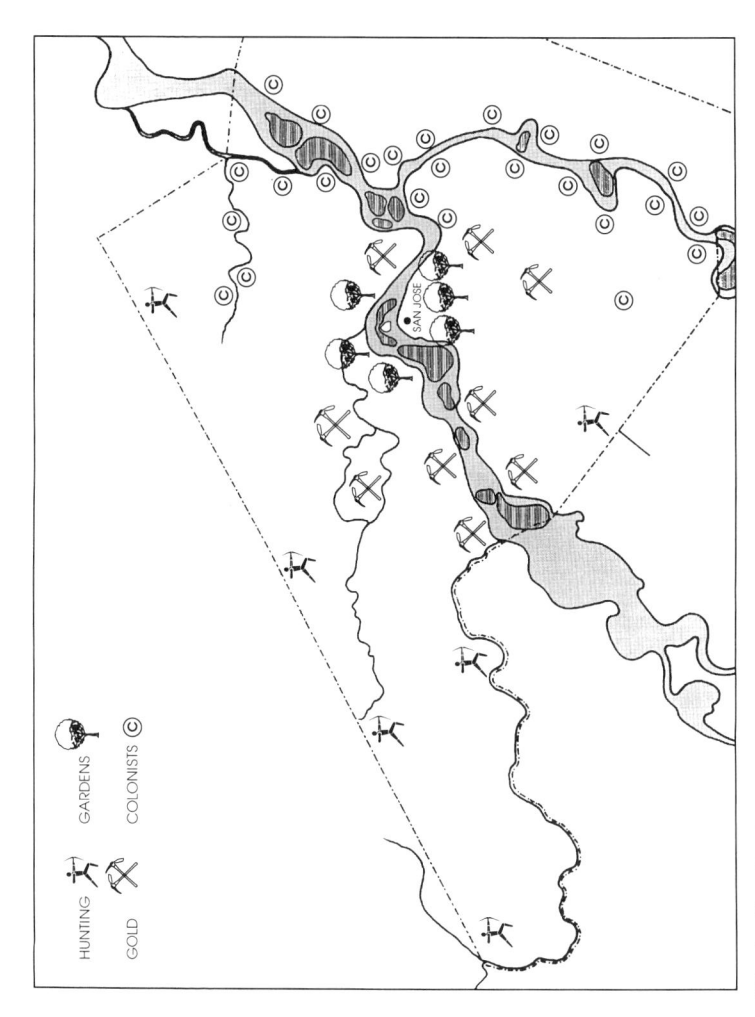

Map 4 Resource Use in San José

territory. The gold mining camps are in the closest hunting, fishing, and gathering areas to the village. These activities constitute the furthest circle of territorial utilisation.

Hunters try to keep their expeditions to within a day and so, on the whole, keep within the territory titled for the community. They go to a series of four salt licks which lie at the extreme point of the territory, which attract some of the animals up from the Ishiriwe where they propagate. Fishers will use any stream near to the community, but collective fishing expeditions which take place in the dry season progressively start from the streams closer to the village and move out to the extreme parts of the territory, particularly the Pukiri. Gathering expeditions are primarily organised by women and follow the periods when the forest fruits ripen. Occasionally a family will go to cut down some *kotsi* (aguaje) or peach palm from old gardens not belonging to any current villager.

Gathering materials for house-building can be burdensome, particularly crisneja leaves for the roof. These leaves have been overharvested in the environs of the community because the Arakmbut have lived in the same place for longer than they would do prior to contact with the missions. A tendency has been to replace leaf roofs with corrugated iron which is more easily assembled. However most Arakmbut, when questioned, prefer the leaves, but find a one- or two-day expedition to find them and bring them back to the house site too time-consuming.

In spite of the fact that hunting, gathering and fishing take place all over Arakmbut territory, the activities nearer the community such as garden and gold work mean that the flora and fauna are quickly depleted and so people move to the furthest circle around the community – coterminous with the community boundaries – for their supplies of meat, fish, or wild fruits.

Occasionally, at least once a year, most households travel to the Pukiri or the Ishiriwe for hunting or fishing expeditions. This is the equivalent of a vacation. The group makes a small camp and fishes and hunts, relaxing and enjoying the proliferation of wildlife which is not so apparent around the community itself. These areas, particularly the Ishiriwe, are the homeland of the Arakmbut and provide older people with an opportunity to remind the youth of their history.

The utilisation of Arakmbut territory is thus a series of areas stretching from the main village including gardens, gold placers, and hunting or foraging activities. The whole of the area is known and used by the people and who occasionally make trips further afield. This complete area, most of which is titled, is recognised by the community as their traditional territory. The resources are available for any member of the community to use. However, this 'usufruct' aspect of land use is only the first aspect of the relationship between the Arakmbut and wandari.

2. *Territory as possession*

One Saturday afternoon in June 1992, a shout went up in San José and several men went running to the port. They jumped into their dugouts and poled downriver to a beach where a hunter was calling for help. He had killed a tapir *(keme)* and needed people to help him bring it up to the community. They dragged the dead animal to a canoe and brought it back to the village where it was cut up and distributed by the hunter's wife. Whereas close relatives in the same clan or alliance group received their share, those young men who had helped bring in the meat went away with a good cut.

When a person has killed an animal or found a gold placer, the meat or work area belongs to him. However, all those who helped to find the gold source or the animal share in the spoils. Thus goods belong to the hunter, gatherer, or discoverer when they are ready for converting them into items for consumption. Before this they are potentially available to anyone in the community.

Possession of territory operates in the same way and is based on control over access. The Arakmbut consider the land to be available to all the members of the community. This includes all Arakmbut who live in the village and who consider the community as their centre. Each adult Arakmbut male and female has access to the territory by virtue of the fact that they are part of the collectivity 'Arakmbut who live in San José del Karene'. This is not a system of 'shares' between individuals, it is a collective body. Decisions regarding territory are taken in the form of direct democratic decisions based on consensus (the subject of chapter six).

The collective responsibility for the territory of the community thus rests on its potential use. During the clearing season households scout out areas which look potentially productive. The Arakmbut weigh up factors such as convenience, proximity to the community, access to thieves, ownship of neighbouring gardens, and whether anyone else wants the area. They will not discuss the area openly until they stake a claim; then they will offer a casual phrase such as 'the soil down by the bend of the river next to by brother's might do, I will work there tomorrow.' If no one objects, they will set to work.

As soon as someone converts the potential resource into an actual commodity for consumption, the resource changes from potential to actual and moves from the collective to the particular. The collectivity is thus embedded in the possibility of use in the future, not in the actual use of the present. The usufruct notion of hunters or gold diggers utilising resources misses out an understanding of what the people are utilising. The Arakmbut constantly shift from the collective control of a territory to the individual or household control of the products and gardens as they become incorporated into social life. Production is therefore a conversion of a collective possession defined by access to the resource into an individual possession based on labour.[8]

The Arakmbut awareness of their territory and the fact they ought to have prior access to its benefits is an example of collective possession. They hold their territory, not only by utilising it, but by trying, wherever possible, to keep outsiders away. This takes various forms according to what is owned. For example, a visitor to San José will sometimes see a mandarin tree outside a house surrounded by thorns to keep predatory children at bay; Arakmbut regularly visit their gardens to check no human or animal is taking the crops; on a larger scale, the community of Barranco Chico has even moved a section of the community close to the boundary to protect it from invading colonists.

Possession is not just utilising an area or territory, it is holding that area and controlling it. Although the Arakmbut are not always successful in denying access to outsiders, they still know that the land on which they live belongs to them and should they have the means to, they will defend it with vigour.

To demonstrate possession means looking at the limitations placed on the use of and access to territory. The Arakmbut allow any of their people to enjoy the resources of the environment. For example, I could fish or gather as I wished while living there, and anyone living in the community with permission of the Arakmbut who wishes to fish or gather is allowed to do so. The Arakmbut are uncomfortable about allowing outsiders in the community to hunt (this is probably connected to the complicated spirit relations involving the hunter and the species of the dead animal), but if someone

---

8. It might be tempting to look at this as a transformation from nature to society. However, I have misgivings about this (Volume 1, Part II) because the Arakmbut have no single concept of nature, but see the world as a differentiated series of domains and species outside of the community. Similarly we could not say that the Arakmbut 'own' or 'possess' nature, whereas their territory is something else.

they trust has a gun and knows what he is doing they will not complain if he goes to look for game.

However, someone who does not live in the community and has entered their territory without permission is heavily criticised by the Arakmbut for using their resources. This is not to say that the community necessarily has the power to stop such intruders. Nevertheless, the Arakmbut are extremely angry about colonists who come onto their lands, mine gold, make gardens, hunt, gather, or fish. If the Arakmbut had the means, they would either expel the colonists directly or expect some form of rent or compensation for forcing access to what they consider to be their own indigenous resources.

3. Territory and ownership

Since the recognition of land titles to community territories in 1986, the Arakmbut have a ready-made imported justification for their claim to own their territory using national law as a basis. An argument could then be made that prior to 1986, they had no notion of ownership on a collective basis and that therefore this idea of territorial ownership is a feature of integrative forces from the national society imposing individual proprietary notions onto people who traditionally held land by usufruct. This argument sounds convincing. There is no doubt that the rigid boundaries for Arakmbut territory arose from taking advantage of legal protections for a bounded area. By holding a recognised legal map of their territories, the Arakmbut of San José can claim collective property rights over their lands without further discussion.

A few members of the community are knowledgeable about the details of Peruvian law, some knowing articles from the Law of Native Communities by heart. However the relationship with their territory is based on something fundamentally Arakmbut, rather than simply national legislation.

The initial expression of the relationship between the Arakmbut and territory comes from the creation myth Wanamey. The case study of the Pukiri and the discussion of the spirituality of wandari showed how territory was formed by different animals and birds after the fiery flood subsided. Human settlement took place at the end of the myth when the woodpecker provided the Arakmbut with fire and knowledge of clans and relationship terms. They travelled downriver to form communities such as exist today. This spiritual origin of the environment and social existence is constantly present in Arakmbut life in two ways, one with animal spirits and the other with the spirits of dead Arakmbut.

(a) Animal Spirits

The Arakmbut have a complicated relationship with animal species. Throughout life each person builds up contacts with the spirit world through dreams and visions. Those with the capacity to communicate easily and freely are recognised as having shamanic qualities (wayorokeri). The introduction of the hallucinogen ayahuasca in the 1970s has facilitated this capacity. With such a variety of techniques to enter the invisible world and to experience its dimensions so directly, no Arakmbut would ever question its intense vitality and meaning for living.

Life and death consist of an exchange with the invisible world via the animal species of the forest and river domains. In order to live, human beings need meat which provides them with the strength to survive. However, meat is potentially harmful and so has to be controlled. The spirits of the species help a hunter find animals, birds, or fish through the beneficial female ndakyorokeri (good dream people), but it is extremely important not to overhunt or over-consume or the spirits of the species will attack a person, leading to sickness or death.

After death a person associated with the species will go to the underworld, but part of the soul of a good hunter with shamanic qualities will also 'go to the species' with which the person had contact during their life. The soul-matter becomes so dispersed that the spirit of specific people is not identifiable. However, spirits of animals receive sustenance from humans in the same way that humans receive sustenance from animals.

This relationship between species and humans is not ready-made. It is created and developed throughout a lifetime. As people learn to contact spirits and develop the techniques of hunting, fishing, and gardening, their ties with the invisible world increase. Knowledge of hunting areas is crucial in this respect because hunters gain knowledge of where the saltlicks are and other areas where animals pass to find fruit trees or to go and drink. This arises from a familiarity with the landscape. The spirits which help hunters find their prey must also know the landscape and the Arakmbut language, in order to communicate their knowledge. In this way, through information from the spirit world the Arakmbut gain the meat which enables them to survive.

The knowledge of the spirit world (often thought by the Arakmbut to reside in the wachipai, or leader of the species) constitutes the potential of resources in a particular territory. The spirit world informs the Arakmbut how much they can take, and chastises them if they misuse the information.

The boundaries of hunting and gathering territory are the limits of Arakmbut spirit presence. At this point one enters the realm of hostile spirits and hunting becomes dangerous. For example, the Wandakweri like to hunt in the headwaters of the Ishiriwe, which was the site of their old malocas. They are not keen about hunting or travelling into the headwaters of the Kipodnwe, where they say that there are 'Inca spirits'.

Spirit definitions of territory are not made with precise boundaries such as the community demarcation recognised by Peruvian law. In fact, the spirit relations stretch considerably further than the community and constitute more of the area recognised as the Harakmbut homeland within the proposed communal reserve. Outside of this area spirits of other language groups appear and the essential contact necessary for survival is difficult if not impossible.

The exchange of meat for spirit thus only takes place in areas which are exclusively Arakmbut. As was noted above, 'e'e' (being or life) is the relationship of a person's nokiren and an object. A territory is the basis of Arakmbut life and is consequently 'owned' through the relationship between their nokiren and the invisible world of spirits. Ownership is thus a spiritual relationship.

(b) Human Spirits

This feature is also apparent with human spirits. When a person dies a good death, the body is taken to the riverine underworld. For this to happen, all the ancestors of the dying person come to his or her house and lead the nokiren away. Dying people often recognise deceased relatives who call them to the afterlife. The spirits are called *wambetoeri* and are beneficial in that the death is good, but dangerous if a living healthy person sees them. They are consequently feared. When someone dies the deceased's name is not mentioned directly for many years and references to dead people are kept to a minimum.

Nevertheless, the Arakmbut need the wambetoeri because they take a person to the underworld from where life can continue. In the cases of shamans and good hunters, this means that the whole process of spiritual renewal can only take place with the participation of the spirits of dead Arakmbut.

I have noted among the Arakmbut a strong reluctance to move away from the community if someone who is expected to die becomes ill. People do not like the idea of taking the two-day trip to Puerto Maldonado hospital because they say that they will die there. Part of the reason is that they want to be home with their relatives, but they also do not want to die away from the community. People want to be brought to the underworld by the wambetoeri when they die, and their nokiren may not know the way back to Arakmbut territory to meet the wambetoeri. This is seen in the references which the Arakmbut make to the fact that their territories are the sites of their dead ancestors.

During death, relations with the spirit world are important and the visible territory of the Arakmbut is connected with an invisible territory of the spirit world. As a person moves into unknown areas, the presence of beneficial spirits is less apparent and the world becomes far more dangerous. In the same way, harmful spirits can enter Arakmbut territory, and threaten members of the community with illness and death. They can only be repulsed by shamanic means. The flexible and pragmatic boundaries of Arakmbut spirit relations reflect the pre-demarcation notions of territoriality discussed earlier in this chapter.

The ties which the Arakmbut have over their territory are based on a relationship between the souls of visible and invisible spirit worlds. The Arakmbut do not pick up the soil and talk about 'mother earth' as do some indigenous peoples. The territory belongs to the spirits of those ancestors who are dead and those Arakmbut who are living, and provides the potential life for those who are yet to come.

The relationship between the invisible spirit world and the living visible world uses the species of animals living in wandari as a vehicle for the continuation of the Arakmbut through time. Without territory this cannot happen. Arakmbut territory provides a potential which is collectively possessed and which each person or household converts into actual commodities for consumption. Arakmbut spirits provide knowledge of possibility or potentiality in the world. They know the past, present, and future, and can inform people of the consequences of their actions and also regulate the utilisation of resources. The Arakmbut use resources and convert them from a potential resource which is held collectively to actual personal property. But in fact this takes place because spirits have the regulatory power of invisible potentiality within the territory.

Territory mutually binds the visible and invisible worlds through the nokiren of each Arakmbut. Ownership is precisely this tie. On the one level the territory draws together the visible and invisible worlds of spirit and human into a collaborative exchange between life and death which perpetuates the cosmos. On the other hand the collective possession by the Arakmbut of their territory provides the means for them to remain exclusively in contact with the invisible spirit world and ensures continuity of life. The spiritual aspect of Arakmbut control over their territory provides the legitimacy of ownership. This relationship with the spirit world demarcates not only the territory but the human beings who should benefit from its resources. Outsiders are not welcome to pillage resources. Only through Arakmbut spirits can potential become actual and collective ownership become individual property.

In this way collective ownership of wandari exists for the Arakmbut, but instead of the law acting as guarantor or legitimation of the ownership, the power comes from the invisible spirit world, which patrols the boundaries of acceptable behaviour for the Arakmbut. Sickness, death, or misfortune are the actions of spirits causally connected to previous behaviour. This provides more evidence that 'the law' for the Arakmbut rests in the spirit world. In this sense the legal basis of ownership of Arakmbut territory is spiritual, not judicial.

These findings from the Arakmbut relate to those of Hocart (1970). He argues that the principal value of human activity is life. He sees ritual organisation as providing parallel structures to government and also argues that law arises initially from the control of the natural world. The activities of the spirit world and shamanic interpretation of events are Arakmbut ways of controlling their territory. This reflects the collective responsibility for the well-being of their community and its resources not only for now, but for future generations. When Arakmbut say *'oroedn wandari'* (our territory) they are aware of its spiritual implications.

Whereas I have used the terms use, possession, and ownership, I have not yet used the term 'property' to refer to territory. In this sense I have followed Cobbett in saying that property arises out of use, possession and ownership:

> 'The land, the trees, the fruits, the herbage, the roots are, by the law of nature, the common possession of all the people. The social compact, entered into for their mutual *benefit* and *protection* ... gives rise, at once, to the words *mine* and *thine.* Men exert their skill and strength upon particular spots of land. These become *their own.* And, when laws come to be made, these spots are called the property of the owners (Cobbett Weekly Political Register 8 May 1819 cited in Williams 1983:32).

However, for the Arakmbut, property is ultimately guaranteed not legally but spiritually. If we want to talk of collective property for the Arakmbut we have to juxtapose property based on an internal spirit definition of ownership, with outside recognition, whereby community titles are recognised legally by the Peruvian state. This external recognition is based on the Law of Native Communities. However, Arakmbut ownership from an internal perspective is the already-existing spiritual recognition of territory. Outside colonists unfortunately do not usually recognise indigenous peoples' definition of their ownership of their territories. Thus only by converting it into 'legal property' can it be defended in the courts, which the colonists recognise. This is particularly important with regard to the colonisation of Arakmbut territory which has taken place over the last fifteen years.

Arakmbut collective relationship to their territory combines our notions of use, possession, and ownership. Use refers to the way in which the Arakmbut cover all their territory to convert its resources into products. Possession refers to the exclusive access to the resources which the community controls, while ownership refers to the specific spiritual dimension of the relationship between humans and territory. Property relates to all three.

These three concepts together constitute the dynamic process of production. Production is the practical utilisation of resources which transforms collective possessions into personal possessions under the sanctioning gaze of the invisible world. Indeed the strength of these relations between people and things stem from the spirit world, where ownership is legitimised. By focusing on the spirit world, it is possible to challenge the view that property is exclusively non-indigenous and legal. The Arakmbut legal system itself operates entirely on the basis of sanctions from the invisible spirit world. Territorial control is no different.

Colonisation and Territorial Rights

The case study on the river Pukiri showed how, after the gold rush began in earnest in 1978, the history of the area consisted of a constant increase in colonisation. This unprecedented invasion was compounded by the existing colonists, who expanded their lands and production, bringing in some cases as many as fifty peons from the highlands, some in conditions tantamount to slavery. Many of these poor labourers were fleeing economic problems and, in the 1980s, the warfare between the Peruvian armed forces and the guerilla organisation Sendero Luminoso. The increase of colonists between 1979 and 1991 was as follows:

Table 3.2 Colonists on the territory of San José

1979	60 people
1981	150 people
1985	300 people
1991	490 people

Similar increases took place in the other Arakmbut communities, where there are now 120 in Puerto Luz, 457 in Barranco Chico, and 95 Boca del Inambari. The total comes to 1155 colonists in the gold mining communities of the Madre de Dios.

The population of San José has remained consistent at about one hundred and thirty people, including children. The number of colonists is so much greater than that of the community that it has seriously affected the morale of Arakmbut resistance. In spite of a successful attempt to stop a local patron taking over San Jose's gold placers in 1985 (Gray 1986:60-68), resignation is frequently the dominant feeling within the community.

The first demarcation map of San José was made in 1979 and the title was eventually approved in 1986. Within this area the Arakmbut try to defend themselves from more invasions. In spite of the large number of colonists on their lands, several outsiders did leave the area when they realised that the lands were the collective property of the community.

The case study showed the effect of the increase in colonists on San José. The Arakmbut are unable to travel through their own territory without receiving threats passed by rumour. In addition to the fear inspired by these threats, the invasions have other consequences for the Arakmbut. The colonists indiscriminately log the trees, frighten the animals with the gold workings, plunder their gardens, and steal their gold deposits. The effect of the colonists is to reduce the potential for production within the community. As we have seen, this potential is regulated by the spirits, in which case the invasion of colonists is no less than a desecration of Arakmbut territory.

On my visit in 1995, the decrease in gold production, probably as a result of overproduction by the colonists in Huaypetue, meant that a few gold colonists had left the area. However the majority have remained, supplementing their gold work with logging and agriculture. The area of the communal reserve is now also being encroached by colonists, non-indigenous hunters, and loggers. Economically, the Arakmbut communities are at the onset of a crisis which will engulf them completely if there is no initiative to alleviate the situation.

The confrontation between the Arakmbut and the colonists is a permanent struggle for access to dwindling resources, with the colonists denying indigenous peoples the legal right to their territory. The problem is that apart from the occasional success, the Arakmbut have found it impossible to throw the colonists off their lands. The reason for this is twofold.

In the first place the law, while recognising their rights, cannot implement its provisions in such a remote area unless there is a strong will to do so. A legal case takes as long as two years and costs a prohibitive $2,000 on average. To pursue a case, the community has to pay the military and police to give permission and support for the authorities to travel into the interior. Thus the laws are not upheld.

The second factor is that the Arakmbut are not powerful enough to attack the colonists. The invaders are well armed; they have the backing of most of the state institutions in the area and would inflict considerable damage on the Arakmbut. Considering that they have already lost 95 percent of their population over the last century (Gray 1983:11) – which is in line with Denevan's statistics on indigenous deaths after contact in lowland Amazonia (1976:221) – the Arakmbut of San José are reluctant to enter a war which would mean the end of their people as a whole.

During the 1993-94 visit, I looked, with FENAMAD, into the possibility of finding strategies which would attract the gold colonists away from indigenous lands to the equally lucrative gold-bearing areas of the Madre de Dios river, below Boca Colorado. An initiative of this type would involve considerable preparation and planning, but on the basis of the success of providing colonists with compensation in the central Amazonian Ucayali region of Peru, it is not impossible. However, this strategy would need to be part of a territorial defence programme, combining legal actions with managing the communal reserve.

The colonists' presence constitutes a violation of Arakmbut territorial rights. But we have to look more closely as to what this means. The term 'wandari' and 'territory' are broadly coterminous in Arakmbut and Spanish. However, the notion of a right is something which we do not encounter within Arakmbut language or culture, while everyone talks about their rights in Spanish. The articulation of territorial rights emerges at the moment when territory is threatened. Donnelly (1989:27) argues that 'lists of human rights emerge out of the political struggle for human dignity and indicate the principal directions of that struggle.'

Territorial rights emerged with colonisation as indigenous peoples became aware of the frontier and the consequences of invasion. This is not to say that indigenous peoples had not been invaded before: in the pre-mission period, there was considerable fighting between peoples, but this was not couched in the framework of rights.

Rights originated, as noted in the first chapter, out of the western liberal tradition. What Donnelly says about these origins relates perfectly to the Arakmbut before contact: 'Prior to the creation of capitalist market economies and modern nation states, the problems that human rights seek to prevent, either did not exist or were not widely perceived to be central social problems' (op.cit.:64). Such rights were, in fact, embedded in the Arakmbut social formation (see chapter one).

Indigenous rights are claims or entitlements by oppressed indigenous peoples to challenge existing institutions, practices, or norms, to ensure that they are treated with dignity by the state. For a people who are so oppressed that they cannot resist an invasion against their territory, the main hope is the implementation of their territorial rights. Should these be recognised legally, the people have some grounds for asserting their ownership. The notion of rights to Arakmbut territory has emerged explicitly because the land invasions for gold resources have established permanent settlements and extracted Arakmbut resources. This weakens the potential for self-sufficiency and threatens to break the spiritual relationship between the Arakmbut and the invisible world which underlines the notion of territorial ownership. There seems to be no immediate solution within their socio-cultural repertoire.

The Arakmbut often say that the Christian God produces diseases but also the medical means to cure them; human rights are seen in a rather similar manner. The national state and the market economy have produced a form of colonisation from outside which stands to destroy the Arakmbut. At the same time, the external world, which has been oppressing indigenous peoples for centuries, has the notion of human rights, which provides a moral basis for resistance. Whether they work or not remains to be seen, but some Arakmbut are using them as a tool to support their claims for justice. Nevertheless, most Arakmbut are frankly sceptical, hovering between resistance and resignation to their fate (Gray 1986:99-100).

This chapter has questioned the strict separation by non-indigenous peoples of the relationship between human beings and their environment into different substances – territory based on political relations, lands based on economic relations, the earth based on spiritual relations, and landscape based on historico-geographic semantics. For the Arakmbut, the notions of wandari covers all of these and the meaning shifts according to context. Any legal provisions dealing with wandari should include all of these aspects. The current draft Declaration of the UN achieves this by making one article refer to the general philosophy behind territorial rights, while the subsequent article looks specifically at the use, possession, and ownership factors.

In the same way, the frequent distinction between use, possession, and ownership of resources is, for the Arakmbut, a distinction between different aspects of the relationship between people, products, and their environment. For the Arakmbut, a personal relationship has aspects of the person invested in the product, whereas a collective relationship is a recognition of the potential inherent in an area for production. The regulators of production are the controllers of potentiality – the spirit world. Ownership and property for the Arakmbut are bound up with the invisible spiritual world.

The effect of the gold rush on the Arakmbut communities has been invasions of their territory and a desecration of their potential to produce and live in peace. In spite of their legal title to territory, the possibility of the establishment of a communal reserve, and some successes at opposing the colonists, the Arakmbut have no means to expel the intruders. They conceptualise their position in terms of a violation of their territorial rights. This provides a basic moral position on which to challenge the forces which threaten to destroy them.

In an Arakmbut context, the standard-setting procedures of the ILO and UN which resist the term territory are nonsensical. To ignore the notion of territory is to carve out the political control of resources from the integral concept wandari. This control provides the only solid legal protection for the Arakmbut, and indeed all indigenous peoples, against invasions and violations of their territories. The historical and sacred aspects of a territory and access to its resources can be protected and controlled by the Arakmbut by recognising their rights. Full recognition of their rights to territory and implementation of these rights is the foundation on which the Arakmbut can ensure their survival for future generations.

◈ *Chapter 4* ◈

PEOPLES, PERSONS, AND PLURALS

'S'
Sign on a Poster of Protest by Indigenous Peoples

At the International Conference on Human Rights in Vienna in April 1993, a strange protest took place. Demonstrators marched up to government representatives with banners marked only with the letter 'S'. After queries as to whether this was some new human rights sect or a group of fastidious etymologists, it become apparent that these were indigenous protesters complaining vehemently that the final resolution of the meeting referred to 'indigenous people' and not to 'indigenous peoples'. This chapter looks at the issues behind the missing 's' and its significance for the recognition of the rights of indigenous peoples.

Over the last ten years, a debate in the international field of standard setting has discussed the relative merits of the terms peoples or populations. The question was illustrated in the Peruvian government statement to the UN in chapter one. The basis for the debate is that according to the UN Charter and the Conventions on Human Rights, all *peoples* have the right to self-determination. Governments, who interpret self-determination in the very narrow sense of the term as external independence, are reluctant to recognise this right and consequently seek other euphemisms, such as *populations*, to circumvent it. Indigenous peoples on the other hand, see self-determination as the right to control their destiny and insist on the term 'peoples'.

In 1988 the Aboriginal caucus at the ILO meeting on revised Convention 169, said:

> 'Based on our historical and continuing experiences, it is essential for the development and strengthening of our diverse but highly vulnerable societies that we be referred to and recognised ... as "peoples". We are not and have never been mere "populations"' (IWGIA 1989).

The United Nations still persists in referring to indigenous peoples as populations in the formal title of its Subcommission Working Group, although the draft Declaration uses 'peoples'. Over the last five years, however, the term populations has gradually become unacceptable to governments too. At the 1986 meeting of experts at the ILO, the Chairman, Rudolfo Stavenhagen, explained the difference was between the quantifiable demographic concept of 'population', in contrast to 'people', which involves social organisation, culture, and some unitary social formation (Gray 1987:80). At the revision of ILO Convention 107, the new text qualified the term peoples by saying in Article 1.3, 'The use of the term "peoples" in this Convention shall not be construed as having any implications as regards the rights which may attach to the term under international law.' This phrase has reappeared in a draft declaration on the rights of indigenous peoples from the Organization of American States (OAS).

The indigenous observers at the ILO meeting walked out when this phrase was adopted, because they considered that there was an intent to establish a two-tiered system between 'ordinary people' who have the right to self-determination and 'indigenous peoples' who do not. Their reaction was later expressed by Dalee Sambo of the Inuit Circumpolar Conference as follows:

> 'A provision was added in an attempt to qualify the use of the term "peoples" when it refers to the world's indigenous peoples under the revised convention. We feel that it is unfair and racially discriminatory to try and limit our human rights as peoples under international law' (1990:201).

Thus as matters stood after the ILO revised Convention 169, the term 'peoples' was only recognised to the extent that the term can be reconciled with the present existing exercise of state power (Berman 1988). The next discussion of the concept of indigenous peoples arose at the Earth Summit in Rio in 1992. There, in Agenda 21, the term 'people' was used extensively referring to indigenous peoples. The following year, the indigenous 'International Year' was proposed. Normally UN years belong to specific groups, such as the 'UN Year of Women', for example. However, after a proposal by the government of Canada, the year was named 'The International Year for the World's Indigenous People'. The criticism of this title has been that the year is 'for' not 'of' which is deemed paternalistic. Secondly, the title suggests that indigenous peoples belong to the 'world', rather like a common heritage. But the main criticism has been the word 'people'. This word was agreed by governments because it reflected indigenous individuals but did not reflect collectivities.

Having moved from the term populations, to a qualified peoples, the international debate now focuses on the term 'people'. At the UN Human Rights Commission on the draft Declaration on the Rights of Indigenous Peoples in November 1995, Brazil fought strongly to have the 's' removed from the name of the meeting and the report. However, several governments agree with indigenous peoples, and the battle is by no means lost.

The reason for governments seeking alternatives to 'peoples' rests largely on their narrow definition of the word, linking it exclusively with self-determination. However, self-determination, which we will look at in chapter eight, is only one aspect of the concept of peoples. This chapter will look at the other important aspect of the word 'peoples' – that it refers to a collectivity – and trace its importance with respect to the notion of identity. The difference between 'peoples' and 'people' is that 'indigenous peoples' refers to a singular collective noun such as a 'community, tribe, race, or nation', whereas 'people' in the other sense is a plural noun referring to individual persons belonging to a 'place or forming a company or class etc.' (Concise Oxford Dictionary).

The term peoples, which is fundamentally collective, is neutralised when replaced by terms such as populations, groups, or people, based on individual subjects. Liberal universalist notions of human rights are couched in individual terms; they do not question the basis of state legitimacy but ensure the continuation of state power over indigenous people – who become 'integrated' into the state through citizenship – exactly as expressed in the Peruvian government statement to the UN in chapter one.[1]

---

1. In both the eighteenth and nineteenth centuries, several philosophers considered that individuals were the basic blocks of social life. The eighteenth century political philosophers linked the notion of peoples to individuals within the framework of the idea of 'social contract'. Locke (1993:305) saw a people as a unity of individuals who form civil society. Rousseau (1968:61) thought of a people as the act of individuals forming a community into a whole. In the nineteenth century, writers such as J.S. Mill (1991:427) considered that a people or nationality had certain common elements: co-operation, desire to be under the same government, common sympathies, race, descent, territory, and history but 'none of these circumstances however are either indispensable, or necessarily sufficient

The anthropological discussion on the notion of 'people' illuminates some of the elements involved in identifying the term. The nineteenth century anthropologist, Lewis Henry Morgan, attempted to place the distinction between a people and a state on an evolutionary scale where a people consisted of the highest level of 'barbarism', below civilisation and the state. He resolved the ambiguity of the collective term 'people', by placing it on an evolutionary framework where he put 'a people or nation *(populus)* as a confederacy of tribes which is not yet distinguished as a state *(civitas)*' above groups of individuals (Morgan 1977:6-7). Governments who deny the 's' on peoples would, on this basis, place indigenous people somewhere in the level of savagery.

With the rejection of evolutionary anthropology in the 1920s and 1930s, the concept of 'a people' was treated as an aspect of sociopolitical classification. For example, Evans-Pritchard (1940:5) says, 'By "people" we mean all persons who speak the same language and have, in other respects, the same culture, and consider themselves to be distinct from like aggregates.' He later explained that 'peoples' can live in continuous territories, be distributed widely, or form 'congeries' of tribes which form loose federations. Thus, rather than being an evolutionary model of progress, the notion of 'a people' became a synchronic feature of socio-political classification. This term relates to the concept of 'peoples' used by indigenous representatives in international fora.

Yet apart from its collective or individual orientation, the lack of analytical precision of the term 'people' has been of concern to anthropologists. Lucy Mair (1962:15-16) saw 'people' as a way of avoiding the unpopular term 'tribe' or the term 'nation', which can refer both to a state or to an ethnic unit. The ILO Convention 107 uses the term tribe, although most indigenous peoples ignore the term preferring the word 'nation'.[2]

---

by themselves'. Mill distinguished between a people and a nationality which had the potential to form a state. Those governments that deny indigenous peoples a collective identity, differ from these writers in that, while they accept the notion that individuals are the basis of collective relations, to them, collectivities all become subsumed within the state in the process of nation-building. This combination of the individualist and statist approaches wipes out all intermediary social bodies, a position to which even the 'progressivist' and 'evolutionary' theorists of the last two centuries did not adhere.

2. The overlapping concepts of nation, people, and tribe strongly resist encapsulation within one logical framework because of the complex connotations which arise in their use. The term 'tribe' has at least three distinct areas of meaning:

The anthropological concern about the term 'people' is that it is vague (Mair ibid.). Leach also refers to the disappearance of the word 'tribe', and his comments parallel those of Mair:

> 'As a consequence, all kinds of euphemistic circumlocutions are now used in place of the simple term "tribe". The most common are "people" and "traditional society". "People" seems to me to be too vague' (Leach 1989:34).

However, in spite of its vagueness, the term 'people' is a convenient and standard way of referring to a human collectivity sharing language, culture, and a sense of separateness from others which has significant implications in international law. 'Peoples' should not be treated as a universal unit of social classification, but rather a politically neutral term which draws together indigenous peoples rather than differentiating between them analytically. Possibly a task for the future is to build a new decolonised vocabulary which reflects particular contexts and circumstances.

An anthropological escape from the problem of peoples, tribes, and nations has been to investigate the issue from its content. This angle uses the term 'ethnicity'. In spite of its long historical ancestry

---

a) An anthropological concept based on the ideas of Morgan and Maine referring to a 'primitive social group' consisting of several communities bound by a common culture with a political organisation. In the United States tribe became part of an evolutionary theory (Steward 1973:44).

b) An administrative unit used in certain countries such as the United States (Dunbar Ortiz 1984:182) or India (Fürer-Haimendorf 1989:39) to define legally the indigenous peoples of the country.

c) A colonial term used for classifying peoples, which is now considered to be a method of imposing order on a multi-ethnic population within a colonised territory (Ranger 1983:248). The pejorative connotations and artificial nature of the term, particularly in Africa, has led to its rejection.

The term 'nation' also has several meanings:

a) In its original meaning, the term referred to the first peoples encountered by travellers in different parts of the world. The native peoples of North America were first called 'nations' (Deloria & Lytle 1984:263). I have also encountered the term in the Amazon at the turn of the century as well as among the hill peoples of Southeast Asia in the eighteenth century. The term 'nation' is growing in popularity among indigenous peoples.

b) For anthropologists, a nation was a specific term referring to a group of tribes which have confederated and have a centralised political system. This is the meaning which Evans-Pritchard gives to the term in the Nuer (1940).

c) The dominant use of the term by states refers to the synthetic creation of national identity before, during and after the formation of the state (Kedourie 1985).

Indigenous peoples, unless they benefit directly from the legal implications of the term, usually reject the word 'tribe' as pejorative. On the other hand, the term nation is more popular with indigenous peoples because it has the connotation of self-sufficiency. Nevertheless because of its collective and self-determining connotations, the word 'peoples' has now emerged as the most general term.

from the word 'ethnos', ethnicity has arisen over the last twenty-five years as an alternative term for 'race' or 'tribe' (Tonkin et. al. 1989:14-16). Indeed, it has been so overused that some writers would prefer to abandon the term altogether. However, the criteria used in writings about ethnicity are illuminating here because they go beyond lists of features such as cultural values, language, socio-political organisation, and self-reproduction.

Barth (1969) criticises the idea that ethnic identities are isolated units of classification, but sees inter-ethnic relations as defining factors for a people. The critical criterion for Barth is self-identification (1969:24). This is now recognised as an important factor of indigenous rights in both the ILO Convention 169 and the Martinez Cobo definition of indigenous peoples. Edwin Ardener (1989:68) agrees with this but adds the corollary of identification by outsiders. The dynamic interaction between these two perspectives, inside and outside, articulates a series of concepts which change with the socio-political circumstances and are quite independent from demographic populations.

Boundaries are critical in looking at identity. They exist not just at the edge of indigenous social life, they operate at all levels of the social formation, distinguishing all relationships whether organised by gender, residence, age, descent, marriage, community, or the people as a whole. Indigenous social life is an articulation of social and cultural relations through the crossing or avoidance of boundaries. Inside and outside, from this view, become relative to the particular social unit under discussion. The paradox is that no notion of identity can appear static without its articulation, and this takes place through the dynamic activity of creating, transgressing, or avoiding boundaries.

This dynamic approach to ethnicity has been developed by Southall (1976) in his work on the complicated differentiations among the Nuer and neighbouring Dinka in the Sudan. He considers that Evans-Pritchard's classification was somewhat static and argues that ethnicity reflects historical change and a constant shifting of identity. This is important when looking at the fact that identification as an 'indigenous people' is part of the history of relations between peoples and the state. As indigenous rights become more prominent, more peoples are identifying themselves. Cohen (1978) considers that ethnicity is more than classification, but 'also reflects an ideological position claiming recognition for ethnicity as a major sector of complex societies and points the way to a more just and equitable society' (p.403). This is a pertinent comment relating to the rise of the indigenous movement.

The result of this discussion has produced a concept of 'people' which is, on the one hand, a reflection of culture, social organisation and common perceptions of history and identity. Yet, on the other hand, it is a concept connected to a notion of ethnicity, which is a situational, relativistic, and political phenomenon.

These points can be illustrated by looking at the Arakmbut in what is the sequel to the events which took place at Boca Colorado, described in chapter two.

The Fall-out from the Storming of Boca Colorado

The Arakmbut returned to San José and Puerto Luz on the evening of Thursday 2 April 1992. The sense of victory could be felt throughout the communities; they had retrieved the materials for the school, the food hand-outs, and the medicines which were justly theirs. The food and medicines from the civil defence fund were distributed meticulously to each household and the corrugated iron roofing material left for the schools. In San José, the households which had participated drank some beers.

The conversation shifted from pride in how in spite of the Incas, Spanish, and Peruvians no one has yet conquered the Arakmbut to fear that the Municipality would get their revenge. For two days the community shifted from pride at the victory to fear of the consequences.

On the Sunday, the news came of Fujimori's coup and the closing of Congress; but that day was to bring its own coup for San José. At midday a boat arrived bringing the two schoolteachers who had worked in the community for eight years, and a new teacher. Accompanying them was the head of education of the region. Apparently, two young leaders of San José had requested a change of teacher for the community and the educational head wanted to know why. A meeting was planned for the evening.

Throughout the afternoon, the young leaders discussed the matter with their allies in the community. Clearly there was a division of opinion. The youth of the community considered that it was time for a change from the lay teachers who had taught them. They objected to the influence which non-indigenous people could build up within a community. However, the older parents were less certain. Several of them had been drawn into the Peruvian ritual kinship obligations of *compadrazgo* with the teachers and were reluctant to criticise them. Furthermore many of their children had reached secondary school standard through these teachers.

Within two days, of the victory at Boca Colorado, San José was debating its educational future. At the meeting, the accusations were made by young men and, in response, the elders, who were effectively adjudicating the session, slowly began to walk out. The older parents, who had supported the teachers, followed. The teachers had to leave. The decision was made, but the community was split on the matter. The head of education was not pleased. As he left the next day, he fired his parting shot:

'By the way, the storming of Boca Colorado is being discussed throughout Puerto Maldonado. The Act of Agreement signed with the governor is being used against the signatories. The mayor has denounced your action as robbery, and it is only a matter of time before the Guardia Civil will be taking the community by force'. The next day an item was broadcast on Radio Madre de Dios: the Council offices of Boca Colorado have been ransacked by native delinquents backed by 'infiltrators' (a term referring to guerilla supporters). Four indigenous representatives were held responsible: Nicolás Iviche and Antonio Iviche (San José) and Daniel Sarike and Eziquiel Moque (Puerto Luz).

On the Tuesday evening, in spite of the tensions and ill feelings which were raging through San José because of the change of teachers, the elders of the community met with the young leadership outside the house of one of the old men. While someone passed cigarettes around, it was decided that representatives from Puerto Luz and San José should go directly and confront those opposing them in Puerto Maldonado. Three young men from San José were chosen to go, the two who had been denounced on the radio and a student, and one representative from Puerto Luz. I was invited to go as a witness to the proceedings, and they teased me: 'Maybe you can write yet another article about all this, Wamambuey'.

On the Sunday the community had been completely divided, but in twenty-four hours everything had changed and the elders of the community had signed a blank piece of paper to denounce the mayor and those criticising the community. Then a letter was written authorising the group to travel to Puerto Maldonado in the name of the community. This was considered by some of the old men as an extra safeguard, should they have any problems with the police. This was a wise precaution.

On Thursday the San José and Puerto Luz representatives went down to Boca Colorado en route to Puerto Maldonado. They had to spend the night there and went to visit the governor. He did not recommend going down to Puerto Maldonado and drawing attention to the problem (it was clear that the Governor was afraid that the breach in security would be put down to his incompetence). Nevertheless, the group travelled on downriver, arriving in Puerto Maldonado on the Friday afternoon.

The Fujimori coup had taken place in a context of corruption among elected representatives; the case of Boca Colorado had suddenly become news. A journalist latched onto the representatives and on the following day they made a broadcast justifying the storming of Boca Colorado and denouncing the mayor. The tide had turned and the response was immediate; the mayor appeared and asked to see the representatives, promising 440 bags of cement, a chain-saw to cut wood for the school, and radios for the communities. He arranged for the indigenous commission to eat freely at his restaurant and confirmed that he had never issued a warrant for the Presidents of the communities. Things seemed to be going well.

Wherever you travel in Peru, documents are essential. In the Madre de Dios, travelling from the Karene to Puerto Maldonado can be fraught with difficulties. There is a checkpoint when arriving and leaving from Labarinto and when entering Puerto Maldonado. Those without documents are cross-examined and sometimes detained and interrogated. Centro Eori and FENAMAD managed to put a temporary stop to this discrimination for the indigenous peoples of the area, who are mainly those without electoral cards. However after the Fujimori coup in April 1992, restrictions became more severe.

On the Sunday, three Arakmbut, members of Centro Eori, and myself took a break from some work and went for refreshment to a cafe in Puerto Maldonado. It was 10 in the morning. Suddenly a truck drew up outside of the restaurant and two armed police burst in demanding that the Arakmbut show their electoral cards. One had his, but the other two did not. They were rounded up and taken away to the police station. Even though the rest of us protested vociferously, it was to no avail.

We followed immediately to the police station and tried to find out where the two Arakmbut were. After a wait and negotiations with the authorities we were allowed to speak to the commandante, who said that the 'people' were being interrogated because, maybe, they were terrorists. The letter from the elders of the community was produced and the commander said that it had to be photocopied (a difficult job on a Sunday in Puerto Maldonado). While people were looking for a photocopier, he sent the Arakmbut out to the garden and set them to do a hard day's clearing.

After strong protests they were released from hard labour. The police said that they were looking for terrorists or drug traffickers (neither of which were prevalent in Puerto Maldonado at the time). The two Arakmbut said that all those rounded up had been hit, except for the Arakmbut because they had friends waiting outside. This all occurred because they had no electoral cards.

The same phenomenon occurred again the following day. People without documents were rounded up and allowed to leave if they were prepared to pay money to the police. This police tactic is not confined solely to indigenous people, but is used on all poor and disadvantaged people who have not had the opportunity to become recognised 'individuals' under the state apparatus. During 1991, through an AIDESEP programme working with FENAMAD, it was possible to register most of the Arakmbut with electoral cards as part of a national programme. However the colonists in Peru have claimed that this is an 'unfair advantage' for the indigenous peoples.

After this strange mixture of experiences, the Arakmbut decided to return to their communities, shaken by their capture, but pleased with the radio interview and the gift of a radio from the mayor. The promises of cement and a chain-saw were as hollow as most of the other offers from the authorities.

This case study tries to give a flavour of the interconnectedness of Arakmbut life. The four incidents: the storming of Boca Colorado, the expulsion of the school teachers, the successful lobbying in Puerto Maldonado, and the random arrest by the armed police were all separate events but entwined in a complicated causality which occurs every day among the Arakmbut. The materials are taken from Boca Colorado, the teachers tell the community of a warrant for the arrest of the young men who promoted their removal, the Arakmbut defend their case in Puerto Maldonado, but at the last minute they are arrested (probably by chance).

Two different aspects of Arakmbut identity emerge in this scenario. When dealing with the perceived injustices of the authorities at Boca Colorado, the communities of San José and Puerto Luz are united indigenous peoples, asserting themselves as Arakmbut. This is manifest in the comments of the elders about the Arakmbut never having been conquered by outsiders, whether by the Inca, the Spanish, or the Peruvian state. At the same time, each community has quite strong lines of internal conflict. In this case the tension was between young men (either not married or with small children) and older adults (with children in the school system), and was mediated to a large extent by the elders who were parents of both groups.

The speed with which these conflicts arise and disappear can be seen in my own attitude during these events. When the rumour of the warrant for the President of San José and his brother broke, the conflict in the community was so great that I could not see how it would be resolved in the short time needed. My comment at the time was: 'Yesterday the community was divided about everything and we thought it would go badly, but there was a meeting outside Ireyo's house [the elder of the community who tells myths]. Everyone ... agreed that someone from San José and Puerto Luz should go to Puerto Maldonado.'

The reason for this shift was that the Arakmbut are not simply individual units who join together to form a collectivity, but are persons defined by multi-stranded social relationships expressed through culturally recognised semantic and affective indicators of identity. This can be demonstrated by looking at the term 'Arakmbut', which has several different meanings. When you ask them who they are, they say 'Arakmbut'. The word Arakmbut does not distinguish between singular and plural. In this case you can use it to refer to a person or group, separately or together. In order to distinguish a particular group or person you name them.

Arakmbut from Within

The starting point for looking at the internal perception of the concept of a people is through the word Arakmbut, which they translate into Spanish with the words *gente* and *pueblo*. From the people I spoke to in the community, there are several different contexts in which the term Arakmbut can be used:

1. Language

All the people who speak the Harakmbut language are called 'Arakmbut' by the people of San José. This includes the Wachipaeri, Sapiteri, Toyeri, Pukiricri, Kisambaeri, and Arasaeri. Although the different languages and dialects of Harakmbut are difficult to understand, they form one family compared to people such as the Arawak-speaking Matsigenka or the Tacana-speaking Ese'eja.

Other indigenous peoples are sometimes called '*gente indígena*' or '*pueblos indígenas*', but more often they are referred to as *nogn* Arakmbut (other Arakmbut). In the Madre de Dios this refers to the ten other indigenous peoples in the area, while in the Amazon it means the other forest peoples. When travelling internationally they refer to all indigenous peoples as 'nogn Arakmbut'. However, when Arakmbut representatives from the Madre de Dios participated at the Working Group on Indigenous Populations, the term became even broader. At the UN meeting there is a clear distinction between indigenous and non-indigenous peoples, and I was aware that for the Arakmbut representatives from the Madre de Dios, the term Arakmbut easily became coterminous with indigenous peoples as a whole.

2. *Amarakaeri*

The second use of the term Arakmbut is specifically for the group of Harakmbut speakers who are called Amarakaeri by outsiders. These are the people from Shintuya (who are not Wachipaeri), Puerto Luz, San José del Karene, Barranco Chico, and Boca Inambari. Arakmbut also refers to all members of these communities even if they live in different parts of the Madre de Dios or are being educated in Lima. This is the most common use of the term Arakmbut, and it parallels the outside word Amarakaeri.

When this meaning of the word Arakmbut is dominant, the other indigenous peoples who speak Harakmbut are not referred to as Arakmbut, but as nogn Arakmbut or 'Taka'. This means someone who is a foreigner and lives in proximity, but in practice, as other Harakmbut speakers are those in closest proximity, the term Taka refers primarily to them. It was clear, in 1991, that the term Arakmbut in the sense of Amarakaeri was the use preferred by the older members of the community.

3. *Patrilineal Clan*

Smaller social units internal to the five communities mentioned above can be given the term Arakmbut. There are two main contexts in which the word is applied internally. The main example is with the patrilineal clan which many Arakmbut refer to as *onyu*. This word actually means 'pure' and refers to the common substance of all members of the group. The clan is the purest social grouping, as physical and spiritual continuity comes through the male line without being mixed. I have heard that the clans can be called *ndoedn* Arakmbut and all the names of the clans are given the epithet Arakmbut.

Thus the Singperi who have the name keme (tapir) are also called keme Arakmbut.

I have also been told that the word Arakmbut means that the people as a whole is onyu (pure). Both clan and Arakmbut both share features of being named groups with clear definable means of inherited recruitment that distinguishes the inside from the outside. Other social units are never referred to as Arakmbut. The wambet, for example is an alliance category consisting of a mixture of paternal and maternal relatives and so is not 'onyu'. Similarly the community or the communal house is not referred to as Arakmbut. Presumably this is because a community constantly has a shifting mixture of people from outside who marry in, move out, and change allegiances. Whereas a community and a wambet can change over a lifetime, particularly over marriage, the clan and the Arakmbut as people do not change.

4. Animals

There are a few examples of the term Arakmbut being used in the context of certain types of animals. Two examples which I have heard are capybaras *(akidnet)* and white-lipped peccary (akudnui). These animals live in herds and show examples of sociality. I have been given detailed accounts as to the social organisation of the peccaries – the herd consists of women surrounded by males and a *wakeriskeris*, which is the guide who checks that all are together when they move off on the trail. On the whole, Arakmbut refers to human beings, but in these rare contexts, the term can be applied to animals.

Through looking at these different usages of the word Arakmbut we can see a cluster of features which connect to form a general orientation to the meaning of the word. In the first place Arakmbut refers to a certain type of social activity. It is not simply sociality; there are many creatures which are social but which are not called Arakmbut. Ants, termites, bees, or shoals of fish are not seen as Arakmbut or even as similar to human beings. Partly this is because of their size and the quantity of soul-matter, which is so small that it connects them more closely to plants. Secondly, the peccaries can communicate with each other through their language. However, animals such as monkeys, agouti, and birds can also talk to each other, but they are not Arakmbut. The sociality of the peccary is more than simply living in groups and speaking a language. It is the combination of both in action. Arakmbut identity is not only being Arakmbut but acting as an Arakmbut. This means sharing certain human features such as the capacity to co-operate for mutual benefit and to organise themselves to protect their family and offspring.

Nevertheless, white-lipped peccary are not human; rather, they share certain characteristics with people. The only words which are juxtaposed with the word Arakmbut are the names of the clans. This brings the onyu purity as a factor behind the notion of Arakmbut and people. The combination of social and cultural characteristics along with a distinct 'purity' or sense of identity in distinction to other groups or categories are the prime elements in defining Arakmbut.

Arakmbut have a cluster of social and cultural features coupled with a shared sense of identity which differentiates them from outsiders. The term is, in its daily sense, used according to the context of clan, ethno-linguistic group, or language family. However, the reference to the ethno-linguistic group is the most important for the Arakmbut themselves.

Arakmbut from Without

The internal notion of Arakmbut is parallelled from the way in which they are referred to by non-indigenous people. Officially, the term indigenous does not exist in Peru, but for the communities of the rainforest, the term *nativo* (native) is considered appropriate. The Arakmbut do not use this term, usually saying *paisano* or *paise* when referring to themselves in Spanish. Non-indigenous Peruvians use the term 'nativo', but occasionally one hears the more derogatory *chuncho* or *indio* with *tribu* as a collective term. These generic terms are most common, but throughout Arakmbut history there has been a discussion as to what they should be called specifically.

The Arakmbut have had two names given to them from outside. Mashco was first used by Padre Biedma in 1687 (Amich 1854:104) although the word was spelt 'Maschcos'. This word referred to a group of Piro in the Mishagua river to the north of Manu. Over the years the term spread to the Madre de Dios where, in 1807, Padres Busquests and Rocamora were referring to the Guirineris (presumably Sapiteri called by their Wachipaeri name Sirineri) who were members of the 'Mashco' nation (Maurtúa 1906, Vol. 12:166). Until the 1970s, the term Mashco was used to refer to all the Harakmbut peoples.

However, various publications in the 1970s (Lyon 1976; Moore 1979; Torralba 1979) demonstrated that the term Mashco was an inappropriate term as it did not reflect either language or cultural factors and that the preferred term was Harakmbut. The Harakmbut peoples themselves supported this strongly. When I first arrived in San José del Karene in 1980 I was told clearly that the term Mashco was an insult imposed from outside by other language groups such as the Amahuaca (Panoan speakers).

The term Mashco has not disappeared, however. The group of women contacted in the Manu National Park during the late 1970s have been labelled Mashco-Piro while peoples in the Purus region who are unknown to the national society, bordering on the northern extreme of the Madre de Dios, have also been named Mashco. It would appear that the name Mashco is still used to label any people which has been recently contacted.

In the late 1970s, Harakmbut replaced the Mashco Nation as the general term for all those who spoke Harakmbut languages. The internal names of the seven peoples (Wachipaeri, Sapiteri, Pukirieri, Arasaeri, Toyeri, Kisambaeri, and Amarakaeri) became standard ethnographic terms. Each of these were names given by other Harakmbut groups. For example the term Amarakaeri is first used in the literature in 1907 by Olivera, a member of the Junta de Vias Fluviales, who heard of a people called 'Maracairis' who lived in the interior of the river Colorado (Olivera 1907:421).

During the late 1970s and 1980s anthropologists and people working with the Amarakaeri thought that the term was a descriptive reference to where they came from (for example, the Arasaeri came from the River Arasa and the Toyeri from 'downstream' and the Pukirieri from the River Pukiri). It was thus assumed that Amarakaeri referred to a hill called 'Amara' (Barriales & Torralba 1970:5). According to Califano (1982:58) it comes in fact from a Wachipaeri name for the stone *(amaraca)* from which they originated. As Califano says (ibid.), the Amarakaeri have accepted this name, even though they use the term Arakmbut among themselves. For this reason most people accepted the term Amarakaeri as an appropriate name.

It therefore came as a surprise in May 1992 when I was talking to several elders about these matters at a meeting between San José and Puerto Luz. They told me that they were not happy about the name Amarakaeri. They said that it had been imposed on them by outsiders, particularly the Matsigenka, who used it as a word meaning stupid – someone who did not know how to make masato (yuca beer). The Wachipaeri use the word Amarakaeri to refer to the Arakmbut as killers. The particle *arak* means 'kill' in the Harakmbut language. The old men preferred to be called Arakmbut.

When I checked this later with some Wachipaeri, I was told that a few generations back the word Amarakaeri had prejudicial connotations, although now they were not so apparent. When I asked the older men where the name Amarakaeri came from, they told me that the word had been given by the Papa. The Papa were white cannibals who roamed through Harakmbut territory in mythological times, killing and eating humans. They then gave the following explanation: 'The Papa existed before Wanamey. One day the Papa said, "I will show you how to hunt sloths *(mbu)*. Mbu! Mbu!" he called. Many sloths came down from the trees. Then Papa called the Arakmbut. "There you are, kill them. You are Amarakaeri!" The sloth is an easy animal to hunt because it is so slow. So for the Papa to help the Arakmbut kill sloths is in itself an insult.' (Indeed sometimes Arakmbut tease bad hunters by saying that they are 'hunters of sloths'.)

'Amarakaeri' is thus insulting because it refers to the Arakmbut not as proud killers, but in the ironic sense of being killers of animals that anyone can hunt. On the other hand the word Arakmbut, which also has the particle arak meaning 'kill', has a more positive sense of courage and hunting skills and is consequently preferred.

The disquiet with the name Amarakaeri appeared in 1992, yet those with whom I spoke about this had been aware that the name was ambiguous before. However they had not raised the question or given it a very high priority.[3] The context in which the discussion arose was through the publication of my material on the Arakmbut. The question which they asked was whether I would mind referring to them in future as Arakmbut because this is their real name.

The significance of this change relates to the two forms of identification noted above; one comes from within (Arakmbut) and the other from outside (Amarakaeri). Both names are dynamic processes of identifying what is a people, rather than strict classifications. The Arakmbut want the world to perceive them as they do themselves. The imposition of a name is one aspect of colonial activity; indeed, throughout colonial history, tribal identity has frequently been classified by the outsiders. The Arakmbut realised that the term Amarakaeri was imposed, but until recently were not aware that it mattered or that they could do anything about it.

3. I learned during this time that when the term Amarakaeri became used regularly in the 1970s, an old priest, Padre Elias, who met the first Arakmbut from San José del Karene to visit Lima in 1981, said that he was amazed to hear that they had accepted being called by that insulting word 'Amarakaeri'. Thus the potential for the insult was not something invented over the last few years.

The Arakmbut of San José and Puerto Luz reacted to the upheavals in their lives and identities caused by colonisation and the gold rush by asserting their own self-identity. The more the classification from outside becomes connected with colonisation, the more they resist and assert their own identity. For this reason, colonisation actually creates a fixed notion of a 'people'. This is a critical shift in the way names have been seen hitherto. Arakmbut has various different contexts of use, each of which refers to a quality of sociality, cultural communication and a common heritage distinct from those of other peoples. The implications of using the word Arakmbut are twofold.

In the first place a term which is used in several contexts will become primarily a name which identifies the people from outside. This is their name for people. Thus they want to be known objectively as 'people' and not by an epithet created by outsiders. This will have the effect of crystallising the term and turning a common noun into a proper noun.

The second implication is that the identification of the Arakmbut from inside is positive and they feel that from the outside it has always been negative. They want to assert their self-identification and project that onto the outside world. The result of this is that they are grasping a reflexiveness whereby they should be respected by outsiders and not accept imposed labels.[4]

In the 1970s the Arakmbut complained strongly about the general term Mashco for all seven groups, which was replaced by the term Harakmbut. In this way they perceived themselves as insulted by peoples outside of their language group. Now, they see Amarakaeri, which is a term internal to their language group, as also pejorative. They realised that through people, such as myself, who publish information concerning their current situation, it would be possible to change their name. In accordance with their wishes I now refer to those whom previously I called Amarakaeri as Arakmbut.

This change of name is significant because it demonstrates a desire that they are recognised as a people from outsiders, not simply as a named group. The request to be referred to as Arakmbut is thus a

4. This should not be seen as something which only occurs to the Amarakaeri. The Kisambaeri are named after a berry which grew near their maloca in the headwaters of the Karene in the 1940s. The oldest surviving member of this people told me that he never liked being named after a berry. It was insulting. The correct term should be Amaiweri because their place of origin was the Amaiwe river in the headwaters of the Inambari.

political assertion of self-identity to bring into focus the perspectives from inside the community and outside.[5]

The definition of the Arakmbut as a people is consequently a clash of perspectives. The term in their language which relates most clearly to the idea of people is the name they want universally recognised. Even though the Arakmbut in San José del Karene are not in touch with the international setting of standards for the rights of indigenous peoples, they are defining their identity according to their word for people, which they consider appropriate.

In principle, there is a marked difference between the idea of an identity which is imposed from outside and one which arises from the people themselves. An identity can be a classificatory label imposed as a means of distinguishing a people from others, or else as a way of placing them on a hierarchy based on prejudice. Both the names Mashco and Amarakaeri were used pejoratively by other indigenous peoples to label the Arakmbut. For this reason the Arakmbut themselves, who knew and understood the terms as derogatory, reacted negatively, even though in many cases the words were not intentionally used pejoratively but as a labelling device. The concern seems to have arisen with the increasing publicity given to their plight and the importance of avoiding a name which they consider derogatory being spread throughout the world.

A parallel can be made with the defining of the boundaries of the term Arakmbut by the elders and the increasingly fixed boundaries of the wandari. In both cases a term which was, and to some extent

5. Two authors have used these 'inside and outside' arguments. Anthony Cohen (1985) argues that the constant element in community definition comes from the shared symbolic model provided by the members through their definition of its boundaries: 'Rather than describing analytically the form of the structure from an external vantage point, we are attempting to penetrate the structure, to look *outwards* from its core' (p.20). Anthony Smith (1986:3), in contrast, argues in his historical view of the origin of nations that when looking at a broad canvas we have to place a static model over events in order to clarify the complexities of social dynamics. 'Inevitably, this requires us to endow nations and ethnic communities with more static "solidity" than closer investigation at any point in time might warrant.'

However, in an indigenous context, relying too much on external classificatory principles runs the risk of imposing neo-colonial structures, whereas analysing shared criteria for self-identification risks ignoring the broader socio-historical principles of identity creation. For indigenous peoples, boundaries are never fixed because colonisation and relations with the state are dynamic and permanently shifting. Smith's boundaries stem from socio-historical models, while Cohen's boundaries are presented as symbolic. In an Arakmbut context, it is possible to see how outside and inside are not fixed boundaries, but highly charged political distinctions which can easily change.

is, flexible and relative, has taken on absolute features in order to distinguish Arakmbut from the constantly encroaching forces of colonisation. This shift from relativity to absolute is can be found within Arakmbut personal and social life.

Peoples and Persons

The case study ends with the arrest of the Arakmbut for not having their electoral cards. This is significant because it indicates that there is a clear distinction between the state notion of an individual, based on documentary proof, and Arakmbut idea of a person. After having stressed the importance of collective identity and collective rights, it should not be thought that the Arakmbut have no sense of individuality. This could not be further from the case; each Arakmbut person is highly individualistic and in fact, after several years living in a community in the Amazon, it is no exaggeration to say that indigenous people often have greater freedom to express themselves than their counterparts in a Peruvian city or a European country.

For the Arakmbut, identity is an expression of what it means to be a person. However, the word for person is also 'Arakmbut'. Linguistically, therefore, the Arakmbut do not distinguish between themselves as a people and as people. When they talk of persons, they place them within a series of social co-ordinates constituting a flexible multi-faceted identity. Each Arakmbut person is made up of three elements. The material aspect of the person is the body (waso) which consists of bones, fat, blood, flesh, and various body organs.[6] The visible part of the person is distinguished from the invisible part constituted by soul-matter (nokiren). The nokiren animates the body and receives its form from the body. The waso and nokiren are bound together through the name (wandik). The name ties the two elements of the person and ensures the unique identity of each Arakmbut.

However the waso and nokiren do not have a permanent unchanging relationship; at night during dreams the nokiren can leave the waso and a more intense separation occurs at orgasm. The relationship between waso and nokiren also changes over life. It is particularly weak for children and elders who are prone to wanderings of the nokiren, while through adulthood, the two parts of the person are more firmly tied together. Occasionally the separation can become

---

6. A detailed description of the Arakmbut person is presented in Volume 1, chapter six.

too great and the nokiren becomes disorientated or lost, as in an illness, when someone loses consciousness, or during a fit. The ultimate separation takes place at death (e'mbuey).

The name can also change through life at important moments such as in the past, during initiation for boys, after an illness has taken someone close to death, or after an encounter with a spirit who utters the new name. Names take various forms: children's names or nicknames are part of the informal internal life of the community, Spanish names are used to connect the Arakmbut to non-indigenous people, while the personal names relate the waso and nokiren together to the spirit world. Whereas all names can be dangerous if misused, the personal name is by far the closest to the person's identity as distinct from another. Personal names are not unique, although I know of no two living people with the same names.

Although the Arakmbut have a very dynamic notion of person, there is a word which could be translated as 'individual'. The word watawata means 'individual' while watawatawe means 'not individual'. This refers for example to a dance or presentation which is done by one person or which is done in a group. On the whole, watawata refers to people who sing songs in private, while watawatawe refers to songs where the group joins in for the refrain or even for the whole song. This word has the idea not just of an individual person, but of something done in private as opposed to in public. The meaning also has a connotation which is physical. The person is tied to the others but is physically separate. For this reason, we could just as easily use the word personal or private to translate watawata. Individual for the Arakmbut is associated with a notion stressing separateness and privacy and would be better translated as 'personal'.

Arakmbut personal identity is not based exclusively on individual separateness but it is in constant flux. Some aspects of life, such as the physical features, nokiren, and personal name are constant over long periods of time. The personal 'I' *(ndo)* remains a constant throughout life. It is distinct from everyone else and constitutes the subjective self. The names bind the ndo into a person, while expressing its relationship with other aspects of the social and spiritual world. This parallels observations from other parts of the world which see within the person an aspect of personal self (the Maussian *moi*) and the social person (the Maussian *personne*) dynamically operating within each individual (Carrithers et al. 1985; Leinhardt 1985:145). Thus within the person there are constant discrete aspects and flexible and relational attributes.

This contrast is even more specific in interpersonal relationships, and is particularly apparent with the use of pronouns. There are two ways of using pronouns in Harakmbut. The first is to use the words ndo (I), *on* (you), *ken* (he, she, they), *oro* (we) *opudn* (you plural) with prefixes referring to factors such as emphasis (*a*), or to/for (*ta*), or of (*edn*). However another way consists of placing the pronouns within the verb. This is done by using forms of the verb which reflect relationships. Should the subject of the verb be unclear the pronoun is included:

Table 4.1 Examples of relational pronouns

onane	I tell you, you tell me, you tell us (s)
ononane	You (p) tell me/us, I tell you (p)
omanane	We tell you (s & p),
menane	He tells me, he tells you (s)
monane	He tells us, he tells you (p), they tell you (s,p)
menonane	They tell me/us

(s = singular; p = plural)

Pronouns utilise verbs either to separate persons or to draw them together within a relationship. The result is that at any moment the Arakmbut, through utilisation of pronouns or not, make statements about their relationships in a way which incorporates people into each other. It is thus impossible to see the Arakmbut as consisting only of isolated individuals within a society. Furthermore it is equally impossible to see them as a collectivity without any individual distinction. The two elements are so entwined that different aspects of a multifaceted personal and collective identity emerge at any moment. The use of the word Arakmbut in the singular and plural thus reflects the complexity and subtlety of collective, interpersonal, and personal identities.

The person contains distinct constant elements mixed with more flexible relative notions of personhood, connected to the state of soul, body, and name which are reflected in social relationships as a whole. On the one hand, the person has a unique identity, but at the same time he or she is bound to other people and has a position in the world which is relative to the rest of the Arakmbut. This distinction between named discrete identities and categories of relatedness constitutes the uneasy tension which makes the social formation a process as much as a structure.[7]

---

7. The following sections are necessarily brief; for a full description of these aspects of social organisation, see Volume 1, chapters two, three, and four.

1. Clan, wambet, and terminology

The seven exogamous, patrilineal clans provide a fundamental aspect of personal Arakmbut allegiance. People defend their clan's name and reputation vigorously, even to the point of fighting for its honour. Clans at one time were thought to have certain physical characteristics which passed down through the patriline. The names of the clans are the basis of an association for each person with animal and plant species. The clan and its members have a special relationship with the invisible world which is based on a form of communication of heightened consciousness from dreams or visions. Clan names remain the same throughout life, even though interpretations of the world can vary from one clan to another.

Physical descent passes through the patriline and the clans, although the emphasis on the predominance of the clan weakens from time to time as the alliance arranging unit, the wambet, becomes more focused (see Volume 2). The wambet contains relatives of both parents and has a *de facto* cognatic element in its application. The wambet, however, is not a named group and any relationship which it identifies is based on the application of the relationship terminology, operating according to a principle of symmetric prescription. The wambet is connected to the terminology because it consists of certain relationship categories which differ according to the speaker.[8]

Every Arakmbut is related to everyone else through the relationship terminology. This consists of five levels of terms which are related primarily through a series of equations which imply sister exchange. In practice, however, sister exchange is comparatively rare and not always encouraged. The terminology thus consists of a 'grid' which relates the Arakmbut through a system of categories consisting of a formal system, a reference system, and a direct address system, all of which are used according to context and the social status of the persons talking to or about each other.

8. Volume 2 looked at the dynamic nature of Arakmbut life in terms of the tension between the wambet and the clan. Whereas the patrilineal clan continues through time from its founding at the time of Wanamey, the wambet provides a closer connection between households at the level of neighbourhood. At different periods in Arakmbut history, the emphasis on clan or wambet changes, resulting in a dynamic socio-cultural system which undergoes shifts between a relatively concentrated spatial organisation based on the clans and the community, and a more dispersed organisation based on the wambet. Indications show that over the last hundred years there have been several shifts of emphasis within these poles. The use of the terms wambet and onyu may change according to the community, but the distinction between clan and cognatic/alliance category is consistent among all the Arakmbut communities (c.f.Helberg 1993:115).

The relationship terminology is based on a system relative to an ego. In the same way as the wambet, no two persons share exactly the same use of the terminology (even suffixes of age grade will distinguish the way the terminology is used by same-sex siblings). This relativistic system shifts according to who is talking and also changes at different times in one's life. The relationship terminology is consequently different from the clan system, which is made up of named groups. All Arakmbut are members of clans and their membership is fixed from birth to death whereas, in contrast, the relationship terminology expresses not only a framework of relatives which changes over life with marriage, but includes terms which differ according to sex, age, and affinity. Furthermore, the use of the terminology in practice is also related to affective connections where people related by marriage, but who are close friends, will often refer to each other as siblings rather than affines.

2. *Space and time: insiders, outsiders, and maloca groups*

The Arakmbut have terms which define a person as a close member of the community. A *wanakeri* who comes from the community (insider) is distinct from an outsider *(esweri)*. However, the application of who is an insider or outsider depends very much on who is talking and how close they are to the person under consideration. In Volume 1, chapter three, it was noted that women who were considered insiders to the community had their names associated with their gardens, whereas those from outside had their husband's name associated with the gardens until the new wives became self-sufficient. However, on talking to the Arakmbut, the higher status of insider women meant that the closer the relative, the more likely they would associate her gardens with her name.

In contrast to this relative sense of social space, each community has two fixed names; one refers to place and the other to people. The community name is usually in Spanish (San José del Karene, Puerto Luz etc.), while the Arakmbut within the community have designations which correspond to the old maloca names:

Table 4.2 Names of maloca groups associated with each community

Shintuya: Shintapoeri;
Barranco Chico: Kotsimberi;
Boca del Inambari: Kipodniritneri;
San José: Wakutangeri;
Puerto Luz: Kipodneri.

Twelve names of pre-contact maloca groups are still used within the communities in certain contexts such as recounting history or tracing genealogical connections; the older people remember them more than the younger Arakmbut, who use the current group names. Place names are fixed and refer to specific houses and so accurate are they that they provide fixed points in social space and time because, for the Arakmbut, time is determined by space (see chapter seven).

When an Arakmbut wants to refer to a period, he or she will refer to the time when they lived at a certain maloca. Although this form of time-reckoning is relative by the standards of a clock, it is fixed in the sense that it refers to a specific moment in time (even though the moment may have consisted of several years while the group lived in any one place).

3. Age, sex, and gender

Whereas the distinction between male and female is absolute in human physical terms, several contexts relate gender to other aspects of life and these are more complicated. For example, age distinctions have two terms which do not mark gender: *wasipo* and *watone*. *Wasipo* means child of either sex, whereas after puberty the gender distinction appears with *muneyo* for girls and *wambo* for boys. *Wetone* and *wambokerek* are terms for woman and man as adults, whereas gender disappears for the older people (watone). Thus according to age the gender relationship becomes more similar (at the extremes of life) or distinct (adulthood, when sexual relationships take place).

Another way of connecting gender is through the exchange of elements. Traditional prestations prior to marriage involved a woman presenting her husband's household with a string bag, associated with trees by the river from which the bark string is found and which is washed in barbasco fish poison. In return the man would make a set of bows and arrows and hunt *chindoi* meat especially to betrothal which would take place on acceptance of the gift.

This exchange of male and female elements appears mythologically, through the daily cycle of day and night when the master of the underworld of the river is the moon (pugn) who is male, is juxtaposed with the sun *(miokpo);* the original mistress of the forest was a now extinct female sun. A further example took place at the lip-piercing male initiation ceremonies (no longer performed). In order to have sexual relations without danger, a man's lip was pierced with a peach palm splinter; in the myth which comments on this rite, the splinter is made from the pubic hair of the culture hero Marinke's grandmother. The man is thus impregnated by a female sexually-charged object (inverting male/female sexual relations).

Rather than gender being tied absolutely to any specific domain or ceremony, the effect is a mixture of the fixed distinction of sex with a more relative distinction in which elements of maleness and femaleness can be juxtaposed. This is an engendering process by which a mixture of male and female, usually in form of an exchange or sexual relations, provides the dynamics of creation.

When looking at the Arakmbut person and his or her relationship with the broader social formation, it is necessary to distinguish between relations which shift according to the person and context as opposed to those which are more fixed named social groups and categories. The dynamic process of Arakmbut life could be seen as a relationship between absolute and relative which connects social categories and groups, time and space and gender. Although this is the case, all Arakmbut socio-cultural life is relative in some degree because, at a systemic level, named groups demonstrate a relativity of perspectives (see Volume 1, chapter four). For this reason I prefer to see relatedness ranging from more flexible (more relativistic) criteria which define a person or group according to the current relationship with others, and the fixed (more absolute) names which refer to specific persons or groups. All of this encompasses the concept of Arakmbut from the person through social and cultural phenomena to the notion of a people itself. The following table summarises this information:

Table 4.3 Distinctions between flexible and fixed social criteria

Flexible Categories	Fixed Categories
relational pronouns	personal pronouns/names
relationship terminology/wambet	clan (onyu)
insiders/outsiders	maloca groups
older/younger	age grades/ maloca sites
gender	sexual identity

All of these aspects of being Arakmbut are, in daily life, superimposed on each other. This multi-systemic organisation makes any overall description of the Arakmbut personal identity and social formation extremely complicated, but these features can be found expressed in Arakmbut practical activities. In this way each person has some constant and some changing elements which place everyone in a unique position in the world as Arakmbut. This is the personal space which provides the Arakmbut with considerable room for self-expression.

The flexible categories are unique for each person and place him or her in a position connected to but separate from others. The groups, on the other hand, place each Arakmbut person together with some members of the community and distinguish outsiders. Thus at the same moment each person is both connected to everyone or separated from them according to one scheme or another. The flexible categories (relationship terms, wambet, gender, pronoun connections) are largely seen as embracing and comprehensive overlapping concepts, whereas the groups tend to be conducive to stronger divisions (clan, age-grade, or sex, for example).

The concept of Arakmbut as presented above covers both relatedness contexts (socio-linguistic features) and shared fixed notions of identity which do not change much over a lifetime (a people). When the Arakmbut face threats to their identity and their territory, the shift is from a more relative to a more absolute categorisation. This reflects both personal and social shifts and constitutes a form of boundary maintenance which is both assertive and defensive.

The Arakmbut as Peruvians

The final aspect of the case study referred to a clash between Arakmbut personhood and Peruvian individuality. The arrest of the young representatives from San José demonstrates the importance of national documentation but also the extent of Arakmbut ambivalence to Peruvian national life. In certain contexts they will recognise themselves as Peruvian – as when, for example, they are in contact with a foreign person or are called upon to demonstrate their loyalty to the state at a time of war, when they will refer to themselves as Peruvians. However, at other times, the Arakmbut refer to 'Peruvians' as non-indigenous members of the state of Peru, as if they were quite independent. This point was discussed in chapter one.

'Nativos', which is the official Peruvian term for lowland indigenous peoples, is rarely used by the Arakmbut. 'Pueblos indígenas' is occasionally used in a political context by those familiar with the indigenous movement. However, when defining themselves in Spanish within a Peruvian context, the lowland term 'paise' is used (a shortened form of 'paisano' or countrymen). 'Paise' reflects a relationship of coherence between Peruvian and Paisano because within a national context 'paise' is a substratum of Peruvian. In contrast

Arakmbut is not a Peruvian word. Arakmbut is something completely separate and, as noted earlier, is the term they use to distinguish themselves as indigenous peoples from others.

Spanish names, which were imposed by missionaries initially but which now all Arakmbut take on, reflect the need to establish a 'Peruvian' identity vis-á-vis the outside world; however, they are not frequently used within the community. Spanish names are those with which a person is registered officially and by which he or she is identified on electoral cards. An electoral card grants status for an individual to become a state-recognised person.[9] The 'indocumentados' are a sizeable proportion of Peru's population and, as noted in chapter two, they find life very restricted.

The legal perspective of the Peruvian state considers the Arakmbut as individual Peruvian citizens who internally do not need electoral cards. As soon as they leave the community, however, the Arakmbut must have their electoral cards. Peruvians are expected by law to vote at elections. However, we have seen above that the local authorities have been extremely reluctant to assist the majority of the Arakmbut to obtain electoral cards in case they outnumber the colonists and take over the state municipality at Boca Colorado.

Each card is processed in a district where the bearer can vote. The district for San José is the District of Madre de Dios with its municipal centre at Boca Colorado. Any Arakmbut with a card is consequently not registered as indigenous but as a Peruvian citizen. Several inconsistencies arise with the cards which were issued before the recent registration programme. All male card holders were required to have done military service or had to pay a fine if they were to get an electoral card without being in the armed forces. One way of getting around this was to declare the people concerned illiterate and carry out registration in Puerto Maldonado, which is in a different district from where the Arakmbut live. In any election, this left the Arakmbut in a minority. A particularly strange inconsistency arose from this when I saw a fourth year Arakmbut university student in Lima with a card registered with the information that he was illiterate. (The military rule does not affect women, but they have also registered as illiterate in the past to save time and money in getting an electoral identity card.)

The Arakmbut live on the boundaries of state society and have a definition of person and collectivity quite distinct from the individual

---

9. In order to avoid complications, when talking of Arakmbut notions of people, I have kept to the more neutral term 'person', and when talking of the Peruvian state identity I have used the term 'individual'.

identification of Peruvian citizens. The difference from an Arakmbut perspective is that the card ties up personal space into one individual identity with a number, distinct from the person with the next number on a separate card. This is, as has been demonstrated above, totally different from the personal and relational connections within Arakmbut social life. This is not to say that other Peruvians do not have multiplex relationships, just that underpinning the state view of individual is a discrete entity, separate from others. This is not the Arakmbut view.

In spite of this, outside of the community, the Arakmbut need an identity based on Peruvian citizenship in order to survive. Without a card, a person appears as a threat to the state – a potential guerilla. All travel is checked with reference to the electoral card; without a card no one can travel freely outside of the community, vote for state officials, or generally participate in public life as a Peruvian. Furthermore, without an electoral card, it is not possible to travel outside of the country. Personal freedom as a member of a state is incumbent on shifting an indigenous notion of multifaceted identity into being an individual unit, crystallised in the card.

The result is that each individual Arakmbut with his or her Spanish name can now become a citizen in the 'liberal democratic' Peruvian system, providing that the electoral card is available. This is not so easy. Unless special dispensations are provided, a person has to travel to Puerto Maldonado, pay several sums to the national bank, and first take out a military card. After a process of several days queuing and negotiating, the lucky ones can become registered as Peruvian citizens.

According to Donnelly (1989:76), the main bases for human rights are human dignity and moral worth, which are based on a liberal conception of the individual in his or relationship with the state. However, for the Arakmbut, those unable to receive recognition as Peruvian citizens suffer enormous discrimination, as the case study above testified. It also illustrated an important principle with regard to the rights of individuals. If citizenship is the recognition of individuality by the state, what happens to the human rights of those who are not able or willing to become citizens of the state? The human rights violations in this case took place because the Arakmbut were *not* recognised as citizens. They were therefore discriminated against because they were different.

Indigenous identity is not only about personal relations within a collectivity, it is also about being distinct. The Arakmbut in the case study were discriminated against on an individual basis because they were different on a collective basis. This example shows that to be recognised as an individual in Peru is not enough to obtain recognition of one's basic *individual* human rights.

Another aspect of discrimination against the Arakmbut over voting rights has occurred in the District of Madre de Dios (the local municipality). The colonists are aware that should all the Arakmbut vote together, they could control the Municipal Council. For this reason an incredible number of obstacles have been set up to prevent indigenous people registering for their cards. The Arakmbut are not informed when the registrar visits the area and the registrars do not usually come to the communities.

In order to ameliorate the problem, in 1992 a campaign took place through the national indigenous organisation, AIDESEP, whereby all the indigenous communities in the Madre de Dios were visited and cards were distributed to many Arakmbut. This caused great concern among the colonists because they feared that an indigenous mayor might take control of the district. However, by the time of the elections in November, the communities had not had the time to organise their candidate sufficiently and, with a small sleight of hand on the part of the local authorities (who brought in people from a neighbouring district who had been registered there 'by accident'), the Arakmbut narrowly lost the position of mayor to a colonist.

The AIDESEP electoral card campaign is deeply ironic when we realise that the Arakmbut were only granted citizenship because an indigenous organisation lobbied the Peruvian government to secure registration for indigenous peoples. The bureaucracy was simplified because the Arakmbut were an indigenous collectivity, but if they had not been an indigenous people, defining their individual rights would have been even more difficult.

But have the Arakmbut been treated in a privileged position over other individuals who cannot get their electoral cards? This basis of human rights is frequently discussed in terms of equity. Brownlie (1993:73) expresses this concern as follows:

'Against this background, and from a strictly legal point of view, the approach based upon the concept of indigenous people has the considerable drawback that it represents a claim not of equality but of priority and privilege. It is one thing to obtain some advantages within a flexible application of equality and within a regime of restitution of land rights; it is quite another thing to operate categorically within a regime of privilege and exclusiveness.'

According to this perspective, there is a potential contradiction between equality before the law and being different. The indigenous organisations of Peru managed to stop discrimination against non-registered Arakmbut by offering them the chance voluntarily to become citizens. This did not affect their indigenous integrity as a people, but rather ensured a defence against random discrimination on behalf of the authorities. By rights, this event could be seen from Brownlie's view as granting priority and privilege, considering that there are poorer and more deprived individuals in Peru than the Arakmbut.

However, Brownlie's notion of priority and privilege is very questionable from an indigenous perspective because to recognise Arakmbut rights involves no discrimination against any other Peruvian. The Arakmbut do not receive recognition of their rights as indigenous peoples at the expense of others' human rights. In fact, using this argument in any context in which indigenous peoples are defending their territories and cultures is like saying that a thief who takes lands from indigenous peoples has the right to his loot.

The problem with an approach which sees indigenous peoples as privileged is that it confuses discrimination and difference. There is no reason legal equity cannot be preserved with recognition of the right of distinct peoples. Difference does not mean automatic discrimination. There is no doubt that racial or any other discrimination is based on the principle of converting difference between one people and another into pejorative treatment through exploitative power. However, to argue that indigenous peoples do not have the right to be different would be discriminatory in itself, as this reinforces the existing inequalities which give rise to the discrimination.

The problem with discrimination is not difference but social injustice and inequality. One of the main features of the definition of the concept 'indigenous' is that indigenous peoples are not equal to others in a state and thus need and deserve legal protection and support to ensure that what they have in terms of territories, resources, culture, and social life is not taken away from them. For this to happen they need to ensure that their rights as peoples are respected.

Individuals in the nation state have the right to be different from each other while remaining equal in the eyes of the law. But no one can understand the Arakmbut if they are seen only as individual citizens. Every Arakmbut person is bound to the Arakmbut people. The Peruvian individual identity only operates in contexts outside of Arakmbut territory. The Arakmbut do not need Peruvian citizenship to hunt, garden, work gold or generally live as an indigenous people. However, they need to be Peruvian to travel, to gain further education, and to vote. All of these activities take place in the context of defending their lives as a people. For example, education and travelling are strategies to ensure that members of the community can manage to deal with illegal colonists. They want the vote to try to ensure that friends of those same colonists do not take over Arakmbut territory and discriminate against them.

In this way Peruvian citizenship is an aspect of Arakmbut identity in that it reinforces or acts as an added protection. However, to suggest that individual citizens' rights are sufficient to protect the Arakmbut people as a whole is plainly false. On the contrary, their recognition as a people comes prior to their rights as individuals. Furthermore, there is another aspect of Peruvian society which is not only based on citizenship but on collective action, this is largely articulated through the popular movement.

The work of Louis Dumont (1986) is pertinent here. He argues that there are two definitions of the term individual:

'Regarding the human individual, or 'the individual', we must distinguish:
1. The empirical subject, indivisible sample of the human species, as encountered in all societies;
2. The independent, autonomous moral and, thus, essentially nonsocial being, so encountered first of all in our modern ideology of man and society' (Dumont 1986:279).

The first category covers all human beings, while the second is relevant to the individual citizen within the Peruvian state. Dumont also contrasts 'holistic' ideologies, which valorise the social whole and neglect or subordinate the human individual, with individualism, which valorises the individual in second sense over the social whole.

Dumont's contrast is illuminating here because, whereas the individual and collective are in tension in state society, for the Arakmbut the collectivity embraces individuality through personhood within a broad space which enables each person to be highly individualistic. However, when the Arakmbut take on state citizenship, they find the non-social autonomous being is not part of their Arakmbut identity but provides a context within the Peruvian state for each person to move safely.

As the Arakmbut take on Peruvian citizenship, they also face the excessive individualism of the state. The popular movement exists as collective set of organisations to challenge state individuation and restore the complementarity between person and people which exists in their community. For this reason the Arakmbut ally themselves to the collective forces of the indigenous movement, through organisations such as FENAMAD and COHAR. In this way the Arakmbut, on the boundaries of their social formation, utilise Peruvian individualistic identity as well as the holistic identity of the popular movement when they resist state interference into their lives.

The Arakmbut have a distinct way of life, but at the same time they are conversant with the Peruvian state. Both the state and the Arakmbut have in their ways created boundaries and forms of identification distinguishing the Arakmbut as a people from outsiders, yet at the same time they are potentially Peruvian citizens allied to the popular movement. Thus the distinction between inside and outside should not be seen as a fixed, objective division, but rather as something which is created through the conflicting perspectives of the Arakmbut and non-Arakmbut.

This distinction between individual versus the state and person as part of an indigenous people draws attention to the inside / outside distinction. Recent writings (c.f. Urban & Sherzer 1991:1) have remarked that the anthropological emphasis on describing communities as if they were isolated has had to change in recent years.

> 'Decolonisation requires abandoning the assumption that indigenous societies are autonomous cultural isolates and recognising that, faced with colonial and state domination, they are inevitably altered by their relationship to dominating forces' (Abercrombie 1991:95).

However, this conclusion can lead to a difficulty when looking at the notion of a people. If people cross boundaries so easily, can indigenous peoples be clearly and consistently different from the state in which they live? Furthermore, if peoples change their identity in relationship to the state then perhaps they are no longer 'authentic', but living in an 'invented tradition' (Hobsbawm and Ranger 1983:1).

The question of authenticity and identification leads us to a dead end. The assumption that there is some authentic element of indigenous peoples implies that they are unchanging and are never affected by any outside influence. On the contrary, changes take place constantly in all social formations and the only way in which authenticity is accepted or not is whether the people concerned themselves accept it is so (Friedman 1992). Once again the argument returns to self-identification.

One way of overcoming this difficulty is to distinguish between words such as 'distinct', 'different', and 'discrete', which acknowledge outside relationships, and 'isolation' which implies minimal communication with an outside world. There is no question, for example, that the Arakmbut are considered different by the Peruvian state and that the state is considered different by the Arakmbut. Acceptance of citizenship, connections to the national economy, or social relations with local colonists do not necessarily mean automatic integration into the state, but can just as easily clarify the boundaries between the Arakmbut and those they consider to be outsiders or non-indigenous.

Without the option of citizens' rights, the Arakmbut stand to be destroyed by the Peruvian state as aliens. But if they are not recognised as an indigenous people, they stand to be denied the means of protecting their very existence as Arakmbut – territorial rights, sociocultural formation, access to resources, and control over life. Without acceptance of these aspects of peoplehood, the Arakmbut would find their collective identity split from their persons and they would become individuals within the state and, quickly, oppressed members of the proletariat.

Peoples, Collectivity and Self-Identification

This chapter has raised the importance of self-identification and traced the process whereby Arakmbut elders openly determined how they wanted to be named. The term Arakmbut has undergone a shift in meaning. Whereas it was a term which linked the person to the collective, this was an internal self-identification which did not relate to the labels placed from outside. Now that has changed. The elders want their internal view recognised nationally and internationally. Thus, in the same way as the word wandari has gradually shifted its meaning over the last thirty years to cohere with the notion of territory, the word Arakmbut, which means people in a multitude of contexts, has also gradually become crystallised primarily around its meaning of an indigenous people.

This change has taken place during a period when the Arakmbut have been most threatened as an indigenous peoples. The process of colonisation, the increasing importance of Peruvian citizenship and the indiscriminate labelling from outside, whether as Mashco, Amarakaeri, 'Indio', 'chuncho' or 'nativo', are all threats to their identity. The word Arakmbut asserts a particular form of relationship between the person and the collective which the state does not grasp.

There could be a connection between the first signs of the Arakmbut wanting their identity objectified with the massive plan for arranging for every member of the community to receive citizenship with electoral cards. In this way they are emphasising the boundaries of their indigenous identity while accepting that in order to increase control over their lives they must accept citizenship. Thus, instead of citizenship becoming a threat, it has served to reinforce their ethnic identity by placing a stronger marker between them and the rest of Peruvian society. As the state encroaches increasingly on Arakmbut life (whether their territory or their identity as a people), the effect is an assertion of their rights. In the Arakmbut case this means recognition as an indigenous people with self-identification and auto-nomination combined with the freedom to take part in the national society, if they so desire.

The self-identification of a people is a multifaceted aspect of human activity which is economic, symbolic, and, in an indigenous case, particularly political. For this reason all the elements which are used to define peoples – territory, culture, language, social organisation, and political action – are not static elements of definition but dynamic features which constantly shape and reshape the content of the categories. It appears through daily activities and can be encapsulated in specific events, such as those recounted in the case study. Through the dynamism of daily life, the notion of people becomes increasingly important as a central focus of identity.

The indigenous reaction at the Vienna Conference on Human Rights to the idea of talking only about indigenous people without the 's' was strong protest by delegates. The use of the individualistic terms 'population' or 'people' demonstrates states' over-reliance on individual rights above notions of collectivity. Furthermore, this statist model of society is made up of individuals and not collectivities. In the first place, this refusal to recognise an indigenous people as a collectivity risks falling into the evolutionary framework of the nineteenth century. There individuals who had not formed themselves into a people were trapped in the backward stage of 'savagery'.

The second consequence of governments rejecting the ethnic identity and collectivity of indigenous peoples is that it ignores the whole social and cultural dynamics of their lives. The idea behind the use of the terms 'population' or 'individual people' is that people's rights are respected as individual citizens and can be dealt with under existing human rights law (Donnelly 1989; Brownlie 1993). However, the idea that all collectivities are made up of juridically separate and discrete individuals is an ethnocentric projection of state citizenship theory and fails to grasp the complexity of indigenous peoples' identity, leaving dangerous gaps in protecting their rights.

The term 'peoples' is vague but this is not necessarily a disadvantage, for it is a catch-all word which indigenous peoples all over the world can use for their expression of self-identification. At the same time, it reflects the collective aspect of indigenous life, which is fundamental for each culture's own expression of personal identity. The term 'peoples' is here to stay, and by ignoring it we disregard a crucial element in the definition of indigenous persons, which is that their personal identity is set within a context of a collective identity separate from the state. According to Howard Berman:

> 'The current system for the protection of human rights, centring on the relationship of the individual to the jurisdictional state, is incapable, even if fully implemented, of protecting the elements essential to the survival of indigenous societies. Fundamental issues of land rights, self-government, control of natural resources, environmental protection and the development of self-determined educational programs are necessarily *collective in nature and arise from the communitarian character of indigenous life*' (Berman 1987).

For those who follow the individualist theories, each individual person is the basis for human rights. However, individualistic reductionism is neither a necessary nor an appropriate way to understand Arakmbut social and cultural life. The main relationship for them is not between individual and state but between the person and the people. The relationship of citizen to the state may be an added protection, but it can never substitute the all-embracing notion of Arakmbut.

On the international stage, the discussion of indigenous rights often centres around the importance of collective rights. This has been emphasised here because the human rights world places so much stress on individual rights that the collective aspect quickly fades from view. Only by pressing for the collective dimension of indigenous peoples' rights will it be possible to avoid the Arakmbut person becoming exclusively an individual citizen and the Arakmbut people disappearing into the state.

This chapter has looked at the notion of difference from the co-ordinates of inside/outside and person/people. These are not fixed oppositions for the Arakmbut but aspects of their lives which are flexible. However, with the continuing encroachment of the state, the distinctions have become more apparent and the Arakmbut, while accepting them in certain contexts, have established protective barriers through asserting their rights as distinct peoples with a territory. Being different is more than simply considering oneself different. This chapter has reviewed the relationships between Arakmbut and others. It is time now to look more at the content of those differences, at the features which the Arakmbut are protecting from outside interference. These constitute important indications as to the content of their cultural identity.

Chapter 5

KNOWING YOUR PLACE
Cultural Heritage

'We are not like white people.' Arakmbut comment on the influence of colonists.

For indigenous peoples, the meaning of 'the right to be different' lies within culture. Yet there is controversy over the question as to whether there can be a right to cultural identity.

Donnelly (1989:158) says: 'Cultural identity is not something that can be provided to individuals by the state or by any other group; it is not a good, service, or status that can be given to people.' The author argues that a way of life is not a right and that the only way in which culture can be protected is through recognition of individual human rights as members of a community. This is in contrast to Thornberry, who says (1991:141): 'Granting minorities a right to defend their special identity, their unique characteristics that distinguish them from other members of the human family is an important task for human rights.'

The fundamental difference in the approach of these two writers is that Donnelly does not see the need for recognising and protecting collective rights. This, as was noted in the previous chapter, is far too limiting for considering indigenous peoples' rights, which recognise the person within the context of peoplehood and conceptualise culture as a shared experience.

Until the discussion of the ILO Convention and the UN Working Group's Declaration, the principal reference to cultural identity came from the 1966 International Covenant on Civil and Political Rights. In Article 27 there is a clause referring to minorities, which has been used on several occasions by indigenous peoples:

'In those States in which ethnic, religious or linguistic minorities exist, persons belonging to such minorities shall not be denied the right, in community with the other members of their group, to enjoy their own culture, to profess and practise their own religion, or to use their own language.'[1]

In spite of its individualist orientation, according to Thornberry (1991:171), the article is a hybrid between individual and collective rights and includes culture, religion, and language. These three factors are retained in the appropriate sections of the draft Declaration on the Rights of Indigenous Peoples (Articles 12, 13, and 14 respectively). However, a new element in the Declaration comes in Article 29, which says that

'indigenous peoples are entitled to the recognition of the full ownership, control and protection of their cultural and intellectual property: sciences, technologies and cultural manifestations, including human and other genetic resources, seeds, medicines, knowledge of the properties of fauna and flora, oral traditions, literatures, designs and visual and performing arts.'

The factor which links these items is knowledge and its manifestations.

The discussions of the draft Declaration's provisions on cultural, scientific, and intellectual knowledge has not been particularly controversial. However, the discussion has become more intense in another international instrument which relates to this question of indigenous knowledge: the Convention on Biological Diversity (CBD). This document was passed at the Rio Earth Summit in 1992 and contains a mixture of advantages and disadvantages for indigenous peoples. The most problematic aspect of the Convention is the emphasis which it gives to state control over resources.[2] Indigenous peoples are referred to a few times in the Convention, particularly in Article 8j under the topic of 'in-situ conservation'. This article refers to 'indigenous and local communities embodying traditional lifestyles'. It argues that 'subject to national legislation' the state will

1. Two cases have been brought to the Human Rights Committee under Article 27 of the Convention of Political and Civil Rights. In 1977, Sandra Lovelace, a Maliseet, complained that under the Indian Act of Canada she had lost her rights as an Indian when she married an outsider. Her complaint was upheld. However when Ivan Kitok, a Swedish Saami, complained in 1988 that he had lost membership of his community and rights to reindeer herding because he had left the area for three years, the Committee did not uphold his complaint because it claimed his exclusion did not affect the minority as a whole.
2. This arose as a result of a deal between states from the North, who want access to resources in the South, and states from the South, who want recognition of sovereignty over these resources.

'respect, preserve and maintain knowledge, innovation and practices of indigenous and local communities relevant for the conservation and sustainable use of biological diversity.' Furthermore, the state will 'promote their wider application with the approval and involvement of the holders of such knowledge, innovations and practices'.

The discussion over this article centres on the positive interpretation of recognising the collective aspect of indigenous communities and agreeing to their approval before this knowledge is used further afield, although this is all subject to national legislation. The context of the CBD is the protection and sustainable use of biological diversity, and so it has a different emphasis from the broader indigenous rights focus of the draft declaration.

Identifying the rights which protect such a mixture of phenomena is difficult. Various attempts have been made to draw them together. The Chair of the Working Group on Indigenous Populations has produced a report which uses the concept of 'cultural heritage' (Daes 1993b). She argues that this term links together material culture, religion, language, and knowledge, and that the best protection is through recognition of indigenous rights in general, particularly rights to lands, territories, and resources, because this controls access to and use of knowledge.[3]

This chapter looks at Arakmbut cultural heritage in a very broad sense that encompasses material culture, language, knowledge, and religion. However, unlike the concepts of territory and people, which cohere with the notions of indigenous rights discussed internationally, the Arakmbut do not have a generalised sense of cultural heritage. For this reason, their methods of relating to non-Arakmbut influences are diverse. One way of grasping this is to look briefly at different approaches to culture, in order to provide an orientation to this ephemeral concept.

Culture – a Shifting Concept

a) Culture Traits

In the nineteenth century, culture became increasingly connected with the discipline of anthropology which was collecting and com-

---

3. Posey (1995) uses the term 'traditional resource rights' to cover this broad spectrum which involves an analysis of international instruments complementing the indigenous rights regime with specific *sui generis* intellectual property approaches which reflect the needs of each state and people. For a summary of these points and a review of the main indigenous declarations on this subject, see Gray, 1995a.

paring traits from different peoples.[4] Particularly influential was the work of the German writer Gustav Kelmm who made an ethnographic study of non-European societies which in its title referred to 'Kultur'. The first all-embracing notion of culture was defined in 1871 by Tylor, who knew Kelmm's work, as: 'That complex whole which includes knowledge, belief, art, morals, law, custom and any other capabilities and habits acquired by man as a member of society.'

This descriptive approach to culture provides a list of traits which is observable empirically and can be analysed and dovetailed into the positivistic attitudes of the nineteenth century which Tylor shared by classifying different peoples on a progressive evolutionary scale. His definition emphasises the phenomena 'acquired by man as a member of society'; thus culture is not only a set of traits, but functions to connect persons to their collectivity as a whole by constituting a shared view of the world.

However, this approach to culture was too static for later anthropologists such as Kroeber, who considered that culture expresses the continuity and discontinuity in social life.

> 'Now the mass of learned and transmitted motor reactions, habits, techniques, ideas, and values – and the behaviour they induce – is what constitutes *culture*. Culture is the special and exclusive product of men, and is their distinctive quality in the cosmos' (Kroeber 1963:8).

Like Tylor, Kroeber continued with the notion of cultural traits which can be studied. However he considered that culture was learned and transmitted over time. For culture to transcend the life of any person living and expressing it, an observer has to see it as a pattern or form which is above individuals – 'superorganic'. Here he supported the idea of a holistic worldview according to which culture draws a people together and distinguishes it from others through both time and space.

The problem with this approach is that it assumes that culture is something tangible which is continuous and bounded. There seems to be no room for differences of opinion or interpretation. The areas of protection indicated in the UN documents reviewed above stem largely from this framework, in which traits such as material culture, language, knowledge, and religion are protected. However, this lim-

---

4. During the late eighteenth and early nineteenth centuries the idea behind culture was the 'improvement and ennoblement of the physical and spiritual qualities of person or a people' (Thompson 1990: 125). This view of culture continues today with the notion of someone being 'cultured' or participating in 'high culture' but does not concern us here.

ited approach should not be the basis for a discussion of the protection of cultural heritage because it leads to a folkloric, static notion of cultural heritage, buried in 'tradition'.

b) Culture as Meaning

Culture is also about meaning (Hanson 1975). Traits in themselves are not distinct or unique unless they have meaning for the peoples themselves. The work of Clifford Geertz has been influential in this area: he considers culture as a web of meaning which must be interpreted. He defines culture as: 'An ensemble of texts, themselves ensembles, which the anthropologist strains to read over the shoulders of those to whom they properly belong' (1973:452). However, Geertz' approach does not break away completely from the idea of an objective description of traits; he sees culture from an aesthetic angle which blends logic, meaning, and value into an ordered worldview and style of life (which he calls *ethos*). Culture acts as a template for behaviour which stands behind social forms and processes, providing meaning.

More recent postmodernist writers on culture go further to take meaning away from any notion of an objective 'scientific description' of cultural traits. The patterns of meaning which are 'described' are really interpretations. Ethnography thus becomes a re-interpretation of indigenous perspectives of the world, and the authority of the anthropological account has to be questioned (Clifford 1983:132-33). The recognition of meaning and interpretation in questions of cultural heritage is important because it allows for flexibility and innovation. Culture is no longer a static reproduction of tradition, but something which is lived.

However, using this interpretative approach can lead to an overly relativistic sense of what is reflected in culture. From a somewhat static and traditionalistic view, cultural relativism, taken to extremes, undermines any sense of cultural heritage altogether, leaving only flux and aesthetics.

An important factor which the interpretative approach does not consider is how cultural heritage relates to the identity of persons and peoples. Although close, the relationship between a people and culture is not necessarily isomorphic. Peoples is a concept which is embedded in social life and constitutes some notion of society or sociality. Culture is not the same as society, but rather is acquired and expressed socially. Bidney (1953:26) expresses this as follows:

> 'The category of the social and that of the cultural are not identical, as is commonly supposed, since there may be social phenomena which are not

cultural facts such as the size of a given population, and cultural phenomena which are not social, such as the creation of a poem by an individual.'

To reflect cultural heritage in its full sense, a sense of process connecting culture to social and political contexts is necessary.

c. Culture and Process

Several writers have tried to draw together the social aspects of cultural transmission and change by looking at processes. Wagner (1981) argues that rather than being constantly interpreted, culture is regularly being created. He also provides clear examples of the ethnocidal implications of this dynamic view of culture:

> 'If our culture is creative, then the "cultures" we study, as other examples of this phenomenon must also be. For every time we make others part of a "reality" that we alone invent, denying their creativity by usurping the right to create, we *use* these people and their of life and make them subservient to ourselves.' (1981:16)

This approach makes the power difference between interpretations crucial.

Scholte (1986:10) posits some of the questions which should be raised in this context by suggesting that we should ask not what cultures mean but how they are produced and maintained as authoritative systems. Whose version of the culture is treated as 'authentic'? In many cases outsiders' interpretations impose themselves hegemonically upon indigenous peoples. Scholte's critique offers a perspective of culture as interpretation and meaning, but placed within a social and political context. This worldview relates persons to the collectivity as a whole and demarcates boundaries between peoples, but different perspectives of culture, both internally and externally, lead to social and political conflicts.

The protection of culture in this context concerns the capacity of indigenous peoples to assert their own cultural views over and above those of outsiders. A socio-political dynamism is incorporated into the analysis of cultural heritage which draws in questions such as invasions of territory, disintegration of identity, and the clash between indigenous and non-indigenous. This, from an indigenous perspective, is significant because it shows that cultural protection cannot be isolated from the other aspects of indigenous rights (Gray 1995a).

These three different approaches to culture are all relevant to an understanding of cultural heritage. The traits approach expresses the imagery of culture while the hermeneutic view allows for flexibility. However, the notion of culture as process is important here because it looks not only at creation, but also at the conflict between different cultural perspectives. This is the heart of the problem facing indigenous peoples such as the Arakmbut.[5]

Friedman (1989) links together the concept of culture in the different forms above into a process which is a useful starting point for reflecting on the Arakmbut. He divides culture into three aspects, where culture does not mean a fixed bounded entity, but spheres of influence and processes of creation and tradition. He calls 'Culture I' the 'culture of the social analysis'. It is imposed from outside and consists of the interpretations and traits noted by observers and then transformed through analysis or political ideology into an 'objectified' account of a people. This relates to Wagner's concern in the quotation above, in which he points to our perspective of culture oppressing indigenous conceptualisations. This can take two related forms: one is a hegemonic set of interpretations of culture which are imposed on indigenous peoples, while the other is the presence of an alien culture used to destroy or diminish the local indigenous cultural worldview. Both use the form of cultural traits as a means of classification.

Indigenous culture Friedman calls 'Culture II'. This is indigenous self-identification of culture, distinct from outsiders' conceptualisations. It is constructed on the basis of local interpretations and traits without any necessary reference to outside influences, although clearly the dynamics of cultural change will account for flexibility and innovation based on external influences. Indigenous culture II is under the control of local people and is life carried on without threat or hindrance. This is where the notion of culture as meaning becomes relevant.

'Culture III' refers to the moment when indigenous peoples use their cultures as a basis for demanding their rights. The result is a distinct culture which is not only different from those of other peoples, but also from the state in which they live. This consists of an assertion of culture, in which imagery and information become elements in an act of self-determination against colonisation. Here culture becomes a politically dynamic process.

Rather than see this classification as three types or even aspects of culture, in an Amazonian context they form part of a tension which

5. Thompson has tried to draw together the breadth of criteria which can be seen as cultural as follows 'Meaningful actions, objects and expressions of various kinds – in relation to the historically specific and socially structured contexts and processes within which, and by means of which, [they] are produced, transmitted and received' (Thompson 1990:136).

is never resolved. The clash between Culture I and Culture II is that between cultural perspectives of the national society and the indigenous community. It provides the context from which Culture III can emerge. When external cultural hegemony begins to threaten the internal indigenous culture, a shift takes place by which Culture III becomes self-aware of the indigenous Culture II. It is no longer taken for granted, but becomes incorporated into the indigenous struggle.

This phenomenon appeared earlier in the discussion on peoples and territory, and can be used as an example of the process whereby the Arakmbut became aware of their rights at the moment that they sensed outrage at injustice. There the conflict between the Arakmbut and the outsiders led to the formation of a political consciousness and an assertion of their territory and identity directly aimed at the national society.

This chapter continues by looking at culture in an Arakmbut context. Rather than using one detailed case study, the approach is to reflect the fragmentary nature of culture by presenting scenarios, rather as in a slide show. In each case the Arakmbut have taken a different course in relating to external views of themselves. However, before reviewing these areas it is useful to look at how the Arakmbut see culture.

Arakmbut Culture

Scene one: Ireyo

'Ireyo o'nopwe' (Ireyo knows). With these words, and maybe a slight chuckle, the Arakmbut of San José will point the freshly picked anthropologist in the direction of a house which veers sharply to one side. The house looks as if a strong wind almost blew it over one day, which is what happened, but that is another story (see chapter eight). Ireyo might be sitting at a seat outside of his house, or the visitor might catch him gingerly treading his way back from a gold beach or a garden. He limps, he is almost blind, he his hair is receding, and he is an elder.

Ireyo is in his seventies. He is a Yaromba Wandakweri from the Wakutangeri maloca and remembers the first time the Arakmbut encountered a white person, Padre José Alvarez. He has a striking hole in his nostril which comes from his having passed through the first initiation ceremony (*e'ohot* – nose-piercing), although he says he had no wish to have his lip pierced in the second stage of initiation. He lives with his brother and another bachelor, but he is close to a neighbouring household, run by a woman in the same clan. She is fond of him and offers him food, and he cures for the household. She often prompts him to tell a story or discuss different species and, although not as vocal as he, she also has an extensive knowledge of Arakmbut cultural life.

Arakmbut elders are often the butt of jokes; they are given nicknames and mercilessly teased. But they give as good as they get and are respected for their knowledge. Ireyo is no exception. From my first visit to San José in 1980, Ireyo was chosen by the community as the teller of stories. Initially, this may have been because the other elders could not be bothered to devote time to visitors, but as he had no children and earned little gold, he managed to gain a few things from the relationship. Ireyo never asks for money; however, a small gift or something useful is never refused in return for a story or song.

In 1980, Ireyo began to teach me about the Arakmbut by singing some songs. I had wondered about myths and asked if he knew any. 'Oh yes', he said with a smile. After I had been in the community about six weeks, he came one day and said 'Wanamey, ijmbajpagai' (I will tell Wanamey). The tape recorder was ready and the process of learning about the Arakmbut entered a new phase. Every month or so he would come with another myth, until after eighteen months, he had stretched out the information he wanted me to have to coincide with my stay.

This was the first time that he had told the stories into a tape-recorder. When I had left the community, other visitors came, also asking for myths. Ireyo then hit upon a useful ploy. He acquired a tape-recorder from a departing guest and proceeded to tape his myths. As the next visitor arrived, he offered to play the tape (for a small gift, 'not money', he would insist).

During the 1991-92 period, I saw Ireyo outside his house one day and we began discussing species of plants. Before I knew what had happened, he had me with my notebook (usually the Arakmbut do not like researchers to use a notebook unless they suggest it) giving lists of plantains, yuca, fruits, and pineapples. He knew, for example, seventeen types of pineapple, far above the three or four used by Peruvian agronomists. A few days later, he came to our house and said, 'I want to sing you the curing songs'. Then he began to chant a dozen or so, each of which attracts the spirit harming the patient by listing species after species of animal, tree, plant, bird, or fish, sometimes in their own animal language. At the climax of the chant the harmful spirit is frightened away by calling out the name of a predator. Hundreds of species passed his lips, each one with its place in the performance. A few nights later he cured the small child of the woman in the neighbouring household.

Ireyo is not a prepossessing shaman, he is a quiet, unassuming man who knows what he needs to survive. He is one of the repositories of Arakmbut knowledge, and through his understanding and sensitivity he keeps all those facets of life which could be termed culture alive in his person. Already there are a few younger men to whom he is trying to pass on his knowledge through informal instruction; however, the men and women who live nearby pick up a considerable amount of information from Ireyo on a daily basis; Arakmbut knowledge is being passed on.

Ireyo brings together different cultural activities: singing, storytelling, knowledge of species and curing chants. He is a living illustration of the areas addressed in this chapter. On the whole, a visitor talks more to Arakmbut men than women, because they are the people most oriented outwards from the house and to some extent act as a barrier around the household. This is not to say that women do not have equally diverse knowledge, but they would be reluctant to tell a myth on a tape-recorder and usually cure or tell stories within the household. When Ireyo was telling the information about plant species, the woman of the household was sitting with him, prompting and learning from him at the same time. The fact that women are less open about their knowledge does not imply that they are not experts in Arakmbut cultural activities.

The Arakmbut rarely talk about cultural rights. Indeed I have not heard anyone talking about culture who has not been involved politically or who has not completed the Peruvian school system. On the occasions when they mentioned 'culture' they used the Spanish word *cultura* to Spanish-speakers because there is no overriding concept of 'culture' in Arakmbut. This is not to say that the Arakmbut do not have a culture. It is one thing not to have a word for a concept and it is another to lack any equivalent.

Several of the features which have been mentioned above in the discussion of culture have names in Harakmbut. *Atay* means language, while *waha* means 'Arakmbut words'. Language is a fundamental feature of Arakmbut identity, and binds together all the members of a community. No outsider has found learning Arakmbut easy, and one has to be careful when attempting to learn the language that one is not encroaching on other peoples' identities. All the Arakmbut can speak their language to some extent, but the complexities of the words mean that there are specialised features of the speech which only older people really understand.

Speech is a useful starting point for cultural self-identity as Arakmbut, although it is not the only factor in identity. Several people who speak the language are not Arakmbut but Matsigenka, while there are a few Arakmbut who do not speak their language but who are genealogically Arakmbut and are consequently recognised as such. However in spite of these exceptions, language is extremely important for the Arakmbut and it is an initial marker for defining someone as the member of one of the communities.

Being Arakmbut is not simply speaking the language, it also refers to knowing *(e'nopwe)* about phenomena which are only available to Arakmbut. This means not just knowing the words (waha) of the language, but the names (wandik) of classification. Someone who is familiar with Arakmbut cultural life can demonstrate the knowledge of these names in different ways. Ireyo is a prime example. To be able to speak *(e'apak)* knowledgeably involves knowing not only words but names. In the same way both words and names are needed to tell stories *(e'mbachapak),* to cure *(e'manoka'e)* or to sing *(e'machinoa).* Unlike words, names contain a spiritual dimension.

Arakmbut mythology shows that the power of names come from the spirit world.[6] In the first myth Ireyo told me, after the descent of the tree Wanamey, the woodpecker Mbegnko named the clans and the relationship terminology. Other names of important animals, trees and people arise in stories and curing chants. Mbegnko also has the form of the Inca Manco, who once appeared at a cave in the headwaters of the Ishiriwe, from where he taught the Arakmbut how to grow maize and make chicha (maize beer) and axes. Knowledge is not simply the capacity to think but also the skill to carry out certain activities.

Arakmbut knowledge comes originally from the spirit world, to which people can supplement their knowledge with observation and experiment. However knowledge is exclusively Arakmbut, and is taught to the young by the elders. The ability to understand the world and to utilise this knowledge for the benefit of the community arises from a mediating relationship of the Arakmbut between the spiritual invisible and material visible worlds. The visible and invisible worlds in themselves are not Arakmbut, but the way in which

---

6. When I returned to San José in 1985, I presented my thesis to the community. The old men were not too interested in the descriptions and explanatory models of the text, but they were very interested in the *wandik* – the names of mythological persona, clan names, the terminology, songs, aspects of the spirit world. All these names were fundamental to knowledge.

human beings interrelate with them produces and reproduces a corpus of knowledge which would be incommunicable to non-Arakmbut without some explanation.

Knowledge and skills grow throughout a lifetime. The way in which they are received, adapted and used is all part of the repertoire of Arakmbut culture. Whereas the source of knowledge comes ultimately from outside, its learning reception, processing, interpretation, and use is all a part of internal Arakmbut cultural activity. Knowledge refers to both human and non-human phenomena. Classification is therefore a part of Arakmbut self-identity, even though its origin stems largely from the spirit world, particularly social classification which originated at the origin period of Wanamey. However, knowledge is not just classification but its concrete application.

All production activities involve the practical application of names based on a blending of visible and invisible factors. For example, the term e'nopwe can be used to connote skill in activities such as hunting, fishing, gathering, tending chacras and even working gold. Although Ireyo is too old to be a hunter, he does some fishing and gardening; however, his strength is in his knowledge of species, which is useful for curing and cultivation. Furthermore, any form of craftsmanship, such as making bows and arrows, string bags, or canoes, involves knowledge which is Arakmbut in style and manner. Articles of material culture are products of the relationship between Arakmbut, the invisible spirit world, and the visible material world.

In the past the Arakmbut had a vibrant material culture which has been described in detail by Califano (1982). This not only included artifacts but body painting, which expressed both social and spiritual relationships. To some extent material culture constitutes a non-verbal form of communication. The person who made the artifact invests part of his or her nokiren (soul) in the material and consequently part of that person's personality and skill can be evaluated on the basis of the finished product. Similarly, a hunter's marksmanship, a fisherman's ability to predict fish movements, a gatherer's memory, and a gold worker's sense for a dried up river bed are all faculties which demonstrate a person's knowledge.

Knowledge which comes from the outside invisible and visible worlds is combined with language to provide the means to utilise the material potential in the world and to ensure good health *(ndak)*. Ndak means 'good' and also 'healthy'. When you meet someone you can ask them 'pa ndak i'e?' which means 'are you well?' This signifies not just good health but also well-being. Health is the sign that the Arakmbut universe is in order. The primary signs of good health are a reliable supply of meat and garden produce provided without upsetting the spirit world by overkilling or over-eating prohibited species. Furthermore health means complying with social expectations and not transgressing the prohibited categories of sexual relations and appropriate behaviour towards people in respective relationship categories.

Health is a primary preoccupation of the Arakmbut because well-being is also a state of contentedness. When people are well the universe is well too, but the forces fighting against that healthiness are numerous. In the first place, there are harmful spirits (toto) who attack transgressors and anyone they come across by chance in the forest or river. Secondly there are non-indigenous people (wahaipi, meaning highlanders, or Amiko, meaning foreigners), who are also dangerous because they bring sickness and threaten the community with encroachment and invasion. The case of Ireyo shows how health is connected with knowledge; only through understanding species and their relationships is it possible to diagnose sickness and choose the right chindign for curing.

In order to place the features described here within an Arakmbut cultural context, it is impossible to say that religion + language + knowledge + technology = culture. This would be to fragment the way in which the Arakmbut relate to the visible and invisible worlds and forcibly to dissect their culture into constituent parts. Instead, a more useful approach is to see the word e'nopwe covering three dimensions:

1. E'nopwe means knowledge of the words and names of language. Through language, the Arakmbut define themselves while referring to the visible and invisible worlds.
2. E'nopwe refers to skills which, by acting on the material world, can transform the potential of the environment into products for Arakmbut well-being.
3. E'nopwe includes spiritual experience, by which the Arakmbut learn from communication with the invisible world how far they can utilise the potential in the environment without transgressing the health of the cosmos. Furthermore the spirit world provides the power for transforming the material visible world and the names for controlling that power.

These three types of activity provide the connections between the visible and invisible worlds, linking human beings, natural resources, and spirituality. The position of the Arakmbut means that they have the task of trying to balance the cosmos as much as possible in order to ensure their continuation and reproduction.

Instead of a culture consisting of language, religion, material culture, and knowledge, the Arakmbut link linguistic, spiritual, and production activities by bringing together the visible and invisible worlds through e'nopwe. Well-being and good health for the Arakmbut consist of the shamans' striving to ensure a constructive relationship with the spirit world.

Each Arakmbut person learns through life the knowledge appropriate to his or her age, gender, and clan affiliation. This knowledge is shared according to the social co-ordinates which were reviewed in the last chapter. At the broadest level of basic language skills everyone shares identity as Arakmbut but this becomes more differentiated, particularly with age. Older people know more of the subtleties within the Arakmbut language and are often capable of conversing with different species and spirits through the curing chants (chindign). Men and women learn gender-specific techniques of production and knowledge from elders of the same sex who teach them chants, ways of planting, and hunting or gathering techniques. Knowledge is not limited to members of the same clan. Women's knowledge in a patrilineal clan system will always change clan as it is passed down from mother to daughter. However, curing and other spirit techniques are most frequently passed down by males of the same clan, which causes information to cluster among the members.

Knowledge not only ensures health for the community, but also establishes its potential for reproduction. A continuity of knowledge connects the generations, with each adult passing on the information which he or she learned from his or her parents. This collective memory builds up a corpus of information which each generation can take on, develop, or reject according to its own experience and inclination. Ireyo's desire to teach his knowledge to younger generations is crucial for the continuity of Arakmbut identity.

The sharing of knowledge, language, and expertise draws people together as Arakmbut in a shared identity, but at the same time distinguishes people from each other within that framework. These cultural activities operate on the basis of the same social distinctions and categories of classification mentioned in the previous chapter, such as gender, age, residence, patrilineal descent, kin, and marriage relations.

The broad notions of culture analysed in this chapter are thus buried within the general term 'Arakmbut'. In order to see what culture could mean for the Arakmbut we have to unravel the word Arakmbut itself. There is no single word for culture or society because they are fused within the notion of 'people'. It is not that culture and society do not exist, but that they are embedded in different terms.[7]

The name Arakmbut unifies the fragmented notion of culture and society by connecting the identity of each person to the Arakmbut people as a whole, through knowledge. There is, as yet, no connection between the notion of e'nopwe and 'culture', but the terms could be seen as equivalent. However, until that connection is made, the notion will remain within Arakmbut identity. This section began with a profile of Ireyo; he is a prime example how the fragmentation of phenomena that is culture can be brought together in an Arakmbut person.

Another area in which Arakmbut cultural fragmentation is brought together is through the physical landscape of territory. All myths, songs, species knowledge, and curing chants relate to specific places in the forest or by the rivers. The connection between the concept of Arakmbut and their territory is critical for grasping the unity of their sense of identity. For this reason, the notions of territory and peoples discussed in the last chapter should be seen as providing the co-ordinates for drawing cultural fragmentation into a coherent framework.

Ireyo presents Arakmbut cultural activities and knowledge in the form which Friedman (above) would refer to as Culture II – practical knowledge and meaning around how the Arakmbut relate to each person within the identity of a people rooted in their territory. However the threats to cultural identity come primarily from outsiders, and this is where the Arakmbut have devised forms of protection.

Arakmbut Culture – Destruction, Protection, and Reformulation

Scene 2: The Entertainer

On Sunday 5 October 1991, a strange incident occurred in San José. At about five in the afternoon an man in strange dress appeared in the community. Presumably he had come upriver with some trader, but no one knew who he was. His apparel was very flamboyant – fake gems sparkled on his multi-coloured jacket; his bright trousers, with massive flares, hung at half-mast, and were covered in pearl-like stones; his wide-brimmed hat, wellington boots, and portly demeanour

---

7. When trying to translate terms from Arakmbut, an apparent lack of equivalent concepts does not mean that such concepts do not exist, but that they are subsumed within other terms.

made him appear as a mixture of highland and old-Spanish players. Brandishing his *churanga* (stringed instrument made out of an armadillo), he strummed from house to house shouting and singing, 'I am the entertainer! I will play my churanga with two hands, feet, and teeth!'

The schoolteacher, not renowned for her sense of the absurd, told him not to be so ridiculous and to change his stupid clothes. But he refused and, with a mixture of bluff and charm, got permission to use the school for a performance. It was dark, and Raymundo from the shop was persuaded to take his petromax lamp from his shop and go to the classroom. The entertainer then stood at the school door charging the people half a sol entry ($1). Everyone laughed and gathered around. The teachers ushered the children into the classroom; but the adults waited outside and looked through the slats. I vied with the old man Aika to get a glimpse. But the entertainer was sitting down on a seat. 'No pay. No entertainment.'

The tableau remained static for ten minutes. The children sniggering inside, the adults chuckling outside and an increasingly irate entertainer. Mumbles of 'I told you so', came from the teacher. Eventually, fed up, Raymundo removed the petromax and went home. As the light disappeared so did the Arakmbut. Feeling sorry for the entertainer, Isaias invited him to his house for a bite to eat and a bed to sleep in – in return for a performance.

'He was a load of old rubbish!' said Isaias the next day, and the entertainer disappeared as quickly as he had arrived.

This bizarre story demonstrates several aspects of the Arakmbut attitude to outside culture (Culture I). They are suspicious, sceptical, and by no means receptive to new ideas without good reason. The ability to ridicule external cultural influences is in itself a defence against unwanted imposition. Culture I in this sense places the Arakmbut at the bottom of a hierarchical set of traits. The entertainer could not understand why the Arakmbut were not attracted to his strange appearance and skills; however, he did not realise that the history of colonisation does not automatically attract the Arakmbut to outsiders, particularly those they consider charlatans.

Another feature in the scene which caused a reaction was the entertainer's desire to charge for his performance. This is something which Ireyo regularly reiterated; people should not charge for providing entertainment and carrying out cultural activities. The person who shares his or her knowledge and skills gains prestige in return, and this should be sufficient reward in itself. The effect is that the

Arakmbut are opposed to the commodification of knowledge. This is significant when considering that benefit-sharing is the assumed procedure for compensating indigenous peoples for their knowledge according to Agenda 21 from the Rio Summit and the Convention on Biological Diversity.

The Arakmbut dealt with the entertainer by ignoring him until he left. They knew that they had the upper hand, because he was a travelling individual. However there are different problems when external cultural influences involve aspects of the quality of life which the Arakmbut desire, but which are tied to hegemonic control. The picture of Arakmbut culture becomes more complicated when taking into consideration the transformation which it has undergone over the last forty years and the way they have incorporated aspects of national life and lost some of their own cultural practices. Particularly influential have been three areas: new technology; western medicine; and education in Spanish. In each case the Arakmbut have managed the delicate relationship according to their own values.

These new elements from the culture of the national society have had the effect of introducing phenomena which are potentially destructive for Arakmbut culture while providing material and services which they need and desire. The result is that the discussion of Arakmbut culture blends together two different aspects of human rights: the protection of the Arakmbut from cultural genocide, and their right to facilities and services, such as health and education, which should pertain to all living in the country. This chapter will now look at three different ways in which the Arakmbut have overcome the conflict between their culture and the forces of the state.

Technology

Scene three: A visit from Chino Walter

Chino Walter, a non-Arakmbut trader, is almost part of the Karene landscape. He has drifted through the area for years, never settling in one place for longer than it takes to fall out with his neighbours. Chino wears his ubiquitous khaki shorts and a variety of tee-shirts, which sets him apart from other traders and colonists who prefer the less-sporty longtrousers and plain shirts. His main characteristic is to dazzle his listeners with a barrage of extraordinary stories and opinions. He stands with his head slightly cocked and looks his listener straight in the eye.

'Honest, I tell you, it's true', he said to me one day at Boca Colorado as he nabbed me along with a young Arakmbut man with Matsigenka relations from Puerto Luz.

'At least a metre across, every one of them ... Never have I seen coca leaves like them ... Up in the headwaters, they are ... Near that group of Matsigenkas ... Incredible, they are ... Two and a half metres high at least ... Savage? I'll give you savage ... They could shoot you blindfolded ... Before you know you where you are ...'

'I can imagine', said our Arakmbut companion inscrutably.

Chino's latest wheeze is to take a video and screen around to the communities and show films. Powered by a small generator, Chino asks for a general sum from the community and shows his latest collection of films about Alien, Commando, Rambo, or other examples of international culture. Particularly disconcerting for the fresh anthropologist, unwary of Chino's arrival, is to be sitting quietly in an evening, listening to the insects, toads, and other beasts of the night, only to have it interrupted by the deafening ululations of Tarzan and an elephant trumpeting from a few houses away.

Chino made a visit to San José late in May. It was a Friday evening and he negotiated with Pedro, a community leader, to show a few films at his house, which was the largest in the community. Aliens, Tarzan, and Rambo were on the agenda; Ireyo and I sat in the cool evening, smoked, and talked. Sheila, Robbie, and everyone else crowded into the house to watch the films until late into the night. Tarzan got the greatest response; it was received as a comedy – everything was totally unreal. The twenty-minute fight with the anaconda had the Arakmbut rolling in the aisles.

The following day at breakfast we discussed the other films with several Arakmbut. The comments came thick and fast:

'Fantastic film, that Rambo. Very exciting,' said one man.
'Is it true?' asked another.
'No.'
'But I thought it was a documentary. Do you mean the film is a lie?'
'It's not true.'
'If that's the case, the film is rubbish. It is just made up.'
'By the way, we should get a video and generator in the community.'

Chino Walter brings entertainment – someone in the community who has found more gold than usual will often pay for the evening and so most people see the films for nothing. The Arakmbut enjoy themselves and use the films as a means of learning about the outside world. Areas where the Arakmbut had experience, such as the rainforest, made them amused at the Tarzan film, but in other contexts, where there is no basis for comparison with experience, distinguishing truth from fiction becomes difficult. This mixture of enthusiasm, scepticism, and acquisitiveness is common with new technology and has followed then since before they ever saw a white person. The end of the description above shows the Arakmbut eager to try out new technology. Throughout their history, they have been open to innovation, but based on a pragmatic sense of use and danger.

a) Technological incorporation

The greatest technological effect on the Arakmbut came in the 1950s with the introduction of metal tools (Califano 1977:186). I was told by an old man in the community of Barranco Chico that the first machetes and axes of metal made a considerable difference in cutting chacras and building houses. The effort and time taken to cut a tree were both reduced. The first move by the Wandakweri to the headwaters of the Ishiriwe was in search of metal goods.[8] The word *siro* was employed for metal and with the morphemes of shape, the Arakmbut were able to create words in their own language for the new technology such as *siropi* for pin or *siropo* for pot (Hart 1983).

Metal goods were used to attract the Arakmbut during their first contacts with the missionaries. Initially goods were dropped upon the Ishiriwe area in the early 1950s by plane. The Arakmbut elders can remember the first planes and thought that they were suspended from the sky by creepers. The most coveted articles were machetes (which were divided by cutting them with sharp stones), knives, and cooking pots. Some shot was also dropped, with which the Arakmbut experimented until the detonators went off.

However people began to die as a result of dealing with these new goods (Wahl 1987:256). Old men in San José gave me a long list of people who died at this time. Initially people thought that sorcery was to blame and some women were killed who had fallen under suspicion. Meanwhile, Arakmbut who received the goods thought that they were dangerous and tried to bury or wash the pollution away. Thus metal goods were seen as something positive and cov-

---

8. Califano (1977) gives several explanations of the origin of metal goods from Amiko of various colours which connect with the origin myth of Wanamey. This was not familiar to Arakmbut in San José and possibly comes from another group

eted, but at the same time something to be feared as they brought disease and death.

This was further proven as the entry of metal goods increased strife between the Arakmbut and other neighbouring peoples. The Sapiteri and Wachipaeri fought over metal goods, and there is a story of how one man discovered that metal goods could kill more effectively than stones and used them as weapons. The Arakmbut began to move their malocas towards the upper Madre de Dios because they thought that the source of the goods came from that direction. The Sowereri from that area fought a particularly bloody war with the Arakmbut over the goods during the early 1950s. Only one Sowereri survives today.

The introduction of new technology, however, did not see the end of the Arakmbut or their material culture. Whereas certain tools disappeared (stone axes, wooden digging sticks, fire sticks, and ceramics for cooking) two elements of Arakmbut material culture remain significant. For a man, these are the bow and arrows which every youth should learn how to make by acquiring the skill from an elder. Women, on the other hand, continue to make their *wenpu* string bags from bark string and weave them on their knees.

The survival of these artifacts is important because they are definitions of adulthood for men and women. Before missionary contact they were exchanged at marriage and all parties would assume that the couple would have these skills. They are the most useful Arakmbut artifacts, because whereas not all men can afford a gun and shot, bows and arrow are particularly apt for fishing or killing animals. At the same time, the string bags are the most practical method of bringing products home from the chacras. Thus the bows, arrows, and bags are still needed.[9]

The effect of metal technology was to make many of the old skills redundant. Nowadays only the old men know how to make and haft stone axes. Some of the younger men know about making fire without matches but only practise the art for amusement. The loss of knowledge about the manufacture of some aspects of pre-contact technology has, therefore, not resulted from any ethnocidal attack by outsiders. The more efficient and convenient technology has replaced the previous methods and no one looks at these changes as a serious loss.

9. I have noticed that Barranco Chico no longer make the string bags and use cloth or other material to bring their products from the chacras. Some people in San José make wicker and rush baskets, but these appear only occasionally.

b) From generosity to dependency

Rather than the dangers of death, new technology, has brought another danger – dependency. The attraction of new technology, was a major force of missionisation. In the early days, when missionaries gave gifts to the Arakmbut, the priests behaved in the same way as beneficial spirits or powerful and generous human beings. Exchange took place through barter, but the Arakmbut were the beneficiaries. José Alvarez (1953:47) describes one Arakmbut as saying:

> 'Brother-in-law, give me a machete. I come with my wife. If you kill her I will be angry. I give you pineapples in exchange for machetes and rope. I have no chacra because I have no machete. I will be hungry. Others were angry because you have not given them machetes.'

The exchange consisted of food in return for machetes. This barter still provided the priests with the means to demonstrate their power by generosity. Generosity is the mark of a beneficial spirit or white 'Amiko'. Furthermore it is the Arakmbut prerequisite for receiving respect as a powerful person. There are many examples of Arakmbut descriptions of good Amiko who came with gifts for them and were stopped by misfortune, or bad people who wanted to divert the benefits elsewhere. The importance of generosity is something which lies at the heart of the Arakmbut political economy in complete contrast to the saving orientation of the non-indigenous economy. Arakmbut expectations of Amiko stem from the fact that they are a source of power (Gow 1991).

The goods initially appeared as gifts, but after a few years, the Arakmbut became dependent on them as commodities for which they had to work and behave appropriately:

> 'The Dominicans, then, do not just attempt to progressively turn highly desired goods from gifts into commodities but, correspondingly, "mystify" the social processes by which this is accomplished – posing these as a matter of "correct" behaviour above all' (Wahl 1987:268).

The overall effect was a dependency which has been described in detail by Fuentes. He argues (1982:68) that the metal tools, and later guns and motors, had the effect of breaking traditional Arakmbut production and internal distribution practices.

The Arakmbut still have a continuous demand for new technology. In San José, for example, the late 1970s saw the Arakmbut working gold with buckets of water poured over their sieves, but from

1979 the community began to work with a motor pump, and ten years later they are looking at the possibility of using dredges. All jumps in technology are costly; most people do not have the money to obtain them immediately and eventually buy them from itinerant merchants on a long-term debt repayment. The result is a dependence which has taken over from the debts which occurred during the period at the mission of Shintuya. However, the Arakmbut communities in the Madre de Dios do not work for other people and so at least they are free from the enslavement of labour debt bondage which plagues other indigenous peoples of the Peruvian Amazon (Gray & Hvalkof 1990).

The goods introduced from outside provide advantages for the Arakmbut in terms of increased production and easier working conditions. However at the same time they can be the cause of unfair trade and indebtedness; unscrupulous merchants can bind a household into monetary commitments way beyond their means. The negative effects of technological innovation has consequently been primarily social and economic rather than cultural. The advantages have to be weighed in the light of dangers of becoming economically bound to creditors.

The Arakmbut have largely consented to changes in their material culture. However this is not to say that the Arakmbut are prepared to drop their own cultural identity simply to gain material goods and access to the power of the Amiko. With technology, the Arakmbut have taken a risk and incorporated many elements of non-indigenous technology into their lives. This has had little effect on their sense of identity but has brought socio-economic risks.

Religion and Health

Scene four: Ametra

One morning in June 1992, Isaias invited me to come into the forest with him to look at some plants for curing. I was somewhat taken aback; the Arakmbut cure primarily with curing songs based on animal characteristics. Plants such as tobacco and isanga nettles are occasionally used, and women elders are familiar with resins and leaves which they use for bathing patients. Nevertheless, compared to the Shipibo or Matsigenka, the Arakmbut do not have a large pharmacopoeia.

We set off and he pointed out some plants, liana and leaves. 'That is our ayahuasca. My brother and father plant it, because it is increasingly hard to find'. I assiduously wrote as much as I could remember and tried to understand why I had never heard this information before. Clearly I had misunderstood Arakmbut health methods – I must have been stupid to have missed all this. We continued walking through the forest, and after about twenty minutes began to return to San José.

'I had no idea you used these plants'.
'Oh yes', he said.
'But who taught you them?'
'Oh I learned at a course on traditional medicine in Puerto Maldonado a few years ago. You know – the Ametra project'.

Then I began to grasp what was happening. In 1986 a traditional medicine organisation called Ametra was established in the Madre de Dios to promote herbal medicines among the indigenous communities of the region. Based on the experience of the Ametra traditional medicine project in Pucallpa with the Shipibo, the Shipibo of the Madre de Dios and the Ese'eja worked together to build up a basic catalogue of plants and their effects which can help to cure diseases without recourse to non-indigenous western medicines.

Various people from San José had been on the courses, and the information which they had learnt was being incorporated into the health practices of the community. Exactly the same thing had occurred with ayahuasca, the hallucinogen, in the late 1970s, when a Shipibo from Tres Islas, a community near Puerto Maldonado, taught several young Arakmbut men how to prepare and use the visionary vine. They brought the technique to the San José and now it has become a part of Arakmbut curing practices.

I returned to the household where we stayed most of the time and spoke to a group of men. 'Oh yes', one said 'Ametra is useful. But these plants – you have to watch them, the information comes from other peoples who use them for sorcery. What is more, white people have been near the mission in Shintuya and they are taking these plants away. Soon all our knowledge will be taken away and people will make money out of us. Whatever you do you can't win.'

This series of conversations about Ametra bring together a range of contradictory opinions about health and religion.[10] When interested, the Arakmbut learn new information and incorporate it into their

---

10. Alexiades (1987) and Lacaze & Alexiades (nd.) provide a background to the project which has since been taken over by FENAMAD as part of its indigenous health programme.

medical practice. However, curing is intimately related to the spirit world, and any knowledge which comes from other indigenous peoples can be potentially dangerous because it could be connected to sorcery practices. Furthermore, white people are famous for wanting to commercialise plants for their own purposes, and an Arakmbut concern is that outsiders will steal and then commercialise knowledge. Acceptance, rejection and fear of exploitation are the three connected reactions of the Arakmbut to new knowledge.

Ametra combines all of these concerns because it promotes a 'traditional medicine' which is distinct from Arakmbut practices, but it also brings into relief the difference between indigenous and white medicine. For the Arakmbut, Ametra is primarily a Shipibo initiative (some of the original trainers came from Pucallpa and many of the ideas are Shipibo-derived). This makes the traditional medicine programme dangerous but capable of being incorporated into Arakmbut practices, while white medicine cannot be so easily incorporated. This distinction marks a contrast to the incorporation of non-indigenous technology into Arakmbut life.

a) Arakmbut health and western medicine

The Arakmbut spirit world is one of a potentiality which animates the visible world from which it receives its form (see Volume 1, chapter eight). The order of the universe is manifest in health (ndak) through a regular supply of food and commodities from production activities. Furthermore, an understanding of the spirit world by means of passing on myths and philosophical speculation helps to keep people in good health.

Arakmbut illnesses have physical symptoms but spiritual causes. Elsewhere (Volume 2, chapters three to five) I have described in detail the spiritual aspects of Arakmbut curing which comes from the wayorokeri (dreamer shamans) and the wamanoka'eri (curing shamans). A healthy person is one who has a constructive relationship with the spirit world. A sick person has fallen out with the spirits for three possible reasons:

1. Sorcery. In this case a wayorokeri or wamenoka'eri from another community has attacked the sick person by spiritual means. There is little which can be done to cure the patient.
2. Spirit attack. The patient in these cases has transgressed the accepted behaviour by overhunting, carrying out unacceptable sexual relations, or treating the forest or river without respect.

3. Accidental spirit encounter. This takes place in the forest or river and is considered an unfortunate accident.

Healing consists of a shamanic process whereby these different causes are discussed and sometimes even fought over in the search for a cure. During this process, different treatments are used until a successful cure is found. This may involve Arakmbut curing chants or visions and some Ametra plant remedies. Whereas these approaches might be difficult for an outsider to distinguish, western medicine is clearly distinct.

The connection between the spirit world of the Arakmbut and Christianity began when the Arakmbut were first attracted to the mission for material goods; the need for medicines was a fundamental incentive. During 1956 a yellow fever epidemic hit the Arakmbut communities of the Ishiriwe. There was a difference of opinion within the communities. Some Arakmbut thought that sorcery was responsible and several women were killed. Others however had a different theory; they thought that the deaths had been caused by the Christian God and that they had to go to the mission for medicines. The 'long march' from the Ishiriwe was a tragic event in Arakmbut history. One typical story was told to us by a woman in San José. Her mother became ill with yellow fever. Her father decided to try to reach the mission and carried his wife there in his arms with his children following. When he arrived at Shintuya his wife was dead from the disease, and he himself died soon afterwards.

The missionaries provided the medicines and, to a large extent, reduced the death rate of the Arakmbut. However for the first few years in Shintuya people continued to die regularly. It was interpreted that the medicines of the priests were powerless against certain illnesses.

The explanation was that during the rubber boom at the turn of the century, many Toyeri were murdered by white colonists and their souls moved into Arakmbut territory seeking victims. This explains why, even though other indigenous peoples' medicine such as Ametra is used, sorcery plagues traditional medical work in Arakmbut communities.

Whereas white people were the original causes of most Arakmbut illnesses, only Christian diseases can be cured by God's medicines, spirit diseases have to be cured by the wayorokeri and wamanoka'eri. The result is a clear division of powers between the Arakmbut and the Amiko medical systems. Ametra provides a form of 'alternative indigenous medicine' which can supplement Arakmbut medicine, but it does not alter the basic division between spiritual and Christian illness.

b) Ceremony and health

The hegemonic pressure of the priests has had a considerable effect on Arakmbut religion, particularly the ceremonial features connected with providing health and strength. Over the last forty years several features of Arakmbut culture connected with religion and ceremonial rights have disappeared:

1. The communal house (maloca), which has been replaced by individual houses, contained at the centre a ceremonial space which was used for feasts and rituals. These no longer take place. The songs are remembered by some of the old men who sing them at fiestas but the dancing is very rarely performed.
2. All of the material features of Arakmbut ceremonies have similarly disappeared. The *tayagnpi* (feathered stick for coca lime), *tangka* (headresses), *machinoa* (feathered shoulder ornament with snail shell rattles for dances), and *tombi* (snail rattles without the feathers) are rarely made except for the curiosity of outsiders such as anthropologists.
3. Body paint continues in rough red (achiote – *mantoro*) or black (huito -*o*) patches on the body to protect the nokiren and waso from spirit attacks. However, the detailed body designs which were reproduced by Califano (1982) no longer exist. Furthermore, without the ceremonies, no young man have perforated noses or lips which were once marks of their initiation.

Contact with missionaries consisted of moves to 'civilise' the Arakmbut by providing them with clothes, settling them in the mission, teaching them Spanish and training them in farming and carpentry (Aikman 1994). The Dominican priests had a theoretical explanation for this process and, in the 1930s, they carried a series of articles in their journal about 'savagery and civilisation'. According to Osende (1933:230) savagery is the way in which human beings imitate their environment; their learning models are based on animal behaviour, particularly monkeys. The key point in this philosophy is that 'man always adopts an interior attitude which corresponds to his exterior' (ibid.). The missionary task was designed to replace the 'savage imitation' of the environs with a higher model based on Christian morality. Thus the starting point for missionary influence was to provide the Arakmbut with clothes, work on the gradual eradication of all visible aspects of their culture, in the hope that they would eventually abandon these external trappings of culture and change internally into 'civilised Peruvians'.

This religious philosophy provides the means to understand why so many visible attributes of Arakmbut culture disappeared during the first five years of life at the mission. The priests provided the means of protection against the sickness and death which surrounded the Arakmbut communities, while at the same time dangled the prospect of material goods in front of them. The esteemed position of the missionaries was taught, and is still taught, at the community schools, while it receives fundamental reinforcement from the attitudes of colonists who live around the Arakmbut.

However, the Arakmbut are a strong people who are not easily intimidated into abandoning important cultural aspects of their lives. Ascertaining from the Arakmbut why their ceremonies disappeared while they were in Shintuya is not easy. Some people say that the priests forbade the ceremonies, but others say that they were *e'mbira* (embarrassed) by their customs and traditions and so voluntarily stopped them. These positions are not necessarily contradictory. Most are in agreement that embarrassment was the main cause for stopping the ceremonies while the embarrassment itself derived from the non-indigenous 'Amiko'. However, whatever happened, the attraction which the Arakmbut had for goods and medicines when they first went to the mission drew them into a set of relations with a very strong hegemonic power which considered them inferior.

A important part of the rejection of the old ceremonies by the Arakmbut was that they seemed no longer efficacious after the enormous number of deaths which took place in the 1950s. In some way, western medicine provided an alternative approach to health. Yet, the Arakmbut are not negative when they talk about their ceremonies. When I discussed the question in San José with several people, the old men and women were genuinely sorry that the Arakmbut no longer dress up in feathers to dance and sing. They commented how enjoyable the ceremonies were and that the feathers and paint were beautiful *(urunda)*.

During the period in the mission, Arakmbut conceptions of religion and health underwent a change. Curing methods of sicknesses caused by spirits continued as before while the ceremonial factor of health control, which the priests did not like, was abandoned in return for which the Arakmbut assumed that the Amiko should assume responsibility for providing medicines. Medicines are still coveted by the communities as a simple way of disposing of superficial sicknesses; when missionaries, teachers or anthropologists come to the communities, they usually bring medicines with them which are distributed to those in need. However, should they be in short supply, the Arakmbut have to go to the trading post of Boca Colorado to buy medicines. Underlying the use of non-indigenous medicines is the conviction that outside diseases are caused by outside forces. For this reason, outsiders are to blame for the sickness and so teachers, missionaries and anthropologists should provide medicines freely. The community frequently complain when they have to buy medicines.

The cause and cure of outside sickness comes from the same source – the Amiko. Underlying Arakmbut thought on this matter is the notion of an exchange. They have taken on the trappings of Christianity and in return expect the means to preserve their health. When non-indigenous peoples are in the community and do not provide medicines, the Arakmbut complain because the exchange is not balanced. The issue here is that health facilities are owed to the Arakmbut and it is their right to receive them. In this context I have never heard an Arakmbut person claiming that their right to express their culture has been denied to them, but I have heard them complaining that they are not receiving medicines and are dying as a consequence.

In contrast to western technology, which is incorporated and blended into Arakmbut daily life, western medicine has a distinct conceptual place separate from spiritual curing. With proliferation of non-indigenous illnesses, the Arakmbut replaced their ceremonies with the visible trappings of Peruvian Christian practices, and they received medicines in return. However, when the medicines are not available, they feel cheated. In this sense medical facilities are a right which they expect for paying respect to the national society and its religion.

Knowledge and Education

Scene five: The school show

On Saturday 30 November 1991, the school concert was put on by the two indefatigable teachers of San José, who had put considerable work into the event. For several weeks, strains of music had frequently wafted from the school and parents had been asked to find bits of cloth or buttons for costumes.

As the evening drew on and people had eaten, Raymundo, as usual, brought over the petromax from his shop and all the community filed in sitting around the edges of the room. The teachers had curtained off part of the room where the children changed, but they made frequent forays onto the central performing area to chastise the occasional erring child. A student who had arrived back from Lima strung a massive collar of snail shells around his neck and became Master of Ceremonies.

The performance started with a young boy, wearing a charcoaled moustache, miming a Mexican number on an old guitar. Then a young girl was Little Red Riding Hood; the wolf didn't frighten her enough, but one of the teachers succeeded where the wolf failed by standing in front of the heroine, arms akimbo until she started to snivel. Clowns tumbled, cockroaches sang, and pigs danced to the delight of the audience. They laughed and cheered as the children appeared and the teacher, unable to resist checking all was in order, emerged to order the children about on the stage.

The climax of the evening was a 'native dance' which the teachers said came from the central rainforest. All the boys and girls were dressed in banana leaves, with feathers in their hair and paint on their faces, dancing in lines and circles. Everyone was delighted. When it was over they all went off to find some beer and celebrate.

This scene is the antithesis of the description of the entertainer above. Here the school put on a performance which was almost as obtuse, and had absolutely nothing Arakmbut in it whatsoever. However, the Arakmbut were delighted with the entertainment, they loved the absurdity and were proud of their children. The fact that none of the items were Arakmbut was quite appropriate, because the school is the centre for all that is not Arakmbut in the community. All of the meetings which take place there are in Spanish and involve non-Arakmbut visitors. Occasionally, the village meets there, but usually, if the weather is dry and bright, they sit outside.

The teachers run the school and have the key to the door. In some respects the school is an aspect of the state which focuses on the non-indigenous element of Arakmbut life. Yet it is at the centre of the village and the communities vie to persuade the local authorities to ensure that the school is in good condition. Indeed, in chapter two, San José and Puerto Luz were prepared to take on the local authorities because they did not support the school. However, the school is about outside knowledge. Arakmbut knowledge is quite different.

a) Arakmbut education and continuity

The continuation of Arakmbut knowledge over time contains two distinct processes of attaining knowledge which have a tense relationship to each other. The first is to learn from older people the ways of the spirits and ancestors who provide the skills and techniques necessary for the continuation of life. These include hunting, fishing (primarily male organising activities), agricultural techniques (particularly important for women), curing, interpretation of dreams, and knowledge of the stories, myths, songs, and dances which constitute Arakmbut historical traditions.

Learning is not an activity which only concerns children and young men, but one which lasts throughout a lifetime. Children learn from their parents and close relatives the basic elements of daily living such as collecting water, gathering, making a fire, looking after babies, and the outlines of stories and songs. As they grow into adolescence, young women learn more about cooking, growing, and tending their gardens, while men learn the rudiments of hunting, fishing, and the way of the forest.

By the time a man and woman marry they are capable of producing children but there is still much they do not know. When a man eventually wants to make his own house there is an extensive knowledge of different tree species which are appropriate for particular features of the building. For example, certain species are avoided by termites and ants, others are good for floor, wall, or roof beams. Certain leaves last longer than others. A well-constructed house can last for up to ten years with the occasional refitting. Similarly a young man will constantly listen to the stories told in the evenings by other hunters to see if it is possible to learn new techniques or skills which will help with his hunting.

A woman will gradually increase her independence as she grows older and will begin to diversify her gardens. Women are knowledgeable about different species of yuca, plantains, pineapples, and other crops. By inter-planting different species of the same crop, the return from the garden is known to be more secure. More difficult crops such as barbasco are particularly important for women to learn. Usually a woman will be independent and mature before she begins to take on the responsibility for the special caring needed. The same goes for peach palm. Probably this is because both crops are semi-domesticated and grow for many years in the purmas (old chacras) and have a sense of being wilder than the species usually consumed.

When a person is a full adult with an independent household, both men and women continue to learn. The very old members of the community teach the younger ones the secrets of curing through chanting, songs, and how to tend gardens with special orations. When an Arakmbut person becomes old, he or she inevitably loses power as they begin the descent to death. However, knowledge does not weaken. An old person will teach a younger adult and try to help him or her carry out a cure or an oration. The difficulty with old age rests in the contradiction between old people and knowledge in contrast with younger people and power. Fusing these two strengths is difficult. Whereas older people do not want to lose their monopoly of knowledge which gives them prestige within the community, they are not strong enough to keep the society healthy. Consequently they need the power and strength of the younger men and women to help them. This is the only way in which knowledge is passed down from one generation to the other. Normally the line of learning passes within the clan from father or uncle to son. However, when there is no older person in the same clan, a maternal grandfather will sometimes teach a younger one. Older men usually prefer to keep their training sessions to one younger adult.

The second way of learning is through revelation. This takes place in the form of dreams or visions (wayorok). All knowledge ultimately comes from the invisible world. The information and experience passed down from one generation to the next stems from relationships between the ancestors when they were alive and the potential world of the spirits. Each generation adds to the knowledge received from the past by means of his or her own experience. Dreams are a frequent way of contacting the spirit world, as are spontaneous visions. The skill at developing new information and having that accepted by the rest of the community, and in some cases, beyond, depends on the reputation of the person (see Volume 2, chapter three).

The recognition of a person's skill in contacting the other world goes a long way to establish his or her reputation as a specialist. The main specialists are dreamers (wayorokeri) and curers (wamenoka'eri), the former who have knowledge direct from the spirit world and the latter who learn the difficult curing chindign. Everyone has some contact with the spirit world when they dream at night. However, the information which they receive is of relevance only to themselves and their close relatives rather than to the community as the whole, which is the responsibility of someone who has more shamanic qualities.

While with the Arakmbut, I discussed in several communities the problem of how knowledge was passed down through the generations. There currently appears to be a crisis among the knowledge specialists of the Arakmbut. Old people say that the youth of today are no longer interested in the old ways. They are interested in making money and listening to rock music, and do not respect the old ways. Whereas this is the case with some young people, when challenged on this point, the young people I spoke to had a different perspective. They explained that they were very keen to learn the chindign and stories of their elders. However, there were many difficulties. In the first place the myths, songs and chants were very difficult to remember and they kept making mistakes and forgetting. The elders were not patient with them, and other younger members of the community thought that they were trying to be too smart by learning the old ways which only the elders should know. Others said that it was difficult to find elders who were prepared to teach the old ways. Some of them felt that the older people had respect in the community which arose from their knowledge, and they did not want to lose this by making it widely available. In particular some old men cured with chindign and charged for the sessions. This supplied them with the basis for their money income, as they could not work gold. If the younger people gained this knowledge the elders would have no means of making money to play their part in the fiestas and to contribute to the households in which they lived.

It is difficult to know whether Arakmbut knowledge is disappearing or not. Clearly one can see that older people are more knowledgeable than younger members of the community. In some cases older members of the family are trying to teach their knowledge to the young ones. There is a perceived crisis. The question we have to consider is whether this has not always been the case. Are younger people not learning the rudiments of hunting or is it that as people get older they learn more anyway? There are arguments on both sides. However, when discussing this question with people in San José, both young and old, it seemed that Arakmbut knowledge could continue, providing that both parties become more tolerant and trusting in one another and that there are opportunities to help both parties in the transmission of knowledge which in many cases may be disappearing. A major factor in the balance of destiny of Arakmbut knowledge lies in education.

b) The school and village – distinct institutions

Education has taken place in the Madre de Dios since the Dominicans first established a school at San Luis del Manu in 1908. The first school at Shintuya was opened in 1956. It was for boarders, but since the 1970s the mission has allowed the children to return home at night. In the communities the school lasts on average from eight to one and consists mainly of Spanish (reading and writing), mathematics, and religious education. No Arakmbut community has any bilingual or bi-cultural system of teaching. The teachers are either lay-missionaries (Shintuya, San José, Puerto Luz, and Boca del Inambari) or provided by the state (Barranco Chico).

The emphasis in the schools is on literacy. Reading and writing in Spanish are considered the main tasks of education. Grammar and spelling are taught by copying into notebooks and repetition.[11] Material is considered learnt when it has been copied and memorised. The subject matter is in fact, for the Arakmbut, irrelevant to their daily activities, but they consider that schooling is important for them to gain some insight into the power of the Amiko, which most think stems from education. The Arakmbut consider education to be extremely important but clearly separate it from the Arakmbut life of the home, where the indigenous language is spoken and the world of the school rarely penetrates.

The effect is similar to that of the discussion on health, noted earlier. Aikman (1994) draws attention to this distinction between home and the school and shows how it clearly separates different contexts of learning. Arakmbut indigenous learning is done by observation, listening, and imitation. Eventually people begin to try out what they have seen. They should not do too much or they will be ridiculed. However, if they gradually demonstrate that they are picking up the skill or technique they will realise from the lack of comment that they are gaining in knowledge.

A part of the division between the young and old in San José comes from different educational expectations. The methods which are used in the school are clearly different from those of the elders. The teachers in the school expect pupils to recite, copy from the blackboard, and be judged right or wrong. The Arakmbut method is to avoid mistakes as much as possible by not rushing the process of learning and enabling the pupil to grow into the knowledge at an appropriate pace. Furthermore, learning for the Arakmbut never stops, whereas in the world of the Amiko it only lasts during childhood. After education is complete, adulthood begins. This may also

---

11. Aikman (1994) provides a detailed study of the education in Arakmbut communities of San José del Karene and Puerto Luz, in which she compares traditional education with the teaching methods used by secular missionaries. This analysis is based on her material.

account for the tension among the youth, who feel they ought to learn everything while they are still young.

The threats to Arakmbut knowledge which have come from education (largely an assault on oral culture) and the outside influence of the Amiko are not usually raised within the communities as violations of their rights. However, as with health, education is seen as something which the mission or the state is obliged to provide to the community. Furthermore, if the behaviour of the teachers or the results of the students are not acceptable to the community as a whole, complaints quickly arise. The Arakmbut consider that teachers and schools are theirs by right. Should there be any question of the state or the mission not providing materials for constructing a school or not sending a teacher to the community the protest is vociferous.

Education and health are both sources of power for Amiko which the Arakmbut need in order to survive. Medicines help protect Arakmbut from the 'diseases of God', while education provides the means to deal with the Amiko on their terms. However, whereas health operates according to a conceptual distinction, education is physically divided by the separate contexts of the school and the house. In each case, technology, health, and education are, to a considerable extent, under the control of the Arakmbut, who protect their culture from unwanted influences from outside.

In the story of Aiwe and the Papa (Volume 1, chapter nine), the Arakmbut hero Aiwe escapes from the cannibalistic white people called Papa utilising their knowledge and technology. When he returns to his community he follows the advice of a friendly Papa to grind white bones and make a chicha drink out of them. Should he drink the brew in moderation he will be strong and able to resist their threats. However, in his eagerness to become powerful as the white Papa he drinks too much and dies.

This myth is a pertinent illustration of the dangers of excessive cohabiting with non-indigenous culture. The new technology, the state, Christianity, health, and education are all important for the survival of the Arakmbut but have to be taken in moderation or else they will become dangerous and destroy Arakmbut culture. Thus, too little innovation, health, and education will leave the Arakmbut prey to the dangers of outside influences, while too much will also lead to destruction. By separating these worlds the Arakmbut manage to ensure that they are controlling the entry of outside culture into their own lives. Eventually, however, as people become more used to managing the two worlds, their blending will probably become more contextual and flexible (Volume 2, chapter ten).

Conclusion

This chapter has looked at the multifaceted aspects of culture and the ways they are subsumed within the notion of the identity of the Arakmbut as a people and framed with the co-ordinates of territory. However, unlike in the chapters on peoples and territory, in which the Arakmbut respond to a sense of injustice by asserting their rights, with 'culture' they react more to the lack of services which they consider they are owed rather than for any loss to the indigenous culture itself. This is probably due to the fact that most of the changes which have taken place have done so with their consent.

Technological changes from contact with the missionaries in 1950 to the present day are conscious decisions by the Arakmbut. Those elements which are still useful or of personal importance, such as bows and arrows or string bags, remain, while the stone axes or digging sticks no longer exist. The disappearance of these can hardly be seen as ethnocidal.

The physical attributes of Arakmbut religion which have disappeared such as dances, painting, and the malocas, and the ceremonial taking of coca and tobacco, were either actively discouraged or despised by the missionaries and Amiko in the Madre de Dios. The Arakmbut no longer practise these and are prepared to change their lifestyles accordingly. To some extent this has been ethnocidal, because with encouragement and understanding, rather than the cultivation of embarrassment, the Arakmbut might have felt more comfortable practising their ceremonies.

Education and health are important alternative entries into the power sources of the world of the Amiko. The Arakmbut consider that the Amiko, who have discouraged Arakmbut religious ceremonies and regalia, have a duty to provide an alternative solution to the destruction they have wrought. This reaction on the part of the Arakmbut to any lack of school and medical facilities is more than a desire to take advantage of the benefits of Peruvian state services; it is seen as an obligation on the part of the national society to replace what they have taken from the Arakmbut. Technology, health, and education have each inspired an increasing concern in the Arakmbut to distinguish between their cultural view of the world and the influences from outside.

The Arakmbut have not lost all their ceremonial practices, however. From 1990, the Harakmbut students in Lima from ADEIMAD have devised a project with FENAMAD to gather together tapes, films, and transcriptions of the myths, songs, dances, and ceremonies of the Arakmbut. The reaction to this has not been one of embarrassment. The clear enthusiasm among the older members of the communities has opened out the possibility that many of the old ways may not have been completely lost and can be captured on film. Indeed, the elders of Boca del Inambari have agreed to organise an *e'mbaipak* ceremony and are planning to reconstruct a maloca to teach young men from the other communities how to dance (Sueyo, 1995).

Another context in which the physical aspect of Arakmbut culture appears is when they take assertive action. The paints, feathers, and dances provide a strength to the Arakmbut when they fight for their rights. Several examples of this were the attack on Sumalave's camp in 1985 (Gray 1986) when they put on paint and feathers, singing at Boca Colorado before storming the Municipality, the wearing of paint and feathers when the National Commission of investigation visited the Karene in 1992, and dancing during the formation of the Consejo Harakmbut at the FENAMAD Congress in 1993.

Arakmbut religion is far stronger in practice than it superficially appears to the visitor to a community. Apart from on rare occasions an outsider would have little indication that Arakmbut spirituality still exists, but the invisible world of the spirits is, without doubt, a constant presence.

The Arakmbut still have a strong sense of their identity as a people using their distinct knowledge and cultural practices as indices of self-identification, providing a meaning for life and expressing an inner identity linking each person to the people as a whole. In spite of the disappearance of most ceremonial aspects of their lives, they have not forgotten them, and the slightest interest demonstrated by a young man or woman or an outsider is received with much enthusiasm. Furthermore, at moments of great importance they use these older cultural attributes to provide strength. The main concern is that these older people will die without passing on their knowledge to their children and grandchildren.

Thus, in the face of cultural hegemony by priests and education, the Arakmbut determine their cultural heritage to a remarkable degree. They use various strategies for ensuring that unwanted cultural features are dropped, while dangerous elements are avoided or else carefully incorporated into their lives. Many elements of white culture are kept at a distance but utilised under the control of institutions such as the school or in a clearly marked, separated context.

However this does not mean that Arakmbut culture is not under threat in the longterm. The gradual eradication of oral culture by the education system which is so strongly based on literacy, the increasing instances of inter-marriage with non-Arakmbut speakers, and the attraction of western styles of speech, clothing, and attitudes could lead to a rejection of Arakmbut cultural identity and the failure of knowledge of the old ways to pass on through the generations. Referring back to Friedman's three cultures, all his options co-exist among the Arakmbut. Arakmbut self-knowledge is surrounded by the outside reformulation of their lives through religion, education, and technology. The emergence of Culture III, the assertion of a self-reflective indigenous culture, exists among the Arakmbut but in controlled contexts, three of which have been reviewed here, revealing Arakmbut culture as multi-faceted, flexible, and, above all, a process of self-assertion arising from the prospect of colonisation.

Culturally, the Arakmbut do not appear to fight for protection of their culture through the language of rights. This is because, as yet, they are largely in control of this area of their lives. However, they do articulate their concern over the lack of services for health and education. This is a claim for a balanced life in which they can benefit from the positive elements of the national society while protecting and preserving their own identity.

Any future development work with the Arakmbut therefore has to combine a re-strengthening of the old ways with the introduction of the new. In this way they will be able to blend their own cultural identity with the outside power of the Amiko.

♪ *Chapter 6* ♪

ARAKMBUT GOVERNANCE

'We must organise ourselves while we still have the chance'
Arakmbut community leader

To witness collective decision-making in an Arakmbut community is a fantastic experience. For maybe one hour, adults with particular points of view will make brief explanations of their positions to the occasional comment from the rest; then, gradually the elders, women, and the silent ones begin to speak louder and make their opinions known; others join in until a murmur catches on in the meeting; this gentle movement of sound slowly becomes a rumble until at the climax of the decision-making everyone is talking or shouting at once; the decision is made by acclamation. Consensus is reached, the persons who are not in agreement reluctantly back down to put their case another day, and the decision is made.

The rumble of Arakmbut decision-making could not be further from the notion of majority voting systems. The Arakmbut try to avoid loss of face, and have a flexible and highly subtle form of preparation prior to reaching decisions which is distinct and has served them throughout the turmoil of the last forty years of colonisation and probably for centuries before. This chapter looks at the Arakmbut political system and demonstrates that it is a crucial basis for their survival as a people. The discussion reflects theoretical and practical approaches to governance and indicates how the Arakmbut have blended two separate systems together in order to protect their political integrity.

Indigenous peoples assert the right to govern themselves and recognition of their own institutions is fundamental to this aim. In the Working Group of the UN Commission on Human Rights in November 1995, some state governments were uneasy about this question because they see it as a challenge to state authority; meanwhile, indigenous peoples see it as a protection from excessive state interference.[1] The draft Declaration on the Rights of Indigenous Peoples states in Article 19 that

> 'Indigenous peoples have the right to participate fully, if they so choose, at all levels of decision-making in matters which may affect their rights, lives and destinies through representatives chosen by themselves in accordance with their own procedures, as well as to maintain and develop their own indigenous decision-making institutions.'

This is a recognition of indigenous governance.

Government and States

The word 'government' comes from the Greek 'gubernaculum', meaning 'steersman' or 'ruling'. It usually refers to those who comprise the executive and its offices or those who declare and enforce the law (A. Vincent 1987:29). Indigenous peoples argue that they have their own forms of government, whereas national authorities claim that governments are the prerogative of the state. This discussion has a considerable history.

The state view of government goes back to Greek times, when Aristotle saw types of government as city-state constitutions (Aristotle 1992:239). During the Enlightenment, Locke considered that government was associated with civil society outside of the state of nature (Held et.al.1983:10). By this reasoning, indigenous peoples (whom Locke considered within the state of nature) would not have had government. Rousseau also saw government tied to the state. It was 'an intermediary body established between the subjects and the

---

1. This is often termed 'indigenous self-government'. Self-government has several meanings. It has been used to refer to a specific aspect of British colonial rule, and subsequently the international mandate system, where dependencies eventually gained self-government (Hall 1948:94). In an indigenous context there are two broad meanings: the first refers to indigenous peoples' right to govern themselves, as seen in Article 31 of the draft Declaration, which refers to indigenous peoples' right 'to autonomy or self-government in matters relating to their internal and local affairs'. Alternatively, it can be seen as a state-imposed political framework designed to enhance integration, as in ILO Convention 169 in Article 2, according to which governments are responsible for developing the 'full realisation of ... these peoples ... their customs and traditions and their institutions.'

sovereign for their mutual communication, a body charged with the execution of the laws and the maintenance of freedom, both civil and political' (1968:102). Sovereignty is the basis of government for Rousseau and is bound up with state structure. During the nineteenth century, the connection between government and the state continued among markedly different thinkers. Hegel, for example, saw the constitutional monarchy of Prussia as an apex of governmental development; Godwin, on the other hand, saw government as bound to the oppression of the state as a whole (Philip 1986:169).

A more historical approach saw government as something which emerged through history and took different forms. David Hume, during the Scottish Enlightenment, replaced the notion of social contract with a theory of gradual change, where the rudiments of government existed in all societies through three principles of justice 'the stability of possession, its translation by consent, and the performance of promise' (Hume 1972:266). Hume sees these three principles as arising from the need for people to co-exist in the face of scarcity, while the need for government arises as a political structure for administering justice.

The anthropological ideas of the nineteenth century included government in the evolutionary system, but unlike Hegel, who connected it totally with the state, others saw the concept as more widespread. For example, Part II of Morgan's *Ancient Society* is titled 'Growth of the Idea of Government' and presents government as developing on a line of social development from the *gens* (1877:6).[2]

Whereas Hume and Morgan did not link the notion of government specifically with the state, from Morgan onwards an anthropological discussion arose in Britain as to whether government was a feature of state societies or could be present in any form of social organisation. In the collection of papers *African Political Systems* (1940:5), Evans-Pritchard and Fortes divide state societies with government from stateless societies without government. Those with no government 'lack centralized authority, administrative machinery, and constituted judicial institutions'.

Since then, a more flexible notion of government has emerged in the discussion of African systems. Lucy Mair (1962:36) distinguishes between 'government' (similar to the term governance) and 'a government'. The functionalist definition of government is that: 'It pro-

---

2. The 'gens' is a term which the historian Grote used to refer to a cluster of families with a common origin, common name, and common ceremonial rites. For Morgan, the gens was the first aspect of society above the family.

tects members of the political community against lawlessness within and enemies without; and it takes decisions on behalf of the community in matters which concern them all, and in which they have to act together' (ibid.:16). By using the notion of government in this broad sense of 'governance', Mair follows the work of Schapera (1956) and McIver (1947:156). She distinguishes minimal government in societies with little or no institutional manifestation of government from diffused government, by which councils in different communities take decisions but are not centralised. These are distinct from the more centralised forms of government that are associated with a state.

Mair's work shows that government can operate on a local level outside of state structure in order to fulfil two activities. The first is to protect the community from lawlessness, and the second is to organise a decision-making procedure. These can easily be embedded within the socio-political relations within a community without any necessary institutional manifestation. Mair's observations on government are relevant in the case of San José, where indigenous government is based within the activities of persons who are respected for their ability to make decisions or for their shamanic knowledge.

However, the difficulty with any form of typology about government has been discussed by Balandier (1979:44), who sees problems arising from transitional cases and a lack of appreciation of the dynamic capacity of political organisation. Nevertheless, it would seem reasonable to argue that government need not be seen as synonymous with the notion of 'state' because 'if government were totally identified with the State, then each removal of government would entail a crisis in the State' (A. Vincent 1987:32). During the 1970s there was a shift in interest from functional analyses, and interest waned as to whether the term 'government' was of any relevance at all. However, in the context of Amazonia, the distinctions which Mair made are not completely anachronistic if used imaginatively, possibly because they were written in the context of the decolonisation process. Nevertheless, this chapter uses the term 'governance' inter-changeably with the general notion of 'government' because its connotations reflects a political life which is not rigidly systematised and institutionalised.

Indigenous Governance in Latin America

In Amazonian studies, the concept of government has hardly appeared at all. Clastres (1977) has argued, from an anarchistic perspective, that indigenous communities are societies without government and this has been similarly noted in the work of Thomas among the Pemon (1982). The question then becomes that if societies have no government, do they govern themselves? This self-governing aspect of indigenous peoples is crucial and demands a notion which is considerably more flexible than the state notion of institutional government.

In a legal context, the presence of government among the indigenous peoples of the Americas has been extremely important. According to Falkowski, the jurist Vitoria was one of the first to express the importance of self-government: 'In refutation of those who asserted that Indians were slaves by nature because of the incapability for self-government, Vitoria contended that the Indians constituted sovereign nations and had dominion over their land' (Falkowski 1992:22). Las Casas reaffirmed this when he said: 'All men who are self-governing, under whatsoever form are sovereign ... The law of nations and natural law apply to Christian and gentiles alike, and to all people of any sect, law, condition, or colour without any distinction whatsoever' (cited in Hanke 1959:47).

However the wishes of the Spanish theologians of the sixteenth century who defended indigenous peoples' right to govern themselves were not carried out. Although during certain periods Spanish colonial rule recognised indigenous communities, such as the cabildos community councils in Colombia, the usual situation of indigenous peoples is that they find themselves in a territory within a nation state which is constantly trying to encroach upon their lands and resources. Nevertheless there are several ways in which indigenous governance has developed in Central and South America which are relevant to the Arakmbut.

1. Indigenist Approach

The indigenist approach is governance based on a state-monitored form of self-government. According to this model, the national government recognises community social organisation and sends development workers to ensure that they are organised appropriately. State intervention can range from useful support to unwanted interference. In Mexico, for example, representatives of the National Indigenist Institute (INI) work directly with communities in the form of development workers.

This form of work enables governments to create direct links with communities, often through their indigenist institutes. Problems can arise because the approach is primarily top-down and, by concentrating on communities, has the effect of weakening other forms of indigenous political organisation. The Peruvian Indigenist Institute has become increasingly interested in this approach since the revision of the Constitution and the promulgation of the controversial Land Law, and has on several occasions advocated dealing directly with communities rather than with indigenous organisations.[3]

2. *The Corporatist Approach*

In Peru the Law of Native Communities, established by the Velasco government, included provisions as to how Amazonian communities should organise themselves. The idea was to draw indigenous communities closer to the state while providing them with an autonomous political organisation for self-government. By connecting the community organisation with its other provisions on land protection and recognition of legal personality, the majority of the indigenous peoples of the Peruvian Amazon supported the move.

The law was passed without taking into consideration the indigenous political system of each people (see chapter two), and can be seen as the imposition of a form of self-government. This system provides more autonomy for each community than the indigenist solution, assuming that the local community can incorporate it into a framework which reflects their political organisation.

3. *Federation and Organisation*

Indigenous federations are particularly common throughout the Amazon. Whereas these organisations are not governing bodies, they represent the self-governing communities. In Peru alone there are at least forty organisations made up of representatives chosen from each com-

---

3. Unlike international trust relationships (such as those established by the United Nations), which are meant to pave the way to a decolonisation process, the domestic trust relationship is considered as a dependent relationship, in which the state government considers that it has the ultimate authority to override indigenous self-government. An example took place in Canada in 1982, when the Department of Indian Affairs and Northern Development outlined a 'devolutionary approach to self-government' which consisted of the government recognising indigenous constitutions. The criticism of this approach (IWGIA 1984:64) is similar to those raised at the United States' government's Indian Reorganisation Act, which established 'self-government' according to a scheme initiated and planned by the Federal Government through the Bureau of Indian Affairs in 1934 (Dunbar Ortiz 1984:148).

munity at an assembly which meets every few years to elect a leadership. The hierarchy of federations connects community organisation to the international movement though bodies such as the Indigenous Coordinadora of the Amazon Basin (COICA) and the International Alliance for the Indigenous Tribal Peoples of the Tropical Forests.

Federations are based on several different organisational principles. The two most common are those of locality, by which communities in a particular area join to strengthen their collective activities, and of ethnicity, by which members of the same people join on a community basis to defend their rights and promote their development.

4. Indigenous Peoples

All peoples, to some extent, continue to recognise their identity as peoples, and this links into their organisation. Sometimes this takes the form of a people in an area, such as the Brazilian Kayapó or the Xavante who mobilise on a community basis. In these examples, there is no federation or other form of indigenous organisation outside of the community.

The most common form of a peoples' organisation is the internal form of governance of each community. Very often this is completely distinct from the other three forms of organisation and relates to the socio-cultural formation of the people as a whole.

These four aspects of governance demonstrate that there is no clearcut division between the state and indigenous peoples; rather, indigenous peoples have a multi-layered form of governance which varies according to the relationship between each community and the state. The following case study from the Madre de Dios illustrates the complexities of indigenous governance but shows that they are self-governing on many simultaneous levels.

Case Study: Governance among the Arakmbut

On 25 May 1992, there was a historic meeting at the Arakmbut community of Puerto Luz in the Madre de Dios. The Arakmbut of the Karene had decided to call the 'First Meeting of the Arakmbut People'. The initiative had arisen from both San José and Puerto Luz, and the Arakmbut convened in order to discuss those issues and problems which affect the Arakmbut people and present them to the local indigenous federation (FENAMAD). FENAMAD was fully in favour of the meeting and sent two representatives to attend, as well as Felipe Pacuri and Thomas Moore from the Centro Eori.

Arranging the meeting involved several informal meetings. The Arakmbut visit each others' communities occasionally when preparing joint actions, such as the storming of Boca Colorado or an inter-village kermesse fiesta, often focused on raising school funds. Yet in San José and Puerto Luz, community meetings are not common; consultations take place, through countless encounters during the day – at meal-times, while the women work in the gardens or the men at the gold placers, during evening strolls around the community. At these times, casual conversation informs, tests opinion, and prepares decisions. Formal meetings are usually acclamations of questions which have already been decided.

The initiative for the meeting in Puerto Luz started about two months previously when several issues were simultaneously worrying the communities of Barranco Chico, San José, and Puerto Luz. The Arakmbut from Barranco Chico and Puerto Luz often pass by San José on their way to Boca Colorado: Barranco Chico and San José were both very concerned about the road which threatens to slice through their communities (see next chapter), while San José and Puerto Luz were worried about the continuing presence of an armed foreign colonist on their territory (see chapter eight).

The communities decided that a meeting of Arakmbut should be called in the presence of FENAMAD and the advisory institute, Centro Eori, to explain the problems they faced and seek ways to solve them. The preparations for the meeting involved several trips from San José to Puerto Luz, the first taking place when the two communities were preparing their attack on Boca Colorado (chapter two). On these occasions, the communities discussed who would cover the petrol costs, who had time to go, and when they arrived how they would formally enter the community.

Originally the May meeting was to have included Shintuya, Boca Inambari, and Barranco Chico, but a shortage of funds meant that these three more distant communities could not attend; they asked that the other two establish a plan of action sent messages of support.

The meeting lasted three days and covered a considerable range of problems. The first discussion concern whether the Arakmbut preferred to be called Arakmbut or Amarakaeri. Arakmbut was preferred, but several participants recognised that Amarakaeri was what outsiders were used to. A group also advocated changing the Spanish names of the communities to Arakmbut names; this was left pending as no one had any alternatives to hand.

Discussions then moved to the problems of colonisation. The increasing numbers of invasions of the Amarakaeri Communal Reserve were of great concern, as were the growing number of colonists coming from Huaypetue to the territories of Puerto Luz and Barranco Chico and others from the Madre de Dios moving onto the territory of San José. The activities of Michael Dianda, the German adventurer, were scrutinised. He had fast become a symbol for all the colonists in the area, primarily because he was so conspicuous (see chapter eight).

There followed a detailed technical discussion of the changes in policy for obtaining gold concessions in the wake of the new mining law, which is designed to open up as much land as possible for companies to mine. This continued until the second day, when the topic turned to the colonists living in the headwaters of the Karene. The final part of the meeting consisted of a discussion with representatives of the mining colonists living in Puerto Luz's lands as to who should stay there and under what conditions. Other topics covered included secondary education, the desire of the communities for health initiatives, and the local election. Plans were made to register the communities to vote and to agree on the candidate for mayor of Boca Colorado.

After the meeting, the Arakmbut celebrated their discussions with a fiesta attended by all the participants. The meeting had taken place in Arakmbut and had asserted their organisational strength as the largest indigenous people in the Madre de Dios. The Arakmbut from San José returned, inspired to take the initiative further.

FENAMAD supported the local meeting, drawing together the ideas and opinions of specific areas of the Madre de Dios in order to work more closely with the communities. However FENAMAD was facing difficulties responding to so many problems at such great distances from one another; Puerto Maldonado is two days from San José and four from the communities on the upper Madre de Dios.

The Arakmbut in the upper Madre de Dios (Shintuya in particular) were particularly aware of this problem of distance, which had repercussions on the traditional health programme which FENAMAD took over from Ametra in 1991. A Centro Oamanokkae had been established in Shintuya as a base for the health project, but this gave rise to various logistical problems in transferring money from Maldonado by boat and opened the couriers to risk from thieves. The distance, coupled with a reluctance by those FENAMAD representatives living in Shintuya to move to Puerto Maldonado, contributed to a feeling of separation from the main FENAMAD office.

This was not lost on the priests at the mission, who have never been in favour of FENAMAD and who were broadly in favour of reducing FENAMAD's influence in the upper Madre de Dios.

There were consequently two developments during 1992. The first brought the Arakmbut together within FENAMAD to discuss their problems. The second was an increased sense that FENAMAD was physically separate from the upper Madre de Dios and that there should be an initiative to become more independent from FENAMAD.

Within this context the FENAMAD Congress took place in El Pilar in August 1993, where the two aspects of organisation clashed. The Arakmbut were more united than they had been for many years and wanted to ensure that there was a permanent representation of Arakmbut leadership in FENAMAD. The discussion about who should be candidates for the election dominated the final day of the meeting, resulting in a conflict between the lower and upper Madre de Dios which broadly took the form of Arakmbut versus the rest. The result was that the Arakmbut left the meeting en masse and decided to form their own Consejo Harakmbut (COHAR).

After an extended meeting between FENAMAD, the Arakmbut, and the support NGOs, and several days negotiation, a compromise was reached whereby the Consejo Harakmbut would be established as an autonomous body within FENAMAD. In spite of a tense relationship for the first year, the COHAR/FENAMAD relationship improved. In December 1996, Antonio Iviche from San José was elected President of FENAMAD and the two organisations dovetailed more smoothly. The Arakmbut had formed an ethnically-based body.

This case study demonstrates the complications which arise when juxtaposing community organisation with ethnic identity and indigenous organisational representations. The tension which existed within FENAMAD and the communities had two dimensions. One was the ethnic distinction between the Arakmbut and the others; the other was the extent to which FENAMAD could remain centralised without making those living further from Puerto Maldonado feel comparatively isolated.

The gradual restructuring of FENAMAD by the formation of the Consejo Harakmbut was an attempt to decentralise the indigenous organisation, seeking a level between the community and the regional body to co-ordinate Arakmbut needs. The current structure of indigenous organisation in the Madre de Dios is now based on community organisation, ethnic federation and local federation. The process of organisation is one involving permanent tension between government (community and territory) and organisation (federation and region), based on different principles (ethnicity and locality).

Indigenous governance in the Madre de Dios is paradoxical because communities, which are self-governing, are represented at a higher level by indigenous organisations, which are non-governmental. The term indigenous government could be used in the context of communities because it reflects the sovereign control which each community has (or rather, is entitled to have) over its territories. The reason that FENAMAD cannot become a centralised indigenous government is that it holds no continuous territory. All the communities co-exist with non-indigenous people and the state which holds lands in between them. However, the Arakmbut, through their ethnic organisation and the existence of the Amarakaeri Communal Reserve, have a sense of territory and peoplehood which goes beyond the sense of organisation.

The case study demonstrates that the different aspects of organisation mentioned above all co-exist. The corporate structure of the community as recognised in the Law of the Native Communities co-exists with the internal Arakmbut community governance, which is based on their own political organisation. At the same time their sense of indigenous identity also persists through the presence of COHAR. The indigenist element is not emphasised in the Madre de Dios, although since 1995 the Indigenist Institute of Peru has tried to wrest the initiative of the Amarakaeri Communal Reserve from FENAMAD and COHAR and to establish a controlling committee made up of community leaders and colonists. (This was even under discussion as a condition for recognising the reserve.) If this were to happen, then the top-down indigenist approach will add a further complication and probably undermine the delicate relations between the communities and organisations currently existing in the Madre de Dios.

The Arakmbut do not discuss the notion of 'government' or 'governance' among themselves. Like the question of culture, it is embedded in other concepts such as those of 'people' and 'territory'. Their capacity to make decisions and to resolve disputes internally is not yet under dire threat from the outside world. However, as external threats become more serious or the internal 'minimal government' becomes weaker, community government will need to become stronger in order for the Arakmbut to assert their identity in the face of a hostile outside world.

The Arakmbut of San José are still free to make decisions about their own internal affairs, but consistently find their power to make decisions relating to external factors weakened by colonisation. The indigenous communities of the Karene have not been strong enough to take on the outside world separately and consequently led to the meeting between San José and Puerto Luz. The formation of the Consejo Harakmbut was a continuation of this process. This chapter now looks in more detail at the different forms of governance both within and outside of the Arakmbut community.

Arakmbut Governance – Minimal Government

The political organisation of the Arakmbut is based on the community and covers two important dimensions: decision-making and conflict resolution. Minimal government here looks at the process by which the Arakmbut reach acceptable decisions through informal consultations and how, as far as possible, they avoid destructive conflict. This refers primarily to the way in which households, clans, men, women, and other groups within the community discuss and formulate information and ideas.

Within San José it is possible to see two political systems operating simultaneously. The most visible is that which operates under the Law of the Native Communities, yet this is, to a large extent, the more superficial. The other political system, which operates within each community, has no officers or councils and is very informal, basing its activities on the encounters which each person makes with others during the day and night.

1. Decision-making

Every member of the community of San José builds up opinions on the basis of meetings with others (Volume 2, chapter eight). The way in which a community reaches decisions is difficult to see except over a period of intense observation. This is because influential Arakmbut sound out opinions and views before they make suggestions which, if analysed and observed correctly, encapsulate community opinion.

During the night and early morning a married couple discuss within the house, while the household as a whole meets at mealtimes in the kitchen where, after eating, information is exchanged and analysed in conversation. Day is the time when men and women separate; the men to work gold and hunt, the women to garden, prepare food, and weave their string bags (wenpu). While carrying out their daily tasks, people talk, discuss, and gossip; incidents are described and reviewed, and opinions are formed. The talking and chatting provide the basis for information exchange and comments which gradually pass from one person to another, until it is possible to gain a rough idea of community opinion.

The most important part of the day comes in the evening (baysik), when the people go to wash before eating. As they return from the river, men, women, and children cluster in small informal groups before and after the meal and pass on the information and ideas on which they have been reflecting during the day. These discussions vary and quickly shift from one topic to another: subjects range from gold work, gardens, health, and threats to the community to amusing incidents. Influential members of the community use these informal gatherings to sound out public opinion.

On the basis of constant discussion and monitoring, these influential people can build up opinions which reflect the desires of the others and put initiatives into action. All of this is done in an informal way without any voting, and is separate from any reliance on the juridical political organisation of the community.

The informal encounters discuss matters relevant to all aspects of community life, yet decisions are made according to the particular social interests involved, such as gender, age grade, clan, or marriage relations. For example, decisions as to which crops will be grown where in the chacra, or who will eat what and when, are decided by the household, with women, men, and grown children involved in the discussion. Work groups of Arakmbut decide on their method of production and where, when, and how they will organise their gold mining. When people decide where to work their chacras, there appears to be little community discussion or approval; the Arakmbut find a spot and begin to clear it. Possibly there will be some informal mention of the fact dropped casually into the conversation at an evening meeting, but people are usually sensitive to each other's needs and avoid conflict whenever possible. Furthermore, no one wants to keep their chacras too close to the village or else they will become easy prey for lazy robbers on the prowl and so conflict over space is minimal.

Decisions as to who should marry whom are made by the people involved with support from the alliance arranging unit (wambet) and the members of the clans. This spreads throughout the community and people, particularly women, who are very knowledgeable about genealogies comment on the connection between the couple, whether there are incidents in their backgrounds which could affect the well-being of the match, or whether they are suited. If the match is not controversial there will be little comment. However the whole community will sift through all the information and public opinion will demonstrate its approval when people meet at fiestas. Should a young man be turned down by a potential bride's family, this can lead to a serious rift between the groups which can spread throughout the community.

Periodically, members of the community who have had success in their gold work will distribute their profits with a fiesta for the rest of the community or for a substantial number of allies. During these all-night drinking sessions, generous members of the community are able to heighten their prestige by buying beer or liquor, and use the occasion to discuss serious matters at length. These fiestas are important for reconciling opinions and explaining actions to others. However, they can also be moments of tension. Much of the way of communication at these fiestas takes place through the medium of songs (e'machinoa). The Arakmbut have several types of song, but the most significant in this context are the personal songs, which are designed to express opinions and ideas which cannot be spoken. The songs refer to specific incidents and are improvised by the singer; they are often the basis for someone learning the real opinions and feelings of another and can frequently lead to altercations.

The household, work, evening meetings, and fiestas are constant occasions during daily life when men and women can gain access to the opinions of others to build up their knowledge and develop decisions. The first element of government, decision-making, is thus dispersed throughout the social activity of the community. The informal methods of deciding and resolving conflicts are carried out with the people directly involved as far as possible and under the 'minimal government' system, the fiesta is the largest informal meeting which draws together any questions. However, there are certain decisions concerning external matters which are discussed at the informal encounters, but which need to be made at a more formal level. Here the community meetings are important.

Informal encounters also take place between Arakmbut communities through visits between households. The most frequent visits occur between households or persons who pass by one another on the way to Boca Colorado or meet there for a drink. These trips provide an opportunity to exchange information about the affairs of each community and the general political situation of the area and are consequently fed into the internal minimal informal government. The communications from visits can also provide the preliminary preparation for the more formal meetings between communities at which matters are decided, such as those described in the case study.

2. Resolving Disputes

The second element of government which the Arakmbut practise in an informal manner is their way of resolving disputes. In the same way that people can build up common opinions through the informal encounters, they can also fall out. In spite of being proud, they will avoid conflict for as long as possible. Sometimes this is because the information which they receive cannot be substantiated publicly, while in other cases they do not want to cause splits within the community. Much household discussion concerns people who might be stealing from chacras, or who might be taking areas of gold which belong to someone else. Property discussions are important and are frequently causes of disputes.

The most serious area for dispute, however, arises from marriage; eligible women are in great demand in the community and there is fierce competition between men for wives. If marriage negotiations break down and a young suitor is rejected by the woman's relatives, or if a couple should elope or separate, repercussions can be vindictive and frequently violent.

If a dispute arises between persons, the households quickly become involved. Should there be any affinal connections between the parties, they will sometimes try to mediate, or else, if the situation is very hostile, will keep out of the quarrel. Initially the parties will try to stay apart. Some differences linger in the form of avoidance, and certain people can keep away from enemies for considerable periods of time, particularly as so many of the Arakmbut live outside of the village in gold camps for months on end.

If the quarrel becomes acute, violence often breaks out. If the dispute takes place within the household one of the parties will leave the community on a temporary basis. Usually when a fight breaks out between husband and wife it is the wife who leaves. Otherwise fights usually take place at the fiestas which are the largest meetings among the Arakmbut. People sometimes discuss their differences and resolve disputes at these fiestas. However, should the discussions break down and violence ensue, the ramifications can spread throughout the community. If fighting takes place on a regular basis, one of the parties will eventually leave.

Disputes are resolved within the same framework and, as with the decision-making procedures, the community does not discuss internal problems in public meetings. The resolutions of conflicts within the community all take place informally through the casual encounters which take place through the day and the channels of information which involve a communication flowing between the households.

The consequences of this fluid way of making decisions and solving disputes within the community means that if there is no real emergency, a community can take a long time to formulate an opinion on a matter. For example, unless someone feels very strongly about expelling a colonist and considers that they have the capacity to send them off San José's lands, the community will spend weeks or even months monitoring the person, seeing what he is doing and the suddenly pounce – much to the surprise of the colonist, who thinks that there is no opposition to his presence on community lands (see case study in chapter eight).

Qualities of Leadership and 'Origins' of Government

Hume and Hocart have two complementary views on the basis of government within indigenous communities which are relevant here. According to Needham, Hume demonstrates that: 'Government is not necessary, and in certain conditions of society it may in fact not exist, but where it has been established, it is originally and essentially a jural institution' (Needham 1970: xxvii). Hume sees the origin of government as stemming from the authority which a people creates when it organises itself in defence against others. The result of Hume's approach is that government is not tied to the state but arises out of practical necessities. He explains this as follows:

> 'I assert the first rudiments of government to arise from quarrels, not among men of the same society, but among those of different societies ... This we find verified in the American tribes, where men live in concord and amity among themselves without established government; and never pay submission to any of their fellows, except in time of war, when their captain enjoys a shadow of authority, which he loses after their return from the field ... This authority, however, instructs them in the advantages of government' (Hume op.cit.:266-7).

Hocart (1970:35), in contrast, argues that there is an evolution in society from ritual organisation to government. He considers that the structure of ritual processes provided the basis for hierarchical organisation, specialisation of offices, and institutional continuity. Whereas both of these approaches initially seem rather too developmentalist and structured for the Arakmbut, the importance of political decision-makers and shamanic relationships with the invisible world in protecting and controlling the community is extremely important. For this reason, both Hume and Hocart are complementary sources of inspiration when looking in more detail at Arakmbut political organisation.

This process of opinion-forming is conducive to the very low key leadership structure which exists in the community. Volume 2 contains a detailed description of how the Arakmbut recognise positive qualities in each person. Among these are the following: shamanic capacity to communicate with the spirit world by dreaming; knowledge about Arakmbut traditions, particularly myths; the ability to amuse, sing, or cure; and taking responsibility for others. Politically speaking, a person's successful initiatives are manifestations of his or her positive contacts with the spirit world and ability to put advice to positive use. However, the most important political quality is responsibility *(matamona)*, which gives someone the authority to ask someone else to do something. The meaning of the word includes the senses of determine, order, and decide.

A respected person is responsible for his or her actions. For example, if a man finds a gold deposit not far from the community, he will inform the others. A group of kinspeople will join him to prepare the area. Should it turn out that there is insufficient water to wash the gold, the prestige of the person will drop. He will have wasted time and effort and be accused of posturing. Furthermore, others will not take much notice of what he says in the near future. On the other hand, if the person is successful and demonstrates his generosity by sharing his find with others, his position will rise within the community.

Whereas within the Arakmbut communities there are no real offices as such, people who are respected receive certain titles. We have seen the terms wayorokeri and wamanoka'eri used for people endowed with shamanic qualities. In certain circumstances the terms *wantupa* and *ohpu* are used for political leadership. The terms come originally from warriors in the times when the Arakmbut fought the Taka. The ohpu was a leader with spiritual qualities enabling him to convert into a jaguar, which made him invincible. The wantupa was the head of maloca, usually in times of war. The word *wairi* means 'honoured person'. This arises as a combination of humility, proven ability, generosity, responsibility, and sacrifice. Wairi is a general term which can be used for someone who is either politically or spiritually skilled and who has the interests of the community as a whole as his responsibility. As with the other titles, wairi is used exclusively for men.

Women have a different set of criteria for respect, based on their knowledge of gardens and the spiritual aspects of growth. They are also considered better than men at curing with plants.[4] The political influence of women stems from their extensive network which crosscuts the patrilineal clan solidarity of the men. Whereas men work together with members of the clan, and also with those immediate affines with whom they have a good relationship, the women who co-operate in the gardens are usually of different clans. They work closer to the community and have more access to information from other parts of the community than the men. Women are therefore particularly powerful in terms of communication flow, and are occasionally accused of being gossips and dangerous because of this. As in many aspects of Arakmbut social and cultural life, the women do not appear prominent on the surface, but their influence runs deep.

The spiritual wayorokeri and wamanoka'eri and the more political wantupa and ohpu could be seen as the rudiments of official positions in an Arakmbut community. However, they are not titles which denote a position. They reflect the qualities of the person to whom they refer. The terms do not grant power or strength. The strength *(tainda)* is already present in the person in terms of the relationship of body, soul, and name which we discussed in an earlier chapter.

Hume's consideration of the rudiments of government in the warrior chief, and Hocart's of ritual specialists, have some relevance here. Both areas provide human beings with qualities which the Arakmbut respect and which grant the recipient of the term prestige and influence. However, the formal institutionalisation of a government is not present in the day-to-day political and spiritual activities of the Arakmbut.

Drawing together the information on Arakmbut systems of political organisation, it is possible to argue without too much difficulty that they demonstrate characteristics similar to what Lucy Mair (after McIver) calls 'minimal government'. By this she means that wrongs are redressed and decisions made largely by the people directly concerned, with public opinion acting as the ultimate arbitrator. Thus government, such as it exists for the Arakmbut, is embedded within the social relations of each community and expressed through the qualities and personal attributes of those with prestige and authority.

4. This may be because some of the women have been outsiders from other peoples with knowledge of plants such as the Matsigenka.

The decision-making attributes and the ability to resolve disputes within Arakmbut communities are informal and minimal, yet no community is an isolated unit. A considerable amount of political activity takes place dealing with the 'outside world'. However, the official institution of the community is quite distinct.

Arakmbut Governance – Diffused Government

Each community, according to the Law of Native Communities, should contain a President, Vice-President, Secretary, Treasurer, and Spokespersons, who are meant to be elected by the community every two years and are legally recognised by state authorities (the Ministry of Agriculture). With its territorial title and juridical personality in the name of its officials, the council appears, from the outside at least, to run the community.

When a non-Arakmbut visitor arrives at the community, or if any outsider wants to make any agreement with its members, the officers, particularly the presidents, are seen as being the representatives with whom one should speak. Colonists and people at the Boca Colorado settlement frequently talk about the President of San José as if he is the spokesperson for all members and can make decisions on behalf of the community as a whole. However, no one person in the community can make decisions on their own initiative which affect everyone.

In spite of these misunderstandings, the council members are not without any position in the community. In the Arakmbut communities, the President becomes the representative of external affairs to the community. He takes on the responsibility of liaising with colonists and the authorities in Puerto Maldonado should a problem arise. The Treasurer of the community is usually responsible for the money which is held for the village as a whole. However, all money-raising activities are aimed at reinforcing non-Arakmbut institutions such as the school or support for indigenous candidates in the local elections.

The officers of the community are not usually the same people as those who are recognised as wairi. Frequently they are younger people with some education and experience with the outside world. Occasionally communities have elected older men, but often they find the outside world difficult to handle and rely on the younger people for advice. However, being a young leader also has its disadvantages, because the older members of the community will not necessarily co-operate when called upon by someone who has less prestige and authority. This can often lead to tensions between the two systems of political organisation.

The councils of the native communities established under Peruvian law provide a different aspect of government among the Arakmbut according to Mair's classification. She calls 'diffused government' one in which there are offices within the system of government but no centralised authority structure for the people as a whole (Mair 1962:78). Thus, both minimal and diffused types of government co-exist within the Arakmbut communities. Each refers to a different area of political life. The minimal government is oriented primarily (not exclusively) to the internal affairs of the community as well as relationships between households in separate communities (such as marriage exchange, for example). In contrast, the diffused government deals with more formal external affairs, relationships between communities as a whole or anything which involves the national authorities. Both systems have different notions of leadership, the former on the basis of quality and the latter on position. The two systems are compared in the following table:

Table 6.1 Arakmbut government

Minimal Government	**Diffused Government**
Arakmbut politics	Modern community offices
Customary basis	National legal basis
Informal encounters	Formal meetings
Leadership from quality	Leadership from position
Recognised by efficacy	Recognised by election
'Internally' oriented	'Externally' oriented
Older men respected	Younger men respected (to a lesser extent)
Arakmbut knowledge	State educational knowledge
Fiestas	Formal meetings in school

By making too sharp a distinction between these as two systems the false impression might arise that the two are incompatible. Rather, they are two aspects of one political system which broadly face in different directions. For example, no formal meeting should take place in San José without a prior procedure of internal discussion. This enables the formal meeting to constitute the ratification or formalisation of opinions which have been emerging in previous weeks, if not months. Furthermore, 'internal' and 'external' are relative concepts. The informal political process itself defines what internal means (whether it is clan, community, or the Arakmbut as a whole), whereas external refers to official decisions, sometimes marked by a written agreement in a book of Acts or with a 'memoria' statement of intention. As a general rule, most formal meetings are about official community matters.

San José rarely meets formally, although this varies according to the circumstances. For example, in 1981 there were meetings on average every month, whereas in 1991, they occurred every two months, unless an emergency arose. Most meetings take place on Sunday, a day when everyone is available and those who live outside the main village settlement visit their relatives.[5] The school is the locale for meetings if visitors such as FENAMAD or local authorities have come, if educational matters are under discussion, or if the weather is cold or wet. When internal questions are under scrutiny, the elders will suggest sitting outside one of the houses by the football pitch. However, the democratic decisions which take place in the meetings are usually already decided on the basis of the informal encounters, at which opinions are sounded out. Meetings discuss school matters and political conditions in the Madre de Dios, particularly the problems of colonists' invasions.

When the Arakmbut make decisions in these meetings, however, there is a moment when the whole process of opinion formation is re-created to legitimise the decision. The word for 'to think' (e'nopwe) is used interchangeably in Arakmbut for 'to know and decide'. At the moment of ratifying a decision, the person leading the meeting asks what the people think. At this point the low murmur, described at the beginning of the chapter, gradually crescendos until all the participants are talking at once and an acclamation or rejection of the proposal emerges from the cacophony. Any vote with hands is a formality. The consensus has the effect of incorporating people into decisions and not alienating them.

This murmur is the blending of both aspects of Arakmbut politics, the one internal and minimal, the other externally oriented and diffuse. The two areas fit together according to the different methods of decision-making and problem solving. The background to a community decision therefore arises through informal encounters and receives ratification at a formal meeting.

The state notion of community works together with the Arakmbut political system because they have determined that this should be so. This parallels certain aspects of non-indigenous cultural factors which the Arakmbut have willingly adopted since the time they

5. Community meetings in Shintuya take place every Friday evening. However, in this case the priests are usually present.

first encountered the missions. The difference here is that the adoption of community political structure is based on their relationship with the state and not through the mission (an institution associated with health and education).

Autonomy and Self-government

The distinction between 'internal' and 'external' affairs should be seen in a relative manner where informal agreements relate to the concerns of inter-household relations and constitute the process for reaching community and inter-community decisions. The formal agreements of the diffused form of governance deal with how the community sees and is seen from outside. Thus, a community need not appear as a divided body incorporating two systems, but as a socio-cultural and political organisation facing in two directions – inside to out and outside to in. This two-directional politics establishes the boundary of the community, where an indigenous notion of autonomy and self-government can take shape through political practice.[6] The notion of autonomy is much discussed in the elaboration of indigenous peoples' rights, but, as with the notion of self-government, it can too often be limited to 'matters relating to their internal and local affairs' (draft Declaration Article 31).

This is a narrow definition, because, as has been described above, autonomy clearly means that the community itself controls its internal affairs, yet this cannot be done without some influence over external matters. The Arakmbut control all political decisions internal to the community concerning critical questions such as access to resources or marriage. However, the main threats to the community come from outside, arising from the wave of colonisation. In order to deal with these outside threats, every community has to decide how it is going to respond. Territorial and cultural defence involve both internal community strategies, as well as collaboration with other communities to strengthen the indigenous presence in an area. This is the sense in which it is possible to understand the concept of autonomy as it applies to the Amazonian communities of Peru.

The Peruvian Law of Native Communities defines indigenous government in terms of autonomous native communities with elected councils, operating throughout the lowlands of Peru. Each commu-

---

6. The term autonomy should be seen here as one of the options of self-determination (see chapter eight) and not as an alternative.

nity is an autonomous unit, running its internal affairs according to its own customs and representing its interests to the outside world through a governmentally approved structure which defines its juridical personality and holds the land title and any other resource in the name of the community as a whole. However, the connections with other communities provide separate dimensions in indigenous political organisation which transcend the internal notions of community implied by the law. By breaking away from community as defined and recognised by national government institutions, such as the Indigenist Institute or the Ministry of Agriculture, the strength of indigenous representation can grow.

The following sections look at how dimensions of Arakmbut community political organisation provide the means for defence of their indigenous rights in a way that is externally oriented.

Community Defence

The Arakmbut reaction to the colonisation of their territory comes in waves of resignation and resistance. The Arakmbut have a warrior tradition, and they were accustomed in the past to take up arms and defend their people and resources. The difficulty now is that, as warriors, they know today that they are outnumbered by the colonists and could easily be killed. After the murder of José Quique in 1987, for example, their response was one of resignation. This was compounded when one of the elders of the community dreamed of blood running from under the doors of the huts in the community. The dream took place in the forest under the influence of a wachipai spirit, which is considered to be an accurate forecast of future events.

The effect of the murder and the dream have made the Arakmbut of San José more resigned to their fate. Yet they are prepared at any moment to take up arms if they really feel that they are approaching their last battle. The shift from resignation to resistance (Gray 1986:99) is part of the constant changes which take place within an Arakmbut community and depends on several internal factors, such as whether community organisation is concentrated or dispersed and whether they feel that they can take on and beat the outsiders.

Several options are open to the Arakmbut on a daily basis for the internal defence of their community. To prevent colonists from settling in San José, the people have tried to disperse their gold-mining activities to cover as broad an area of the community territory as possible. In 1984, the Arakmbut spread settlements from the mouth of the Pukiri (see case study, chapter three) and asserted their presence throughout the area in the same way as neighbouring Barranco Chico did further upriver. This had its difficulties. The old patrons who lived on the Pukiri were incensed at this assertion of indigenous land rights and threatened the Arakmbut as they worked on the beaches. After the murder of José Quique, the community withdrew from the Pukiri and took a much more cautious attitude to the colonists.

Whenever feasible, colonists are contacted when they move onto community lands and, providing that this takes place soon after arrival, they will sometimes move. This occurred successfully in 1981 when a company from Puerto Maldonado settled on the boundary between San José and Puerto Luz. The community has to act quickly to do this, and often time goes by before a decision emerges from the community. Complications also arise if certain members of the community enter into an agreement with the colonist on certain basis or if, as occasionally happens, they establish ritual godparental ties of compadrazgo. This prevents Arakmbut who are in this relationship from opposing the colonists' presence on the community lands.

If the colonist refuses to leave, there are several options. The easiest is to ignore the encroacher and move to another area of community lands. This retreat is effectively what took place on the Pukiri after 1986, and it also explains why the Arakmbut live and work predominantly in their lands on the beaches of the Karene above the mouth of the Pukiri. Sometimes the community hopes that a colonist will lose interest and move of his own accord, but this is rare.

At several points in their history, the Arakmbut have taken up arms against colonists, with broadly successful results (at least in the short term). The powerful local patron, Jaime Sumalave, was thrown off a gold mining area known as Santa Rosa, which he had taken from the Arakmbut in 1985 (Gray 1986 contains an account of this event). However, these events, although initiated from the community, have always needed some support from outside. Campaigns such as the storming of Boca Colorado took place with an alliance with Puerto Luz, while the threat of the road through their lands was opposed in alliance with Barranco Chico. When conflict becomes a possibility, the Arakmbut have to look further afield for alliances.

Inter-community Defence Alliances

The threat from outside is so strong that it is impossible for an indigenous Amazonian community in Peru to be politically self-sufficient without being taken over by colonisation. Defence has to involve alliances, which join the community members with institutions and interests that can potentially be of service to them. The Arakmbut forged these alliances with two groups of indigenous peoples – other Arakmbut, and the indigenous peoples of the Madre de Dios as a whole.

1. Other Arakmbut – Ethnic Alliance

Community alliance

Throughout their history, the first level of co-ordination takes place with other Arakmbut communities. This involves several complicated features. The relationship between malocas in the pre-mission period consisted of positive alliances in the form of marriage exchanges, fiestas, and collaboration in defence; in certain circumstances this meant bringing together the members of two malocas under one roof. In contrast, negative relations consisted of elopements between men and women without agreement from their parents. Sometimes this led to fighting.

In recent years elopements still cause ill feeling. The elopement of women has affected relations between Boca Inambari, Puerto Luz, and Shintuya and still causes resentment in the communities. When a dispute cannot be regulated within a community the affected persons or, in some cases, several families move elsewhere. Between 1984 and 1986 serious problems between several households in San José led to a series of confrontations resulting in several families moving to Barranco Chico, Shintuya, and Puerto Luz.

Positive and negative events such as these mean that the five Arakmbut communities are linked together by a mixture of friendly and hostile relationships. At any moment it is possible for two communities to fall out or form an alliance and, to a large extent, contemporary community politics are reflections of the constantly shifting alliances between malocas in the period prior to 1956. However this also means that alliances are difficult to predict. For example, in May 1992, Puerto Luz and San José were closely allied together with the idea of supporting an Arakmbut mayor in the February 1993 local elections; yet six months later, a colonist based at Boca Colorado offered Puerto Luz, but not San José, substantial advantages if they supported him. This split the vote, preventing the election of the Arakmbut candidate from San José.

Relations between communities operate on the same two political principles – minimal and diffused – which occur within the community, but on a less intense basis. People who are related in nearby communities will meet up with each other occasionally in order to exchange information. On the basis of these informal meetings, positive and negative relationships can spring up. However, from time to time the communities meet on a more formal bases such as at a kermesse, when neighbouring communities are invited to participate in an evenings' entertainment and drinking in support of the school or communal fund. The fiestas can be quite competitive, with each community vying to bring the better band to play music for dancing and to throw a more enjoyable party. The kermesse take place in each community once a year. During them people manage to exchange information, and should the fiesta go well the informal ties are strengthened between the communities.

The 'minimal government' informal political organisation deals predominantly with the concerns of particular sectors of the community such as marriages and visits, whereas the formal meetings connect with the 'diffused' aspect of the political system of the Arakmbut and deal with community concerns such as gold work, colonists, and indigenous control over the local government of the municipality. These more formal meetings, such as those described in the case study, include members of the different councils and the President of the host community.

Institutional ethnic alliance

In 1981, the colonisation of the Karene river began to reach breaking point for the communities of the area. Two incidents were responsible for this development. A multinational company, Central American Services, had negotiated, with dubious legality, a series of concessions for cattle ranching which was stretching throughout the Madre de Dios and threatened the Arakmbut communities of San José del Karene, Barranco Chico, and Boca Inambari (Moore 1980).[7] At the same time, the gold rush taking place in the Madre de Dios increased in 1980 and 1981. Figures for gold extraction in Madre de Dios averaged at two thousand kilos, which constituted two thirds of the national figures.[8] 1980 and 1981 consequently witnessed a race for gold in the Karene.

7. Central American Services also caused considerable havoc among the brazil nut harvesters by breaking up the market and seriously harming the economies of the indigenous and ribereño communities down river from Puerto Maldonado.
8. I emphasise the word 'figures' because in the 1980s experts considered that as much as 90 percent of gold produced in the Madre de Dios crossed over into Brazil illegally. For this reason gold production figures need not reflect the real

The invasion by the Montecarlo company in 1981, for example, was a major influence on the growing political consciousness of the Arakmbut in San José. The sight of a boat full of armed miners caused considerable fear but through diplomatic tactics, the community managed to see off the colonists without bloodshed. Now, most colonists keep themselves downriver from San José, although there have, in recent years, been clusters of non-indigenous miners invited by members of the community to work in a corner of community lands. This gives rise to much ill-feeling internally. However, the anger is reserved for the patrons of the Pukiri mouth, who illegally grant permission for invaders to settle (c.f. case study, chapter eight).

All of these problems caused concern in San José, but similar events were taking place in the other Arakmbut communities; Puerto Luz, Barranco Chico, and Boca Inambari, in particular, expressed similar concerns. In February 1981 a representative from San José went to Lima and met with the national indigenous Amazonian organisation, AIDESEP, and discussed the possibility of forming an indigenous organisation at the level of the Madre de Dios.

On his return to Madre de Dios the representative visited the different Arakmbut communities in the mining zone, and the decision was made to form an Harakmbut Council to represent the indigenous peoples of the Madre de Dios. A month later representatives from San José, Puerto Luz, and Boca Inambari went to Lima and formalised a relationship with AIDESEP. In January 1982 a meeting was held at Boca Colorado at which FENAMAD was formed (Wahl 1985).

The growth of FENAMAD was gradual. For the first few years the Arakmbut were the main initiators of its work, and during the discussions of its formation, they had assumed that the organisation would be broadly Harakmbut. However, from the first meeting, representatives from other indigenous peoples of the Madre de Dios participated fully and the Arakmbut were satisfied that the organisation would be ethnically broad-based.

---

quantity of gold produced, but can give us some indication of increases and decreases in mining. Since Fujimori deregulated gold production in 1990 and closed down the state managed Banco Minero, there are no figures or estimates of gold production in Peru. The Ministry of Energy and Mines has some figures and estimates, but in 1991 representatives were not even prepared to reveal them in confidence (Felipe Pacuri pers. comm.). Discussions with miners throughout the area indicates a strong decline in gold output since 1990. This is caused by over-exploitation in the headwaters of the Pukiri, and, to a lesser extent, in the Karene, and the resulting ecological destruction of the gold deposits.

The first leadership of FENAMAD was largely Arakmbut, but after about six months, it became clear that the organisation's administration needed to be based in Puerto Maldonado, at the central point of access in the Madre de Dios. The Arakmbut continued to be members of FENAMAD and benefitted from its projects in land titling and its education scholarships. However, the centre of gravity moved downriver and the active leadership became predominantly Shipibo, Ese'eja, and Arasaeri. The Arakmbut members rarely came to Puerto Maldonado to work in the office because their communities were so far away and there were few resources to allow Arakmbut leaders to live in Puerto Maldonado.

Apart from relationships between neighbouring communities (primarily Puerto Luz and San José) which brought the Arakmbut together prior to the formation of FENAMAD, the case study described the tensions within FENAMAD which led to the formation of COHAR. This process repeated two of the features of the original founding of FENAMAD. In the first place, the establishment of COHAR was not done on the spur of the moment, but was a subject which communities had discussed for at least a year prior to the 1993 FENAMAD Congress. The formation of COHAR was actually on the agenda of the Congress and was hastened when the Arakmbut felt that the downriver indigenous peoples of the Madre de Dios had taken over the organisation.

The tension between locality and ethnicity was not solved with the formation of COHAR, because although it has been established as an 'ethnic federation' within FENAMAD, its constituency is primarily in the upper Madre de Dios, where there are also Matsigenka and Piro (Yiné) members. Until now, these tensions have not erupted within COHAR, but it is accepted that the Matsigenka will possibly want to form their ethnic federation within FENAMAD at some point in the future.

The Arakmbut consider themselves as a whole to be quite distinct from the other indigenous peoples of the Madre de Dios. They define their cultural uniqueness as an important asset, but this also has certain complicated effects on their relationships with other indigenous peoples. The Arakmbut are proud of having successfully preserved their language, their knowledge, and their traditions. On the other hand, they often feel inferior to other indigenous peoples who can manage the world dominated by the Peruvian national society more smoothly.

Part of this stems from the fact that they were the last Harakmbut people to be missionised, and furthermore, their contact in 1950 was treated as a major achievement, described by the Dominicans as a 'conquest' (Rummenhöller 1985). For the first years of contact, young Arakmbut students were taken to boarding schools and were, according to their testimonies, treated with contempt by the other indigenous peoples for being 'savage' or 'primitive'.

The previous chapter noted that the Arakmbut felt both embarrassment and pride at their cultural identity. The timidity arose in the face of ridicule by outsiders of their spiritually sensitive understanding of the world, while the pride was the satisfaction they felt at having survived forty years of ethnocide. This complicated juxtaposition of pride and timidity in the views of the community as a whole should be coupled with the resistance/resignation conflict noted above.

These attitudes can also be seen not only in the opinions of groups, but within the psychological make-up of persons themselves. This takes the form of the state of the soul (nokiren), which through life relates to the body in a way which strives to avoid the extremes of over-concentration (hatred associated with sorcery – ochinosik) and over-dispersion (a debilitating weakness arising from the soul leaving the body). (This was analysed in detail in Volume 1, chapter six and Volume 2, chapter two.) Resistance and pride reflect strong and confident states of the nokiren; over-concentration is ameliorated by co-ordination with other Arakmbut. On the other hand, resignation and timidity are debilitating and cause the strength of collectivity to disappear.

The two sets of distinctions, resignation/resistance and cultural pride/timidity, are related. When the Arakmbut feel resignation in the face of threats from outside, their view is that they will be destroyed and that their culture can do nothing to save them. When they feel strong in their resistance to threats, the strength of their cultural identity and pride in their heritage comes to the fore, as when the Arakmbut sang, dance, dress in feathers, and paint. It is almost impossible to identify in advance the moment at which resignation and timidity become resistance and pride. The two elements are bound together and can only be understood in retrospect. This tension generates the personal and social dynamics of political mobilisation through the activity of the nokiren.

The organisation of the Arakmbut as a people provides a broader perspective from which to view the relationship between informal minimal government, formal diffused government and the internal/external orientations of Arakmbut politics. Within the community, the political system is predominantly informal, but the formal aspects are emphasised when external factors are under discussion.

However, informal communication continues outside of the community, but this becomes weaker as the more formal attributes of decision-making need to be ratified by larger numbers. The more these two complimentary aspects of the political system become confused, the more conflicts come to the surface.

The effect is a self-government defined in terms of practical activities and politics, with the concept of community and people as the principle factors. The former is defined according to territory and the latter by ethnic affiliation. Thus, as with the concept of culture, self-government is embedded within the notions of territory and people. The dynamics of political mobilisation take place according to the resignation/resistance and timidity/pride conflicts which affect persons, communities, and the people as a whole. However, the importance of FENAMAD as a political organisation over the last ten years has added another dimension to Arakmbut governance – indigenous inter-ethnicity.

2. Indigenous Peoples of the Madre de Dios

FENAMAD constitutes a different level of organisation from the aspects of governance seen hitherto. Whereas one can talk of community government, it is difficult to talk of FENAMAD as a government as it is a representative non-government organisation. In fact it consists of a federation of communities which acts to bring together the diffuse indigenous political organisations in the Madre de Dios. Each community, on its own, is not powerful enough to defend itself against the threats which it faces. FENAMAD works to provide representation and support for community defence, to co-ordinate the diffused community councils, to inform them of the problems which threaten them from outside, and to promote self-help initiatives.

After the 1982 meeting of FENAMAD it became increasingly clear that the Madre de Dios was one of the most complicated areas of Amazonian Peru for the political organisation of indigenous peoples. In other parts of the Amazon, indigenous peoples have large populations. The Asháninka and Aguaruna have at least four indigenous organisations each and the Shipibo three. These are organised geographically. The Madre de Dios is one of the few areas of Amazonian Peru where the indigenous organisation operates on an inter-ethnic regional basis.

The Madre de Dios has nineteen different ethno-linguistic indigenous peoples. Some of them were brought down into the area at the turn of the century by the rubber barons. Others are survivors of the terrible slave raids *(correrias)* which wrought catastrophic destruction on the peoples of the main Madre de Dios, Inambari, and Tambopata rivers. The indigenous make-up of the Madre de Dios is consequently the result of one hundred years of genocide through murder, disease, and forced removal.

In addition to the variety of indigenous peoples in the Madre de Dios, there is a wide spectrum of relationships with Peruvian national society. Some people may call this a scale of acculturation. However, 'acculturation' implies that the defining feature of an indigenous people is how they relate to the nation state. This work takes issue with the categorisation of indigenous peoples from state-based criteria. Each indigenous people in the Madre de Dios has its own culture and indigenous identity which provides a series of specific relationships to the nation state. Describing these in detail is difficult, but a general impression can be gained by looking at factors such as the history of relations with the national society, distance from urban centres, and the juxtaposition of Peruvian and indigenous cultures. The following broad set of distinctions marks four different community/national society relationships in the Madre de Dios, covering geographical, historical, cultural and political factors.

a) Self-sufficient indigenous peoples

In the Madre de Dios there are a few groups of Yora (Nahua) and Mashco-Piro who have been in sporadic contact with outsiders over recent years. They live largely in the headwaters of the river Piedras and are currently at risk from the explorations of Mobil, the oil company. In September 1996 FENAMAD wrote a letter to Mobil accusing their contracted company, Grant Geophysical, of seeking contact and placing these peoples' lives in jeopardy.

Other Mashco-Piro live in the Manu National Park and come to posts such as Pakitsa from time to time to exchange produce for pots and clothes. The Nahua travel in and out of the Park and occasionally visit relatives in the Purus and in Sepahua mission. These indigenous peoples live for periods in native communities and then move on. They speak predominantly their own language and have little or no knowledge of or interest in the outside world.

b) Indigenous peoples with limited national contacts

Within the Manu Park there are several Matsigenka communities, such as Tayakome and Yomibato, which are largely self-sufficient. They speak mainly their own language, but the communities have schools which are run by secular missionaries. Their main contacts with national society come through the priests, the park authorities, and environmental organisations working in the park. Production in the communities is not oriented to the market, although there are some exchanges which involve money.

c) Indigenous people with two worlds

In the Madre de Dios, the other Arakmbut communities are in a situation similar to that described for San José. The internal aspects of the community are run on the basis of the indigenous culture, but the money economy is a part of their daily life, and most community members are broadly conversant in Spanish. The economy is a combination of subsistence activities such as gardening, fishing, hunting, and gathering, and commercial activities such as gold mining and gathering brazil nuts. Some of the Ese'eja, Piro, Amahuaca, and Wachipaeri communities are in a similar position to the Arakmbut communities, although they have been in contact with outsiders for many more years. The gold rush in the Karene during the late 1970s and early 1980s contributed to the juxtaposition of the two worlds – indigenous and Peruvian.

d) The bi-cultural indigenous peoples

These communities in the Madre de Dios are those which are fully conversant with Spanish and the national society. However, they are still indigenous and are aware of their difference from the colonist population. This may not always have been the case, and there are examples of indigenous peoples who only comparatively recently realised that they were different from the Quechuan highlanders. Some of these communities speak more Spanish than their indigenous language, which is confined mainly to older people. The main communities in this relationship are those which have been most traumatised by contact and have suffered most in terms of decimation. The peoples brought to the Madre de Dios during the rubber boom, such as the Shipibo and Santarosinos (Quichuaruna), and those decimated by the caucheros, such as the Arasaeri and some Ese'eja, share these characteristics.

FENAMAD thus represents communities and people from all of these four points in the spectrum of inter-cultural blending. The concept of acculturation is not relevant here in that in no case have any of these communities lost their indigenous identity as they become conversant with different spheres of national society.

There are several correlations between the communities which are closer to urban or small town centres, such as Pilcopata, Mazuco, or Puerto Maldonado. They are comparatively more conversant with the national society and have been in contact with Peruvian life for longer. The communities closer to these centres have taken on most of the active support and work for FENAMAD. The other communities are progressively more distant from population centres and more separate from the national society.

Passing through the spectrum of communities, it is possible to see that those which have the least contact with national society are the most monocultural, with predominant emphasis on the indigenous culture. Arakmbut communities such as San José are conversant in both languages, whereas those closest to population centres have the highest frequency of monolingual Spanish speakers. Along with the cultural differences, it is also possible to see the juxtaposition of the minimal and diffused governments, which co-exist in San José in shifting emphasis. Those with the least contact operate on the basis of more traditional informal minimal community government, while those that have the closest relationship to the national society utilise the community council to a greater extent. This is not to say that the communities such as Tayakome do not have formal community meetings (the schools ensure this), nor does it mean that the communities closer to Puerto Maldonado do not have their own minimal government. The difference is that there is a shift in emphasis between the two aspects of the political system, which relates to the other transformations. These shifts of system are presented in the following table:

Table 6.2 Indigenous communities in the Madre de Dios

Contact	Government	Location	Culture
Little	Minimal	Six days from town	Monocultural
Regular	Minimal mainly	Four days from town	Some Spanish
Constant	Minimal/Diffused	Two days from town	Indigenous/Spanish
Permanent	Diffused mainly	One day from town	Bi-cultural

This table provides a rough model for all the communities of the Madre de Dios. Although it does not illustrate the idiosyncrasies which arise in every community, it gives an idea of the difficulties facing FENAMAD when bringing together the peoples of the Madre de Dios in an indigenous representative organisation.

The case study related the tension which arose within FENAMAD in 1991 between the communities closer to Puerto Maldonado (lower Madre de Dios) and those more oriented to Pilcopata and Cusco (upper Madre de Dios). In this case Shintuya, which has better facilities than most other communities owing to its position as the centre of missionary activity in the area, has actively worked towards a decentralisation of FENAMAD. The Arakmbut at the mission objected to the centralisation of FENAMAD in Puerto Maldonado which, they argued, benefits communities of the lower Madre de Dios.

FENAMAD has worked closely with the environmental and development organisation, Centro Eori, in titling indigenous communities in the Madre de Dios. All of the current land titling and preparation on the Amarakaeri Communal Reserve has been done by FENAMAD and Eori; furthermore, Arakmbut communities have been helped to obtain gold mining permits and to defend their rights against invasions. FENAMAD has achieved recognition as a representative organisation and has had considerable influence within the government of the sub-region. This has been helped by the alliance with the Agrarian Federation, FADEMAD, which has brought FENAMAD into the forefront of regional and sub-regional politics. Particularly fortuitous was the election of FENAMAD's legal advisor, Felipe Pacuri, as the first Vice President of the Inka Region.

In 1991, FENAMAD ensured support from the regionalisation process (which has been dissolved by Fujimori) and, through lobbying contacts, was able to establish a series of secondary school scholarships for community students. A grant from the Norwegian development agency NORAD has enabled FENAMAD to support indigenous university students in Lima. Parallel to these activities, FENAMAD has been working on a traditional health programme and an Arakmbut project for the revitalisation of culture both of which were discussed briefly in chapter five.

In spite of all of its initiatives, FENAMAD has faced many difficulties in its ten years (Gray 1986: 84-87). The great ethnic diversity, together with the variety of communities, make local work difficult. In addition, FENAMAD has had a constant shortage of funds, which means that visiting communities more than one day's distance from Puerto Maldonado has been difficult. The funds cannot support a leadership to live in Puerto Maldonado and run the office, which means that those who work at the headquarters are often those who live in nearby communities.

For this reason, FENAMAD has functioned with a high proportion of representatives from the communities closer to Puerto Maldonado, who are themselves more familiar with the running of the state institutions. This has been an outcome of the conditions in which the organisation is run, rather than any deliberate policy. The effect has been to give the impression to the communities further away from FENAMAD that it is dominated by the communities living nearer to Puerto Maldonado. Indeed, while living in San José, it became clear quite how far away Puerto Maldonado is in the eyes of the community. People are reluctant to go to the town which lies two days downriver and possibly three day's return journey upstream. At the nearest port to Puerto Maldonado, Laberinto, the indigenous representatives immediately come into conflict with the police and armed forces. They demand to see their electoral cards (most of the community have no cards) and also the papers for their boats. Indigenous peoples are exempt from paying tax on their boats but the harbour authorities often try to charge them money. When they get to Maldonado, accommodation is uncomfortable or expensive and getting attention from authorities invariably involves several days waiting. For this reason it comes as little surprise that the community members feel a reluctance to go to Puerto Maldonado unless they really have to.

The effect is that FENAMAD has considerable difficulty keeping close contact with its constituent communities. An initiative to decentralise FENAMAD by opening a traditional health centre in the mission of Shintuya and establishing a network of radios made some initial difference, and now that COHAR is running well as a part of FENAMAD, there is hope that the intricate relations between people and territories will be able to operate smoothly.

Conclusion

Previous chapters have argued that the appearance of the notion of indigenous rights emerges as a result of practical experience of the clear violation of what the peoples concerned consider to be just. The right to government is not the issue in the Madre de Dios because Arakmbut communities are self-governing and, as yet, there is no direct threat to the system. The problems facing the Arakmbut are rather articulated as demands for a more refined and efficient organisation.

FENAMAD has had difficulty drawing together the problems of over forty communities in the Madre de Dios with few resources; the Arakmbut formed their Consejo because they wanted to assert control over the organisation which represents their communities. The Arakmbut acted not because their right to internal community government was affected, but because they felt that their external influence was not strong enough to defend their rights against the encroachments of colonists onto their territory. They wanted political attention to support their struggle. This parallels the Arakmbut approach to health and education noted in the previous chapter; rather than proclaiming right to health, education, or government, they maintain that they have a right to attention which reflects and satisfies their needs.

In conclusion, the Arakmbut do not express the notion of government but are self-governing in practice. They acknowledge the need to make decisions without interference, but they also want to control the support which they receive from outside. Genuine self-government is not something which can be imposed from above, but must be controlled from within. The Law of Native Communities provides a structure for autonomous self-government; however, this would never have worked unless it made practical sense to the communities. That sense came through government recognition of identity as a people and territorial title.

Furthermore, the Arakmbut have incorporated the prerequisites of the Law of Native Communities into their political system in order to transcend community boundaries and establish a broader political organisation through the ethnic and local federations. As far as a people can control their political system, they can be said to determine their decision-making processes. Where a government imposes this system unwanted, indigenous peoples lose their self-determination and become colonised.

The strength of the Arakmbut political system is that it is multi-layered. The minimal organisation of social encounters, the diffuse community council, the ethnically based council, and the regional federation are all aspects of 'self-government'. Government imposed from above has been ameliorated because each community incorporates the external system when it provides a defence from external threats. In this way the imposed community model of the Law of Native Communities has been internalised into the community. Nevertheless, any imposition of external systems of government on top of preexistent political structures inevitably brings tensions, particularly when informal and formal arrangements become confused. In this way, internal community tensions are as much a part of Arakmbut political life as the inter-ethnic tensions are within FENAMAD.

Government and cultural identity have provided a contrast to the chapters on territory and people. Whereas the concepts of Arakmbut and wandari relate closely to the notion of territory and people, those of cultural identity and governance have no real Arakmbut equivalents. This is because culture and government are already embedded in the more all-embracing notions of people and territory. Furthermore, threats to the Arakmbut as a people and to their territory are far more apparent than those to their government and cultural identity, which have both been the sources of innovations adopted by the Arakmbut. Thus, whereas the Arakmbut are aware of violations of their rights to territory and as a people, rights to cultural identity and government are articulated more in the sense of the lack of support, services, and facilities to which they feel entitled. The following two chapters look at two more open-ended concepts relating to Arakmbut indigenous rights: these are self-development and self-determination.

Chapter 7

SELF-DEVELOPMENT
An Alternative to the Impasse

> 'I just want to carry on working gold with my in-laws and have a wife who will tend the produce in the gardens. I need game to feed the household. We want to drink our beer at weekends and enjoy life. But these outsiders take our gold, scare off the animals, and steal our women. The colonists prevent us from living our lives as we want to.'

An Arakmbut elder made this statement at a community meeting in May 1992, which the adults from San José had called to discuss their future. The constant pressure from the colonisation of their homeland has led the Arakmbut to feel a sense of desperation for their future. Whereas the last chapter demonstrated that the Arakmbut are largely self-governing in terms of decision-making and conflict resolution, their sovereignty decreases as their hold over their territory becomes weaker. They want to secure access to their resources, whether meat, crops, or gold; however, the gold rush and colonisation process means that the territory over which the Arakmbut have control is becoming increasingly restricted.

When the Arakmbut discussed their visions for the future at that May meeting, they were entering into a discussion about development issues. Their views are, at first sight, contradictory. The Arakmbut have all agreed with the sentiments of the elder above, who argues for a future that reinforces a quiet and fulfilled lifestyle without interference from settlers. At the same time, several Arakmbut made clear at the same meeting that they wanted to benefit from the same advantages as the colonists living in the settlement at Boca Colorado. One man argued this clearly: 'Why should the wahaipis at

Boca Colorado be the only people in the district with electricity? Why should they be claiming safe piped drinking water when we have to go to the river down a muddy slope? Why should we not have a parabolic antenna to watch the television – even the priests in Shintuya have bought television for the community?'

The Arakmbut do not consider these views contradictory but want to combine the positive aspects of their own lifestyles with those of the settlers. The conflict arises between the Arakmbut, who want to control their destiny through their own forms of governance, and the settlers, whose life-styles are based on the maximisation and indiscriminate extraction of resources. The settler view of development is embedded in the contradictory interests of a state-centred concept of *desarrollo* (development) and unfettered market forces. These ideologies constitute a regular justification for discrimination against the Arakmbut.

Almost all the problems facing the Arakmbut stem from external development initiatives arising from the interests of state-sponsored development and the uncontrolled market forces of the colonising frontier.[1] The pressures on Arakmbut resources grew with the gold rush of the late 1970s. Gradually, during the last fifteen years, the corporate state intervention and control of market forces, which had been the dominant development ideology from the time of President Velasco, became increasingly overshadowed by the influence of neo-liberal economics.

This neo-liberal restructuring of Peruvian capitalism, promoted by the current president, Fujimori, has placed a strong emphasis on enterprise. Using free market principles and minimal state intervention, the idea has been to let markets draw economic development through competition. However, in countries such as Peru, the markets are so fragmented and competition so limited that the effects of

1. The conflict between market forces and the state goes back to the Enlightenment. Hobbes and Locke discussed the conflict between possessive individualism based on market forces and sanctity of property, and the need for social order within the state (Slater 1993:97). The concern of these writers was that the greater the promotion of individual freedom, the more chaos threatens, while if the state imposes too much order, the consequences impinge on individual freedom (Macpherson 1962). Individual freedom was thus pitted against the need for a coherent socio-political organisation. The same discussion continued in the nineteenth century under the liberal promotion of the free market, controlled by a state run on positivistic legal approaches, which was largely taken up by utilitarian thinkers. In the twentieth century, as development has increasingly taken on an economic growth perspective, these discussions have been brought into a framework where the market and the state consist of opposing forces of development (Hettne 1982:14).

neo-liberal economics encourage its detrimental aspects such as high unemployment, increase in poverty, and inequality – the very evils that economic development is supposed to alleviate.

One of the reasons for the recent shift to market forces has been the debt crisis, which places the Peruvian state in a position of dependency on international institutions such as the International Monetary Fund, which vigorously promotes neo-liberal economics. So common has this phenomenon become in Latin America that the 1980s were seen in development terms as *la decada perdida* – the lost decade (Escobar 1993a). The Peruvian government's development policies are bounded by its crippling debt obligations, and the more destitute the state becomes, the more it seeks resources to service its debt from the more distant regions of the country, where indigenous peoples such as the Arakmbut have their territories (Gray 1995b:233). The recent mining and land laws open indigenous territories to exploitation by gold and oil companies while offering untitled rainforest lands to the highest bidder.

In spite of international dependence on a *laissez faire* ideology, however, development aid is by no means dead in Peru; it exists in the form of economic and welfare projects firmly bound into the political economy of multinational institutions such as the World Bank, national development agencies, and non-governmental organisations (Cassen 1994:2). Development is a concept which is connected to state-centred thought (Hettne op.cit. 22) and most of the development aid which goes to Peru passes through the government. The initiatives for development made by the colonists in Boca Colorado, for example, all seek support from the Peruvian state.

Peru provides an illustration of how there are constant shifts between the development poles of state and market (Hettne 1995:9).[2]

2. Hettne distinguishes state capitalist strategies of development: the industrialisation of agrarian economies in newly formed capitalist states such as Russia, Germany, and Japan at the turn of the century; Keynesianism, which is an attribute of entrenched capitalism, by which the state acts as a regulator of the market to ensure stability and growth; and the most extreme state model in which state structures replace the market, as took place in the former Soviet Union and Eastern Europe. This was the model which Velasco tried to establish in Peru.

Market emphases of development range from models where the growth process is more gradual, such as in Peru during the late 1970s and early 1980s, under Presidents Morales Bermúdez and Belaúnde, to the recent extreme neo-liberal wave taking hold in many countries, particularly Peru under Fujimori, which tries to eradicate the influence of the state over the market altogether. Thus in twenty years Peru has shifted from an extreme state-based to an extreme market-oriented model of development.

This has important implications for indigenous peoples who find themselves caught between these forces. Too much state intervention can be as disastrous for indigenous peoples as the unlicensed free market promotion of colonisation, because any initiative which has neither the consent nor the control of indigenous peoples is effectively an invasion of their territory. It is therefore not surprising that so many indigenous peoples consider that development is not so much a solution but part of the problem.

Indigenous Peoples and Development

When looking at the relationship between indigenous peoples and nation states, the concept of development is constantly lurking in the shadows. As with the other concepts reviewed in this book, 'development' is quintessentially Eurocentric and state-centred. Within the framework of development classification, indigenous peoples are categorised as an 'undeveloped' backward sector, hindering national progress. Writers differ as to where these characteristics emerged in European history. Nisbet (1969), for example, traces the history of ideas concerning growth, progress, and development back to the Greeks, Romans, and medieval Christian thinkers. He considers that western thought has consistently combined the idea of genesis and decay through the notion of growth which he defines as change intrinsic to the entity being changed, change as directional, and change as cumulative.[3]

Some writers consider that the roots of current notions of development can be found in the Enlightenment, arising from the emergence of modernity in the form of the political economy as a field of study, the appearance of welfare as a way of ensuring social standards of normality, and the conceptualisation of undeveloped people (Watts 1995:47).[4] During this period, indigenous peoples were

3. Greek philosophers used the concept *physis* (growth) to refer to the principle of generation. With Aristotle, the term became closely connected with causality, which sees development as a process of change present in all existence (Nisbet 1969:29). Whereas Classical thinkers saw growth as cycles of genesis and decay arranged in ages or periods, Christian thinkers, such as St. Augustine, moulded the Classical approaches to growth into an idea of one cosmic cycle under the control of God, starting from the Garden of Eden and moving on to the end of time.
4. The eighteenth century witnessed an increase in the idea that knowledge was cumulative and that life tended towards a gradual improvement. The writings of Fontenelle (Bury 1932) argued that human beings could never degenerate and that there was no end to the growth of knowledge and wisdom. The develop-

used as examples of markers of change; writers such as Adam Smith and Turgot posited a four-stage theory of development: hunting, pastoralism, agriculture, and commerce (Meek 1976). This emerging notion of growth and progress became bound up with the positivism of the nineteenth century, particularly through the Saint-Simonians and Comte, who had such an influence in South America (Cowen and Shenton 1995:32-33). By the second part of the century, progress and growth were blended into the notion of evolution, while development was increasingly connected to the growth of empires and nation-states (ibid.:36).[5] The nineteenth century operated under an evolutionary system of comparative classification, of which Morgan was the most famous exponent, which placed indigenous peoples on a ladder stretching from 'savagery' at the lowest level through 'barbarism' to 'civilisation'.

This approach to what was later term 'undeveloped' continued in the twentieth century. Some writers, such as Wolfgang Sachs (Watts 1995:51), consider that 'development' was created in the late 1940s, following the Second World War, when the Marshall Plan in Europe provided the means for re-constituting the national economies that had been devastated by the conflict. European reconstruction took place largely through a planned programme of investment and, on the basis of this experience, economists began to see the injection of capital as a way of encouraging development in poorer countries.

The economists Harrod and Domar argued that this should take place by mobilising domestic and foreign savings to invest in industry and national programmes. By saving from the gross national product of a country it would be possible to achieve a point where the economy would 'take off' (Todaro 1989). W.W. Rostow (1960) postulated a five-stage theory based on the use of investment: traditional society; take-off into self-sustaining growth; drive to maturity; maturity and the age of mass consumption. The basic tenet of this 'modernisation' approach was 'development as an identifiable process of growth and change whose main features are similar in all countries' (Todaro 1989:77). Traditional societies (primarily agrarian

---

ment of the notion of progress was supported in France by thinkers such as Condorcet, and in Germany a stream of philosophers from Kant to Hegel argued for the inevitability of progress.

5. Using examples from Hegel, Marx, Spencer, and Morgan, Nisbet (1969:165) identifies the facets of evolution which relate to the earlier ideas of growth: change as natural, directional, immanent, continuous, necessary, and proceeding from uniform causes.

subsistence economies), which included indigenous peoples, were obstacles to progress.[6]

This approach consists of an economistic reformulation of the eighteenth century developmentalist and nineteenth century evolutionary stages, but in all cases, indigenous peoples are placed lower on the scale than the rest of humanity. By categorising them into an evolutionary typology, indigenous peoples have become treated as 'survivals' of older peoples. This is effectively a reformulation of the racist and colonialist justifications for the imperial order from the days when Europe dominated the world.

The arguments against these evolutionary approaches are strong. Indigenous peoples today have lived through history in the same way as any other peoples; without interference, their lifestyle would change in a manner appropriate to the world in which they live, not as non-indigenous writers think it ought to 'develop'. The implications of this is that as part of their self-governance, indigenous peoples should live within the framework of their own development.

Another anti-evolutionary argument, used by Nisbet, criticises the metaphor of growth itself, which has dominated Western intellectual thought and been reified onto real lives and events.

'The less the cognitive distance, the less the relevance and utility of the metaphor. In other words, the more concrete, empirical, and behavioural our subject matter, the less the applicability of the theory of development and its several conceptual elements' (Nisbet 1969.:267).

Indigenous peoples can thus be seen to have their own development, or to challenge the whole concept of development. In spite of these critiques, however, the vestiges of evolutionary racism still exist in contexts ranging from the Madre de Dios to the discussions in the United Nations.

Opposition to Progress

Not all writers have seen development as evolutionary progress. Some have taken a more sceptical view. Hobbes, Locke, Rousseau, and Hume each saw the indigenous peoples of the Americas as examples

6. More modernisation analyses appeared in the 1970s, looking at the conversion of 'traditional' agrarian economies into industrial ones. The economist Lewis argued that this involved transferring labour from the agrarian to the industrial sectors through higher wages, whereas, on a more empirical level, Chenery analysed case studies to demonstrate that, as per capita income rises, economies shift from agriculture to industry (Todaro 1989).

of the state of nature or of natural society. Their notion of change was developmentalist, but not based on the assumption of an inevitable improvement which effectively defined other peoples using developmentalist criteria. Rousseau used the idea of progress, but he did not imply a necessary 'improvement'. People in the state of nature were capable of self-improvement through reason, yet the cultivation of land and the establishment of property led to inequality and injustice. Progress only really appears when human beings can re-introduce notions of natural justice and equality reigns (1984:88). Hume was even more sceptical about the notion of progress.

> 'As far, therefore, as observation reaches,' he said, 'there is no universal difference discernible in the human species; and though it were allowed, that the universe, like an animal body, had a natural progress from infancy to old age, yet as it must be uncertain, whether, at present, it be advancing to its point of perfection, or declining from it' (Hume 1993:224).

In the nineteenth century, several thinkers were sceptical of the notion of progress: De Tocqueville queried the inevitable progressive flow of life; Nietzsche saw the industrial world as increasingly decadent and philistine; while the transcendentalists of New England, such as Hawthorne, questioned the idea that time marched into the future and sought an escape route from the presence of decay. Yet the optimistic idea that progress and growth would bring automatic benefits to the target groups became stronger with the modernisation paradigm of development in the post-war period.

A reaction arose to the modernisation approach in the 1970s through the analysis of structural dependency. There have been several different versions of this paradigm, but the common elementis to look beyond internal factors of development to see how modernisation creates underdevelopment. The neo-colonialist dependency model was greatly influenced by Latin American thinkers such as the Argentinean Prebisch and the Brazilian Furtado (Kay 1989). The challenge to the modernisation approach was to see development in the context of the socio-historical expansion of western Europe, as countries of the centre exploit those of the periphery.

This argument was developed by Frank (1967), who looked at modes of domination and dependency between countries, showing how a metropolis survives by expropriating surplus from its satellites. Particularly important in this context is the monopoly capital of transnational corporations, which need to expand to survive. The resources needed for the expansion lead the corporations to act as predators on developing countries. Elites in developing countries usually support this exploitation and gain accordingly. In this way, alliances develop between elites throughout the world who are involved at different points in the development process. Thus for the dependency theorists, development need not be positive, but can have serious negative consequences. Furthermore, underdevelopment is not caused by internal mechanisms but arises from exploitation by outside interests.

Instead of investment, the dependency approach advocates the break of exploitative ties with the developed world and the promotion of self-sufficiency, particularly through improved production. Without this, the discrepancy between poor and rich countries will escalate. Growth is not necessarily the best solution for solving inequality and poverty; what is needed is a change in social, political, and economic structures. Indigenous peoples recognise the idea of dependency when they find poverty increasing as their resources are plundered. But a weakness, from an indigenous perspective, is dependency's state-centred approach.

Over the years, the dependency approach has responded to criticisms of its initial bold formula. The reaction has led to two different directions of thought, each moving away from the state. Some, such as José Matos Mar, argue that dependency is not only something which takes place between countries but within them (Long 1977: chapter four). Local factors, ethnic relations, environmental questions, and scale are all aspects of development ignored by the dependency approach because of its state-centred orientation. The approach of writers such as Matos Mar opens up the possibility of an alternative developments for indigenous peoples.

In another direction, Wallerstein (1979) and many others took the interdependence of countries further by looking at the question of dependency from the point of view of the world as a system. According to this approach, the world system consists of a relationship between the core, periphery, and semi-periphery. As the centre becomes incapable of surviving in the scramble for resources, the semi-peripheral areas stand the chance of becoming future core areas. In this way states, empires, and corporations rise and fall. This globalisation of development theory is significant in the light of the debt problem facing Peru, because to some extent development consists of political economiies shifting within one system, rather than a teleological notion of progress through time.

Modernisation and dependency theories continue a history of development models of growth and decay that have been used for both state and market-run economies.[7] Modernisation theory is the more optimistic approach, seeing growth as progressive and positive, while dependency sees decay and exploitation as the result of developed countries heedlessly following their push for gain. However, both approaches operate simultaneously, because they reflect relationships inherent in capitalism -one treating growth as the natural conversion of resources into wealth, the other as a form of exploitation. However, whereas modernisation follows the tradition of defining indigenous peoples as a low point on an evolutionary scale, dependency recognises their plight but proffers no solution outside of the state. For colonists who are state-centred, the modernisation and dependency approaches may still have some relevance, but for indigenous peoples, the post-dependence notions of development have reached an impasse which can be approached either in terms of alternative development or avoidance of development altogether.

Alternative Development or No Development?

The difference of perspective between colonist and indigenous viewpoints reflects the crises of interpretation which have plagued development work in recent years. Writers on development have recognised an impasse or crisis in development studies since the 1980s (Schuurman 1993:10; Escobar 1995a:212; Leys 1996:19). However, rather than being a victory of neo-liberalism over controlled development, the impasse has consisted of a dispersion of the notion of development into several different areas, which writers often have difficulty combining.

However, most approaches to economic development appear large-scale from the perspective of indigenous peoples. Rather than take the state and markets as the starting point for development, indigenous self-development operates on the basis of an 'alternative' programme or, 'another development', as Hettne calls it (1982:75). Development is frequently perceived as negative by indigenous peoples, who associate it exclusively with the political-economic state-oriented models of growth or as the justification for the neo-colonial extraction of resources from indigenous territories. Yet it can provide badly needed resources to protect and promote their rights. Thus, development is a two-edged sword which can both threaten and offer a future for indigenous peoples.

7. The distinction is fundamental and provides the basis for books as different as Long 1977, Roxborough 1979, Hettne 1982, and Todaro 1989.

In response, some indigenous peoples who accept the notion of development prefer the concept 'self-development', to refer to self-defence against interference from alien models of development. This is an indigenous form of alternative development or 'another development' which Hettne (1982) bases on the Cocoyoc Declaration: it is need-oriented, endogenous, self-reliant, ecologically sound, and based on structural transformation. Self-reliance is a particularly important goal of alternative development proposals.[8] In addition to self-reliance, however, the scale of development is an important issue. The original aim of alternative development was to look for practical ways to break through dependency ties. For this reason non-government organisations and smaller development agencies began to turn to projects which looked at the local implications of development work, rather than the large-scale state level approaches.

During the 1980s, as the neo-liberal approach to development began to take hold in developing countries, alternative approaches to development also became more prominent to counteract this *laissez faire* tendency. The publication of the report of the World Commission on Environment and Development (WCED) 'Our Common Future' (1986:43), argued for the concept of sustainable development which is 'development that meets the needs of the present without compromising the ability of future generations to meet their own needs'. This concept of sustainability is seen as a move towards alternative development. However, the concept has been used by all sides of the development debate, and cannot yet be claimed exclusively by alternative development models (Adams 1995:99).

Indigenous peoples provide much scope for a discussion of alternative development. Living in predominantly rural areas, they aim for a combination of small-scale, multi-dimensional projects with environmental sensitivity, cultural protection, and sustainable economies:

> 'What indigenous peoples are presenting is an *alternative development* ... The alternative concept means that indigenous peoples can become self-supporting – but not until they themselves feel capable of doing so. The idea should not be one of privatisation of rural indigenous economies but collective or community developments which are determined by the recipients who become the *subjects* not the objects of development' (Henriksen 1989:15-16).

8. Johann Galtung has written of these in the form of hypotheses covering priorities to address basic needs, local participation, creativity, diversity, less alienation, ecological balance, just distribution, solidarity, avoidance of dependency, stronger defence, and bringing centre and periphery on an equal footing (Hettne 1982:78).

Since 1990, an intense discussion has arisen within the framework of indigenous development. The original notion of indigenous development as 'alternative' was a process of self-reliance based on territorial consolidation and culturally appropriate production, which could ensure the sustainability of indigenous communities. In contrast to this position, there has appeared a philosophy of development for indigenous peoples which is based in on the market economy.

This discussion of development is reminiscent of the debate which took place among ecologists in the 1980s. In contrast to the self-reliant approach to ecology, there arose a group of 'green capitalists' (Elkington & Burke 1989). The idea of this philosophy is to utilise the money-making potential of industry to protect the environment. Taken to the indigenous field, this appears in the form of initiatives such as the Rainforest Harvest (Counsell & Rice 1992), whereby indigenous peoples collect crops and sell them to international companies. This provides the companies (such as Body Shop or Cultural Survival Enterprises) with profits and the indigenous people with money.

Considerable scepticism and animosity has arisen in the debate between the approach to indigenous development based on self-reliance and marketing produce as forms of development.[9] The difference between the marketeers and those advocating indigenous self-development stem from two contrasting points. The 'market positions' argue that indigenous peoples need money to escape from their problems, and that their integration into wider socio-economic entities will ensure their protection in the future. Territorial consolidation is important, but secondary. Those opposing this view are critical of the idea that integration and investment will solve the problems of indigenous peoples. Furthermore, they consider that markets which are outside indigenous peoples' control will lead to further dependency.

This current debate has brought the alternative development argument full circle. Within the 'alternative development' approach there have arisen new versions of the modernisation and dependency views of development. Those supporting the idea of integrating indigenous peoples into the market economy are broadly in line with the modernisation advocates which rely on markets and investment; in contrast, the anti-market position starts from the fact that indigenous peoples are caught in a colonial relationship with the

9. For a rundown of the debate see Gray (1991), Corry (1993), and Clay (1993).

nation state in which they live and that development should be oriented to support the greatest amount of freedom from those dependent ties as possible. This would mean that indigenous peoples and the state work out a mutually beneficial relationship.

Another option for indigenous peoples is to seek alternatives to development, rather than alternative development (Escobar 1993b). For indigenous peoples, such as the Arakmbut, this takes two forms. It means opposing hegemonic definitions of development, both in theory and practice, while establishing strategies of development which are not based on economic growth models, but on their own socio-cultural needs. The Arakmbut provide two ways of looking at development which challenge those forms which are state-controlled or based on market forces. Their culturally based, self-controlled development could well be seen as localised alternative forms of 'another development' which by-pass the state altogether (Hettne op.cit. 162); alternatively, the Arakmbut conceptualisation of development could be seen as a rejection of the development paradigm itself – 'not development alternatives but alternatives to development' arising from within the indigenous social movement (Escobar 1995b:219; Schuurman 1993b). These approaches are not mutually exclusive, but, for the Arakmbut, coexist simultaneously. The following case study illustrates these points:

The Planned Road from Boca Colorado to Huaypetue

The enthusiastic initiator of this scheme was Lucho Otzuka from Puerto Maldonado. According to people from San José who had talked to local traders, his plan was to construct a road and colonisation project from Colorado to Huaypetue which would slice through the territories of San José and Barranco Chico. He said that he had received $10,000 from a source, which he did not reveal; but others in Boca Colorado said it came from Abel Muñiz of Villa Carmen, who had plans to 'develop' the area.

It appeared that the settlers in Boca Colorado had formed a Comité Pro-Carretera (Road Committee) and were trying to raise money to take advantage of the new lands which would be opened up by the road. Their aim was to parcel out lands on either side of the road for cattle, wood, and agriculture. This would mean dividing up San José's lands for colonists. The Arakmbut were extremely worried about the road, and it increasingly appeared in community discussions, both formal and informal, from our arrival in October 1991.

Map 5 Planned road through San José

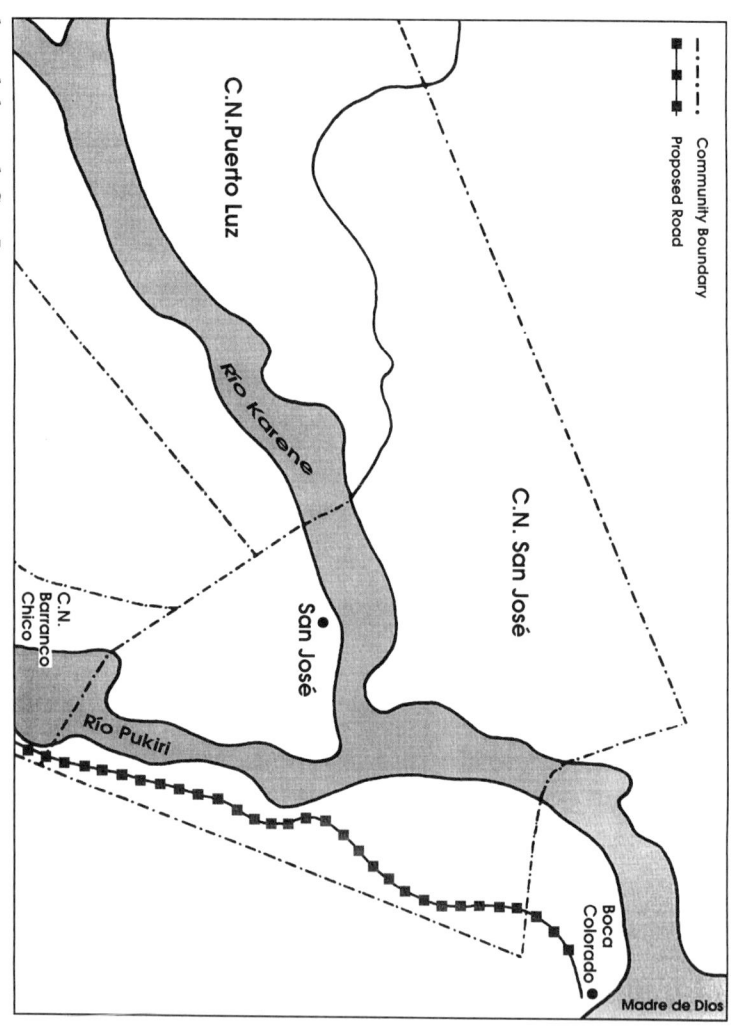

The first definite proof of the plan was when Otzuka brought up a caterpillar bulldozer from Puerto Maldonado and began to clear the road in the first week of November 1991. 'You are studying development, Wamambuey. Why don't you go and find out what he's doing?' suggested an influential man from San José. So on Sunday 3 November 1991, I went with the university student Tomás Arique to Boca Colorado. Otzuka was in his caterpillar and we had a conversation.

He obligingly drew a map of where he thought the road would go and claimed to know nothing of the demarcated community territories. He said that he had $10,000 invested in the project and that it would go ahead because it was in the national interest, a condition that overrides the Law of Native Communities. He said that he would consult with San José and Barranco Chico about the road. He had no worries about their accepting the idea because he would parcel the lands in their territories out for them to use. 'Everyone wants development and this will bring development to the area. Produce can be commercialised and wood or other resources will come to Boca Colorado. This will develop the whole area and help Peru,' he said.

Back in San José an informal meeting of concerned Arakmbut made it clear that they were opposed to the road. 'Originally', said one 'I thought that Otzuka would not be able to raise the money, but the road is only thirteen kilometres from Boca Pukiri and he has $10,000 from somewhere. They will never come and discuss it though, even though they promised.'

However, over the next few weeks it appeared that not everyone in the Boca Colorado was in favour of the road and a split was developing. Comerciantes who got their goods from Cusco via Shintuya were not enthusiastic about the competition from Huaypethue which the road would bring. On the other hand, the settlers with interests in the Pukiri were in favour. The gold in the area was running out and they were looking for ways to develop their economy into wood and cattle. The road was seen by them as a major new development initiative. Several people in the Bajo Pukiri area said that they were attracted to the zone because of the possibility of the road. The powerful Mateus family was keen, and there had been a general threat from the area against the native communities if they oppose the road.

FENAMAD made a visit to the Karene during its preparatory research for the reports to establish the Amarakaeri Communal Reserve spoke to the Comité Pro-Carretera twice. After the first meeting the Comité was informed that there was no official permission to proceed with the road. After the second meeting they said that they would not go ahead. The Comité told FENAMAD that they would be able to move the road outside of San José's territory. However, only a week later, Otzuka said to the Arakmbut that there was no alternative route and that he intended to follow an existing trail made by Shell twenty years ago which avoid the swamp land (aguajales) immediately outside San José's territory.

As a result of FENAMAD's insistence that there be a proper consultation, a member of the Comité visited San José one day in January without giving any notice. No member of the council was in the community; the women were in the gardens and most of the men were working gold. The visitor entered and left the community without attending any formal or informal meeting. The community later heard that they had been 'consulted'.

Concern was mounting, and a delegation from the community arranged to go down to Boca Colorado in February to talk the project over with Otzuka and the Comité Pro-Carretera. Twenty men went down one Saturday to have a meeting with the council of Boca Colorado. When they arrived, Otzuka was nowhere to be seen and all the officials they were meant to speak with were drunk. The elders were furious and decided to reinforce their opposition to the road. A few days later someone from the municipality told visitors from San José at Boca Colorado that it was irrelevant whether San José and the Commission opposed the road or not because the Comité Pro-Carretera was going ahead anyway.

In March, San José met with a group of Arakmbut who came down the Pukiri from Barranco Chico. Their community stands to be affected when the road passes through San José. They stated that they were extremely concerned about the proposed road because it would lead to more colonists entering their territory to take out their resources, in particular wood, and to establish gardens for growing produce. Colonists would then take the resources and market them for their own benefit.

The opposition by San José and Barranco Chico was backed up by Puerto Luz and reported directly to the Comité Pro-Carretera in March. In response, the Comité said that they would review the project, but let it be known to the communities affected that they had no intention of changing their plans. However, the project was temporarily halted because the rainy season and lack of funds provided a major obstacle. This was a respite, not a cancellation – 1994, the new mayor of Boca Colorado announced that the project would resume when money was available.

San José was opposed to the road because it meant an increase in colonisation. However, several of the community members, who had experience with development issues, were not opposed to the idea of a road in itself. As one representative from the community said: 'These outsiders want a road to extract resources from our territories and settle colonists ... We are opposed to any road with this aim. If we want a road, it will be to help us export our produce, such as pineapples or bananas.'

This case study shows that the fundamental features of development for the Arakmbut are based on control over access to their resources and consent over what happens on their territories. The settlers in Boca Colorado who were in favour of the road used national and local development as excuses to override indigenous rights. Development is conceived as a 'thing' which 'comes' to an area in order to improve living conditions and integrate it into the rest of the country. The Arakmbut are not opposed to development, only to those aspects which they cannot control and which threaten their communal resources.

A way through this would have been to bring the parties together and discuss the matter. Otzuka, however, considered that a brief trip to the community was sufficient 'consultation' and that when the project was in operation, he would allow the community to 'participate' in the project by receiving free parcelled plots of their own territory. The Arakmbut were not opposed to a road, but they wanted one which they had approved and which they controlled for the merchandise of their produce, not an attraction to increase colonisation of the homeland. This illustrates the fundamental conflict between development projects based on consent and those which go ahead with only consultation, and between those under indigenous control and those which involve their participation in an external initiative.[10]

The case study also reflects the distinctions which have been drawn above between development as growth and as decay. The settlers in favour of the road argue within a modernisation framework for development of the area in terms of communication and trade. They seek financial and political support form the state in order to open market forces into the area; indeed, when they talk about 'development coming to Boca Colorado' they mean precisely the expansion of trade. In contrast, the Arakmbut see the project as opening up forces which will exploit their lands and resources and which are consequently regressive.

10. This conflict echoes the fight over the concepts of consultation and participation, which indigenous peoples have been waging since the time of the ILO discussions (see Gray 1987a, 1989, and 1990a).

Their response is twofold and demonstrates neatly the complementarity between alternative development and alternatives to development. Their protest at the road took the form of community, inter-community, and native federation meetings and discussions with the Comité Pro-Carretera in Boca Colorado. This was a clear example of alternatives to development organised by the Arakmbut as part of the indigenous movement. This fits with Escobar (1993b) and his notion of social movements challenging the established views of development.

At the same time, the Arakmbut have their own visions of development – their *auto-desarrollo*, as it is sometimes put in Spanish. However in order to understand how an Arakmbut alternative would appear, it is necessary to look at their notion of self-development and to juxtapose this with the perspective of the colonists.

Self-development among the Arakmbut

> 'For many indigenous peoples the notion of development is itself a problem. Development implies motion towards something and usually some connotation of "growth". In relation to societies, growth is primarily seen as an economic concept, and too often development is seen in economic terms.
>
> 'Indigenous self-development is a total phenomenon which cannot be defined only in terms of economics, politics or culture. As all indigenous socio-cultural formations, indigenous self-development has to be seen as a whole, covering many different areas. Unless the terms of development are defined by the people themselves then there is no self-development' (Henriksen 1989:14).

This quote is very relevant to the Arakmbut approach to development questions. Between 1991 and 1992, I had several extended public meetings with the Arakmbut of San José, at which the comments on the following pages were expressed. The Arakmbut have no word for 'development' in their language. Two relevant concepts demonstrate that their own culturally based idea of 'development' is outside of the western framework of progress and degeneration. The first concept is that of 'time'. Arakmbut notions of time have been discussed in detail in Volume 1, chapter three. Particularly relevant in this context is the fact that, for the Arakmbut, time does not flow as it does in non-indigenous thought. The word for time – *o'pogika* (it always passes) – refers to something which goes past a person. People face the past and not the future. The result is that time is something which is active and people change because it passes.

This places the Arakmbut in a position whereby change is the effect of time going by. Human beings do not travel with time and so change cannot be explained by movement. From an Arakmbut perspective, people who travelled in time would not change because there would be no way of perceiving fixed signs marking the difference. Change over time is a spatial phenomenon for the Arakmbut (Nilsson 1920). For example, one can see that time has passed by observing the effects of wet and dry seasons, looking at the sun or moon, or following the budding and flowering of plants. Their change indicates that time has passed.

The other aspect of development which has been highly influential in western philosophy is growth, but the concept is different from an Arakmbut perspective. Growth *(e'kerek)* is not only something which can be seen in a materialistic manner. Human beings change because of a reorganisation of the relationship between their body (waso), soul (nokiren), and name (wandik). Genesis and decay are aspects of this relationship between the visible and invisible worlds.

The whole process of human life begins with sexual intercourse when a man passes his semen *(wandawe)* into a woman; at the moment of orgasm he temporarily dies *(e'mbuey)*. The child takes shape in the womb by the accumulation of semen. After birth, growth takes place by eating meat, by bathing in cold water, and through the use of chants (chindign). This process of growth lasts until a child becomes an adult, when body and soul are strongly bound together. As the adult grows older, the soul and body become increasingly separate until death takes place. Genesis and decay are thus processes whereby the soul and body become separate (e'mbuey) or closer together (e'kerek). Human 'development' consists of genesis and decay juxtaposed as part of the life cycle.

When I mentioned the term 'development' to the Arakmbut and asked if there was any equivalent in their own language, no one could think of one. When discussing what a man and woman want out of life for themselves and their children, most of the people said that they sought new technologies and opportunities for sustaining or recuperating the quality of their lives; but they considered that the purpose of development was to ensure health for the community. The Arakmbut expressed this by saying that they needed adequate supplies of gold, meat, and children in order to be strong and healthy.

Whether or not the Arakmbut, within their own cultural perspective, want to be developed was not the question. When discussing change or improvement possibilities at the public meetings and in private conversations, the older men all said that they wanted to ensure that they and their households had enough to eat and survive in the future. Their main concern was to make sure that outsiders did not take resources which were essential for the community to continue as it always had done. The nearest way in which the Arakmbut, in their own conceptualisation, approach development, is that they want to be able to retain some stability in their lives. They do not want to be 'developed'. As the quotation at the beginning of the chapter says, they want to stay still and change in accordance to the genesis and decay of life as time goes past.

This makes the Arakmbut sound like typical examples of the 'traditional' level of W.W. Rostow: people who are opposed to development and who prevent progress as defined by the state. In fact, the situation in the community is far more complicated. The case study shows that the Arakmbut are not opposed to change, but they want to develop in the sense of retaining control over their lives and to keep in good health. Development comes from outside and can be either beneficial or destructive, depending on the circumstances. If new technologies or aspects of health can be found from the national society that will make life easier, they are certainly in favour. But this has to be something which the Arakmbut give their consent to and which comes under their control – such as a road which serves them and not make them prey to colonists.

For the Arakmbut, development means neither growth nor progress in a western sense, but the achievement of being able to continue life as it has always been led, accepting changes when wanted, and producing children who can continue life after one's own death. This is ultimately a model of self-sufficiency in which external benefits are used to supplement the lack of certain resources within the community. The Arakmbut have always traded or bartered for those things which are not available in any one area, such as bamboo for arrows, or mud for clay, and goods which they cannot produce themselves, whether clothes, foodstuffs, alcohol, outboard motors, or gold technology, are now obtained by exchanging gold.

The Arakmbut internal ideal is therefore based on stability, sufficiency, and control over the environment. However, development in its broadest sense does not consist simply of economic factors, but covers all dimensions of indigenous life – social, cultural, and political. The presence of development, for the Arakmbut, is about access to and utilisation of resources. On the one hand this means defending what they already have while obtaining goods and services from outside. By looking at these 'resources' in more detail, the relationship between the Arakmbut and development issues becomes clearer.

Self-development

Scarcity of Meat and Gold

Since the gold rush, meat has become increasingly scarce and hunters have had to go further afield to find it. Gold miners are penetrating further into their territory in search of new deposits and the animals are frightened away by the noise of the motor pumps and the constant movement of people. The Arakmbut also work gold, but their territory is sufficiently large that they will vary the area where they hunt according to the gold camps where they stay. However as invasions have occurred throughout their territory, the Arakmbut hunters find their options for gold camps reduced.

The Amarakaeri Communal Reserve was designed to improve this situation and ensure a regular supply of meat. Communal reserves are hunting areas, usually in watersheds where animals breed. For the Arakmbut of San José, this takes place at the Ishiriwe river; on this relatively untouched part of their homeland animals are plentiful. Some of the prey come to salt-licks at the edge of the community which provide most game for the Arakmbut hunters. Unfortunately, settlers from Boca Colorado have been going into the communal reserve to hunt animals for sport, and in this way game becomes even more scarce. One man from San José who went on a hunting trip into the Ishiriwe in August 1993 said that game in the reserve had diminished extensively since his hunting trip of the year before.

The game scarcity is now paralleled by a scarcity of gold. The gold that can be found on beaches of the Madre de Dios is a renewable resource brought down every year in the rainy season and deposited in the sand, although inland, more lucrative non-renewable deposits can be found in the dried-out courses of old streams. These areas provide better returns but are becoming far rarer. To work gold, the Arakmbut live in camps several hours by foot from San José village. This is inconvenient for transporting equipment and food to the workers. Combined with the increasingly scarce gold deposits, the colonists, particularly in the Pukiri and in the Karene downriver from San José, do not allow the Arakmbut to work on the beaches and threaten them with fire-arms should they approach (see chapter three).

Income from gold has dropped considerably since the increase in mining activities in the headwaters. In 1993 the average production rate was 1-2 grams daily on the beach ($10) and about double that in the interior; however, more time is necessary to clear the forest-based placers and so the amount produced is approximately the same. This is half of the amount gained in 1992, even taking into account that the money has to be divided between at least four members of the work group. If an Arakmbut has workers (about five out of fifteen households employ between one and four outsiders), he has to cover their food and pay them $3 daily. The result is that most of the households in the gold mining Arakmbut communities with workers cannot make ends meet.

These examples show that the gold rush has had the effect of threatening game and gold – two resources which are essential for human survival. Meat provides the Arakmbut with strength, while gold increasingly provides access to basic necessities which cannot be produced in the gardens. Plant resources have not been so greatly affected by the gold rush, since the land which women use for the gardens lies nearer to the main community. There is some evidence, however, that colonists have been robbing produce from Arakmbut gardens, but so far this problem has not reached crisis point. On the other hand, there is also evidence that the amount of time spent on gold work has affected garden production and several species which were once used by the Arakmbut in the past are now disappearing because of loss of seeds and knowledge of tending.

By looking at production and subsistence as a whole, it is clear that the Arakmbut of San José are entering into a crisis. From 1992, for example, hardship in the community was becoming apparent. With the lack of game, there is less distribution within the community and some households have no meat from one month to another. With the gold production lower than ever, they have not enough resources to buy more than basic food, with the result that they live on yuca and plantains. From time to time, a newly-found gold deposit can temporarily improve living conditions. However, comparing my visits of 1980, 1985, and 1992, subsistence is becoming more difficult than ever.

In the context of a constant decrease in the availability of valuable resources, people say that they want to continue living in a self-sufficient manner. This does not mean a rejection of development in the face of traditionalism, but that the Arakmbut want a development which will enable them to defend their way of life and existence without becoming destroyed as a people. They therefore need to run to stand still. Development, for the Arakmbut, does not constitute any 'take-off' into the realms of progressive modernisation, but is a way to increase their capacity to survive on the resources which still exist within the community. In this sense their approach to development is based on the principle of sustainability, in that they want a world to leave for their children and grandchildren.

Gold: The Development Factor

Whereas territorial control is fundamental for self-sufficiency, the Arakmbut also want the means to obtain goods and services from outside. Gold is the prime means for this. Of all the resources in San José, the most coveted by outsiders is the gold; there is an interest in wood in Shintuya, but as yet this is not seriously in demand except among some colonists on the Pukiri river. The spontaneous invasions by colonists are mainly by poor peasant farmers from the highlands seeking a fortune. In addition, the patrons who have lived in the area for between ten and twenty years regularly increase in population by bringing their families down from the highlands and employing hundreds of workers. The threats by these patrons keep the Arakmbut away from their gold deposits.

Other factors also complicate access to gold resources in the native communities of the Karene area, indeed, of Peru as a whole. Whereas the Arakmbut have exclusive legal rights to the surface resources on their community lands through their territorial title, the state claims all the subsurface resources, including gold. Peruvian legislation is contradictory in that it allows indigenous peoples rights to their lands and resources through the Law of Native Communities, whereas at the same time it offers permission to potential miners to take gold from the same areas. The contradiction has been exacerbated by the removal of the inalienable clause in the Peruvian Constitution and the passing of the Land Law in July 1995 (see chapter two).

Permits for mining gold are organised by the government without any discussion with the indigenous peoples in the area. This has led to the erroneous impression that all gold invasions are legal. In fact, the only gold invasions which are legal are carried out by those people who have completed the whole bureaucratic procedure and have permits. Gold permits are extremely hard to obtain. In the past, indigenous communities, with the help of FENAMAD and Centro Eori, were able to establish rights on several areas of their lands. San José has three mining permits: Huanamey (150 hectares), Huanamey 1 (1000 hectares) and Huanamey 2 (340 hectares).[11]

These permits are based on the Ley General de Minería which was established in 1981, during the time of President Belaúnde, under Decreto Legislativo 109. A public Register of Mining inscribed

---

11. Puerto Luz has four concessions (Amarinke, Puerto Luz 1, Amarinke 2, and Amarinke 3). Boca Inambari has a concession called Rosita which was won from an illegal invader after a massive demonstration of indigenous solidarity in 1978 (Pacuri & Moore 1992:27).

every new concession. However there were many problems, among which were the corrupt officials in the Ministry of Energy and Mines who would issue concessions without hesitation to anyone, issuing one permit on top of another on the same ground. Indeed, one official in Puerto Maldonado received the name 'Dr. Cien Gramos' (Dr. Hundred Grams) because he would charge one hundred grams of gold before authorising a concession.

In 1986, with support from the Senator from the Madre de Dios, FENAMAD and Centro Eori drew up a proposal for a revised mining law. The idea was to stop granting concessions on indigenous lands to outsiders and ensure that indigenous peoples could mine gold anywhere on their territory (Pacuri & Moore 1992:20). In spite of receiving much support in the Congress, the proposal became entrenched in official bureaucracy. Nothing had been decided by the time Fujimori came to office, and he had other ideas.

In 1991 Fujimori passed the Decreto Legislativo 708, which advocated a promotion of private investment into mining activity. All concessions were to be issued on the same basis, whether for a multinational company or a small mining family. Through Decreto Supremo 005-91-EM the Banco Minero was suspended and all gold is now sold on the free market. Gold concessions can now be granted on indigenous territories and protected areas. The Public Mining Register took over from regional mining offices to co-ordinate the concessions which can only be held on the basis of impossible conditions for small-scale miners:

1. Production has to exceed US$100 per year and per hectare.
2. To keep the concession each concessionary has to pay $1 per hectare annually. This is in addition to four other taxes on each concession.
3. Each concession has to be authorised in a system of squares delimited by the system of the National Geographical Institute in Lima, paid for by the applicant prior to approval.
4. All of these actions have to be carried out, checked and paid annually or the concession can be annulled.

'The essence of these rules is that up to 90 per cent of the small-scale miners and the native communities will not be able to seek concessions or will lose what they have until now because it will be impossible to fulfil the legally established requirements' (Pacuri & Moore op.cit.:18).

The legislation further deprives the Arakmbut access to their resources because, at any moment, a company can pay to enter and extract gold within indigenous territory. In this way, land defence becomes even more difficult than ever. The only saving grace in the whole process is that there is not enough gold on San José's land to satisfy the high production rates demanded by the government. However, in order to defend themselves and expel a company, the Arakmbut would have to allow them to mine an area of their land and challenge the right to renew their concession on the technical grounds that they have not mined enough gold over the year. This is contrary to the Arakmbut's desired way of protecting their territory because it risks encouraging environmental degradation from gold companies.

Legislation is therefore no protection and, on the contrary, could be extremely detrimental to the Arakmbut. In the current situation, the Arakmbut have to struggle to preserve their standard of living in the face of illegal miners who enter their lands and threaten them. The interests of the government and non-indigenous miners threaten the capacity of the Arakmbut to utilise their resources and control their own development. There is a fundamental difference between the Arakmbut and those colonists from elsewhere, who are eager to exploit their resources. Whereas the Arakmbut are people from the rainforest and have no other home than the Karene, the outsiders are basically rooted in Cusco. Even those colonists who have been in the area for ten or twenty years still send their children to school in the highlands, where they have their main house which they visit every few months when they need to recruit more workers to replenish their stocks of exploited labour.

Gold provides access to products from the wider local and national social systems, from where goods and commodities ranging from motor pumps for gold mining to beer bought for the fiestas, have become necessities for the Arakmbut way of life. However, the Arakmbut have to be careful only to buy or receive what they can afford. This enables them to control their resources and ensure that the gold is put to a use which benefits each family in the form of commodities and capital investments for gold production, while the surplus can be redistributed throughout the community in the form of beer.

Thus, in addition to the reduction of resources and the limitation of access, the legal obstacles makes gold ever more difficult to gain, with the result that self-sufficiency and buying products from settlers or colonists becomes very difficult. The settlers, then, instead of becoming a source of goods and services, become unwanted invaders. However, the colonists and settlers have their own views of development, which are markedly distinct from those of the Arakmbut.

The Arakmbut and Development from the State

As noted at the beginning of this chapter, people in San José were not opposed to receiving the material benefits from the state in the form of public works, like the benefits Boca Colorado itself has received in recent years. Development from the state was seen by several people in San José as parallel to the gifts of education and health. They argued that material benefits would be useful for the native communities too. The most significant are as follows:

1. A school made of concrete is something for which the community was prepared to fight (see chapter two). Although several suggestions were made by architects and even by leaders of FENAMAD that a school would actually be more comfortable and cheaper to make if it was made of wood and leaves, the reaction was that this 'rustic' building would not be appropriate for the community. This fits in with the analysis in chapter five that the school should be an externally focused institution.
2. San José (and other communities) have several stranded wooden posts throughout the village connected with wires. These are all that remain of the two electrification schemes which the community has tried to rig up over the last six years. The first one was paid for by a colonist who had wanted Arakmbut permission to work gold on community land to counteract the opposition he had received from the patrons. The second came from money offered to each community by President Alan García in 1986. Neither worked for more than a few days. Yet electricity has become symbolic of community development, and the vast majority of the community want it.
3. Hand-outs of medicines and food are common in the Madre de Dios. This food aid usually bypasses indigenous peoples and ends up at the settlements of highland colonists and patrons. The food is mainly powdered milk, soya flour, and oil. In spite of the fact that most Arakmbut do not like the provisions which they receive and are not instructed on how to use the medicines, they consider that they have a right to them, and complain if they do not receive them.

The people of San José have several plans for future development projects which could come from the municipality. They would like a medical post (preferably concrete), and concrete harbour steps which would facilitate access to the village, situated at the top of a steep river bank. The cliff path is in a state of collapse and is treacherous in the rainy season. Other plans are for piped water, bringing clean water from a nearby stream to central points of the village.

These ideas for the future are broadly shared by everyone in the community and reflect an approach to development which relates to the material benefits which Boca Colorado has received from the municipality. These are non-indigenous buildings and facilities which are bought with outside aid. They cost nothing to the community and come from tapping external resources – namely development money.

However, the community itself does not see this as development in the same way as the outsiders. The Arakmbut want development to provide them with the means to supplement their subsistence activities and help them to lead a quiet life. By supplicating in the correct manner, they feel that support should be forthcoming from beneficial sources outside of the community. The Arakmbut see this as just compensation for their resources which have been, and are being, stolen by outside interests. Thus Arakmbut desire for goods and services is not based on modernisation principles of growth, but is a form of reciprocity which could provide the means to make life easier. This is distinct from the colonist's perspective on development.

Colonists on Development

The social stratification of gold production in the Madre de Dios has been analysed by Moore (1985b:180-183). In this article he contrasts various dominant members of the society. Traders *(comerciantes)* who came originally from Cusco are often the same people who are patrons of large-scale mining operations or who own businesses. These people are the most allied with the national state and participate in political parties, ally with the church and/or the military, and ultimately reap most of the benefits available in the region.

The small-scale independent workers come in various forms. These *pequeños mineros* work individually or in small groups to mine gold and may employ a few peons to work for them. They work as artisans on the beaches with sieves and small water pumps. Indigenous miners would come under the category of pequeños mineros. Relations between indigenous and non-indigenous miners are not always good because of the suspicions arising from community land invasions. The majority of indigenous and non-indigenous pequeños mineros are part of the informal sector of the Peruvian economy.

Indeed, many people no longer use money in the Madre de Dios but carry out most of their economic transactions in gold.

The crisis facing the Arakmbut has arisen in the context of a modernising idea of development which has gripped Peru as a whole for the last twenty years. Since the early 1980s, when President Belaúnde spoke of the 'colonisation of the rain forest', the ideology has been strong among conservative politicians that Peru's resources should act as an investing motor to facilitate the take-off of modernising economic development.

The Karene provides a clear example of the consequences of this internal colonialism. In contrast to the Arakmbut multifaceted view of development based on control over resources, the colonists see development in very different terms. I had several discussions on this matter in Boca Colorado, and the testimony of one settler put the case for a development in a particularly succinct manner.[12] He was a married man of about forty years with a family who operated a radio in the settlement; he was by no means hostile to the Arakmbut but had distinct views.

> 'Of all the areas in Peru that I have lived, the most corrupt is without doubt the Madre de Dios. Although the terrorists have not got here, there are terrible problems. My children, what is the future for them? I am Limenian. I came here fifteen years ago. What place is this for the future? My children, when they are old enough, will go to Lima for their education. When they come back, what will they think of their father, living in such a terrible place? We have no sanitation here. Corruption is the main obstacle to development.
>
> 'Development as it should be organised is based on resources. The forest is full of resources, but nobody takes advantage of the wealth. The wood can be sold, cattle can be used, and agricultural crops, like rice, sown. The authorities want prestige projects like shrimp farms. But we would prefer fish farms. The authorities want us to live from hand to mouth. We cannot be parasites on the land. We have to produce something which will provide wealth to the area.
>
> 'A prerequisite of development is communication. As things stand, the only way that Boca Colorado receives goods in and out is from Shintuya. The cost is prohibitive – twenty soles to get down to Laberinto. It now costs more to send rice to Puerto Maldonado than you can sell it for. There is therefore no incentive to produce any surplus for sale. Until transport costs are reduced there will be no development.
>
> 'The solution to the transport problem and the development problem is to build a Huaypetue-Colorado road. This will provide a direct link to

---

12. The Arakmbut use the term 'colonists' to refer primarily to all highland people who live in the area. The distinction I have used here is between colonists, who live on indigenous territory, and settlers, who have not invaded Arakmbut lands. However, their views on development are identical.

Puno. The Cusqueños don't like it because their artificially high prices will be undercut by cheaper Puno prices. The road will bring in goods at cheaper Puno prices. The road will bring in goods at cheaper prices and take out the resources here at a cheaper rate, thereby generating wealth and development in the whole area.

'The problem stopping all of this is political. The corrupt officials are all Izquierda Unida [IU, the largest party of the Left in Peru]. The whole sub-regional government is IU and they appoint everyone else including the mayor here. These leftists are opposed to development. What is needed is a political coalition to throw them out and get things going.'

According to this perspective, which was common in Boca Colorado in 1992, there are two aspects to development. One is the utilisation of resources from the environment to generate wealth, and the second is investment in the means of production and infrastructure necessary to extract the wealth. This, according to the colonist perspective, is in the hands of corrupt state authorities, which are, in their turn, in the hands of corrupt political parties.

The position expressed here was made by a man who supported the free market policies of Fujimori but felt that some state investment was necessary to set the market in motion. For him, it was parasitical to sit on the resources of the rainforest without exploiting them. This modernisation argument expresses the position of the colonists who make their way to the Madre de Dios to make a living. The resources of the forest, in their eyes, are open territory for any one with the initiative to exploit them. The indigenous peoples who live in the area are backward, in their view, and do not deserve to make money out of the resources. They are essentially obstacles to progress.

The objectives of colonist development in the area are less tangible but can be illustrated by the public works which the settlement of Boca Colorado has managed to produce over the last few years. In the first place, during the mid-1980s, the settlement which consists mainly of colonists and traders decided to gain municipality status. There had always been a mayor of the area but, as a full municipality, Boca Colorado has the right to tap into government development funds which are administered in Lima and in Cusco. Party political connections are also important, and before elections party candidates often go around offering small projects to encourage people to vote for them.

The financial support which Boca Colorado received enabled the settlement to change substantially by 1990 from what it had been in 1980 or even 1985. The area in 1990 had two 'hotels', electric lights in the evening, a health post, and a school. This did not improve its general appearance or provide it with the hygiene standards which it urgently needed. However, in the eyes of the settlers, with buildings of cement and electricity, 'civilisation' had arrived at Boca Colorado.

The settlers of Boca Colorado see development as a process through which they can benefit from the material trappings of progress. Transportation facilitates trade, which brings money into the region and with this people can obtain the raiments of 'civilisation'. Where money is not available, the settlers consider that these works should initially be subsidised by government support.

Arakmbut and Colonists on Development

By comparing the view of development from the perspective of the Arakmbut and juxtaposing this with the view of the colonists, in particular those who have been in the area for more than a year, the two perspectives appear as mirror images of each other. For the Arakmbut, self-development comes from within the community and seeks to preserve self-reliance on resources. Positive development in the western sense consists of gifts or compensation for the destruction wrought on their peoples. Negative development consists of the roads which outsiders wish to construct in order to extract indigenous resources and destroy them. Thus development strategies for the Arakmbut consist of two main factors:

1. Anything which enables them to continue to produce for their basic necessities. This notion of self-sufficiency means total control and access to the resources on their own territories.
2. Any activity taking place on Arakmbut lands should take place with their consent. Access to outside resources from abroad, the state, and the municipality would provide them with the basic markings of a 'civilised' community. This consists of certain buildings in concrete, electricity, and water. Arakmbut think that these should be provided freely.

On the other hand, the colonists have different priorities:

1. The resources of the forest are open to anyone, and those with initiative should be able to take them.
2. The state should provide the support for infrastructural means to convert these resources into commodities – roads and electricity, for example. If any other resources are available for schools or health posts, these should be tapped.

3. With the profits that emerge from the results, the colonists then hope to be able to improve their immediate environment by providing what the state will not.

The following table compares these views:

Table 7.1 Difference between Colonist and Indigenous views of Development

	Colonist	Indigenous
Access to forest resources	For Peruvians	Indigenous ownership Control of resource
Access to state resources	For Peruvian citizens	An indigenous right Consent over projects
Purpose of development	Modernisation No self-sufficiency	Self-sufficiency Modernise to ease life

The table shows that the Arakmbut and the colonists have a completely different approach to development, which draws them into the contrast noted in western development thinking. Whereas the colonists want the Madre de Dios integrated into the country as a whole, the Arakmbut want to control their own development, and this can only come through their own self-sufficiency. They want to be able to give their consent before any modernisation happens to their community.

Thus it is too simple to say that the Arakmbut are opposed to modernisation and are exclusively in favour of self-sufficiency. Their concern is to avoid dependence on the colonists and those who oppress or exploit them, and they do not want to have their resources plundered. Their notion of development 'by staying still' is a form of defence against invasions and encroachment. The Arakmbut do not see goods and services as modernisation and growth but as initiatives to enhance their health, well-being, or prestige.

The colonists consider that they have a positive view of development. This involves transferring resources from the forest to Lima and receiving, in return, money through trading and from the authorities, which allows them to become fully integrated into the state. The indigenous perspective, on the other hand, always seems to appear as the negative influence. Indigenous peoples are accused by the colonists of wanting to keep the resources for themselves and to receive state handouts for no work. They are the obstacles to development. Self-defence is interpreted by the colonists as an unwillingness to co-operate. Indeed, the strongest clashes between colonists and indigenous peoples stem from these issues.

A case which has arisen in 1993 illustrates this difference. A local colonist, Sergio López, with other outsiders, tried to form an official Rural Agrarian Settlement at the mouth of the Pukiri (Boca Pukiri) which would have a school, a medical post, a parabolic television aerial, and other facilities. All this was taking place within the territory of San José. The community became furious and vigorously opposed the creation of a colonist community. The local authorities at Boca Colorado were willing to support the colonists with these facilities, even though the indigenous communities have been asking for them for years. The case looked as if it would eventually go to court. However in 1994, San José asked the lawyer at Centro Eori to draft a letter demanding López' withdrawal from the area; he left immediately because, apparently, he had events in his past which he did not want to become public in a court case.

The conflict in the Karene between the Arakmbut and colonists is over resources. Both want to exploit the environmental potential of the forest and gain development money. However, whereas the indigenous peoples concentrate their efforts on promoting their self-sufficiency and consequently base their aims on sustainable notions of development, the colonists have a modernisation approach which is based on the profits of short-term extraction.

The Mission and FENAMAD as Agents of Development

In between the colonists and the Arakmbut there are two intermediary sectors which also work with development. These are the Dominican priests and the indigenous organisation FENAMAD. The priests offer education facilities through the secular mission organisation RESSOP, and there is also a move to initiate a health programme in the communities of the upper Madre de Dios by the mission. San José and Puerto Luz are pleased to receive these services, which they see as aspects of the duty of the mission to the community.

Apart from this, the priests do not offer goods to the community, but they do encourage certain aspects of development such as lumbering and cattle. In Shintuya, wood and cattle projects have been in operation for about ten years. The result has been extensive deforestation and uncontrollable cattle grazing. In effect, the mission has been run by the priests as a farm. However, once the projects were handed over to the community, the Arakmbut quickly lost interest.

The priests are currently planning to sell off the cattle (Fuentes 1982; Wahl 1987; and SERI 1992).

Although the mission has not established cattle and lumbering initiatives in the gold-producing communities, its influence is present everywhere in the Karene. Several households in San José have tried to buy cattle (not from the mission) and establish them on the river bank. One such attempt in 1992 failed as all the cattle died within a week. A herd of sheep met the same fate during the previous year. Whereas Shintuya had the benefit of priests with experience in running cattle farms, the indigenous communities did not. Some of the students at the mission had been made to look after cattle and thought, erroneously, that this was sufficient experience to try it out in their own communities.

The economic programmes of the priests are clearly framed within a modernisation model. Their ideas of production development have rested entirely on creating new initiatives for raising money which can then be ploughed into the community. Their model is that of a hacienda or farm.[13] When looking at their education programme, it is also clear that the aim of the teachers is to facilitate the integration of the Arakmbut into national society (Aikman 1994). Thus the idea of self-sufficiency is not the aim of the work of the Dominicans; integration into the national economy and society is far higher on their agenda.

In contrast to the priests, the work of FENAMAD is oriented in another direction. Since the middle of the 1980s, FENAMAD has been working closely with Centro Eori to title the territories of indigenous communities throughout the Madre de Dios. Rather than production, FENAMAD has started its work on territorial defence and tried to obtain gold concessions for the communities. Furthermore, they have been watching closely the state publication 'El Peruano', where concessions have to be published, and have made several successful appeals against illegal permits on indigenous territory.

One particular case which FENAMAD has been following for San José has been the ownership of concessions on the river Pukiri. For the last five years there has been a conflict between a colonist, Mateus Bejar, and the company CARISA (Compañía Aurífera del Río Inambari), which has taken over concessions throughout the Pukiri from a

13. The hacienda model of missionaries in the Madre de Dios has been a consistent feature of their work since the 1940s. Alvarez (1944) described San Miguel de los Mashcos in Kaichihue in terms of a Spanish-style farm surrounding the chapel. As the Harakmbut became farmers, the 'seeds of Christianity could be sown' (Alvarez 1944:255).

previous company, Ausorsa. The Bejar family control the Pukiri with guns, and wanted CARISA's concessions. However, after five years of appealing to the Ministry of Engineering and Mines, the court came out in favour of CARISA. This satisfied San José because CARISA does not actually work in the Pukiri, and this prevents Mateus Bejar from having any legal right to work gold there except on a very small concession of forty-nine hectares. FENAMAD actively followed the case and lobbied in favour of the community. However, as soon as CARISA won, the company announced that they were to sell the concessions in the Pukiri. This opened up a new problem for the community as it could not afford to buy them, and the fear is that Mateus Bejar will do so instead. Territorial defence is in many ways a thankless task because it is unending. It involves court cases and lobbying, and at the end of the day new problems arise. Nevertheless, FENAMAD's emphasis on territorial rights is the important basis for self-sufficiency in the Madre de Dios.

In contrast to that of the Mission, FENAMAD's initiatives are towards community development based on self-sufficiency and self-reliance. The mission's approach is to emphasise modernisation and integration. However, as the Arakmbut of San José and Puerto Luz take advantage of both strategies, the rivalry between FENAMAD and the mission in many ways turns different aspects of development into a competition. The relationship which the communities have with the priests and FENAMAD makes this even more complicated, because politically divided loyalties are argued out in development terms.

The result is that the Arakmbut have a complex relationship with both the priests and FENAMAD. Support from the community depends on the capacity of the respective organisations to allocate resources efficiently while creating, identifying, and satisfying community desires. This can only be understood by looking at members of the community and their personal allegiance or conflicts with the mission and FENAMAD. All these are acted out and discussed during the informal encounters in the community.

Placing together the different sources of development for Arakmbut communities, it is possible to see how the different sources of power around them can be dangerous but also beneficial if handled well.

1. The Arakmbut recognise the need to be self-sufficient. They need access to their resources, which normally takes place through their relationships with the spirit world.
2. Arakmbut want this self-sufficiency to be reinforced by FENA-MAD's support for territorial defence against colonists' inva-

sions, the utilisation of medicinal plants, and for promoting indigenous culture.
3. The Arakmbut want support from the priests in the form of western education and medicine, which they feel are necessary as a means of defending themselves from the non-indigenous outside world.
4. The Arakmbut want support from the municipal authorities to ensure that they can gain certain prestigious items such as electricity and concrete public buildings.

The breaking of dependency is one aspect of development which the Arakmbut want but, at the same time, they want the prestigious, labour-saving, technical infrastructure, health, and education facilities which non-indigenous peoples in the area receive. The result is a mixture of self-sufficiency and innovation as complementary aspects of development.

Positive development from the state, as the Arakmbut see it, is a system of receiving, rather than doing and initiating. To a large extent this perspective stems from the first relations with non-indigenous outsiders, which was based on receiving gifts. Positive development from outside, for the Arakmbut, is still a relationship with outsiders based on tapping goods for the benefit of the household and the community. Whereas these forces are dangerous and destructive, they provide goods. The knack of dealing with outside forces is to ensure that one learns how to behave to acquire the gifts but avoid the dangers. Relationships with the spirit world and with white people are broadly parallel, because in order to gain access to resources, the beneficial ones have to be treated well and the dangerous ones avoided or deterred (Volume 1, chapters eight, nine, and ten).

Self-development Projects in San José

The question now arises as to what form of development the Arakmbut want and whether there is any way in which these different styles of development can be brought together for their benefit. I participated in several meetings with San José between 1991 and 1995 to discuss the future of the community. In every case the discussions were inspired by concern over what would happen when the gold ran out completely.

The first issue to be discussed was production. The Arakmbut wanted to look for alternatives to gold. As a third of San José's beaches are in the hands of illegal colonists, the gold may not be decreasing in absolute terms and a territorial defence initiative oriented to removing the colonists was considered as an important proposal. From this the discussion moved to how other aspects of Arakmbut production could be reinforced. This involved looking at non-commercial production. In the first place, several people mentioned that there are species of vegetable and fruit which are not grown any more in the gardens, and that these could be identified and reintroduced from other areas. Furthermore alternative species of plantains, yuca, and other crops have also been lost.

The community agreed that the protection of the Amarakaeri Communal Reserve would be a good start to ensure a consistent supply of game for hunters. They they wanted to explore ways in which wild animals can be monitored and protected from non-indigenous hunters who kill for sport or commercial purposes. Similarly, fishing stocks need to be monitored and controlled. Several people felt that the Arakmbut should stop selling barbasco to highlanders, which only encourages them to fish in community rivers.

The Arakmbut buy many crops from colonists which they could grow themselves if they knew the right soils and how to protect them from predators. In particular, the Arakmbut expressed interest in tomatoes, onions, carrots, and rice. The overall idea in the meetings was to supplement the gold work so that there would be a diversification of the Arakmbut economy, enabling them to become more self-sufficient. However, every household needs some money to survive, and the necessary entrance into commercialisation is particularly difficult in the Madre de Dios. However, the Arakmbut realised that markets are available but that before moving into trading products, they need more experience. Several people mentioned that the community wanted the knowledge and expertise to control the fluctuations of the market as much as possible so that on a local level it would be easier to take note of shifts in demand and changes in supply. The Arakmbut would prefer to direct their buying and selling to local markets such as Boca Colorado, rather than the more distant centres such as Puerto Maldonado or Cusco.

The net result of the discussion with the Arakmbut was that they wanted to blend a more efficient subsistence production with a diversification of commercial products which can then lead to a broad spectrum economy. In this way, a reduction in the price of one item can be compensated by promoting another product. The community as a whole would initially work as independent households or groups of neighbours and close relatives, with the possibility of alliances forming onto a broader level. The Arakmbut in San José and elsewhere consider that community development should begin with subsistence and self-sufficiency. Only when the community has a secure basis of production would the commercialisation process begin to make sense. However the background to all of this is territorial defence.

The priorities within the community are thus: ensuring territorial rights and, from this, building on self-sufficiency. Dealing with development possibilities from the state comes next, because with control over their own development, the community can organise the facilities available from outside in line with their own needs.

Considerable time and patience is needed to enable a community to work out what it needs. The period between 1993-95 witnessed several discussions in San José, Puerto Luz, Barranco Chico, Boca Inambari, and Shintuya, at which these ideas were organised into one framework. This initiative by the communities themselves demonstrated that for the first time the Arakmbut were conceptualising a project which they themselves would run and not simply receive as a hand-out from an outside agency.

The key issue in the community is therefore not simply raising money, as those who advocate commercialisation would have us believe. The issue is to ensure that, prior to a development project, the community is prepared to take the responsibility for it. This can only happen if there is agreement as to priorities. In the end, the conclusion of the meetings with the Arakmbut was that the only way in which a genuine community development project can start is by listing all the priorities and drawing them into a scheme. The result is a series of related themes – in this case territorial defence, self-sufficient production, cultural strengthening and ensuring the availability of basic social services and facilities. In this way, Arakmbut self-development fulfils Henriksen's criterion of being seen 'as a whole', covering many different areas, and being defined by the people themselves. The conclusion which we reached in our discussions was a proposal for community development among the gold mining Arakmbut communities of San José, Puerto Luz, Barranco Chico and Boca Inambari, and other communities around the Communal Reserve.

Working on a development project within an indigenous community is not simply an economic question. It is impossible to promote self-development work without understanding the political, social, and cultural implications of a project. The problem facing a people such as the Arakmbut is that even though they need to reinforce their capacity for self-sufficiency, they have great difficulty putting this into practice. Development support should therefore be oriented to helping them take on this challenge, and therefore the presence of pre-project training is an important condition for beginning this type of development work in the Arakmbut communities.

This chapter has looked at the development theories of modernisation and dependency in the light of small-scale community needs in the Madre de Dios. But is development a right for the Arakmbut to assert? As yet they have not seen development in this sense. On 4 December 1986, the United Nations passed the Declaration on the Right to Development. Indigenous peoples are not mentioned specifically in the Declaration. According to its definition, development is an open concept which embraces potentiality:

> 'Development is a comprehensive economic, social, cultural, and political process, which aims at the constant improvement of the well-being of the entire population and of all individuals on the basis of their active free and meaningful participation in development and in the fair distribution of benefits resulting therefrom' (IWGIA 1988:168).

The Declaration appears largely oriented towards the interests of states, and so in this context development has a negative meaning for indigenous peoples (Sambo 1992:172). This was illustrated in the case study in which a road was to be forced through the territories of San José and Barranco Chico without their consent. Consultation and participation are not sufficient to protect indigenous peoples from the ravages of development. They need to grant their consent to protect and control their own self-development. The destruction of their lands by the road was presented by the perpetrators as development. The right to development must not provide economic interests with the means of walking over the rights of others.

Development is a two-edged sword for indigenous peoples; it can be either destruction or benefit – hence the co-existence of both alternatives to development and alternative development. Until this is understood, it is unlikely that indigenous peoples, such as the Arakmbut, will seek recourse to their 'right to development'. From the perspective of indigenous peoples, both modernisation and dependency are aspects of non-indigenous notions of development. In order to survive in the world, indigenous peoples have to balance the relationship between self-sufficiency and outside sources of development. Modernisation and dependency are not, in fact, opposites. The one is a description of what development could be, and the other is an analysis of its effects. Modernisation and dependency are thus on the same side of the analysis because one promotes and the other analyses a relationship stemming from states and markets. The alternative is based on self-sufficiency through control over resources. This is both an alternative development and an alternative to development.

When indigenous peoples control their development, the outside no longer becomes a threat and self-determination becomes a practical possibility. This leads to the final chapter of this study.

Chapter 8

SELF-DETERMINATION AND ARAKMBUT DECOLONISATION

Article 3
Indigenous peoples have the right of self-determination. By virtue of that right they freely determine their political status and freely pursue their economic, social and cultural development.

From the draft Declaration of the Rights of Indigenous Peoples

The new draft Declaration of the Rights of Indigenous Peoples was approved by the five members of the United Nations Working Group on Indigenous Populations in August 1993. Indigenous peoples have insisted for many years that the right to self-determination is critical for them, and, at last, after eleven years, the Working Group accepted its importance. The wording, which comes from Articles 1 of the UN Covenants on Civil and Political Rights and Economic and Social Rights, constitutes a benchmark in the recognition of indigenous rights.

This orientation of self-determination applies not only to the peoples of territories that have not yet attained political independence, but also to those living within independent and sovereign states. This means that a people 'can decide for independence or choose association with any state ... provided that the new association is freely sought' (Cassese 1981). The right of self-determination, as set out in the draft Declaration, refers to a multitude of features of indigenous life: political status, economic, social, and cultural development, and, consequently, control over resources.

This attempt to outline the right of self-determination draws together the areas of control which a people must have to put the right into effect. The Martinez Cobo report referred to the subject of self-determination in the context of indigenous peoples in paragraph 269: 'Self-determination, in its many forms, is thus a basic pre-condition if indigenous peoples are to be able to enjoy their fundamental rights and determine their future, while at the same time preserving, developing, and passing on their specific ethnic identity to future generations' (United Nations 1984/6).

While the Cobo report was in preparation, the UN hosted two NGO Conferences in 1977 and 1981. At these meetings indigenous peoples themselves went on the offensive, explaining their position on self-determination. The 1977 Declaration stated:

> 'All actions on the part of any state which derogate from the indigenous nations' or groups' right to exercise self-determination shall be the proper concern of existing international bodies'. The 1981 Declaration recognised that indigenous peoples have a 'just struggle for self-determination and for the right to determine the development and use of their land and resources, and to live in accordance with their values and philosophy' (Dunbar Ortiz 1984:31-32).

Throughout the twelve years of the Working Group, the right of self-determination has developed a special significance for indigenous peoples. Draft declarations of both the World Council of Indigenous Peoples and the Indigenous Caucus at the UN Working Group considered that the right of self-determination was a priority. One of the greatest achievements of the Working Group has been the drafting of the article on self-determination and its approval by the Subcommission. Indeed, the legitimacy of the declaration itself rests largely on governments accepting the article, because if a people is not recognised as determining its own way of life, the whole indigenous engagement with human rights becomes considerably weakened.

This chapter looks at self-determination and the Arakmbut from two angles. In the first place, a case study introduces the concept as a multifaceted feature of indigenous life – self-determination in practice. The other part looks at the second aspect of self-determination raised by Cassese, 'choosing a form of association with the state'. The case study covers a series of events which lasted for almost one year, and brought to a head the multidimensional features of self-determination, linking together several of the examples which have been expressed in earlier chapters.

Self-determination in Practice

The presence of one colonist dominated community life in San José while I was there, and he came to symbolise the problems facing the whole community. The painstaking process of realisation, decision-making, and action provides an illustration of how the Arakmbut are self-determining. Whereas the Arakmbut are self-determining all the time, a study such as this highlights the main features of self-determination.

When I arrived in San José in October 1991, I quickly became aware that the community was discussing a new arrival on Arakmbut territory who was different from the normal run of colonists. They were talking about a white person who they had heard was German and had set up camp within their territory. Apparently, during September, the 'Alemán' (German), as he had become known, had come to meet with the community. Most of San José was present. He explained that he had returned in June after several years away from Peru with his wife and small child. They had established a camp near to San José. He wanted to carry out biological research into mercury contamination in the river. This, he informed the community, would be useful for their health.

He negotiated a base at the mouth of the river Kiraswe from the local patron, Jaime Sumalave, to whom he paid $1,000. Sumalave had had serious problems with the community in 1985. When the Alemán told San José this at the meeting, the Arakmbut leaders informed him clearly that this money paid to Sumalave was wasted – the land belonged to the community and not Sumalave. To ingratiate himself with the Arakmbut he promised to donate parabolic antennae and electrification to San José. At the end of the meeting he was given permission to stay on San José's territory to do his studies.

However, as time went on, people began to discuss the Alemán even more at the work groups or during the evening 'encounters'. Several Arakmbut had been to his camp to exchange meat or melons for fishing hooks and medicines. They began to notice that he was not alone with his family. He had five workers at the camp and gossip from the local colonists was that he was planning to work gold.

The Alemán visited San José's kermesse on 8 October 1991 with the Boca Pukiri football team. A large group of Arakmbut from Puerto Luz came down to San José and when, in the morning, the Alemán arrived with his wife they recognised him. They remembered him from 1983-84, when they had turned Miguel (which was the Spanish version of his name) away from Puerto Luz with bows and arrows. Apparently he returned to the Karene a couple of years later, and went back to the headwaters without affecting the community, but since then he had abandoned his camp and equipment in the headwaters.

As Miguel approached the football pitch it became clear that he had a pistol in a holster and bullets in his belt. In their eagerness to avoid him, a farcical routine took place during the football match. As Miguel moved in one direction to greet the Arakmbut, men, women, and children all made sure that they were constantly on the opposite side of the pitch. Eventually, he left, perplexed.

Puerto Luz and San José discussed the matter at the evening drinking sessions. Puerto Luz decided that they would not allow him to enter their territory. Whereas San José were not in favour of the Alemán remaining, they did not want open conflict; as he was not affecting anyone in the community directly, they felt that the best approach was to leave him alone.

Over the next month, though, the Arakmbut became vigilant. During the evenings people would swap news, and those who had been down to exchange produce would give accounts of the numbers of people and the enormous house which he was constructing. On 7 November, the evening's discussion was more detailed. Some wanted to go to Puerto Luz to discuss concerted action concerning the Alemán. Meanwhile, it was decided that a small group would go to the Alemán's camp and discuss exactly what was going on.

On Friday 8 November a group from San José visited the camp. I was asked to accompany them as a witness. When we arrived, Miguel had left for a visit to Puerto Maldonado. We met a man in charge of the camp and visited a large house which was under construction, consisting of two storeys. Inside were four small dredges and tubing for gold mining. To the left, another large house was under construction. The Arakmbut spokesman was Elias Kentehuari, one of the students from Lima. He said that the Alemán had only received permission to do research and had had no authorization from the community to build a permanent structure. All construction work must stop immediately.

We then went to look at a clandestine cemetery which was about one hundred yards away from the house and saw forty tombs marked with pebbles and others unmarked. During this period there had been a considerable scandal in Madre de Dios about the existence of secret cemeteries which contained the bodies of peons, murdered by their patrons. The previous dweller on that spot had been Jaime Sumalave, and during 1991-92 he was questioned several times as to who was buried in the cemetery. I did a calculation of the number of bodies over a period of twenty-five years and discovered that the death rate was higher than that of San José which is, on average, one person per year out of a population of 130. Sumalave's population was at the most eighty, and probably considerably less in the early years. Even taking account of people from nearby camps who might have been buried there, twice as many people were buried in Sumalave's cemetery as in the Arakmbut community during the same period. We returned to San José, musing on the reasons for such a high death rate.

On Sunday 10 November, the local colonist, Sergio López, visited San José. He lived in Boca Pukiri and was a friend of Miguel. He explained that Miguel had support from the Ministry of the Interior to work in the area and had hired helicopters ready to transfer their material to the Wasoroko, thereby passing over Puerto Luz. Miguel had promised López a hydroelectric generator and a fridge for selling cold beer, and so had concluded that Miguel had a lot of money. Furthermore, he had permission from the President of the Republic to be there and the community could do nothing about him. His full name was Michael Dianda from Krefeld, Germany.

With this information the community discussed the case further. Some felt that he was maybe not such a bad person and that to leave him be would avoid problems. Others, particularly those with relatives in Puerto Luz, wanted him out. However, with him currently away from the area, the community decided not to do anything immediately. The rumour spread that he had returned to Germany for the time being. Things became quiet and information passed around the informal circuits between San José, Puerto Luz, and the colonists of Boca Pukiri.

These rumours mentioned how twice he had reported money being stolen, once in Cusco and once in Puerto Luz. In both cases he tried to use events to his advantage and so people wondered whether he was as careless as he appeared. His apparent ease in carrying arms caused much talk, inspiring suggestions of a 'special relationship' with the police or with the military. He did hire a member of the Guardia Civil to work with him; the Guardia had worn a uniform in Puerto Luz which considerably intimidated the community. It was rumoured that the person was off duty and not entitled to appear as a personal police bodyguard.

Without the presence of Dianda to incite the community further, the issue died down until a Commission from FENAMAD came to the community on Friday 6 December. They met with the people in

San José and discussed the main problems. The result was that the community drafted a memorandum to the authorities of all the problems facing them, including the road (see previous chapter), the gold law and the presence of Michael Dianda on San José's lands. FENAMAD passed the memorandum on to the authorities, who took no action.

Meanwhile, Centro Eori did some investigation in the gold mining records. Dianda first came to Peru in 1983, when he took out a mining concession covering 142 hectares in the headwaters of the Karene, which he called 'Michael'. The claim was not completely legal, as the concession was issued prior to the date on which it had been officially published. A period after the publication is meant to allow affected parties to appeal against the claim before issuing the permit. The signatory of the document was 'Dr. Cien Gramos', who was mentioned in the previous chapter as a notorious issuer of concessions.

During December, in Lima, the German anthropologist Klaus Rummenhöller discovered from a friend in Germany that Dianda was home and had been talking on German radio. This tape was highly revealing. In it Dianda claimed to have found kilos of gold in the Peruvian rainforest and argued that by using dredges without mercury he had found a sustainable way to mine gold from the rivers. He claimed to have had no problems with the local indigenous peoples and described his weapons in detail, drawing attention to his gas guns and dum-dum bullets. Subsequently it transpired that he has written three books about gold mining, although none of them relate to this particular case. The tape presented Dianda as an adventurer whose interest is in gold.

In March 1992, a meeting of the Arakmbut took place at Puerto Luz to discuss local elections, gold concessions, the road, the materials for the school, and Dianda (see chapter two). The information from Lima about his gold concessions and the interview he had made on German radio renewed the old conviction that he was up to no good. The communities decided to discuss the questions and meet again on 21 March. At that meeting the two communities wrote a memorandum about Dianda and agreed to take it to him on 23 March. They drafted a letter which said:

> 'in a general meeting between the two communities of San José and Puerto Luz it was decided not to allow you permission to enter into the Amarakaeri Communal Reserve or to remain any longer on communal lands of San José del Karene ... You are declared *persona non grata* and are invited to leave in a peaceful manner from these lands as quickly as possible and to avoid consequences which we might later regret'.

On the 22nd, the night before the visit, there was a storm. Several Arakmbut were afraid that the weather portents augured conflict with Dianda and danger for the community. Several mentioned the dream of the wachipai which had augured a bloody fate for the community; Dianda and his weapons seemed a likely threat. Eventually representatives from both communities went to Dianda the next day to hand over the letter; once again I was invited along as a witness. This was the first formal meeting with him since the community meeting the previous September.

A large delegation of over twenty people went to his camp. Prior to discussions, he handed out knives as gifts and tried to talk apart with those he knew. He explained that mercury poisoning was affecting the communities and he wanted to help the children. He had one hundred and twenty-five new plant species which would support the communities and, furthermore, he offered to pay money to remain there. The Arakmbut asked him why he was not affiliated with an institution and why he did not respect the law and leave. 'The law does not have effect here', he said. When asked why he was armed, he explained he needed guns because of the value of his equipment. The meeting ended in stalemate. He received the letter and the Arakmbut said that he should discuss his case with FENAMAD. If FENAMAD considered him honest, the communities would reconsider the case.

San José did not know exactly what to do. The communities agreed to wait and discuss the matter with the state authorities at Boca Colorado when they went on Monday 30 March to insist on receiving their school materials (see chapter two). The meeting with the authorities was very revealing. In spite of the fact that Dianda was in violation of the Law of Native Communities, the Governor and Judge refused to comment on the rights and wrongs of his presence on San José's territory. They claimed total ignorance of the matter, even though they knew Dianda and had spoken about him to members of the community before.

In April, representatives from San José and Puerto Luz went to Puerto Maldonado to defend themselves against accusations of taking the school materials by force (see chapter four). At the same time they alerted FENAMAD to the problem with Dianda. FENAMAD, Centro Eori, and the community representatives then drafted a series of denunciations to the Sub-Prefect of the Province of Tambopata and the head of the Armed Forces in Madre de Dios. A few weeks later Dianda visited the offices of FENAMAD and met with the leadership, several lawyers, and other representatives of the community who happened to be in Puerto Maldonado. The strength of opposition was so powerful that he eventually agreed to sign a document admitting that his occupation of San José's lands was illegal and that by 31 May he would have left the area.

On 25 May, Dianda moved camp. He hired a helicopter from the Peruvian Air Force and flew all his equipment, not out of the forest, but further upriver, beyond Puerto Luz. The helicopter, full of armed soldiers, landed in San José del Karene, causing damage to houses, particularly that of Ireyo, which was left at a permanent tilt (see chapter five). The shock traumatised a sick woman who died the following day. Several Arakmbut commented that the portents had been correct, his presence was threatening the lives of the Arakmbut.

But Dianda had left. He was now outside of Arakmbut community lands but continued to work gold within the communal reserve area, designed to protect the environmental heritage of the Arakmbut peoples.

On 10 July, a national commission of investigation, including representatives from AIDESEP and COICA, visited San José and Puerto Luz to look at the appalling situation of gold mining among the indigenous peoples of the Madre de Dios. They were highly critical of the way in which the authorities had ignored the presence of Dianda and also of the Armed Forces, which had even allowed him to hire a helicopter to move from his base further upstream into the Communal Reserve.

The effect of expelling Dianda from San José's lands was mixed. The community felt no euphoria. A woman had died, he was still in the area and the whole process had taken them eight months. On the other hand, the colonists were in considerable turmoil. Several who lived on the river Pukiri moved out of San José's territory upriver – only to add to the problems of neighbouring Barranco Chico. However the struggle against Dianda was an example of San José and Puerto Luz successfully exercising their self-determination in practice.

Between 1991 and 1992, Michael Dianda became a symbol for both the colonists of the Karene and the communities of San José and Puerto Luz. Considering that there are almost five hundred colonists on San José's lands, it may seem strange that one man should have caused such attention and discussion. However, looking at his character, his clear intention to override community decisions and, above all, the threat from his weapons, it becomes clear that he was seen by indigenous and non-indigenous alike as the most powerful person in the area. Whether Dianda intended to intimidate the communities is not the question here; from the perspective of the Arakmbut he was terrifying – yet he also brought promises of benefits.

The colonists hid behind Dianda's power in order to justify their position on San José's lands, while the authorities would not commit themselves to denouncing him because they wanted to avoid problems. Furthermore, both colonists and authorities were afraid of him because they realised that he had contacts with the armed forces. For the Arakmbut, however, the relationship was more complicated. Initially they had given the man the benefit of the doubt and, on the whole, San José and Puerto Luz are positive towards researchers. However, the gradual awareness that things were not as they should be took some time to work its way through the community. Partly, this was because some of the community had agreed to his temporarily remaining on their land to research and did not want to go back on their word.

When the Arakmbut were convinced that Dianda had double-crossed them, those who had originally welcomed him were the most vociferous in opposition to his remaining there. At the same time, the Arakmbut were afraid of him; he was armed and the community felt that they had no hope of taking him on alone. The alliance with Puerto Luz and the subsequent support of FENAMAD were crucial in the stages leading to his expulsion. Eventually the attack from all sides made Dianda realise that his days on San José's territory were numbered.

This case study provides several points of illustration regarding the discussion of self-determination, and embraces the different aspects of indigenous rights discussed throughout this book. The presence of Dianda consisted of a violation of the territorial integrity of the Arakmbut. While he was researching or writing, the Arakmbut had little concern, but once it became clear that he was taking their gold resources and establishing a permanent settlement, San José and Puerto Luz felt cheated. As they considered that their territory had been invaded, the Arakmbut began to assert their determination to get rid of him. However, this was complicated by opposing factors. The community was angry and felt deceived, but at the same time they feared the potential violence which might ensue if he were angered. Dianda became symbolic of colonisation because he stood out above the other invading colonists, all of whom supported him.

Throughout the conflict, the identity of the Arakmbut as an indigenous people became increasingly relevant. Whether as Arakmbut of San José, as Arakmbut living in the Karene or as indigenous Arakmbut throughout the Madre de Dios, all were opposed to Dianda.

This process took place because, as the battle for the expulsion of Dianda progressed, the boundaries between internal and external grew. What had been a community struggle for those of San José became a common problem for San José and Puerto Luz after the kermesse. This brought the case to an Arakmbut level. Indeed, Barranco Chico agreed to support San José and Puerto Luz on the matter because they feared that Dianda might flee onto their lands. Finally, by bringing FENAMAD into the case the issue became one of indigenous peoples as a whole. The meaning of internal and external shifted several times during the campaign, and by the end all of these different contexts of community, ethnic identity and indigenous peoples operated simultaneously to dislodge the colonist. The struggle eventually became identified as a conflict between colonists and indigenous people.

Dianda was a danger to the Arakmbut, and they saw his person as the possible manifestation of an augury made by the wachipai spirit. As the Arakmbut asserted their identity, the spiritual expression of their predicament became increasingly apparent. The elder's spirit dream of San José in ruins with Arakmbut blood coming under the doors was discussed several times during conversations about Dianda. The storm before the visit to his camp and the arrival of the military helicopter were all seen as signs of potential destruction. When the old woman died the day after the helicopter arrived, they saw Dianda's anger as partly to blame. The spirits thus operated throughout the period of conflict as advisors and cautionary influences, ensuring that the Arakmbut did not overstep the boundary of appropriate behaviour.

The Dianda case took several months to turn into an indigenous struggle, but during this period, several aspects of Arakmbut governance became apparent. Initially the community of San José waited to see if he would go away of his own accord. This is an example of dormant resistance which was also mixed with resignation based on the fear that they lacked the power to deal with Dianda. On the other hand, as the conflict took shape, Arakmbut governance became more determined. Throughout the case, all aspects of Arakmbut governance were practised – informal encounters, meetings with other Arakmbut communities, and formal meetings with FENAMAD and the authorities at Boca Colorado. At each case, the Arakmbut used their forms of government to decide their next move and assert their right.

The benefits which the colonists hoped to reap from Dianda were signs of modernisation development. He was admired for his money, power, and influence. However, the Arakmbut wanted to remain independent from Dianda. Whereas he offered them temptations in the form of electricity and parabolic antennae, the residents of San José were afraid of becoming indebted to him and then finding themselves obliged to keep him on their lands permanently. In spite of this, when he left, a few Arakmbut wistfully wondered if he might have brought some benefits to the community.

The case of Dianda illustrates the multifaceted notion of self-determination: Dianda's threat resulted in the Arakmbut asserting their rights to territory and resources, asserting their identity as a people and their culture, carrying out decision-making, and striving for self-sufficiency. These have been the main themes of this book and are the main features of self-determination.

The most public expression of this took place during the storming of Boca Colorado, described in chapter two. When the municipal offices were taken over, several Arakmbut representatives from San José and Puerto Luz made speeches asserting their rights as indigenous peoples; a key factor in these speeches was that they were going to take on Dianda and expel him. The Arakmbut are a self-determining people, and all of the features discussed here are present in their lives on a daily basis. The case study of Dianda is significant because it threatened the Arakmbut to such an extent that they had to assert these aspects of self-determination and thus they become visible to outsiders.

The case study illustrated a practical way in which indigenous peoples are self-determining; it shows how they assert their right to self-determination because it is the only concept which embraces the holistic scope of their diverse political, economic, social, and cultural formations. However, indigenous peoples also demand international recognition of this right as a protection against colonisation. This recognition defines the particular relationship which each indigenous people has with a state.

Self-determination and States

Of all the concepts discussed in this survey of indigenous rights, self-determination seems to cause the most difficulty for governments. According to an influential report on indigenous peoples, the concept of self-determination 'challenges the absolute sovereignty of nation states' (Independent Commission on International Humanitarian Issues (ICIHI) 1987:36). However, to call self-determination a challenge begs an important question. In practice, a state hardly ever has 'absolute sovereignty' over its territory. In Peru's case, reviewed in chapter two, the reality of state sovereignty was limited economically, politically, and militarily, and yet the rights of indigenous peoples present no challenge to the existence of Peru as a state.

International law is based on 'principles and rules of conduct which states feel themselves bound to observe' (Starke 1984:3) and so state sovereignty can never be absolute because authorities are obliged to behave within certain standards if they are to be recognised as part of the international community (Bull 1947). Human rights constitutes one area in which states are sometimes obliged to regulate their actions. Recognising the rights of indigenous peoples at the United Nations, which is itself constituted by states, is illustrative of this self-regulation. Thus both internally and externally, states have limitations on the exercise of their power.

However, within the concept of self-determination there is a breadth of application which refers to the integrity of states and to the rights of peoples at the same time. The concept of a people is broader than that of a state, and so the effect is that a political space appears between them which is pregnant with misunderstanding, if not conflict. The word 'self-determination' has appeared in widely different contexts at some of the most important junctures in the history of Europe: it refers to the protection of peoples within states; it refers to the formation of states during the process of decolonisation; and it refers to the integrity of the state when established. The term arose in the nineteenth century writings of German philosophers, but the meaning to which the term refers has reverberated throughout the history of peoples seeking to control their destinies. Examples have been given of the formation of nation-states in the seventeenth century (Chen 1976:214) and the external secession and internal revolution of North America and France in the eighteenth century.[1]

1. The significance of this approach to indigenous peoples rests on the way in which the concept of self-determination can be traced in retrospect to the French and American Revolutions, during which where the word had not yet gained political currency. Taking this position, there should be no difficulty in applying self-determination to indigenous peoples who do not all articulate the concept in their own languages. However, Ofuatey-Kodjoe warns: 'The use of the term "self-determination" by writers to describe historical phenomena which occurred before the term came into use are products of the way in which such writers define the term. Therefore, the validity of such descriptions depend on the validity of their definitions of self-determination. Since the generally accepted definition of self-determination has been undergoing change, such descriptions are likely to be open to serious question, In any case, such descriptions should be validated case by case, not accepted *a priori*' (1977:199).

Like 'self-development', the concept of 'self-determination' is not a static term, and refers to a process which undergoes shifts according to historical circumstances. At the turn of the century, for example, self-determination had three areas of orientation, each of which looked to the struggles of peoples in history. According to Ofuatey-Kodjoe (1977) 'self-determination' in this period could be divided into three approaches :

a) The 'Plebiscite Theory' sees self-determination as the consent by citizens to be members of a state and to acknowledge the legitimacy of a government. Some voting method would be the most appropriate way to ascertain the will of the people based on the principle of popular sovereignty.

b) The 'National Determination Theory' arose with the formation of nation states in Europe during the nineteenth century, particularly Germany and Italy (Ronen 1979:27). Here new states were created through an integrative process based on the national identity of a people. During the German unification process, the concept of self-determination became a political source of mobilisation. Fichte defined national self-determination as the right of each nationality to constitute an independent state in the form of national sovereignty.

c) The 'National Equality Theory' stemmed from the Second International when another approach to self-determination arose. Lenin saw self-determination as connected to the oppression of nations (Lenin 1971:159). It applied to overseas colonies of European nations (such as Britain); nations under domination by land empires (Austria and Russia); and semi-colonised countries (Persia and China). Self-determination for Lenin meant achieving the equality (non-oppression) of nations through regional autonomy, federal union, or independence. The result was a regional sovereignty.

The national determination approach to self-determination is about state formation, whereas the national equality theory is about the decentralisation of states. The plebiscite theory is more a process of decision-making, but one which takes place within the context of an already existing state. These three options relate to the different applications of self-determination mentioned by Kingsbury (1992): relating to states in themselves; to the formation of states and non self-governing and trust territories; and to other relations between entities and states. The two world wars provided catalysts for changing the meaning of self-determination. The end of the First World War put the three approaches to self-determination to the test.

Post-World War One

When the Ottoman and Austro-Hungarian empires broke up, the map of Europe was redrawn by the victors, who had the power to create states and add to those which already existed. Realising the significance of national minorities as part of the origin of the First World War, U.S. President Woodrow Wilson was active in securing protection of racial and national minorities. For Wilson, the concept of self-determination was rooted in popular sovereignty, and he thought that the territorial restructuring of Europe should follow this principle.

There was considerable discussion as to whether this would mean holding plebiscites in each country (Wilson's model followed the plebescite theory of self-determination). However, in practice there were few referendums because the allies established national territorial boundaries taking the majority populations into consideration, and arranged for a series of treaties to be drawn up with these countries to ensure that they respected the rights of any minorities.[2] In addition to the national self-determination dimension of the work of the League of Nations, self-determination also appeared in its mandate system (Falkowski 1992:41). According to this system, members of the League became responsible for the well-being of native peoples under colonial control.[3]

With regard to indigenous peoples, Article 23 (b) of the Covenant guaranteed 'to secure just treatment of native inhabitants of territories under their control'. This constituted a statement recognising the responsibility of League members for the peoples under their jurisdiction. Indeed, in 1931, Liberia was warned under Article 23 (b) that it would be expelled from the League if it continued to treat the nomadic peoples of the interior inhumanely (Falkowski op.cit.:42).

2. Minorities were guaranteed full rights of citizenship and freedom to use their languages. Fourteen treaties were drawn up, of which the five largest, with Czechoslovakia, Poland, the Serbo-Croat-Slovene State, Romania, and Greece, were called the 'Minority Treaties' (Heinz 1978:26). They were signed and kept by the League of Nations. For details of the Treaties see Thornberry (1992:42).

3. Fourteen Turkish and German territories were included under the system. Class A Mandates were in the Middle East, Class B in East, West, and Central Africa, and Class C, Southwest Africa and the Pacific. Furthermore, the Mandate system was meant to move towards self-government of these territories, although there was no mechanism for this. Only Iraq, Lebanon, and Syria achieved independence during the lifetime of the League.

In practice, however, the mechanisms of the League for self-determination of states with minorities and mandated territories were not wholly successful. The League was dominated by the Allies and Associated Powers, and the arrangements which were made complied largely with political conveniences of the time. The complaints or 'petitions' from minorities were not dealt with effectively by the League and decreased markedly by the end of the 1930s. The mandate system also operated on very cautious lines. Furthermore, when indigenous leaders such as Chief Deskaneh from Canada and the Maori leader, Ratana, tried to petition in the League in the 1920s they were rejected out of hand.[4]

The main threat to the League's work on self-determination came from a resurrection of the second theory of self-determination (nationalist self-determination), which argued that each nation should have a state. The League supervised a system whereby Germany was separated from Austria and large German minorities lived in Czechoslovakia and Poland. By whipping up discontent among these German minorities and arguing for a German 'national self-determination', Hitler and the Nazis used the inconsistencies of the Versailles agreement as a pretext for their European conquest. Furthermore, according to Falkowski, 'Hitler saw the settlement of the New World and the concomitant elimination of North America's Indian population by White European settlers as a model to be followed by Germany on the European' (1992:44).

The aftermath of the Russian Revolution brought the Bolsheviks to power. The Russian Empire was reconstructed and the self-determination argument became state policy. Whereas Lenin's view on self-determination was primarily anti-imperialist, there was another current in Bolshevik policy which was influenced by Stalin and contradicted Lenin's position. According to Stalin, only nations had the right to self-determination. A nation had to be a historically stable community with a common language, occupying a single piece of territory, organised by a coherent economy, and belonging historically to the epoch of rising capitalism (Blaut 1987:148). This narrow definition of 'nation' considerably limited self-determination in practice. By connecting the definition of nation to so many factors and tying it to a lower, non-socialist, stage of capitalism, any claim by a nation for the right to self-determination could easily be seen as revi-

4. The League received petitions on minority rights in varying degrees. Between 1930 and 1932 petitions were at their peak and numbered 305; of these, about half were considered. However, by 1939 only four petitions were sent and the League did not respond to these at all (Thornberry 1992:47).

sionist or counter-revolutionary. Furthermore, Stalin considered that any non-nation (national minority) should be assimilated into the state as a whole. In this way, Lenin's approach to self-determination based on liberation and equality of nations did not feature in the practical formation of the Soviet Union.

The three approaches to self-determination failed for different reasons. The plebiscite system was managed ineffectively by the League of Nations until it eventually petered out. The theory of nationalist self-determination was discredited and considered untouchable after Hitler and the Nazis used it as a pretext for genocide. The theory of national equality, although advocated by Lenin in a positive manner, was transformed by Stalin into a form of oppression. In all cases indigenous peoples were either ignored or destroyed.

The period after the First World War dealt with self-determination in two main contexts: peoples within states wanting their right recognised (minorities) and peoples on the process to becoming self-governing (mandates). Indigenous peoples straddled several of these options, and clearly staked their claim to self-determination during the period, as mandated peoples, native peoples, and through the attempted representations of indigenous leaders to the League.

Post-World War Two

The Second World War acted as another catalyst for the concept of self-determination. After the dissolution of the League, self-determination gradually re-appeared in a new guise with the establishment of the United Nations. While still at war, Churchill and Roosevelt signed the Atlantic Charter of 1941. In two principles they advocated the principle of self-determination based on the Wilsonian model of the League of Nations, according to which 'no territorial changes should take place that do not accord with the freely expressed wishes of the people concerned', 'the right of all peoples to choose the form of government under which they wish to live'- must be respected, and 'sovereign rights and self-government [must be] restored to those who have been forcibly deprived of them.'

Whereas this statement was applicable to Eastern Europe in 1941, the United States, concerned at the rise of colonial nationalism in Africa and Asia, began to consider that the Charter should apply to the right of independence for colonial peoples. Whereas the Soviet Union and China were in agreement, the British, French, and Dutch considered colonial questions to be internal matters. Prior to the founding conference of the United Nations at San Francisco in 1945, a compromise was reached by which a notion of trusteeship was incorporated into the UN Charter, linking the intentions of national liberation to the notion of self-determination. The effect was a shift in the concept of self-determination, combining the plebescite approach with that of the national equality theory (Ofuatey-Kodjoe 1977:104).

The principle of self-determination is specifically mentioned in Articles 1 (2) and 55 of the Charter. In these Articles, self-determination is attached to 'peoples'. There was some disagreement at the San Francisco meeting as to whether the self-determination of peoples actually acknowledged the right of a people to secession and exactly to whom the principle applied. These two questions were left open and the General Assembly in 1949 passed a resolution to establish a Special Committee to examine them.

Two issues dominated the self-determination debate over the next forty years which parallelled the two aspects of self-determination - mandates and minorities – recognised after the First World War: one was the question of independence for overseas colonies and the second was self-determination for peoples living within nation states. Throughout the 1950s a series of General Assembly resolutions were passed defining the rights of non self-governing territories more clearly. Independence was clearly recognised as a possible option of for non self-governing territories in General Assembly Resolution 648 (VII) in 1952. In the same year the Human Rights Commission was given the authority to include the right of self-determination in the drafts of the Human Rights Conventions.

In 1960, Resolution 1514 (XV) the 'Declaration on the Granting of Independence to Colonial Countries and Peoples' and Resolution 1541 (XV) were passed, accepting the idea of independence for geographically separate colonial peoples, but in certain cases allowing for trusteeship to continue until the people acquired the capacity for self-government.[5] The purpose of the Resolutions was to create a climate whereby new states could join the UN with ease and would have their territorial integrity guaranteed. Within ten years, the decolonisation process was largely over and the UN passed Resolution 2625 in 1970: 'Declaration of Principles of International Law Concerning Friendly Relations and Cooperation among States'.

There has been some discussion over whether the Declaration recognises support for the rights of peoples living internally to

5. Bennett (1978:13) gives several examples in which indigenous peoples could be defined as 'geographically separate' even though they do not strictly live across salt water from the colonial power. Examples range from the Arctic to deserts and rainforests.

states (Thornberry 1992:19). The Declaration guarantees the territorial integrity of states provided that they do not treat their peoples with discrimination:

> 'Nothing in the foregoing paragraphs ... shall be construed as authorizing or encouraging any action which would dismember or impair ... the territorial integrity or political unity of sovereign and independent states ... possessed of a government representing the whole people belonging to a territory without distinction as to race, creed or colour'.

Although one must be cautious not to overstate this qualification on territorial integrity, the establishment of 'safe havens' among the Kurds in 1992 shows that a flexible interpretation of the term is possible where there is a political will. Furthermore, the question of discrimination is very important when looking at the application of the term indigenous peoples to self-determination. At the United Nations, several representatives have made the point that not to be recognised as indigenous peoples is discriminatory and runs against the Declaration of Friendly Relations.

The rights of non self-governing peoples within nation states was raised by Belgium in 1954 in what became known subsequently as the 'Belgian thesis'.[6] The question was subsequently taken up over the next twenty years through the Commission on Human Rights' discussion in the Covenants and later in its discussion on indigenous peoples. This provided a political space for discussing the self-determination of indigenous peoples within states and led to the opportunity for indigenous peoples to approach the United Nations in 1977 to assert their claim for self-determination.

The acceptance of the right of self-determination for indigenous peoples by the UN Working Group on Indigenous Populations in Article 3 of the draft Declaration completes the picture of the development of the concept of self-determination as it has emerged over the last one hundred years. In spite of its shift of emphasis, self-determination has always referred to the rights of peoples within states as well as to the rights of those forming states. Thus indigenous peoples are the appropriate subjects of self-determination both logically and historically. After the draft Declaration, the approval of self-determi-

---

6. Belgium argued that colonies did not only have to be overseas; some peoples who were colonised lived within the boundaries of states, and they should also receive protection. This argument would have included indigenous peoples (as currently defined) within the framework of trusteeship, and consequently raised the question of their right to self-determination. The proposal was rejected but the idea did not disappear.

nation is now a central pillar of the document's legitimacy in the eyes of indigenous peoples.

The main problem for indigenous peoples is that some states in the UN limit the term self-determination only to the formation or secession of states; however, this limitation is widely considered unrealistic (Brownlie 1988; Hannum 1990; Kingsbury 1992). To demonstrate the indigenous right to self-determination in a manner which is relevant to states, misunderstandings have to be ironed out and an area cleared to establish the grounds for a positive, non-colonial relationship.

Issues Arising from the Concept of Self-determination

State concerns about self-determination cover four main areas: territorial integrity, sovereignty, external self-determination, and the rights of peoples. By grasping these features from an Arakmbut perspective is it possible to deconstruct the way in which the state tries to monopolise the terms relating to self-determination and thereby seek ways in which the relationship between the Arakmbut and the Peruvian state can become more constructive.

1. Self-determination and Territorial Integrity

A frequent concern regarding the self-determination of indigenous peoples is that recognition will mean the violation of the territorial integrity of nation states. The fear is that indigenous peoples, armed with the right to self-determination, will constitute a threat or even cause the break-up of the states in which they live.

Self-determination and territorial integrity are not mutually exclusive, but a pair of concepts in dynamic relationship connecting indigenous peoples and the state. The Arakmbut illustrate this clearly. The state of Peru has a set of geographically recognised boundaries which are recognised by the principle of territorial integrity. Yet at the same time, Arakmbut territory is part of their own indigenous inalienable heritage. During their history, the Arakmbut have never ceded their territory to the Peruvian state and, as noted above, at fiestas they proudly claim that they were conquered neither by the Incas nor by the Spanish and that they are owners of their own homeland.

Both the Arakmbut and the Peruvian state have a form of territorial integrity. Conflict arises when the state considers that it has exclusive rights to Arakmbut lands and resources. The result is a clash of perspectives. From the state view, it might be possible to argue that the Peruvian authorities are powerful, that they have international recognition of territorial integrity, and that in practice they exercise control over Arakmbut territory. Indeed, the Peruvian state itself has threatened the territorial integrity of the Arakmbut in several ways: it has unilaterally declared that the Arakmbut, along with all other indigenous peoples of Peru, no longer have inalienable rights to their territory; it has unilaterally claimed all sub-surface resources, allowing national and multinational companies access to Arakmbut gold; and it refuses to defend the Arakmbut from invasion by colonists. Of particular concern here is how the government is trying to destroy the indigenous land base. By offering credits to communities at 26 percent interest, the local authorities know that many indigenous people will become in debt to their creditors. These creditors will be able to force indigenous communities to mortgage and sell what was once their unconquered territory. What the state cannot take by force they will take through induced poverty.

The consequences of this are suspicion of the state, conflict with the international and national companies which enter Arakmbut territory, and hostility to the invading gold colonists. The more exclusively the state asserts its authority over the Arakmbut, the more tension and conflict arises. In response, the Arakmbut assert their own territorial rights as indigenous peoples and the zone risks becoming an area of violence. This is the current situation in which the Arakmbut find themselves.

However, this need not be the case. From an Arakmbut perspective the state's cavalier attitude to indigenous territory is an abnegation of responsibility in what should be a trustworthy relationship. No one denies that Arakmbut territory lies within the boundaries of Peru, and Arakmbut lands are recognised by the Peruvian state. The Law of Native Communities has been a mutually acceptable way for lands to be demarcated, titled, and recognised. The law may not be perfect, but it is a mutual agreement. The purpose of titling is to have a territory recognised legally by the Peruvian state in order to protect it from invasion.

The Law of Native Communities is effectively a 'treaty' between indigenous communities and the state. Each community and the state have to agree to the boundaries, and the Arakmbut have rights to all surface resources. Peruvian law does not consider that the Arakmbut violate state territorial integrity; on the contrary, the Law of Native Communities is an acknowledgement of indigenous rights to self-determination over their territories within the framework of the state.

The choice is stark. The more the state and the processes of colonisation assert national territorial integrity in order to deprive the Arakmbut of their rights, the more conflict will increase. On the other hand, the more the state recognises that territorial integrity concerns relations between states, and that indigenous territorial rights should be respected, then self-determination becomes not only something practised by communities, but understood by all. The result would then be a much more harmonious relationship between the state and Arakmbut.

In a recent book on peoples and minorities (Brohlmann, Lefeber, & Zieck 1993) several articles look at the tension between the concept of self-determination and territorial integrity. Franck puts it as follows:

> 'Where title to territory is concerned, two related but different principles had become the parameters of international law's unceasing, if illusory, quest for certitude. One is the static principle of *uti possidetis* or 'territorial integrity'. The other is the dynamic principle of self-determination' (1993:4).

Franck is not writing specifically about indigenous peoples but refers to the national minorities, yet his main point is relevant here because he argues that territorial integrity is never absolute.[7]

Indeed, the history of the last twenty years has provided several examples of the weakness of the notion of territorial integrity. Examples range from the break-ups of the Soviet Union and Yugoslavia to Bangladesh and Ethiopia. These countries demonstrate quite clearly that if the political will is present in the international community, the territorial integrity of states can be redefined. However, these examples concern prexistent sub-states separating from a larger state. Indigenous peoples rarely seek separation from nation states, although there are cases in which a state's claim to territorial integrity has to come under scrutiny. Chen says: 'The principle of territorial integrity must not serve as a shield for tyrants, dictators or totalitarian rulers, it must not become a cloak behind which human deprivations are justified, condoned and perpetuated' (Chen 1976:243).

A second example of the lack of an absolute notion of a state's territorial integrity comes from indigenous peoples who signed treaties with European powers before the nation state was formed. Whereas

---

7. West Papua and East Timor constitute clear examples in which a state (in this case Indonesia) has invaded and occupied another country at an early stage of independence. To consider West Papua and East Timor as violating the territorial integrity of Indonesia is absurd because Indonesia's invasion was itself a violation of the territorial integrity of West Papua and East Timor.

Canada argues that it controls the territorial integrity of the state as a whole, indigenous nations such as those in Treaty Six argue that they signed their international treaty with Britain and have never been part of the state of Canada. The question is therefore not whether Canada's territorial integrity has been violated by Treaty Six, but whether Canada has a right to impose its sovereignty on an indigenous people.

The concern of states that self-determination threatens their territorial integrity can be seen by the Arakmbut in terms of two factors. State territorial integrity cannot be absolute, and to define it, some form of treaty or other constructive agreement is one way of avoiding conflict. These points are not unique to the Arakmbut, but can be seen in other parts of the indigenous world.

2. Self-determination and Independence – the Question of Sovereignty

A common concern about the right of indigenous peoples to self-determination is that they will all declare independence. This is another way of looking at the territorial integrity of states reviewed above; however, this argument presupposes the unrealistic possibility of thousands of different indigenous peoples all seeking seats at the United Nations. Most indigenous peoples are not seeking independence, and those who do want their own state are seeking liberation from invasion.

From an Arakmbut perspective the idea of independence clearly seems absurd. Eight hundred or so people in the Amazon could hardly form their own independent state. However this 'statist' view of independence does not alter the fact that in many ways the Arakmbut are independent from Peru. They are culturally distinct and socially different, operating on their own community-based customary legal principles based on reciprocity, personal relationships, and ties to their territory and the spirit world. Furthermore, they are markedly self-sufficient provided that they have access to their resources.

A more useful term than independence, which places the subject in a clearer context, is that of 'sovereignty'. Sovereignty is:

> 'The unrestricted right of groups of people to organize themselves in political, social, and cultural patterns that meet their needs. It is the right of a people to freely define ways in which to use land, resources and manpower for their common good. Above all, sovereignty is the right of people to exist without external exploitation or interference' (Myers, cited in Kickingbird et.al. 1977:2).

Sovereignty is a European concept which refers to the supreme power from which all specific political powers are derived. For writers such as Hobbes, this rested with the monarch by the Divine Right of Kings, whereas for Locke it rested with the people. The term has been used by indigenous peoples who see sovereignty arising from their identity as a people. The discussion in this book relates the notion of a people with its territory, and in the Arakmbut case with spirituality. These three domains interact so that the Arakmbut as a people are tied to their territory on the basis of an ownership based on spiritual legitimacy. This spiritually recognised ownership of territory provides the dynamics behind Arakmbut sovereignty (see Volume 2 chapter twelve). Sovereignty, therefore, does not exist through external recognition; it is a series of relationships which arise from the people themselves. Sovereignty is an aspect of self-determination because it focuses on the power base with which a people controls its resources, lives, and destiny. In the Arakmbut case, the spirit world provides that fundamental power.

The principles governing Arakmbut sovereignty and the Peruvian state are different. The sovereignty of the state is based on a standardised legal system, territorial integrity as defined by boundaries, citizenship, and cultural homogeneity.[8] Although states might consider that sovereignty is synonymous with independence, many indigenous peoples, particularly those in Peru such as the Arakmbut, consider themselves Peruvians in the national state context while accepting their own sovereignty as a people. This consists of an identity based on a shared language and religion, a common cultural framework, a sense of territoriality, and their own political and legal system, all of which we have reviewed in previous chapters.

When the Peruvian government recognised the Arakmbut in law, that was a step in the direction of recognising their sovereignty. However, as was noted with the concept of territorial integrity, the notion of state sovereignty cannot be absolute. The Peruvian state and the Arakmbut have different sovereignties which can be combined or related. The exclusivity of state sovereignty denies indigenous identity as a people and leads to integration and assimilation of Arakmbut. This leads to resistance and a

---

8. Some writers such as Hannum (1990:15), argue that sovereignty is a state prerogative: 'One principle upon which there seems to be universal agreement is that sovereignty is an attribute of statehood, and that only states can be sovereign'. Needless to say indigenous peoples, particularly those from North America, would argue that sovereignty is an attribute of nationhood rather than statehood and does not need the recognition of states to exist.

stronger desire for the Arakmbut to assert their distinct identity, which can be seen at times when they come under threat, such as the conflict with Dianda or at the storming of Boca Colorado when the communities joined together as Arakmbut, or when the Consejo Harakmbut was formed.

The constructive way of avoiding conflict is for the state and Arakmbut to enter a process of mutual recognition of each other's forms of sovereignty. This means dealing with the colonisation which takes place on the lands of San José and the arbitrary change of the Peruvian constitution which threaten indigenous sovereignty. Myers talks above of the sovereign right to 'exist without external exploitation or interference'. Sovereignty does not mean total isolation but is a recognition that an indigenous people can control unwanted interference in their own affairs.

Indigenous peoples' demands for self-determination vary from internal autonomy to independence. The Arakmbut are an example of autonomy, but there are other expressions of self-determination which range from various forms of association with the state to full independence. One feature noted throughout the world is that the greater the oppression under which they suffer, the more wide-ranging indigenous demands become. In the Chittagong Hill Tracts of Bangladesh, for example, the indigenous peoples seek a regional autonomy which, in itself, is no greater than statehood in India. However, the Bangladesh government has responded to this demand with horrendous oppression. During the visit to Bangladesh of the Chittagong Hill Tracts Commission, several people said that if the oppression did not stop soon, many hill people would seek independence simply as a means of escaping the horrors to which they are subjected.

The Declaration on Friendly Relations says that gross discrimination could be a reason for separation from a state. This question has been discussed by Erica Daes in her 'Explanatory note on the draft declaration on the rights of Indigenous Peoples':

> 'Once an independent State has been established and recognised, its constituent peoples must try to express their aspirations through the national political system, and not through the creation of new States. This requirement continues unless the national political system becomes so exclusive and non-democratic that it can no longer be said to be "representing the whole people". At that point, and if all international and diplomatic measures fail to protect the peoples concerned from the State, they may perhaps be justified in creating a new State for their safety and security ... "Self determination" is a continuing dynamic right, in the sense that it can be reawakened if, at any moment, representative

democracy fails and no alternatives exist for the defence of fundamental rights and freedom' (Daes 1993a:4).

This opinion is significant because it demonstrates that the right of secession is an option for indigenous peoples who are oppressed and discriminated against to a point where their survival is at stake.[9] However, the majority of indigenous peoples are not in a position to become independent by forming a new state. For this reason, whereas the option of forming a state is open to all peoples, in practice this does not mean an explosion of applications to the United Nations:

> 'Recognition of the right to secede does not automatically mean that every nation or people have a duty to secede; indeed the fathers of this right believed that the very recognition of the right to secede and democratic treatment of all nations and nationalities within a particular state lead to a situation of voluntary union of nations rather than secession. For, to emphasise once again the right [of self-determination] belongs to an oppressed nation and if a nation is not oppressed, that is to say, it is treated democratically and accorded equality, both the reason and rationale for secession disappear' (Shivji 1989:84).

The fear of secession is largely unwarranted in the context of indigenous peoples because potential secessionists need a state structure and this pre-supposes a particular form of organisation which most indigenous peoples do not have. A vision of the world swamped by thousands of new states trying to squeeze into the United Nations is clearly groundless (c.f. Hannum 1990:454).

In the same way that self-determination and territorial integrity are not absolute opposites but rise and fall flexibly according to historical conditions, state and indigenous sovereignty need not enter into conflict unless the peoples are exploited or suffering unwarranted interference. For a state to deal with indigenous sovereignty it has two choices: one is to exterminate the indigenous peoples, physically or culturally, and the other is to recognise sovereignty in the context of a multi-cultural system.

If a state tries to exterminate an indigenous people either physically or culturally, this grants that people the right to secede or defend themselves. A constructive way for a state to act is to recognise the importance and value of a multi-national and multi-ethnic state where human and peoples' rights are fully recognised.

---

9. A similar point was made at the UNESCO meeting of Experts on Ethnodevelopment and Ethnocide in 1983 (IWGIA 1984:83).

3. Internal and External Self-determination

An approach to reduce the controversial aspects of indigenous self-determination is to promote 'internal' self-determination of indigenous peoples as opposed to 'external' self-determination of states. The logic of this is to emphasise the territorial integrity and sovereignty of states, while providing the political space for indigenous peoples to come to constructive agreements appropriate to their circumstances.

This subject has caused much discussion in the UN Working Group on Indigenous Populations. Initially the de facto approach of the Working Group considered that their forum was not appropriate for the decolonisation procedures of peoples wishing to become states and they would be directed to the New York Decolonisation Committee. Indeed, this is the reason why peoples such as the Tibetans and the East Timorese are less interested in the Working Group. Nevertheless, when the draft declaration, in an earlier version, tried to limit the notion of self-determination in 1992, there was a rare vociferous protest by the hundreds of indigenous delegates present, and the current text was adopted to avoid the controversy by using the wording of existing instruments on self-determination in international law (Kingsbury 1992:390).

The Arakmbut illustrate the complexities of this question and demonstrate that, as a people consisting of self-governing autonomous communities, notions of internal and external exist but are entirely relative.[10] Throughout these three volumes there has been constant recourse to the notion of Arakmbut versus outsiders. The argument has been made that the Arakmbut are neither isolated fossilised communities, nor integrated into the nation-state. Their relationship with the state of Peru is one which constantly varies according to circumstances.

Externality can be people from another clan, people from another community, other indigenous peoples, non-indigenous people, Peruvians, or foreigners. The way in which these are classified as internal or external depends entirely on the social relations under review. At the fault lines of conflict, this volume has seen that identity is asserted at different levels. Thus in the case of Dianda: San José opposed him, then became allied with Puerto Luz, and later with all the Arakmbut communities. FENAMAD's presence demon-

---

10. In Canada, for example, self-sufficient independent nations within the boundaries of the state (such as some Treaty Indians) provide a contrast to indigenous provinces of Canada itself (such as Nunavut).

strated that the case had become so notorious that it became an 'indigenous' campaign.

The crucial point for the Arakmbut is that 'external self-determination' is relative and is not defined by an absolutist state. The distinction is meaningless. Both internal and external self-determination exist for them; the question of independence is predicated on a state-based political organisation, and clearly the Arakmbut are not states. The Arakmbut are a people and they relate to the Peruvian state. This is a more relevant distinction regarding self-determination than 'internal' and 'external' defined by the state itself.

In practice, there are several ways in which the different perspectives of Arakmbut and Peruvian government perspectives have come together. They have developed a legally guaranteed manner of coexistence which should allow the Arakmbut free expression of their right to 'external' self-determination within the framework of Peruvian national society. The Law of Native Communities recognises a formal political organisation for each community; the system which operates in Peru consists of a series of federations constructed on the principle of representatives from each community. Local, national, regional, and international organisations carry these concerns way beyond the 'internal' community or even peoples-oriented political organisations. In this way indigenous peoples, through their negotiating both nationally and internationally, are struggling to gain control over their own lives and resources.

Another area in which indigenous peoples are increasing control over external factors is through their gradual influence in the local municipalities. The Arakmbut are a majority in the District of the Madre de Dios. If there is no subterfuge by colonists in the future, they will eventually take control of the municipal council in Boca Colorado. This would be, from the Arakmbut territorial viewpoint, external self-determination, and they will be have the opportunity of incorporating elements of the national state into their political system. Yet from the perspective of the state it is internal self-determination.

Another area in which 'external' and 'internal' factors can be drawn together is with the creation of communal reserves. Current Peruvian law only recognises Arakmbut territory from the perspective of indigenous communities even though the Arakmbut themselves recognise a territory which transcends community boundaries. By use of the communal reserves, both sides can be accommodated. The state considers the land of the communal reserves as its own but held by the indigenous peoples in perpetual trust. On the other hand, the indigenous peoples see the reserved land as their own, but agree to protect it on conditions agreed nationally. After two years, the Arakmbut are still waiting for the government to finalise the establishment of the communal reserve.

The Arakmbut show that the distinction between 'external' and 'internal' self-determination may be absolute for states, but it is relative for indigenous peoples. The weakening of the right to self-determination for indigenous peoples is not only discriminatory but could have serious repercussions on a local level, where the relationship between state and people is being organised in practice.

In her position paper of 1993, Erica Daes, Chair of the UN Working Group on Indigenous Populations, explains this relationship in the context of indigenous peoples:

> 'Indigenous peoples have the right to self-determination, and that this means that the existing State has the duty to accommodate the aspirations of indigenous peoples through constitutional reforms designed to share power democratically ... Furthermore, the right of self-determination of indigenous peoples should ordinarily be interpreted as their right to negotiate freely their status and representation in the State in which they live' (Daes 1993a:5).

The dimension which Daes raises here is that of democracy. This is significant because indigenous peoples' demands are for the broadening of the notion of democracy to reflect their needs and desires. As Hoffman says, 'the analysis of democracy in terms of pluralistic identity, must turn on the question of displacing statist force by government co-operation' (1995:214). Indigenous peoples can offer an approach here by being given the space to work out their own relationship with the state.

According to Cassese (1981) and Critescu (1981), external self-determination consists of the right of political independence and sovereignty over natural resources, while internal self-determination is the right of a people to choose under which government they live. Both of these aspects of self-determination are state-oriented, and give rise to the danger that indigenous incorporation into the state becomes integration.

Self-determination within the state is not a matter of integrating into national political processes:

> 'indigenous peoples' organizations today are claiming not just short-term special measures to allow them to integrate; they are claiming long-term differential status as distinct peoples, with their own base on land or other resources, and the ultimate right of self-determination of their political destiny' (Nettheim 1988:126).

Self-determination of the state and of indigenous peoples is markedly different. In each case internal and external mean different things, although the rare indigenous demands for independence draw the perspectives closer together. However, internal and external self-determination cannot be treated as mutually exclusive. Each implies the existence of the other. In some cases indigenous peoples will seek external state self-determination under circumstances of occupation or gross violations of human rights. In other cases they seek a relationship with the state from within. But between these extremes a range of options exists.

Once again, the conclusion is that indigenous rights discussions on self-determination are too often couched in absolute terms, by means of which the state controls all the discussions. Territorial integrity versus self-determination, independence versus decolonisation, internal versus external self-determination – all have become either/or problems in which indigenous peoples inevitably lose out. But indigenous peoples are so diverse that the form which self-determination takes will vary considerably.

Pomerance argues for flexibility:

> 'Such complexity can only be handled by means of a flexible approach which sees self-determination as a *continuum* of rights, as a plethora of possible solutions, rather than as a rigid absolute right to full 'external' self-determination in the form of complete independence' (Pomerance 1982:74).

When the Arakmbut are not treated with the respect which they feel a self-determining people ought to receive, the result is heightened discontent and social conflict. Only by expanding democracy 'beyond the state' (Hoffman 1992) can processes be seen for enabling indigenous peoples to determine their political status in a constructive manner.

4. Self-determination: Peoples Revisited

The right of self-determination is recognised for all peoples in the UN Human Rights Covenants. This is probably the main reason for some states refusing to acknowledge the 's' in indigenous peoples. In chapter four, the meaning of the word 'people' was covered in a sociological and anthropological sense. Daes puts the point succinctly (1993:2):

> 'Indigenous groups are unquestionably "peoples" in every political, social, cultural and ethnological meaning of this term. They have their

own specific languages, laws, values and traditions; their own long histories as distinct societies and nations; and a unique economic, religious and spiritual relationship with the territories in which they have lived.'

However, the connection between peoples and self-determination is also critical. The Daes list of the criteria involved in defining a 'people' can be supplemented by Falk's account of the rights of indigenous peoples (1988:20). He argues that the assertion by indigenous peoples of their rights as peoples is 'in many instances a cry of help from those confronted by the terrifying prospect of genocide'. The importance of the term 'peoples' is critical because it recognises indigenous peoples' self-determining capacity and provides them with moral and political support in defending their rights. The Arakmbut illustrate this connection between peoples and self-determination.

Whereas 'Arakmbut' is the closest articulation of the term people, there is no word, as yet, which means 'self-determination' in Harakmbut. However, this does not necessarily mean that there is no relationship. In spite of the variety and relativity within Arakmbut social and cultural life, there remain factors which they all recognise and share as linking them together. These are language, customs, and spirituality. The Arakmbut are self-determining in their daily lives and this aspect of their lives becomes particularly apparent during campaigns, such as the conflict with Dianda mentioned in the case study. What connects Arakmbut to this notion of self-determination is that they have a distinct way of determining their lives which demarcates them conceptually from other peoples who live in different ways.

The concept of Arakmbut is therefore not only a labelling device for categorising a people, it is a dynamic aspect of identity which is used to delineate the particular entity of existence which is self-determining. As was pointed out in chapter four, although the term can refer to several different indigenous contexts, nevertheless, as the elders explained, Arakmbut has taken on a primary meaning of referring to the five communities which share socio-cultural features and determine their lives in similar ways. This is the main Arakmbut self-determining entity in Peru.

According to Halperin and Scheffer (1992:1), 'at its simplest the principle of self-determination accords people a right to govern their own affairs'. For most of their daily lives the Arakmbut do govern their affairs (see chapter six), but state authorities and colonists challenge this when they undermine ownership rights or invade their territory. This invasion of territory leads inevitably to a response from the Arakmbut in the form of resistance or resignation. On the whole, after much deliberation, they assert themselves, but deciding how to respond to the colonists is difficult because the Arakmbut are weary of the constant struggle for survival and nervous of unleashing even more destructive forces against themselves.

At the moment of assertion they will publicly demonstrate physical manifestations of their cultural identity which they would normally be reluctant to show to outsiders. They paint themselves, wear feathers, sing, and dance in public at critical moments in their history. When important decisions need to be made, or when it is necessary to demonstrate unity among themselves, the Arakmbut reveal aspects of their ceremonial culture. These activities have rarely been practised since their years in the Dominican mission of Shintuya during the 1960s. However, their political assertion as a people and the cultural manifestations of their identity as a people are both closely bound together.

Thus, self-determination in practice, both on a daily basis and in the assertion of rights, is about the identity of the Arakmbut as a distinct people, but this can also come into conflict with the Peruvian state. On the basis of the statement reproduced in chapter one, the state recognises the Arakmbut as individual citizens. This is because the state claims that the collective right of a self-determining people is the sole prerogative of a state. The only people in Peru, on this reckoning, are the 'Peruvian people'. Once again this illustrates the conflict of perspectives between a state, which claims an absolute monopoly over terms such as 'peoples', and indigenous peoples who feel effectively ignored and discriminated against, even though they live within its national boundaries.

Yet the situation is not one of stalemate. Each demarcated title in Peru is given out not only in the name of the community but in the name of a particular people. Thus, to some extent, the ground is already prepared for the recognition of the indigenous peoples of Peru as peoples. What is needed is the goodwill to provide grounds for a common-understanding of and constructive approach into indigenous-state relations.

The case studies in this volume show that the more unwanted interference the Arakmbut receive, the more they will assert their identity as a people. As their distinctiveness becomes critical, the term 'Arakmbut' becomes politically mobilised and brings people together in a common cause. This assertion of identity only arises because they are not recognised. The more the rights of the Arakmbut are recognised, the more self-determination will refer to the daily activities of governance and living according to their distinct social and cultural premises.

Self-determination and Awareness

Falk (1988:27ff) calls indigenous self-determination 'self-determination (with an existential self)'. By this he means that a people is defined by the practice of the right. For this reason, the activities involved in determining one's own life define the criteria for self-awareness and identity as a people, which, when threatened, is reasserted. In this way the relationship between a people and self-determination can be seen more clearly in concrete practices than in ideological discourse. However, the right of self-determination inhabits both these areas and the process whereby self-awareness emerges within an indigenous people is critical for understanding political mobilisation.

This view of self-determination is consistent with the notion of intransitive and transitive features. The 'intransitive' aspect of self-determination refers to Arakmbut control over social and cultural life, economic production, access to resources, and political status, and it exists 'in itself'.[11] The right to self-determination is in this sense 'inherent' for the Arakmbut in that control over these activities takes place from day to day without the need for conceptualisation. However, when I say that self-determination is inherent, I do not mean that some metaphysical notion of self-determination is ready-made and hidden within the Arakmbut, waiting for a chance to escape. Self-determination is the ability to control life which, for most daily activities internal to the community, takes place spontaneously.

In contrast, the 'transitive' aspect of self-determination operates in relation to what the Arakmbut consider to be outsiders: outsiders to the community, to the Arakmbut people as a whole, or to indigenous peoples generally. As this form of political activity is directed towards a non-indigenous world, the conscious notion of self-determination 'for itself' becomes increasingly relevant.

The Arakmbut do not have a term for self-determination. It is a non-indigenous word that they have learned from other representa-

11. Many indigenous peoples have commented that, for them, the areas of self-determination in the Covenants are weakened by the lack of the term 'spirituality'. As we have seen in this work, spirituality and religion in fact pervade all aspects of indigenous life.

tives in the indigenous movement. Several of the more educated Arakmbut recognise the term in Spanish and this demonstrates their growing indigenous self-awareness. The word 'self-determination' has strong political connotations and indigenous peoples all over the world rally around its potential for liberation. The Arakmbut have no difficulty in understanding what the term means when they hear it explained. For example, the young man quoted at the beginning of the Introduction did not know the meaning of the concept, but when it was explained, he quickly grasped its implications. The reason for this is that it expresses a predicament which is common to them all – the threat from colonisation.

The invasion of territory (wandari) and their assertion as a people (Arakmbut) are the two all-embracing concepts which the Arakmbut recognise (see chapters three and four). The notion of self-determination is intimately bound to their territory and peoplehood because colonisation is the main threat to both. The concepts of 'wandari' and 'Arakmbut' thus set the framework for understanding self-determination. The word in Spanish is not 'alien'; it arises from the colonising experience.

Self-determination is the capacity of a people to control their destiny and this is embedded within the political mobilisation of the concepts of wandari and Arakmbut. When their existence as a people is threatened by outside exploitation and interference, then the term self-determination becomes relevant and will be articulated by the Arakmbut. This arises for two reasons: first because they become involved in the national indigenous political movement, in which the term is a regular part of the vocabulary; but more importantly because the term is meaningful.

The Arakmbut could utilise a word to blend in with the meaning of self-determination (just as wandari means 'territory' and 'Arakmbut' people). A possible candidate would be the words 'Arakmbut matamona'. This means 'we Arakmbut decide/order/determine/assert'. Perhaps this, or some other term, will gain currency as the Arakmbut's tie with the indigenous movement grows. In this case political discourse in both Harakmbut and Spanish will become coherent, and the inner aspects of Arakmbut resistance will become isomorphous with indigenous rights coming from outside.

The Arakmbut consider strength and assertion as linked to the concentrated or dispersed aspect of soul-matter – nokiren. The more dispersed the soul within the body, the more cerebral the person; the more concentrated, the more emotional. Too concentrated soul matter leads to the danger of sorcery and hatred, too dispersed and the person dies of weakness and debilitation. The shift between resistance and resignation in the face of threats is part of the same phenomenon on an Arakmbut collective level.

Self-determination can be seen in a similar manner. In ordinary daily life when the Arakmbut are self-determining, these multifaceted aspects of identity and control are dispersed through a multitude of activities. People do not reflect on them. However, during periods of danger the community either becomes dispirited or concentrates its efforts in resisting the threats. In the past, prior to the contact with missions in 1950, the Arakmbut united under a war-leader (ohpu) and fought against their enemies. Now, when resisting colonisation, they unite under community and federation leaders, and unifying concepts such as self-determination becomes increasingly more relevant. The result is that the label of self-determination makes sense to the Arakmbut when they talk of resistance; the more they recognise what the term means, the more the right is articulated.

Self-determination is thus not simply something which reacts to outside elements; it is a label given to the coalescing of resistance to colonisation from the outside. For most indigenous people this means members of the state in which they are living and also the authorities which constitute the national bureaucracy. Indigenous self-determination is thus difficult to grasp because it contains within it such a broad inter-connected spectrum of social, cultural, economic, and political life. The main factor, however, which links these areas together is the spirit world which connects each person to the rest of society, Arakmbut culture, and the environment as a whole. This will be discussion in the conclusion.

The Content of Self-determination

According to the United Nations Human Rights Covenants, the right of self-determination covers political status; social, cultural, and economic development; and disposition of natural resources. The phrasing on resources has its origins in the earlier Declaration of 1962, which discussed the permanent sovereignty over natural resources of nations and peoples (General Assembly Resolution 1803 (XVII)). The draft Declaration recognises all of these attributes in its reference to self-determination and rights to territories and resources.

To a large extent, the divisions of self-determination in the Covenants are arbitrary, but they do provide a framework both for peoples as self-determining entities on a daily basis and as self-determining their association with states. The Arakmbut provide a clear example of how so many elements of life are interconnected. Each aspect has reverberations and connotations which pass through their whole social and cultural life. This connectedness of life is paramount for the Arakmbut, although nothing is so structured that they lack room for creativity and improvisation.

By looking at the areas in which Arakmbut self-determination is apparent in relation to those set out in the Covenants, it becomes possible to trace themes from this and previous volumes in the series on mythology and history and on shamanism and politics.

Political status, the first aspect of the content of self-determination, provides a convenient starting point for reviewing the term among the Arakmbut. Two dimensions of the Arakmbut political system face inwards and outwards respectively, combining decision-making with control of behaviour. The informal, internally-oriented aspect of the political system is in contrast to the externally-oriented community council, defined by Peruvian national law. This is an example of the relativity of internal and external political status, which relates both to daily life and to state relations (see Volume 2, chapter eight).

Social, cultural, and economic development is the second set of criteria for the content of self-determination. Political influence is achieved through the collective recognition of generosity, which is a state of the nokiren resulting from distributing the benefits of successful economic activities such as hunting, fishing, well-managed gardens, and finding gold deposits. Reciprocity within the community defines social relations, forges alliances, and facilitates the smooth-running process of decision-making (see Volume 2, chapter seven). In this way, a person's spiritual being is bound up with the collective socio-cultural relationships of production and reciprocity, all of which determine indigenous self-development.

Access to resources, the third criteria of self-determination, arises from spirit contacts who give information through dreams. Arakmbut can only reap the fruits of these resources because of their capacity to tap into the collective knowledge and skills of their cultural heritage (Volume 2, chapter two). This knowledge is not only materially productive but, in a shamanic context, can also help to cure those who have fallen foul of the invisible world, thus protecting not only the patient, but in certain circumstances, the community itself from spirit attack (Volume 2, chapter four). Knowledge and skill in practical activities all show how access to resources is not simply a question of exploitation, but connects person and people together in political, economic, spiritual and socio-cultural dimensions of self-determination.

Politics and shamanism, discussed in Volume 2, are thus closely linked to self-determination in practice because they mediate between daily production activities of households and the decision-making processes of communities while striving to ensure a healthy relationship between the visible human and invisible spirit worlds. They also cover political status; social, cultural, and economic development; and the disposition of natural resources, which are the prime components of self-determination.

However, there is another aspect of Arakmbut life which is connected to self-determination on an even more fundamental level – mythology. In the three main Arakmbut myths discussed in Volume 1 of this series, it was shown that the whole history of the Arakmbut operates in a form coherent with their mythology.

The origin myth Wanamey is about the decision to found communities and to begin the whole process of self-organisation (Volume 1, chapter one); this myth reverberates through Arakmbut history, particularly contact in 1950, life in the missions until 1969, and subsequently the founding of the present communities (Volume 1, chapter twelve). The second myth, Marinke, is about growth, responsibility, and the self-control necessary for daily life to continue without breaking up; in particular it portrays distinct and unique aspects of Arakmbut culture and identity (Volume 1, chapter five). The third myth, Aiwe, explains the ways in which the Arakmbut should deal with white people and avoid destruction (Volume 1, chapter nine); this involves utilising non-indigenous knowledge in moderation while keeping consistent with Arakmbut socio-cultural values. All three myths relate to the capacity of the Arakmbut to assert themselves as a people and to become aware of the dangers encountered when creating their history and forging their destiny.

Mythology thus provides the orientation for self-determination throughout Arakmbut history, while political and shamanic activities carry the lessons from this collective experience into contemporary life. It could be said that the three books in this series provide the background for an understanding of Arakmbut self-determination.

CONCLUSION

On Tuesday 26 March 1996, the oil company Mobil signed a contract with Perupetro for new lots 77 and 78 in the Madre de Dios. The consortium for these areas includes Mobil Exploration and Producing Peru Inc, Elf Petroleum B.V., and Esso Exploration and Production Peru Ltd. The areas of intensive seismic exploration are all in the Madre de Dios and include the upper Piedras River, the upper Karene area, and the southwest portion of the Tambopata-Candamo Reserved Zone within the area proposed for the Bahuaja-Sonene National Park. This agreement was signed in the face of opposition from FENAMAD, COHAR, and the indigenous communities of the Karene.

The seriousness of this situation led the International Work Group for Indigenous Affairs (IWGIA) and the Tambopata Reserve Society (TReeS) to write a letter of protest. It was endorsed by a group of international environmental, solidarity and indigenous organisations which had been following Mobil's plans in the Madre de Dios. This letter contains information which demonstrates that, in spite of the constant presence of invasion, colonisation seems never-ending for the Arakmbut:

> 'As you are aware, the Madre de Dios is one of the most highly sensitive areas of the Amazon rainforest, due to its relatively untouched state. The region contains unique biological and cultural diversity including two major protected ecological areas and nineteen indigenous peoples, several of which are uncontacted.
>
> 'Several cases of extractive activities in Asia and Africa have taken place in areas of ethnic tension in recent years, and these have acted as a catalyst for violence. West Papua, Bougainville, and Ogoniland are only a few examples which come to mind. We are therefore extremely worried that irresponsible exploration activities in the upper Karene will exacerbate already existing conflicts, with serious repercussions for the indigenous Arakmbut who live in the area; this would have disastrous consequences for Mobil.

'The upper Karene is the homeland of the indigenous Harakmbut peoples who have lived in that region since before Inca times. The area has been demarcated as a communal reserve to protect breeding of the animals and birds on which the sub-group, Arakmbut, depend for its subsistence hunting. Furthermore, the reserve contains sacred areas where ancestors of the Arakmbut lived and were buried; it is also the mythological site of the appearance of the Wandakwe Inca who taught the Arakmbut many important aspects of their culture.

'The Karene is home of the Arakmbut communities, but around the reserve there are also communities of Piro, Kisambaeri and Matsigenka. We are aware that, early last year, the Canadian company Walsh did an environmental impact study of the area and visited the Arakmbut communities of San José del Karene and Puerto Luz. Far from allaying their concerns, by August, the communities were extremely worried about the prospect of exploration on their lands and signed a petition (along with the other presidents of communities around the reserve) objecting to Mobil's proposed exploration.

'At several meetings in Puerto Maldonado, on 20/7/95 and 5/11/95, FENAMAD's leadership expressed its serious fears about the proposed exploration in the upper Karene. Furthermore, Mobil's meeting at the Congress of FENAMAD in December did not result in an approval of exploration, but only agreed to continuing 'dialogue' in the future. On this basis, it is clear that the process of consultation with the Arakmbut and the other indigenous communities has been inadequate. They have not consented to what is to take place on their lands.

'Their concern is justified when one considers that if a base camp is to be placed in Mazuco, the only way to travel to the upper Karene, other than helicopter, will be by trail across the native community territories of Barranco Chico and Puerto Luz. Should oil be found in the area, there is no guarantee that a road would not slice the communities asunder and devastate their lands and territories.

'Unfortunately the environmental impact study has not been disseminated; we ask that you release this into the public domain immediately. However, we assume that Mobil realises from this report (if it had been done properly) there are already over two hundred illegal colonists in the upper Karene area who are causing numerous problems to the Arakmbut in both Puerto Luz and San José. There is fear in the communities that the exploration and possible subsequent activity will act as a pole of attraction for yet more colonisation from the highlands thereby leading to more ethnic conflict. The tensions in the area between indigenous peoples and colonists are growing. There have been several killings by colonists in recent years. The Karene as a whole is currently a tinderbox with potential violence between 1,500 colonists from the highlands and five hundred indigenous Arakmbut in the traditional Karene communities.

'We are very concerned that Mobil will continue with its plan of seismic exploration and eventually carry out exploratory drilling in these sensitive areas. If this becomes a possibility, we would strongly suggest that Mobil consider carefully the implications of this action. A new process of consultation should be instigated with international observers from oil monitoring, indigenous and environmental groups. Consent of

Conclusion

the indigenous peoples should be a fundamental principle in all activities of this nature. This approach would ensure that should any further work take place in the Madre de Dios, it is done in areas which are not sensitive, and is carried out in a manner which is environmentally and socially responsible ...

'We realise that on the basis of the agreement you are about to sign you might consider that you have the legal right to explore for oil in any part of the Madre de Dios. However, we are writing this letter to express our serious concern at your proposed activities which, if they go ahead unchecked, will have severe consequences for the environment and indigenous rights. Although Peruvian internal legislation encourages extraction in the rainforest, we would like to draw your attention to the fact that Peru is a signatory of the Convention on Biological Diversity and the ILO Convention 169 on Indigenous and Tribal Peoples. Both of these international undertakings will be violated if you go ahead with your plans for these sensitive areas of the Madre de Dios.

'We are all very concerned about the situation in the Madre de Dios and will be closely monitoring events in the future. In the meantime we recommend the following:

1. Mobil makes clear to the Peruvian government that it will not explore in places where uncontacted indigenous peoples have been reported, any indigenous community territory, or any reserved area which is currently awaiting government approval.
2. Mobil will support the immediate approval of the Amarakaeri Communal Reserve and the Bahuaja-Sonene National Park because the government delay is entirely attributable to Mobil's exploration interests in these areas.
3. If Mobil goes ahead in the Madre de Dios, all its future work, and that of subcontractors, will be completely transparent and have the full and informed consent of the indigenous peoples, their organisations and the environmental community.
4. That Mobil ensures that any of its activities or those of subcontractors conform stringently to national and international environmental and indigenous rights standards.
5. That Mobil postpones signing its contract on Tuesday 26th March until these points have been agreed by all parties.

   Signed Helen Newing (TReeS) and Andrew Gray (IWGIA).'

This development not only illustrates the threat of the continuing colonisation of the Madre de Dios, but also that, even though indigenous rights are couched in terms of state-people relationships, there are, behind states, the economic interests of multinational companies eager to extract the resources of indigenous peoples. Instead of the state and indigenous peoples forging alliances to protect their mutual concerns, the government of Peru, by signing the contract, works in opposition to the desires and aspirations of the Arakmbut. Increasingly, as multinational interest becomes more dominant in the Madre de Dios, the problems facing the Arakmbut will become internationalised and they will be even more incorporated into the political struggles of the indigenous movement.

Already Mobil has penetrated the Piedras river and according to two indigenous employees, its sub-contracted company Grant Geophysical has contacted isolated peoples of the area, putting their lives and the lives of the workers at risk. In October 1996, Mobil, in collaboration with the environmental organisation Conservation International and with the support of the Peruvian government's Indigenist Institute which is officially responsible for guaranteeing indigenous rights, planned to visit the Arakmbut communities to prepare for oil exploration on their territories.

The colonialism which the Arakmbut face is only one example of the threats facing hundreds of indigenous peoples throughout the world. Whereas in this 'post-colonial' epoch the developmental progressivism of the eighteenth century and the positivistic racism of the nineteenth century should be seen as an aberration of history, unless indigenous peoples are vigilant, these influences will continue within their territories. The state and multinationals have simply taken over where the sea and land empires of the past centuries left off.

However, the history of colonialism should not be seen as a monolithic form of absolutist oppression (J.&J. Comaroff 1992:183; Thomas 1994:7). In the period of Spanish colonisation, the theologians of Salamanca such as Vitoria and Las Casas defended the rights of the indigenous peoples; during the Enlightenment, Grotius, Rousseau, and Hume recognised the validity of indigenous political systems, while in the nineteenth century the early indigenists in Peru, such as González Prada, defended indigenous culture from racism. There has, therefore, always been a process of colonisation by states, empires, and multinationals, and resistance from indigenous peoples, thinkers, and progressive state governments and bureaucrats. For this reason, whereas it is possible to distinguish indigenous peoples from other interests, it is not possible to separate the indigenous struggle and the basis of indigenous rights from the whole multifarious panorama of colonial relations.

Indigenous Rights as a Process

This review of the relationship between development, identity, and self-determination has drawn together several lines of investigation which directly affect indigenous peoples today: human rights, the state, territory, peoples, cultural identity, government, development, and self-determination. The concepts have been approached initially through case studies in order to show how they appear to the Arakmbut through practical experience.

At the same time, in comments and footnotes, there has been a discussion of the main concepts used in indigenous fora, particularly the United Nations draft Declaration on the Rights of Indigenous Peoples. These concepts have a history, primarily of European origin, but in many cases, with direct connections to Latin America. They arose out of a struggle against European national oppression over the last five hundred years and were transformed by colonised peoples seeking to overcome European imperialism. Currently they are being used by indigenous peoples to fight back against national and international colonial interests.

Ultimately, the model of the oppression which the Arakmbut face stems from the North, and so it is not surprising that many of the concepts which they use can be found in the history of European political philosophy. However, the United Nations has taken the concepts and, through a collaborative process over the last thirteen years, transformed them into international standards which indigenous peoples have broadly accepted. This book has shown that both Latin American writers and the Arakmbut through their political activities have taken these international concepts and are currently transforming them once again into rights which reflect the specific needs and aspirations of the peoples of Peru. By taking on this challenge, the Peruvian state can place its priorities firmly with its peoples, rather than with, say, the exploitative economic forces of the International Monetary Fund; it can then continue with a process of state-formation that reflects local and national needs and is built on genuine multicultural and plurinational principles.

The Arakmbut demonstrate the way in which human rights concepts emerge from political action and an awarenesss of injustice. San José del Karene in Amazonian Peru shows that rights do not emerge all at once. Whereas certain human rights concepts are commensurable, particularly those based on notions of territory and peoples, others, such as culture, government, development and self-determination, are not part of the Arakmbut daily political vocabulary. This is not to say, however that the Arakmbut lack an understanding of these notions. On the contrary, they have their own way of expressing cultural identity, government, development, and self-determination which leaves no absolute mapping between Arakmbut conceptualisation and non-indigenous terms. Partly this is because, in practice, the Arakmbut still control most of their internal affairs and so there has been no recourse to alien terminology to defend their rights.

Indigenous peoples have their own philosophical views, which are equivalent to non-indigenous notions of rights. However, as the non-indigenous world increasingly threatens indigenous peoples, they utilise the language of rights as a part of their defence. In this way, rights emerge through the experience and sense of injustice which the Arakmbut would translate as 'ndakwe' (bad fortune/ill-health/bad behaviour).

Human rights may have had their origin in the liberal philosophy of Europe, but they now have universal application as a means of curbing the injustices and oppression which operate within that most European of institutions, the nation state. Today, the world is constructed on the basis of nation states and human rights are the major non-violent instruments for defence within this statist framework. It is useless for countries (such as China) to argue that culturally human rights do not apply to them when their whole power structure is based on the model of a state which has its origins in Europe.

Out of the concepts of territory, people, cultural identity, governance, development, and self-determination reviewed here, the only exact mapping of terms comes with the notion of territory (wandari) and peoples (Arakmbut). The other concepts are articulated in different ways. For example, cultural identity for the Arakmbut is recognition of the unique attributes which make a person part of a particular people – linking territory, the invisible world, and human beings, rather than a personal essence linking the individual to society. Government for the Arakmbut is about processes of making decisions and resolving disputes relating a people to their territory, not about institutions of law and order. Development is a question of changing while staying in the same place, not 'progressing'. Self-determination is bound up with living an Arakmbut life on Arakmbut territory.

The six terms, territory, people, cultural identity, government, development, and self-determination comprise three different types of concept. For the Arakmbut, territory and people are concrete material phenomena which can be seen, identified, and defended. Cultural identity and governance are both factors subsumed within the concepts of Arakmbut and wandari. Thus, rather than seek any equivalent term in Arakmbut, it is important to grasp the possibility that a concept may be encased within a word with its broader set of connotations.

The same phenomenon appears with development and self-determination. Development is also a relationship between wandari and

Arakmbut. Wandari links political, spiritual, and economic aspects of territory with access to the resources which are within it. All notions of economic development, production, and land use are bound up in the idea of wandari. Wandari provides the precondition for development because the spirit world is guardian of the resources and controls the potential which should be used at any one time. Development is therefore embedded within the wandari in the form of its potential, which is regulated by the spirit world and actualised through Arakmbut production activities.

Self-determination, in an Arakmbut context, consists of a worldview embracing an independent people who should have control over their internal and external relationships, receive respect for their territorial integrity, and determine their development as they see fit. This is in fact the way in which a nation-state defends its view of self-determination. Thus self-determination is not separated from the notion of peoples, but is embedded within the notion of Arakmbut and the control which they as a people should have over their territories.

The previous two volumes have shown that the invisible world is the potential inherent in the world and constitutes the framework within which all activity can take place. This contrast between potential and actual relates to some of the human rights concepts analysed here. The basic importance of wandari and Arakmbut demonstrates the fundamental significance of territory and people – this is the visible and tangible world of identity and existence. The notions of development and self-determination look at the relationship between the two and the potential for change – a factor which is directly parallel with the power of the invisible world. This fits with the non-indigenous view that both development and self-determination are open concepts – potentialities. Government and cultural identity, in contrast, are not open concepts, but moments of development and self-determination within the framework of territory and peoples.

These rights in an Arakmbut context are not discrete but have to fit into a pre-existent Arakmbut framework which consists of the invisible spirit world of potentiality and the visible world of actuality (see Volume 1, Part II). Whereas the invisible world provides the dynamism for life, the visible world provides the form. The two worlds relate through practical activity. In this case, rights are not imposed or unchanging since time immemorial, but arise from historical experience.

This throws a different light on the anthropological distinction between formalist and substantivist approaches to phenomena. According to the formalists, concepts are universally applicable whereas for the substantivists they have only specific, culturally-based meanings. Here we can see that the concepts dealt with in this report range between both formalist and substantivist meanings. With the threat of colonisation, indigenous peoples can bring their concepts into focus with the language of human rights. Thus formalist concepts are historically produced through movements such as that of indigenous peoples. This relationship can be expressed as follows:

Table 9.1 Comparison of indigenous and non-indigenous views of rights

Indigenous Perspective	Non-indigenous Perspective
Congruent Perspectives	
Arakmbut	People
Wandari	Territory
Parallel Perspectives	
a) Potentiality	
Spirit world	*Open concepts*
Potential of relationship between Arakmbut and wandari In hands of invisible world converted into actuality by human activity.	Development and self-determination: potential for political control over resources, society, culture, economy, government and identity.
b) Actuality	
All assertion of identity and decision-making or conflict resolution takes place within the framework of Arakmbut and wandari and the spirit world.	Government and cultural identity are manifestations of self-development and self-determination.

The Spiritual Dimension of Indigenous Rights in Theory and Practice

Rights are both political and moral. For non-indigenous state governments, indigenous rights are about control over resources, which is fundamentally political; however, juridical legitimation of rights is not sufficient in itself. Injustice has a moral dimension which indigenous peoples use whenever legal means do not assist them. These political and moral aspects of rights arise from the people or from those controlling the state when a clash of interests leads to a perceived injustice.

However, for indigenous people such as the Arakmbut, political and moral power is intimately connected to a spiritual quality of the soul and invisible world, which is neither good nor bad in itself but is manifest in the relationships between people and their environment. Here spirituality is taken further than being the potential of resources and for human activity as discussed in the previous section.

Spirituality is the means of generation whereby the whole social formation can change without destroying identity (Volume 2, chapter twelve). The legitimacy of justice stems from the invisible world, not on the basis of a Christian morality, but on the principle of an unstable balance of power within the universe which has to be constantly surveyed and checked. For the Arakmbut, the boundaries of the acceptable are patrolled by the spirit world, which constitutes a fundamental basis for indigenous perspectives of their rights. When human beings transgress these boundaries, they lay themselves open to the dangers of uncontrolled spirit activity.

The soul of each person reflects the relationship between that person and the rest of the community. When people unite in action to defend the interests of the community as a whole, the assertion is as much one of spiritual strength as of physical strength. The whole community comes together during a moment of cultural assertion, comprising an example of self-determination in its strongest Arakmbut form. They achieve this by putting on paint (which keeps the soul within the body), by dancing (which emphasises co-ordinated personal relations), singing (which directly opens contact with beneficial spirits), and wearing traditional dress (which draws on mythological powers from the culture hero Marinke, the strongest of the Arakmbut). This spiritual dimension of self-determination and self-development goes some of the way to explain why indigenous peoples defend these rights to the end. In a way, the spirit world is the last bastion of defence of the Arakmbut as a people. Once their capacity to determine their own lives, resources, and destinies becomes impossible, they will cease to exist.

The world of the spirit and rights are directly connected. In the chapter on territory, the Arakmbut legitimisation of ownership and property was seen as arising from the spirit world. Rights also provide indications of acceptable behaviour through moral and legal considerations in a manner parallel to the legitimation of behaviour by spiritual means. However, the structure of the relationship which the Arakmbut have with the invisible spirit world parallels that with the non-indigenous world. On the one hand the outside powers, whether spiritual or non-indigenous, are dangerous for the Arakmbut, while on the other hand they can also be beneficial if treated with respect.

The shamanic quest of life is to harness spiritual power for beneficial purposes and to keep danger and threats at a distance. On a spiritual dimension, the Arakmbut defend themselves by means of a double process. Curing and ensuring a healthy community involves contact with the invisible world. The first aspect of the process is incorporating the beneficial aspects of the spirit world. This comes from communication through dreams and visions. The information from beneficial spirits is incorporated into Arakmbut knowledge and used to reinforce the Arakmbut shamanic capacity to keep harmful spirits at a distance. This is apparent in the practice of curing chants, in which the shaman uses detailed knowledge of harmful spirits' weaknesses to frighten them away.

In the same way, the non-indigenous world constitutes a major threat for the Arakmbut, but it also provides some potential remedies. These are the human rights concepts which have arisen from a history of oppression and injustice stemming from Europe. Rights therefore emerge at points in history when gross injustice becomes intolerable for a people who are resisting and defending their existence. San José's external political strategies consist of making alliances with these beneficial sources, both human and spiritual, in order to survive and promote the interests of households, clans, or the community as a whole. With the knowledge they gain, they can reinforce their own assertion of their Arakmbut strength in order to keep threats at bay.

By controlling the relationship between positive forces from outside and inside the community, the Arakmbut strive to achieve a complementarity which generates a dynamic, creative strength. This exchange between external and internal factors enables the Arakmbut to assert their strength and to defeat the enemies which surround them. In this way the objective of a complementarity between inside and outside operates both on the spiritual and non-indigenous dimensions of socio-cultural life and constitutes the basis of indigenous rights for the Arakmbut.

Prospects for the Future

In addition to the different ways in which communities relate to the outside influences, this book has looked at the elements which pull them in different directions. Bodley (1988:5-7) sees integration as the most destructive influence on indigenous peoples. By integration he means, 'preserving the "best" features of the traditional culture and eliminating those features that might be considered obstacles to economic progress' (p.3).

This draws indigenous peoples into the dominant state society and usually integrates them into the impoverished classes, but far from offering them a better life, leaves them with a weakened cultural identity and dependent on the outside world. Even though the ILO in Convention 169 has dropped all advocacy of integration, it is still the dominant state ideology when dealing with indigenous peoples. All indigenous peoples in the Madre de Dios face factors of integration, but those closer to Puerto Maldonado have suffered most from its ethnocidal implications.

Rather than integration, the aim of all the communities, particularly in the Karene, is to become self-sufficient. This is an Arakmbut notion of being independent from the destructive influences from the outside world. They want the freedom to be able to organise their lives and sufficient control over their resources to ensure that they are not dependent on exploiting economies from outside. This can provide them with the freedom to practice self-determination and to organise their own self-development. According to Bodley (op.cit.:5) self-determination and self-development are the antithesis of integration and together constitute a goal for which all indigenous peoples strive.

Integration and self-sufficiency are the opposing forces which surround indigenous peoples all over the world. In the Madre de Dios, each community will seek for its own strategy of self-determination with which to relate to the outside world. The notion of integration is part of a continuum leading to assimilation whereby indigenous peoples' identities eventually disappear. The goal of integration is dangerous because the initiative comes from outside. The state and the national society stake out the framework within which the indigenous peoples will live. The effect is to draw them into a dependent relationship.

Total self-sufficiency may not be possible for all communities. The discussion thus becomes not the particular solution for any community but, by joining forces, to strengthen the capacity for an indigenous people to control its destiny. The distinction is between indigenous peoples deciding for themselves how they want to relate to the state (self-determination) or whether the state determines how that relationship will be organised (colonisation). To take away the capacity of indigenous peoples to decide their future lives is to colonise them. The only way out of this is through constructive agreements with the state and the colonists.

In practice, self-determination is intimately bound up with self-development. The Arakmbut see cultural and territorial defence as fundamental aspects of any future project work in their communities. At the same time, they are extremely concerned about the aftermath of the gold rush, the penetration by Mobil, and their capacity for self-sufficiency. On a community level they continually say that they can only defend themselves if they have the resources to live healthily and are not dependent on outsiders for their survival.

A project proposal based on the discussions set out in chapter seven aims to establish an environment in which the Arakmbut have access to all of their economic and cultural resources and can utilise them for their benefit, providing a solid basis for their future. The proposal includes a process for negotiation with both state authorities and local colonists.

Final Reflections

The easiest way of ending this book would be to correlate everything together as follows: Oppression from the outside forces of the national and international political and economic interests leads to resistance from the indigenous peoples who, by using the supportive forces from the spirit world and from the national and international society, particularly the notion of rights and the potential inherent in development projects, assert their rights and exercise their self-determination.

However, in practice there are many factors which subvert this scheme. The community may not be in complete agreement. Some may advocate one defence strategy while others prefer alternative approaches. Often, in order to avoid internal conflict, no one does anything. The empowerment and co-ordination of the community thus becomes a key point which rests entirely on internal social relations.

This unpredictability is both a strength and weakness. It means that for much of the year the Arakmbut do nothing about the colonists who invade their lands because they do not know how to deal with them. On the other hand, when they do something assertive, such as storm the municipality or expel Michael Dianda, the effect on the colonists is startling because they had not realised that there is a point at which the community will resist. Rights emerge through injustice, but ascertaining when assertion of those rights turns into resistance is difficult.

This unpredictability is reflected on the state side. The Peruvian state presents a contradiction to indigenous peoples. On the one hand it is barely present in the rainforest, yet when the Arakmbut stormed the municipality the threat of the police or even the army was truly terrifying. When Dianda took his materials to the headwaters he used an armed military helicopter, which terrified the community. The presence of armed soldiers was considered to be a contributing factor in the death of the sick woman. State militarisation is a clear form of oppression which can terrorise a community. At the same time, the government sits by and lets multinational corporations, such as Mobil, enter the Madre de Dios with what amounts to a free hand for exploitation.

Yet, even though the state is not permanently present in an area, it holds the possibility of reaching a constructive solution to the tensions between the Arakmbut and the government. This is through the Law of Native Communities. The threat of militarisation only serves to draw the Arakmbut into resistance and resignation. By recognising their rights and protecting them from colonisation, the state would open up the possiblity of enhancing a strong multi-cultural democratic polity, based on mutual respect, rather than mutual suspicion. Paradoxically for the state, the conclusion is that only through recognising indigenous rights can the way be opened for a positive and constructive relationship between state and people.

As long as the state does not live up to its responsibilities, the Arakmbut will defend themselves from injustice by asserting their rights and organising themselves as communities, as peoples, and as indigenous. The first is supported through economic self-sufficiency and control of resources; the second through social and cultural assertiveness; and the third through the political defence of their rights on local, national, and international levels.

At each moment in this struggle, the presence of the invisible world appears, connecting each person to the potentiality of resources, limiting acceptable behaviour, and generating dynamism throughout the universe. All of this provides the Arakmbut with the strength and sustainability to practise their right to self-determination. In this way development, identity, and self-determination are all connected for the Arakmbut through the links between economic self-sufficiency, cultural pride, and political control over their destinies. These areas provide the Arakmbut with the means to put their visions into practice in the face of the ever-increasing threats to their future existence.

ORTHOGRAPHY

The Ministerio de Educación Republica Peruana (1973) has an Arakmbut orthography which was prepared by Robert Tripp of the Summer Institute of Linguistics. This orthography uses an alphabet which conforms to that of Peruvian Spanish. Heinrich Helberg (1984) has adapted this to accommodate the phonetic alphabet. This orthography largely conforms to Peruvian Spanish, but several Arakmbut students have advised me on the spellings they prefer.

Each Arakmbut community has its own accents, words, and expressions, which means that there is no fixed spelling system for the language as a whole. Some of the words written here may well be rewritten in the future, as young Arakmbut find a system which is appropriate for all the communities.

Some Arakmbut vowels can be un-nasalised or nasalised but I have not made this distinction in the text. I have substituted an *'h'* for the Spanish *'j'* or *'x'* and *'w'* for *'hu'* except in quotes from Spanish-speaking authors. Where the 1973 orthography has *'ti'*, I have written *'ch'* or *'tch'*, depending on how strongly the *'t'* sounds; where it has *'si'* I have written *'sh'*. The 1973 orthography recognises that *'b'* is pronounced *'mb'* by the Arakmbut. However, in some cases the *'m'* is more apparent than in others. I have therefore written *'mb'* where the *'m'* is pronounced and *'b'* where the *'m'* is silent. Similarly the *'d'* in the 1973 orthography appears as *'nd'* at the beginning or *'dn'* at the end of a word. I have written the letters *'n'* and *'d'* as they sound because in some examples the *'n'* is silent. I occasionally heard a *'v'* and a *'j'* sound which are not in the orthography but are used here.

Vowels

a as in 'apple' (also nasalised)
e as in 'egg' (also nasalised)
i as in 'into'
o as in 'pot' (also nasalised)
u as in 'moon'

Consonants

b as in 'book' but with varying degrees of semi-nasalisation (*mb*).
ch as in 'church' but also accasionally with a slight '*t*' as in 'pitch'.
d as in 'dog' but with varying degrees of semi-nasalisation as in 'and'. At the end of a word, a '*d*' sounds '*dn*'.
g appears with semi-nasalisation ('*ng*' as in tongue') but often at the end of a word as '*gn*' as in 'gnu'.
h as in 'hat'
k as in 'kite'
m as in 'mouse' also as semi-nasal to '*b*'
n as in 'nature' but also as semi-nasal to '*d*' and '*g*' or after '*d*' and '*g*' at the end of a word.
p as in 'pig'
r as in 'rainbow'
s as in 'sea'
t as in 'top' but sometimes present before '*ch*' or '*sh*' as in 'pitch'
w or *hu* as in 'window'
y as in 'yacht'
'a stop as in the glottal stop before '*l*'

GLOSSARY

akidnet	capybara (Hydrochoerus hydrochaeris)
akudnui	white-lipped peccary (Tayassu pecari)
anenda	olden times
apik	sugarcane
arak	kill
atay	language
barak	ground
baysik	sundown/evening
chindign	sorcery/curing chant
chindoi	meat presented prior to marriage
chiwembet	girl sorcerer
chongpai	ayahuasca/anaconda spirit
e'apak	to speak
e'e	to be
e'ka	to do/make
e'kerek	to grow
e'machinoa	to sing
e'machunka	to hunt
e'manoka'e	to cure
e'mba'a	to work/labour with hands
e'mbachapak	to tell stories
e'mbaipak	second initiation ceremony ceremony
e'mbere	to steal
e'mbira	to be embarrassed
e'mbuey	to die/orgasm
e'mbuey'e	repeated death/fit
e'nopwe	to know/think
e'ohot	nose-piercing ceremony
eri	people from
esweri	outsider

Glossary

e'tae	to have
e'toepak	to marry
hak	house
ho	peach palm (Guilielma speciosa mart)
isipo	child
keme	tapir (Tapirus terrestris)
ken	he, she, they
kotsi	aguaje (Mauritia flexuosa)
kotsimbayo	aguajales
kuka	coca
kumo	barbasco
kurudn (eri)	sky (people)/air
kuwadn	sand
machinoa	feathered shoulder rattle
makoy	bunch of plantains
mantoro	achiote (bixa orellana)
matamona	responsibility, determine
mbakoykoy	warrior initiation ceremony
mbegnko	woodpecker (Melanerpes cruentatus)
mbu	sloth
miokpo	sun
muneyo	young woman
ndak	good, healthy
ndakyorokeri	beneficial (good dreaming) spirits
ndo/ndoedn	I/my
ndumba	forest
ndumberi	forest spirits
nogn	other
nokiren	soul
o	huito, black dye
ochinosik	hatred
ohpu	warrior
on	you
onyu	pure, clan
o'pogika	it always passes (time)
opudn	you (plural)
oro/oroedn	we/our
oteyo	upper gardens
pugn	moon
senopo	meanness/selfishness
Seronwe	underwater riverine world
sipo	younger
siro	metal
siropi	pin
siropo	pot

Glossary

sorok	soil
sorokmbayo	salt licks
tai/tainda	power/strength
Taka	indigenous outsider
tamba	garden (chacra)
tangka	headdress
tayagnpi	ceremonial stick for coca lime
tombi	small snail-shell rattle
tone	older
toto	harmful spirit
Totoyo/Takayo	underground forest world
urunda	beautiful
wachipai	spirit head of animal species
wae	water
wahaipi	highlander
wairi	honoured or respected person
wakeriskeris	white-lipped peccary guide
wakumbogn	bank/cliff
wakupa	undulating ground
wamambuey	brother, (my name)
wamawere	dispersed spirit
wambet	alliance arranging category
wambetoeri	spirits of dead Arakmbut
wambo	young man
wambokerek	man
wamenoka'eri	curer
wanakeri	insider
wandari	territory, earth, land, landscape
wandawe	semen
wandik	name
wantupa	political leader
waso	body
watawata	individual/private
watawatawe	group/together
watone	old person
wawe	river
waweri	river spirits
wayawaya	balanced exchange
wayorok	dream/vision/hallucination
wayorokeri	shamanic dreamer
wendari	lower gardens
wenpu	string bag
wetone	woman
widn	stone

BIBLIOGRAPHY

Abercrombie, T. 1991. To be Indian, to be Bolivian: 'Ethnic' and 'National' Discourses of Identity. In G. Urban & J. Sherzer (eds.) *Nation States and Indians in Latin America.* pp 95-130. Austin: University of Texas.
Adams, W.M. 1995. Green Development Theory? Environmentalism and sustainable development. In J. Crush (ed.) *Power of Development.* pp. 87-99. London: Routledge.
Aikman, S.H. 1982. Informe preliminar sobre hallazgos del Río Karene (Río Colorado), Madre de Dios. *Amazonía Peruana.* Vol. III, No.6. Lima.
Aikman, S.H. 1994: *Intercultural Eduction and Harakmbut identity: A Case Study of the Community of San José in Southeastern Peru.* PhD. Thesis Institute of Education. University of London.
Alberoni,F. 1984. *Movement and Institution.* Colombia University Press.
Alexiades, M. 1987. Tropical Rainforests – An integrated approach to health and conservation. mss.
Alvarez, J. 1944. La Misión de San Miguel de los Mashcos en la actualidad. *Misiones Dominicanas del Perú.* No. 26: 245-256.
Alvarez, J. 1953. Al Kipoznue y Alto Colorado. *Misiones Dominicanas del Perú.* XXXIV: 44-50.
Amich, J. 1854. *Compendio Histórico.* Paris: Librería de Rosa y Bourel.
Ardener, E. 1989. Language, ethnicity and population. In M. Chapman (ed.) *The Voice of Prophecy and other Essays.* Blackwell.
Aron, R. 1965. *Main Currents in Sociological Thought.* Pelican Books.
Asad, T. ed. 1973. *Anthropology and the Colonial Encounter.* London: Ithaca Press.
Aristotle. 1992. *The Politics.* Penguin Books.
Balandier, G. 1970. *Political Anthropology.* London: Allen Lane. The Penguin Press.
Barclay, F. (et. al.) 1991. *Amazonía 1940-1990: el extravio de una ilusión.* Terra Nuova y Centro por Investigaciones Sociológicas, Económicas, Politicas y Antropológicas, Pontificía Universidad Católica del Perú. Lima.
Barnett, C. 1988. Is there a Scientific Basis in Anthropology for the Ethics of Human Rights? In T. Downing & G. Kushner, *Human Rights and Anthropology.* pp.21-26. Cambridge Mass: Cultural Survival.

Barriales, J. & A. Torralba. 1970. *Los Mashcos.* Lima: Santiago Valverde.
Barry, M. 1992. As Indian Moors Obey their Spanish Lords. In D. Levine (ed.) *Americas Lost.* pp. 10-25. Paris: Bordas.
Barth, F. (ed.) 1969. *Ethnic Groups and Boundaries.* Bergen & Oslo Universitets Forlaget. London: George Allen & Unwin.
Bender, B. (ed.) 1993. *Landscape: Politics and Perspectives.* Oxford: Berg.
Bennett, G. 1978. *Aboriginal Rights in International Law.* Occasional Paper 37. London: Royal Anthropological Institute & Survival International.
Bennett, G. 1979. The Developing Law of Aboriginal Rights. *The Review, International Commission of Jurists.* Vol. 22 pp. 37-46.
Berman, H. 1987. Comment in 'Are Indigenous Populations Populations Entitled to International Juridical Personality' *American Society of International Law Proceedings.* 79th Annual Meeting. ASIL. Washington DC.
Berman, H. 1988. The ILO and Indigenous Peoples: Revision of ILO Convetnion 107. *The Review of the International Commission of Jurists.* 41, 48.
Berman, H. 1993. The Development of International Recognition of the Rights of Indigenous Peoples. In H. Verber et al. (eds.) ... *Never Drink from the same Cup: Proceedings of the Conference on Indigenous Peoples in Africa, Tune, Denmark, 1993.* IWGIA Document No. 74. pp. 313-324.
Bidney, D. 1953. *Theoretical Anthropology.* Columbia University Press.
Blaut, J.M. 1987. *The National Question: Decolonising the Theory of Nationalism.* London: Zed Books.
Bodley, J. (ed.) 1988. *Tribal Peoples and Development Issues: A Global Overview.* Mountain View, California: Mayfield Publishing Company.
Bovo de Revello, J. 1848. *Brillante porvenir del Cuzco.* Cusco: Imprenta Libre.
Brohlmann, C., R. Lefeber & M. Zieck (eds.) 1993. *Peoples and Minorities in International Law.* Dortrecht: Martinus Nijhoff Publishers.
Brown, A. 1986. *Modern Political Philosophy: Theories of the Just Society.* Pelican.
Brown, W.J. 1906. *The Austinian Theory of Law.* London: John Murray.
Brownlie, I. 1988. The Rights of Peoples in Modern International Law. In J. Crawford (ed.) *The Rights of Peoples.* pp. 1-16. Clarendon Paperbacks.
Brownlie, I. 1993. *Treaties and Indigenous Peoples.* Oxford University Press.
Bull, H. 1947. *The Anarchical Society.* Basingstoke: Macmillan.
Burger, J. 1987. *Report from the Frontier.* London: Zed Press.
Burgess, H. 1987. Traditional Territories of the Earth: Intervention to the ILO Meeting of Experts on Convention 107. *IWGIA Yearbook 1986.* pp.133-140. Copenhagen.
Bury, J.B. 1932. *The Idea of Progress.* New York: Macmillan.
CAAAP. 1992. *Propuesta Política Educativa: Sub-Región de Madre de Dios.* Centro Amazónico de Antropología y Aplicación Práctica. Lima.
Califano, M. 1977. La Incorporación de un nuevo elemento cultural entre los Mashcos de la Amazonía Peruana. *Relaciones de la Sociedad Argentina de Antropología.* Vol. XI. N.S. Buenos Aires.
Califano, M. 1978a. El Complejo de la Bruja entre los Mashco de la Amazonía sudoccidental (Perú). *Anthropos.* 73:401-433.

Califano, M. 1979b. *Analisis Comparativo de un Mito Mashco*. Entregas de I.T. Instituto 'Ticlan'. Centro de Investigaciones Regionales Facultad de Filosofía y Letras. Unversidad de Buenos Aires.

Califano, M. 1982. *Etnografía de los Mashcos de la Amazonía Sud Occidental del Perú*. Buenos Aires: FECIE.

Cárdenas, C.M. 1988. Dora Mayer de Zulen: Apuntes para un Estudio de su Vida y Obra. *Perú Indígena*. 12(27):141-163. Lima.

Carrithers, M., Collins, S. and Lukes, S. (eds.) 1985. *The Category of the Person*. pp. 141-155. Cambridge.

Cassen, R. (and associates) 1994. *Does Aid Work?* Oxford: Clarendon Press.

Cassese, A. 1981 The Self-Determination of Peoples. In L. Henkin (ed.) *The International Bill of Rights: The Covenant on Civil and Political Rights*. New York: Columbia University Press.

Caufield, C & V. Pino Zambrano. 1985. *Bosque Tropicales Humedo*. Cusco: Centro de Estudios Rurales Andinos 'Bartolomé de las Casas'.

Chen, Lung Chu. 1976. Self-determination as a human right. In W.M. Reisman & B. Weston (eds) *Toward World Order and Human Dignity: Essays in Honour of Myres S. McDougal*. pp. 198-261. New York: The Free Press.

Chirif, A, P. Garcia & R. Chase Smith. 1991. *El Indígena y Su Territorio son Uno Solo: Estratégias para la Defensa de los Pueblos y Territorios Indígenas en la Cuenca Amazónica*. Lima: Oxfam America y Coodinadora de las Organizaciones Indígenas de la Cuenca Amazónica (COICA).

Claessen, J & P. Skalnik (eds) 1978. *The Early State*. Studies in Social Sciences 32. Mouton, The Hague: New Babylon.

Clastres, P. 1977. *Society against the State*. Oxford: Blackwells.

Clay, J. 1993. Marketing and Human Rights: Lessons from the Cultural Survival Marketing Program. *IWGIA Newsletter*. No. 3:pp.4-6.

Clifford, J. 1983. On Ethnographic Authority. *Representations*. 1:2 pp. 118-146.

CODEH-PA. 1983. *La Selva y su ley: lavadores de oro*. Sicuani: Comité de Defensa de los Derechos Humanos de las Provincias Altas.

Cohen, A. 1986. *The Symbolic Construction of Community*. Ellis Horwood, Chichester & Tavistock Publications.

Cohen, R. 1978. Ethnicity: Problem and Focus in Anthropology. *Annual Review of Anthropology*. 7:379-403.

Comaroff, J. & J. 1992. *Ethnography and the Historical Imagination*. Westview Press: Boulder.

Corry, S. 1993. The Rainforest Harvest: Who Reaps the Benefit? *The Ecologist*. Vol. 23. No. 4:148-153.

Counsell, S. & T.Rice (eds) 1992. *The Rainforest Harvest: Sustainable Strategies for Saving the Tropical Forests?* London: Friends of the Earth.

Cowen M. & R. Shenton. The Invention of Development. In J. Crush (ed.) *Power of Development*. pp. 27-43. London: Routledge.

Cranston. M. 1966. John Locke and Government by Consent. In D. Thomson (ed.) *Political Ideas*. pp.67-80. Pelican.

Crawford, W.R. 1961. *A Century of Latin American Thought.* Harvard University Press.
Cristescu, A. 1981. *The Right to Self-Determination. Historical and Current Development on the Basis of United Nations Instruments.* Report for the Sub-Commission on Prevention of Discrimination and Protection of Minorities. E/CN.4/Sub.2/404/Rev.1. New York: United Nations.
d'Ans, A-M et al. 1973. *Problemas de Clasificación de Lenguas No-Andinas en el Sur-Este Peruano.* Centro de Investigación de Linguística Aplicada. Lima: Unversidad Nacional Mayor de San Marcos.
Daes, E-I. 1993a. *Discrimination against Indigenous Peoples: Explanatory notes concerning the draft Declaration on the Rights of Indigenous Peoples.* UN paper for the Sub-Commission on Prevention of Discrimination and Protection of Minorities: E/CN.4/Sub.2/1993/26/Add.1. United Nations.
Daes, E-I. 1993b. *Study on the protection of the Cultural and Intellectual Property of Indigenous Peoples.* E/CN.4/Sub.2/1993/28. United Nations.
D'Entrèves, A. 1967. *The Notion of the State.* Oxford University Press.
Deloria, V. & C. Lytle. 1984. *The Nations Within: The Past and Future of American Indian Sovereignty.* New York: Pantheon Books.
De Jasay, A. 1985. *The State.* Oxford: Blackwell.
De Soto, H. 1987. *El Otro Sendero.* Lima: Instituto Libertad y Democracia.
Denevan, W. 1976. The Aboriginal Populations of Amazonia. In W. Denevan (ed.) *The Native Population of the Americas in 1492.* pp.205-234. University of Wisconsin Press.
Dobyns, H & P Doughty. 1976. *Peru: A Cultural History.* Oxford University Press.
Dodson, M. 1994. Voices of the People – Voices of the Earth: indigenous peoples – subjugation or self-determination? In L. Van der Vlist (ed.) *Voices of the Earth: Indigenous peoples, new partners & the right to self-determination in practice.* Amsterdam: The Netherlands Centre for Indigenous Peoples.
Donnelly, J. 1985. *The Concept of Human Rights.* London: Routledge.
Donnelly, J. 1989. *Universal Human Rights in Theory and Practice.* Cornell University Press.
Dourojeanni, M. 1990. *Amazonía – Qué Hacer?* Iquitos: Centro de Estudios Teológicos de la Amazonía.
Dumont, L. 1986. *Essays on Individualism: Modern Ideology in Anthropological Perspective.* Chicago University Press.
Dunbar Ortiz, R. 1984. *Indians of the Americas: Human Rights and Self-Determination.* London: Zed Books.
Easton, D. 1971. *The Political System.* New York: Alfred Knopf.
Eastwood, R.A. 1916. *A Brief Introduction to Austin's Theory of Positive Law and Sovereignty.* London: Sweet and Maxwell.
Eide, A. 1985. Indigenous Populations and Human Rights: The United Nations Efforts at Mid-Way. In J. Brosted et. al. *Native Power.* Bergen: Universitetsforlaget.

Elkington J. & T. Burke. 1989. *The Green Capitalists: How industry can make money – and protect the environment.* London: Victor Gollancz.
Engels, F. 1973. *The Origin of the Family, Private Property and the State.* London: Lawrence and Wishart.
Escajadillo, T.G. 1994. *La Narrativa Indigenista Peruana.* Lima: Editorial Mantaro.
Escobar, A. 1995a. Imagining a Post-Development Era. In J. Crush (ed.) *Power of Development.* pp. 211-227. London: Routledge.
Escobar, A. 1995b. *Encountering Development: The Making and Unmaking of the Third World.* New Jersey: Princeton University Press.
European Association of Social Anthropologists (EASA), 1995. Informe del Comité de Expertos de la Asociación Europea de Antropologos'. *Antropología.* No. 10. Octubre. pp.190-201.
Evans-Pritchard, E.E. 1940. *The Nuer.* Oxford University Press.
Evans-Pritchard, E.E. 1951. *Social Anthroplogy.* London: Cohen & West.
Evans-Pritchard, E.E. 1956. *Nuer Religion.* Oxford University Press.
Eyreman R. & A. Jameson. 1991. *Social Movements: A Cognitive Approach.* Polity.
Falk, R. 1988. The Rights of Peoples (In Particular Indigenous Peoples). In J. Crawford (ed.) *The Rights of Peoples.* pp.17-37. Clarendon Paperbacks.
Falkowski, J. 1992. *Indian Law/Race Law: A Five-Hundred Year History.* Praeger.
Favre, H. 1988. Capitalismo y Etnicidad: La Política Indigenista de Perú. Instituto Indigenista Interamericano and Centre D'Études Mexicaines et Centramericaines (eds.) *Indianidad, Etnocidio, Indigenismo en América Latina.* pp.113-127. Mexico.
Fernandez Distel, A. 1976 La decoración pintada aplicada a elementos de la tela de corteza entre los indígenas mashco de la amazonía peruana. *Archiv für Völkerkunde* XXX, 5-39. Vienna.
Fortes, M. 1940. The Political System of the Tallensi of the Northern Territories of the Gold Coast. In M. Fortes, & E.E. Evans-Pritchard (eds.) *African Political Systems.* Oxford University Press.
Fortes M, & E.E. Evans-Pritchard. 1940. *African Political Systems.* Oxford University Press.
Franck, T.M. 1993. Postmodern Tribalism and the Right to Secession. In C. Brohlmann (et al.) *Peoples and Minorities in Interntional Law.* pp. 3-27. Dortrecht: Martinus Nijhoff Publishers.
Frank, A.G. 1967. *Capitalism and Underdevelopment in Latin America.* New York & London: Modern Reader Paperbacks.
Frideres, J.S. 1983. *Native People in Canada: Contemporary Conflicts.* Canada.
Friede, J. 1974. *Bartolomé de Las Casas: precursor del anticolonialismo.* Mexico: Siglo Veintiuno Editores.
Friedman, J. 1989. Culture, Identity and World Process. *Review.* 12 (1) 51-69.
Friedman, J. 1992. The Past in the Future. *American Anthropologist.* 94 (4) pp. 837-854.
Fuentes, A. 1982. *Parentesco y relaciones de producción en una comunidad Harakmbut en el Sur-Oriente Peruano.* CAAAP mss.

Fürer-Haimendorf, C. von. 1989. *Tribes of India: The Struggle for Survival.* *Delhi.* Oxford University Press.
Galeano, E. 1992. Othercide. *IWGIA Newsletter.* July-September. pp. 3-5. Copenhagen.
García Hierro, P. 1995. *Territorios Indígenas y la Nueva Legislación Agraria en el Perú.* IWGIA Documento 17. Lima: Grupo de Trabajo Racimos de Ungurahui.
Geertz, C. 1973. *Interpretation of Cultures.* Basic Books Inc: New York.
Gerbi, A. 1973. *The Dispute of the New World: The History of a Polemic 1750-1900.* University of Pittsburgh Press.
Gewirth, A. 1984. The Epistemology of Human Rights. In E. F. Paul, F.D. Miller & J. Paul. (eds.) *Human Rights.* pp.1-24. Blackwell.
Giddens, A. 1985. *The Nation-State and Violence.* Cambridge. Polity Press.
Godelier, M. 1974. *Perspectives in Marxist Anthropology.* Cambridge University Press.
Goldie, M. 1993. Introduction. to J. Locke. *Two Treatises of Government.* London: Dent (Everyman).
González Prada, M. 1974. *Horas de Lucha* Lima.
Gow, P. 1991. *Of Mixed Blood: Kinship and History in Peruvian Amazonia.* Oxford: Clarendon Press.
Gramsci, A. 1988. *A Gramsci Reader.* D. Forgacs (ed.) London: Lawrence and Wishart.
Gray, A. 1983. *The Amarakaeri: an Ethnographic Description of An Harakmbut People from Southeastern Peru.* D.Phil.: Oxford University.
Gray, A. 1984. Los Amarakaeri: Una noción de Estructura Social. *Amazonía Peruana.* Vol.V, No. 10 pp.47-64. Lima.
Gray, A. 1986. *And After the Gold Rush ...?: Human Rights and Self-Development among the Amarakaeri of Southeastern Peru.* International Work Group for Indigenous Affairs. Document 55. Copenhagen.
Gray, A. 1987a. Report on ILO Meeting of experts on Convention 107. *IWGIA Yearbook 1986.* pp. 73-85. Copenhagen.
Gray, A. 1987b. Perspectives on Amarakaeri History. In H.Skar & F. Salomon (eds.) *Natives and Neighbours in South America.* pp.299-328. Goteborgs Etnografiska Museum.
Gray, A. 1987c. *The Amerindians of South America.* Minority Rights Group Report No. 15. London.
Gray, A. 1989. IWGIA at the ILO Conference 1988. *IWGIA Yearbook 1988.* pp.167-178. Copenhagen.
Gray, A. 1990a. Report on the Meeting on the ILO's Revision of Convention 107, Geneva, 1989. *IWGIA Yearbook 1989.* pp. 173-191. Copenhagen.
Gray, A. 1990b. The Putumayo Atrocities Re-examined. Mss.
Gray, A. 1991. *Between the spice of life and the melting pot: Biodiversity conservation and its impact on indigenous peoples.* IWGIA Document 70. Copenhagen.
Gray, A. 1992. 'It is Time to Act!' Say the Peruvian Arakmbut. *Anti-Slavery Reporter.* Series VII, Vol. 13. No. 8: 111-114. London.

Gray, A. 1993. Caught in the Crossfire. *The Ecologist.* Vol. 23, No.4 p.124.
Gray, A. 1995a. Whose Knowledge is it Anyway?: Editorial. *Indigenous Affairs.* No. 4 Oct.-Dec. pp.2-4. Copenhagen.
Gray, A. 1995b The Fight for Indigenous Rights and the Combatting of Social Injustice in the Light of the World Summit for Social Development. In *The Indigenous World 1994-95.* pp.230-237. Copenhagen: International World Group for Indigenous Affairs.
Gray, A. & S. Hvalkof. 1990. Indigenous Land Titling in the Peruvian Amazon *IWGIA Yearbook 1989.* pp. 230-243. Copenhagen.
Gray, A. & J.Dahl. 1991. Report on the Eighth Session of the UN Working Group on Indigenous Populations. *IWGIA Yearbook 1990.* pp.167-173. Copenhagen.
Grisel, E. 1976. The Beginnings of International Law and General Public Law Doctrine: Francisco de Vitoria's 'De Indiis'. In F. Chiappelli (ed.) *First Images of America.* pp. 305-325. University of California Press.
Guillen-Marroquin, J. 1990. El Trabajo Infantil en el Perú: La Explotación de Aluviones Auríferos en Madre de Dios. In J. Boyden (ed.) *La Lucha contra el Trabajo Infantil.* Geneva: International Labour Organisation.
Hall, H. Duncan. 1948. *Mandates, Dependencies and Trusteeship.* London: Stevens & Sons.
Halperin M.H. & D. Scheffer. 1992. *Self-Determination in the New World Order.* Washington D.C.: Carnegie Endowment for International Peace.
Hammergren, L.A. 1977. Corporatism in Latin American Politics: A Reexamination of the 'Unique' Tradition. *Comparative Politics* 9.
Hanke, L. 1959. *Aristotle and the American Indians: A Study in Race Prejudice.* Bloomington: London.
Hannum, H. 1990. *Autonomy, Sovereignty and Self-Determination: The Accommodation of Conflicting Rights.* Philadelphia: University of Pensylvania Press.
Hanson, F.A. 1975. *Meaning in Culture.* Routledge and Kegan Paul.
Harrison, R. 1983. *Bentham.* London: Routledge & Kegan Paul.
Hart, R.E. 1963. Semantic components of shape in Amarakaeri grammar. *Anthropological Linguistics.* Vol. 5, No. 9, 1-7. Bloomington.
Heinz, W. 1988. *Indigenous Populations, Ethnic Minorities and Human Rights.* Berlin: Studien zur Internationalen Politik Band 10. Quorum Verlag.
Helberg Chavez, H. 1993. Terminología de Parentesco Harakmbut. *Amazonía Peruana* 23:107-140. Centro Amazónico de Antropología y Aplicación Práctica. Lima.
Helberg Chavez, H. forthcoming. *Baysik.* Centro Amazónico de Antropología y Aplicación Práctica. (CAAAP). Lima.
Held, D. et. al. (eds.) 1983. *State & Societies.* Blackwell.
Henriksen, G. 1989. Introduction. to IWGIA (ed.) *Indigenous Self-Development in the Americas.* Proceedings of the IWGIA Symposium at the Congress of Americanists. Amsterdam. 1988. IWGIA Document No. 63. Copenhagen.

Hettne, B. 1982. *Development Theory and the Third World.* Stockholm: SAREC Reports.
Hettne, B. 1995. *Development Theory and the Three Worlds.* Harlow: Longman Development Series.
Hirsch, E., 1995. Introduction to E. Hirsch and M. O'Hanlon (eds.) *The Anthropology of Landscape: Perspectives on Place and Space.* pp. 1-30. Oxford: Clarendon Press.
Hobbes, T. 1989 (1651). *Leviathan.* Penguin Classics.
Hobsbawm E.& T. Ranger (eds) 1983. *The Invention of Tradition.* Cambridge.
Hocart, A. 1970. *Kings and Councillors: An Essay on the Comparative Anatomy of Human Society.* Chicago University Press.
Hoffman, J. 1995. *Beyond the State.* London: Polity Press.
Huddleston, L.E. 1967. *Origins of the American Indians: European Concepts, 1492-1729.* Austin: University of Texas Press.
Hume, D. 1972 (1740). *A Treatise of Human Nature, Book Three.* Fontana.
Hume, D. 1993. Of the Populousness of Ancient Nations. In *Selected Essays.* Oxford.
Independent Commission on International Humanitarian Issues (ICIHI). 1986. *Indigenous Peoples: A Global Quest for Justice.* London: Zed Books.
International Labour Organisation. 1989. *Convention Concerning Indigenous and Tribal Peoples in Independent Countries.* Geneva.
Isbell, B.J. 1978. *To Defend Ourselves: Ecology and Ritual in an Andean Village.* The University of Texas at Austin.
IWGIA. 1984. Canada: Minister Introduces Indian Self-Government Legislation. *IWGIA Newsletter.* 39:61-65. Copenhagen.
IWGIA. 1984a. International: UNESCO Breaks New Ground. *IWGIA Newsletter.* 39:82-87. Copenhagen.
IWGIA. 1985. Draft Declaration of Principles for Indigenous Rights Presented to the Working Group. *IWGIA Newsletter.* Nos 43 & 44. pp. 293-298.
IWGIA. 1990. *Indigenous Peoples of the Soviet North.* IWGIA Document No.67. Copenhagen.
Jackson, J.E. 1983. *The Fish People: Linguistic Exogamy and Tukanoan Identity in Northwest Amazonia.* Cambridge University Press.
Kaplan, J.Overing. 1975. *The Piaroa, A People of the Orinoco Basin.* Oxford: Clarendon Press.
Kay, C. 1989. *Latin American Theories of Development and Underdevelopment.* London: Routledge.
Kedourie, E. 1985. *Nationalism.* London: Hutchinson.
Kickingbird, K. (et. al.) nd. *Indian Sovereignty.* Washington D.C.: Institute for the Development of Indian Law.
Kingsbury, B. 1992. Self-determination and 'Indigenous Peoples'. *American Society of International Law Proceedings 86th Annual Meeting.* pp.383-394. Washington D.C.

Kingsbury, B. 1995. 'Indigenous Peoples' as an International Legal Concept. In R.H. Barnes, A. Gray & B. Kingsbury (eds.) *Indigenous Peoples of Asia.* pp. 13-54. Association for Asian Studies. Monograph and Occasional Paper Series, Number 48. Ann Arbor.

Kingsbury, B. and A. Roberts. 1995. Introduction: Grotian Thought in International Relations. In H. Bull, B. Kingsbury & A. Roberts (eds.) *Hugo Grotius and International Relations.* pp. 1-64. Oxford: Clarendon Paperbacks.

Kroeber, A. 1963. *Anthropology, Culture Patterns & Processes.* San Diego: Harvest HBJ Books.

Lacaze, D., & M. Alexiades, nd.: Ametra 2001: An Integrated Approach to Health Care in the Peruvian Amazon. mss.

Lambert, C., 1948. *Music Ho!* London: Pelican Books.

Lawrence, T.J. 1895. *The Principles of International Law.* London: Macmillan.

Leach, E.R. 1961. *Rethinking Anthropology.* London: Athlone Press.

Leach, E.R. 1989. Tribal Ethnography: past, present, future. In E. Tonkin et. al. *History and Ethnicity.* ASA Monographs 27. Routledge.

Leinhardt, G. 1985. African Representations of Self. In M. Carrithers, S. Collins & S. Lukes (eds.) *The Category of the Person.* pp. 141-155. Cambridge.

Lenin, V.I. 1971. *Selected Works.* Moscow: Progress Publishers.

Leys, C. 1996. *The Rise and Fall of Development Theory.* London: James Currey.

Lindley, M.F. 1926. *The Acquisition and Government of Backward Territory in International Law.* London: Longmans, Green and Co.

Lloyd Thomas, D.A. 1995. *Locke on Government.* London: Routledge.

Locke, J. 1993. *Two Treatises of Government.* London: Dent, Everyman.

Lomasky, L. 1984. Personal Projects as the Foundation for Basic Rights. E. F. Paul, F.D. Miller & J. Paul. *Human Rights.* pp.35-55. Blackwell.

Long, N. 1977. *An Introduction to the Sociology of Rural Development.* London: Tavistock.

Lorimer, J. 1883. *The Institutes of the Law of Nations: A Treatise of the Jural Relations of Separate Political Communities.* London: William Blackwood.

Lowie, R. 1920. *Primitive Society.* New York: Boni & Liveright.

Lukes, S. 1993. Five Fables about Human Rights. In S. Shute and S. Hurley (eds.) *On Human Rights* pp. 19-40. New York: Basic Books.

Lyon, P.J. 1976. Tribal Movement and Linguistic Classification in the Madre de Dios Zone. Typewritten corrected version of the paper published in the XXXIX Congreso Internacional de Americanistas. *Actas y Memorias.* Vol. 5, 185-207. Lima.

Lyon, P.J. nd. The Attackers or the Attacked? The Invention of 'Hostile Savages' in the Valleys of Paucartambo, Cuzco, Peru. mss.

Marzal, M. 1986. *Historia de la Antropología Indigenista: Mexico y Perú.* Lima: Pontificia Universidad Católica.

Macpherson, C.B. 1962. *The Political Theory of Possessive Indiviualism: Hobbes to Locke.* Oxford University Press.
Maine, H. 1912 (1861) *Ancient Law.* London: John Murray.
Mair, L. 1962. *Primitive Government.* Pelican.
Martinez Cobo, J. 1986. *Study of the Problem of Discrimination against Indigenous Populations.* Doc.E/CN.4/Sub.2/1986/7/Add.4. Geneva: United Nations.
Marx, K. 1977. *Selected Writings.* D. McLellan (ed.) Oxford University Press.
Maurtúa, V. (ed.) 1906. *Juício de limites entre el Perú y Bolivia: Prueba presentada al gobierno de la república de Argentina.* 12 vols. Barcelona: Imprenta Henrich y Cia.
McIver, R.M. 1947. *The Web of Government.* London.
McGrane, B. 1989. *Beyond Anthropology: Society and the Other.* New York: Colombia University Press.
Meek, R. 1976. *Social Science and the Ignoble Savage.* Cambridge University Press.
Mendoza Marsano, J. 1974. Oro en el Peru. *Minería.* 124, 200-204. 8 Congreso Mundial de Mineria. Lima.
Migdal, J.S. 1988. *Strong Societies and Weak States: State-Society Relations and State Capabilities in the Third World.* Princeton University Press.
Migdal, J.S. 1994. The State in Society: an approach to struggles for domination. In J. Migdal, A. Kohli & V. Shue (eds.) *State Power and Social Forces: Domination and Transformation in the Third World.* pp. 7-34. Cambridge University Press.
Mill, J.S. 1991. Considerations on Representative Government. In *On Liberty and Other Essays.* Oxford University Press.
Moody, R. (ed) 1988. *The Indigenous Voice: Visions and Realities.* (2 volumes.) Zed Press, London & International Work Group for Indigenous Affairs, Copenhagen.
Moore, T.R. 1979. Sil and a 'New-Found Tribe': The Amarakaeri Experience. *Dialectical Anthropology* 4:113-125. Amsterdam.
Moore, T. 1980. Transnacionales en Madre de Dios: Implicancias para las comunidades nativas. *Shipihui* 5 (16):451-462.
Moore, T. 1985a. Informe Preliminar de la Minería Aurífera en las Poblaciones Indígenas de Madre de Dios, Peru. mss.
Moore, T. 1985b. Movimientos populares in Madre de Dios y regionalización. In María Isabel Remy (ed.) *Promoción Campesina, Regionalización y Movimientos Sociales.* Centro de Estudios Rurales Andinos 'Bartolomé de las Casas' y Centro de Estudios y Promoción de Desarrolo (DESCO). Lima.
Moore, T.R. nd. Resumen de la organización social y religión Harakmbut. mss.
Morgan, L.H. 1877. *Ancient Society.* New York: Holt.
Nash, J. 1975. Nationalism and Fieldwork. *Annual Review of Anthropology.* 4:225-45.

Nash, J. 1979. *We eat the Mines and the Mines eat us: dependency and exploitation in Bolivian Tin Mines.* New York: Columbia University Press.

National Indian Brotherhood, 1973. *Statistics on Indian Organisations.* Canada.

Needham, R. 1970. Editor's Introduction. to A.M. Hocart. *Kings and Councillors.* University of Chicago Press.

Needham, R. 1975. Polythetic Classification *Man.* n.s. 10:349-369.

Nettheim, G. 1988. Peoples and Populations – Indigenous Peoples and the Rights of Peoples. In J. Crawford (ed.) *The Rights of Peoples.* pp. 107-126. Clarendon Paperbacks.

Newsweek. 1993. The Fujimori Phenomenon: Anti-Politics is Working in Peru – So Far. May 10th.

Nilsson, G.K. 1920. *Primitive Time Reckoning.* Lund: C.W.K. Gleerup.

Nisbet, R. 1969. *Social Change and History: Aspects of the Western Theory of Development.* Oxford University Press.

Nordenskjöld, E. 1905. Beitrage zur Kenntnis Einiger Indianerstamme des Rio Madre de Dios – gebietes. *Ymer.* 25: e arg., haft 3, 265-312. Stockholm.

Ofuatey-Kodjoe, W. 1977. *The Principle of Self-Determination in International Law.* New York: Nellen Publishing Company.

Olivera, J.M. 1907. Informe. In *Ultimas Exploraciones ordenadas por la Junta de Vias Fluviales a los ríos Ucayali, Madre de Dios, Paurcartambo y Urubamba.* pp. 395-429. Lima. Oficina tipográfica de 'La Opinion Nacional'.

Olsen, J., and R. Wilson (eds.) 1984. *Native Americans in the Twentieth Century.* University of Illinois.

Ortiz, A. 1969. *The Tewa World: Space, Time, Being and Becoming in a Pueblo Society.* Chicago.

Osende, V. 1933. Observaciones sobre el Salvajismo. *Misiones Dominicanas del Perú.* 15 (74): pp. 228-230. Lima.

Ots Captequi, J.M. 1940. *Estudios de história del Derecho Espanol en las Indias.* Bogotá: Editorial Minerva.

Pacuri Flores, F. & T, Moore. 1992. *Los Conflictos entre Mineros Auríferos y el Pueblo Arakmbut en Madre de Dios, Perú.* Centro Eori and FENAMAD, Puerto Maldonado.

Pagden, A. 1982. *The Fall of Natural Man: The American Indian and the Origins of Comparative Ethnology.* Cambridge Iberian and Latin American Studies. Cambridge University Press.

Pagden, A. 1994. *The Uncertainties of Empire.* Aldershot: Variorum.

Paine, T. 1987. The Rights of Man (1791-2). In *The Thomas Paine Reader.* Penguin Classics.

Paredes Pando, O. 1990. *Region Inca: Desarrollo, Posibilidades y Limitaciones 1990-2005.* Centro Promotor de Desarrollo Integral del Campesino Andino: CENPRODIC. Cusco.

Parkin, C.W. 1966. Burke and the Conservative Tradition. in D. Thomson (ed.) *Political Ideas.* pp. 118-129. Pelican.

Paxton, J. (ed) 1987. *The Statesman's Year-Book.* 124th edition. Macmillan.

Pennano, G. 1988. *La Economia del Caucho.* Iquitos. Centros de Estudios Teológicos de la Amazonía (CETA).
Peru Support Group (PSG). nda. *Peru: Democracy in Danger.* A special Publication of the PSG. London.
Peru Support Group (PSG). ndb. *The Debt Lottery: Peru.* PSG London.
Philip, M. 1986. *Godwin's Political Justice.* London: Duckworth.
Plant, Raymond. 1972. *Hegel.* Blackwell.
Plant, Roger. 1991. *Land Rights for Indigenous and Tribal Peoples in Developing Countries: A Survey of Law and Policy Issues, Current Activities, and Proposals for an Inter-Agency Programme of Action World.* Employment Programme. Research Working Paper WEP 10-6/WP108.
Pomerance, M. 1982. *Self-Determination in Law and Practice: The New Doctrine in the United Nations.* The Hague: Martinus Nijhoff.
Poole, D. & G. Renique. 1992. *Peru: Time of Fear.* London. Latin America Bureau.
Posey, D. 1995. *Indigenous Peoples and Traditional Resource Rights: A Basis for Equitable Relationships?* Oxford: Green College Centre for Environmental Policy and Understanding.
Radcliffe-Brown, A.R. 1940. Preface. In M. Fortes & E.E. Evans-Pritchard (eds.) *African Political Systems.* Oxford University Press.
Radcliffe-Brown, A.R. (ed.) 1970. Introduction. *African Systems of Kinship and Marriage.* London. Oxford University Press.
Radcliffe-Brown, A.R. 1977. The Social Organization of Australian Tribes. In A. Kuper (ed.) *The Social Anthropology of Radcliffe Brown.* London: Routledge.
Rädda Barnen. 1991. *Area Chica.* No. 6 Ano II. Lima.
Raimondi, A. 1874-9. *El Perú.* Vol. I-III. Lima: Imprente del Estado.
Ramos, A.R. 1994. The Hyperreal Indian. *Critique of Anthropology.* Vol. 14(2) 153-171. London.
Ranger, T. 1983. The Invention of Tradition in Colonial Africa. In, E. Hobsbawm & T. Ranger (eds.) *The Invention of Tradition.* pp.211-262. Cambridge University Press.
Reichel-Dolmatoff, G. 1971. *Amazonian Cosmos: The Sexual and Relgious Symbolism of the Tukano Indians.* University of Chicago Press.
Reyna, E. 1942. *Fitzcarrald, el Rey del Caucho.* Lima: P. Barrantes Castro.
Ribeiro, D. & M.R. Wise. 1978. *Los Grupos Etnicos de la Amazonía Peruana.* Comunidades y Culturas Peruanas No. 13. Instituto Linguistico de Verano.
Robertson, W. 1817. *History of America.* London.
Ronen, D., 1979: *The Quest for Self-Determination.* New Haven: Yale University Press.
Rorty, R. 1993. Human Rights, Rationality, and Sentimentality. In S. Shute and S. Hurley (eds.) *On Human Rights* pp. 111-134. New York: Basic Books.
Rosengren, D. 1987. *In the Eyes of the Beholder: Leadership and the Social Construction of Power and Dominance among the Matsigenka of the Peruvian Amazon.* Göteborgs Etnografiska Museum.

Rostow, W. 1960. *The Stages of Economic Growth – A Non-Communist Manfesto.* Cambridge University Press.
Rousseau, J-J. 1968. *The Social Contract.* Penguin Books.
Rousseau, J-J. 1984. *A Discourse on Inequality.* Penguin Books.
Roxborough, I. 1979. *Theories of Underdevelopment.* London: Macmillan.
Rummenhöller, K. 1984. Ein Beitrag zur historischen Entwickling der Arazairi, einer marginalisierten ethnischen Gruppe im Department Madre de Dios/Peru *CaMak.* 4, 6-8. Berlin.
Rummenhöller, K. 1985. *Vom Kautschukboom zum Goldrausch Ila wissenschaftliche.* Reihe 3. Bonn.
Rummenhöller, K. 1987. *Tieflandindios im Goldrausch: Die Auswirkungen des Goldbooms auf die Harakmbut im Madre de Dios, Peru.* Bonn. Mundus Reihe Ethnologie, Band 12.
Rumrill, R. 1982. *Amazonia Hoy: Cronicas de Emergencia.* Serie Debate Amazonico/ Ediciones CETA y CAAAP, Iquitos.
Rumrill, R. 1992. *Narcotráfico, Biodiversidad y Amazonía en el Perú: Diagnóstico y Propuesta.* Lima: Acción Andina.
Russell, B. 1946. *A History of Western Philosophy.* London: George Allen & Unwin.
Russell, J. 1985. *Francis Bacon.* London: Thames and Hudson.
Sambo, D. 1990. Statement by the Inuit Circumpolar Conference to the Working Group of Indigenous Populations. *IWGIA Yearbook 1989.* pp.200-202.
Sambo, D. 1993. The Emerging Indigenous Human Right to Development. *IWGIA Yearbook 1992.* pp.167-189.
Sarmiento, D.F. 1883. *Conflicto y armonías de las razas en América.* Buenos Aires.
Schapera, I. 1956. *Government and Politics in Tribal Societies.* London: Watts.
Scholte, B. 1986. The Charmed Circle of Geertz' Hermeneutics. *Critique of Anthropology.* Vol. VI. No. 1 pp. 5-15. Amsterdam.
Schuurman, F. (ed.) 1993a. *New Directions in Development Theory.* London: Zed Books.
Schuurman, F. 1993b. Modernity, Post-modernity and New Social Movements. In F. Schuurman (ed.) *New Directions in Development Theory.* London: Zed Books.
Seri. 1992. *Salúd Indígena: Analisis y Propuestas para la C.N. Shintuya.* Seri Consultores de Salúd. mss. Cusco.
Shivji, I. 1989. *The Concept of Human Rights in Africa.* London: Codesria.
Simon, R. 1991. *Gramsci's Political Thought.* London: Lawrence & Wishart.
Simpson, J. 1994. *In the Forests of the Night.* London: Arrow Books.
Skar, H., 1988. *The Warm Valley People: Duality and land reform among the Quechua Indians of highland Peru.* Göteborgs Etnografiska Museum.
Slater, D. 1993 The Political Meanings of Development. In Search of New Horizons. In Shuurman, F (ed.) 1993. *New Directions in Development Theory.* pp.93-112. London: Zed Books.
Smith, A.D. 1986. *The Ethnic Origin of Nations.* Blackwell.

Smith, R.C. 1982. *The Dialectics of Domination in Peru: Native Comunities and the Myth of the Vast Amazonian Emptiness.* Cultural Survival Occasional Paper. No. 8. Cambridge Mass. Cultural Survival.

Southall, A. 1976. Nuer and Dinka are People: economy, ethnicity and logical possibility. *Man.* ns. 11 (4):463-91.

Starke, J.G. 1984. *Introduction to International Law* London: Butterworths.

Stavenhagen, R. 1988. *Derecho Indígena y Derechos Humanos en America Latina.* Mexico: El Colegio de Mexico.

Stefan, A. 1978. *The State and Society: Peru in Comparative Perspective.* Princeton University Press.

Steinzor, N. 1992. *The Web of Self-Determination: A Focus on Native Americans.* Gothenburg: Padrigu Papers.

Steward, J. 1973. *Theory of Culture Change: the Methodology of Mutilinear Evolution.* University of Illinois Press.

Stocking, G.W. 1987. *Victorian Anthropology.* New York: The Free Press.

Thomas, D.J. 1982. *Order without Government.* Illinois Studies in Anthropology No, 13. Urbana: University of Illinois Press.

Thomas, N. 1994. *Anthropology, Travel and Government.* Cambridge: Polity Press.

Thompson, J.B. 1990. *Ideology and Modern Culture.* Polity Press.

Thornberry, P. 1992. *International Law and the Rights of Minorities.* Oxford: Clarendon Paperbacks.

Todaro, M. 1989. *Economic Development in the Third World.* London: Longman.

Tonkin, E., M. McDonald & M. Chapman (eds.) *History and Ethnicity.* London: Routledge.

Torralba, A. 1979. Los Harakmbut: Nueva Situacion Misionera. *Antisuyo.* 3 Publicación de los Misiones Dominicanas en la Selva Sur-Oriente del Perú. pp. 83-141. Lima.

Touraine, A. 1978. *The Voice and the Eye: An analysis of social movements.* CUO & Editions La Maison des Sciences de L'Homme.

Trend, J.B. 1946. *Bolivar and the Independence of Spanish America.* London: Hodder and Stoughton.

Tylor, E. 1871. *Primitive Culture.* London: Murray.

United Nations. 1982. *Resolution.* 1982/34 of 7th May.

Urban, G. & J. Sherzer (eds.) 1991. *Nation States and Indians in Latin America.* Austin: University of Texas Press.

Vayussière, P., 1988. La politica indigenista del Peru Independiente. in Instituto Indigenista Interamericano and Centre D'Etudes Mexicaines et Centramericaines (eds.) *Indianidad, Etnocidio, Indigenismo en América Latina.* pp.79-85. Mexico.

Vincent, A. 1987. *Theories of the State.* Blackwell.

Vincent, R.J. 1986. *Human Rights and International Relations.* Cambridge University Press.

Wallerstein, I. 1979. *The Capitalist World Economy.* Cambridge University Press.

Wagner, R. 1981. *The Invention of Culture*. Chicago.
Wahl, L., 1985: La Federación Nativa del Madre de Dios: Informe de un Congreso. *Amazonía Indígena*. Ano 5 No. 9.
Wahl, L. 1987. *Pagans into Christians: The Political Economy of Religious Conversion among the Harakmbut of Lowland Southeastern Peru, 1902-1982*. PhD. thesis. The City University of New York.
Watts, M. 1995. 'A New Deal in Emotions': Theory and practice and the crisis of development. In J. Crush (ed.) *Power of Development*. pp.44-62. London: Routledge.
Weber, M. 1978. *Economy and Society*. Berkeley: University of California Press.
Westlake, J. 1904. *International Law*. Cambridge University Press.
Whittaker, A. 1985. Slavery and Gold in Peru. *Anti-Slavery Reporter*. Series VII, Vol.13 No.2.pp.63-70.
Williams, R. 1983. *Cobbett*. Oxford University Press.
World Commission on Environment and Development. 1986. *Our Common Future*. Oxford University Press.

INDEX

Abercrombie, T., 158
Aborigines Protection Society, 53
Acosta, J. de, 41, 45
Adams, W., 245
ADEIMAD (Asociación de Estudiantes Indígenas de Madre de Dios), xv, 21n, 22, 196
age, ix, 26, 27, 145, 150, 175, 191-3, 211
Agenda 21 *see under* United Nations Conference on Environment and Development (UNCED)
AIDESEP (Asociación Interetnica del desarrollo de la selva Peruana), 7, 79, 81, 136, 155, 225, 281
Aikman, S., xv, 4, 179, 187, 194
Alaskan Native Brotherhood, 10
Alberdi, J., 47
Alberoni, F., 12-13
Alegría, C., 50
Alexiades, M., 184n
Alvarez, J., 5, 109, 182, 267n
Amarakaeri, xv, xviii, 2, 138, 141, 142, 159
   change of name, viii, 142-5, 206
   see also Arakmbut, Harakmbut, Mashco
Amarakaeri Communal Reserve, 22, 126, 207, 209, 232, 249, 255, 270, 271, 279n, 312; *see also* communal reserve
Ametra (traditional medicine project), 183-6, 207; *see also* medicine, sickness
Amich, J., 140
Anti-Slavery International, 17n
Arakmbut, viii, xvi, xviii, 2, 5, 21, 24, 25, 64, 88, 98, 112, 137-45, 156, 158, 159, 175, 177, 199, 205, 237, 252, 292, 300, 303, 304, 310, 321
   as Peruvians, 152-9
   relations with Peruvian state, 86-9
   see also Amarakaeri, Harakmbut, Mashco
Arana, J.C., 48
Arasaeri, 3, 5, 21n, 137, 141, 226, 230
Ardener, E., 132
Arguedas, J.M., 50
Arique, T., xvi, 249
Aristotle, 39, 41, 42, 43, 64n, 200, 239n
Aron, R., 47
Asad, T., 12n
Atlantic Charter, 289
Austin, J., 46-7
authenticity, 13n, 158
ayahuasca (hallucinogen), 118, 184; *see also* shamanic practices

Bacon, F., xii
Bahuaja-Sonene National Park, 310, 312
Balandier, G., 202
barbasco, 109, 191 *see also* fishing
Barclay, F., 76
Barnett, C., 18
Barranco Chico (Arakmbut community), 6, 7, 24, 94, 95, 116, 123, 138, 180, 181n, 194, 206, 207, 222-5, 247, 249, 250, 271, 272, 281, 283, 311
Barriales, J., 141
Barth, F., 132
Barry, M., 39
Belaúnde, F. (Peruvian President), 67, 70, 76, 78, 89, 95, 238n, 257, 262

- 343 -

Index

Belgian thesis, 291
Bello, A., 46
Bender, B., 105n
Bennett, G., 14, 40, 50, 290n
Bentham, J., 46, 47, 63
Berman, H., 14, 65, 128, 161
Bidney, D., 166
Biedma, M., 140
biodiversity conservation, 163, 164; *see also* UN Convention on Biological Diversity
Blaut, J., 288
Boca Colorado, xvi, 24, 55-64, 84, 88, 89, 97, 124, 133-6, 153, 179, 197, 206, 212, 217, 222, 225, 236-8, 247, 251, 255, 260-4, 266, 270, 280, 283, 297, 300; *see also* municipality
Boca Inambari (Arakmbut community), 6, 123, 138, 194, 197, 206, 223, 224, 225, 257n, 271
Boca Pukiri (colonist settlement), 266, 276, 278
Bodin, J., 63n
Bodley, J., 319
body, 28, 145, 187, 253, 318
Body Shop, 246
Bolivar, S., 44, 66, 77
boundaries *see under* ethnicity, politics, territory
Bovo de Revello, J., 5
Brazil, 50
Brohlmann, C., 294
Brown, A., 16, 17
Brown, W., 47
Brownlie, I., 155, 156, 160, 292
Buffon, G-L., 42-3
Bull, H., 285
Burgess, H., 102n
Burgos Laws, 40
Burke, E., 18n
Burke, T., 246
Bury, J., 239n

Calderón, M (Asháninka leader), 73
Califano, M., 7n, 29, 141, 173, 180, 187
capitalism, 87, 103; *see also* market economy, neo-liberalism
Cárdenas, C., 49
Carrithers, M., 66n, 146
Cassen, R., 238
Cassese, A., 274, 275, 301
Castilla, R., (Peruvian President), 67, 77

cattle ranching, 266-7; *see also* colonisation, Shintuya
Caufield, C., 75
Central American Services, 224
Centro Amazónico de Antropología y Aplicación Práctica (CAAAP), 82
Centro Eori, 100, 111, 135, 206, 232, 257, 258, 266, 267, 279, 280
change, x, 196; *see also* development, growth
Charles V (King of Spain), 40
Chaumeil, J-P, xvii *see also* plagiarism, victim of
Chen, L., 285, 294
Chenery, 241n
Chirif, A., 101
Chittagong Hill Tracts (Bangladesh), 297
Christianity, 45, 125, 186, 189, 195, 318; *see also* missionaries, missions
citizenship, 34-5, 44, 45, 51, 52, 60, 68, 153, 158, 160, 161
see also identity, Peru, person
civil society, 44, 67, 70, 80, 84-5, 157
Claessen, J., 60
clan, ix, 26, 27, 30, 138-9, 140, 148, 149, 172, 175, 211, 319
clan names, 26, 148
    Embieri, 26
    Idnsikambo, 26
    Masenawa, 26
    Saweron, 26
    Singperi, 26, 139
    Wandigpana, 26
    Yaromba, 26, 169
    see also descent, social organisation
class, 70
Clastres, P., 202
Clay, J., 246n
Clifford, J., 166
Cobbett, W., 121
Cobo, A.M. 15, 34, 132, 275; *see also* indigenous definition, United Nations
coca, 5, 72-3, 75, 196
CODEH-PA, 83
cognatic relationships, 148; *see also* wambet
Cohen, A., 144n
Cohen, R., 132
collectivity, 154; *see also* rights
Columbus, 38, 41

- 344 -

Index

colonisation, xvi, 8, 24, 32, 36, 46, 52, 53, 87, 89, 98, 122-4, 198, 220, 239, 289, 306, 320, 323
    decolonisation, 11, 93-4, 158
    internal colonialism, 262
    colonists, 22, 82, 95, 96, 117, 123, 124, 155, 214, 222, 224, 234, 250, 259-66, 270, 276, 282, 293, 311
    Bejar, M., 267-8
    Dianda, M., 207, 278-84, 297, 299, 303, 321, 322
    López, S., 266, 278
    Pinto, 95, 96
    Sumalave, J., 95, 197, 222, 276, 277-8
    see also white people
Comaroff, J & J., 313
commercialisation *see under* market economy
communal house *see under* maloca
communal reserve, 79; *see also* Amarakaeri communal reserve
community, 321; *see also* Barranco Chico, Boca Inambari, native communities, Peruvian legislation, Puerto Luz, San José, Shintuya
compadrazgo, 133
Compañía Aurífera del Río Inambari (CARISA), 267-8
complementarity, 319; *see also* gender, spirit world
Comte, A., 47, 48, 240
Condorcet, Marquis de, 240n
Consejo Harakmbut (COHAR), 8, 157, 197, 208, 209, 210, 225 226, 233, 297, 310
contribución, 46
Conservation International, 313
cooking, 26, 27
Coordinadora de Organizaciones Indígenas de la Cuenca Amazónica (COICA), 7, 205, 281
Corry, S., 246n
Cowen, M., 240
Crantson, M., 17
Crawford, W., 48
Critescu, A., 301
cubism, xii
Cultural Survival Enterprises, 246
culture, 164-9, 227
    cultural heritage, 164, 166
    definitions, 165, 174

Friedman's three cultures, 168, 198
material culture, 173, 187
curing, ix, xiii, 25, 30, 188, 319; *see also* shamanic practices
Cusco, 7, 81, 231, 249, 259, 261, 263, 270
customary law *see under* indigenous legal systems

development, x, xix, 237, 272, 313, 317
    alternative development, 244-6
    alternatives to development, 242, 247, 251, 272
    Arakmbut development, 256, 269-271
    concept of development, 239-44
    dependency, 182, 242-4, 269
    modernisation, 240-2, 251, 265, 272
    perspectives on development, 264-6
    self-development, xviii, 235, 245, 252-254, 321,
    self-sufficiency, 245, 254, 259, 264, 268, 270, 271, 273, 320, 322
Daes, E., 21, 34, 164, 297, 298, 301, 302-3
Dahl, J., 91
death, 118, 119, 253
debt crisis, 71, 89, 243; *see also* development dependency
decolonisation *see under* colonisation
Declaration of Barbados, 51
Declaration of Cocoyoc, 245
Declarations *see under* United Nations
De Jasay, A., 66
Deloria, V., 131n
democracy, 301, 302
Denevan, W., 124
D'Entrèves, A., 64n
Descartes, R., 43
descent, 148; *see also* clan
De Soto, H., 72
De Tocqueville, A., 242
Dobyns, H., 44, 46, 76
Dodson, M., 18
Domar, E., 240
Dominicans *see under* missionaries
Donnelly, J., 16, 124, 125, 153, 160, 162
Doughty, P., 44, 46, 76

- 345 -

Dourojeanni, M., 75
Dr.Cien Gramos (vendor of gold concessions), 258, 279
dream, 29, 31, 101, 192, 308, 319
Dumont, L., 157
Dunbar Ortiz, R., 131n, 204n

Easton, D., 65
Eastwood, R., 46
Echeverría, E., 47
education, 178, 191, 193-8, 234, 269
  school, 133-4, 136-7, 171, 189-90, 260
  see also culture
Eide, A., 15
Elkington, J., 246
encomienda, 39
Engels, F., 92n
Enlightenment, 42-6, 52, 53
entertainer, 176-8, 190
Escajadillo, T., 50
Escobar, A., 238, 244, 247, 252
ethnicity, 132
European Association of Social Anthropologists (EASA), xvii
Evans-Pritchard, E., 43, 93, 102n, 130, 131n, 132, 201
evolution, 92, 130, 240, 241
exchange *see under* reciprocity
Eyreman, R., 11

Falk, R., 18, 303, 305
Falkowski, J., 14, 39, 40, 51, 203, 287, 288
Favre, H., 46
Federación Agraria de Madre de Dios (FADEMAD), 85, 88
Federación Nativa de Madre de Dios y sus Afluentes (FENAMAD), xv, 7, 21, 56, 85, 88-90, 100, 101, 111, 124, 135, 136, 157, 184n, 197, 205-9, 219, 225-6, 228-9, 230-4, 249-50, 257-8, 260, 266-8, 278, 280, 282-3, 299-300, 310-11
Ferdinand and Isabella of Spain, 40
Fernandez Distel, A., 104
fiesta, 212, 224; *see also* politics
Filmer, R., 44
fishing, 114; *see also* barbasco, production
Fitzcarrald, C., 5
Fontenelle, B., 239n
food aid, 260; *see also* development

forest, 101, 102n, 103, 118; *see also* production, spirits
formalist/substantivist debate, 316-17
Fortes, M., 93, 201
Foucault, M., 45
Franck, T., 294
Frank, A, 242
French Revolution, 64, 285n
Friede, J, 40
Friedman, J., 12n, 13n, 158, 168, 176; *see also* culture
Friends of the Earth, 246
Frideres, J., 10
Fuentes, A., 5, 82, 182, 267
Fujimori, A (Peruvian President), xvi, 67, 70, 72, 78, 79, 83, 84, 86, 89, 133, 135, 225n, 232, 237, 238n, 258, 263
Fürer-Haimendorf, C., 131n
Furtado, C, 242

Galeano, E., 41
Galtung, J., 245n
García, A. (Peruvian President), 67, 70, 78, 80, 81, 89, 260
García, P., 50, 73, 77, 101
gardens, 27, 104, 106, 108-10, 112, 191; *see also* gender, production, women
gathering, 114; *see also* gender, production, women
Geertz, C., 116
gender, ix, 26-7, 104, 110, 115, 149, 150-1, 171, 191, 192, 210; *see also* gardens, gathering, hunting, production, relationship terminology, marriage
Gerbi, A., 42, 46
Gerwith, A., 17
Giddens, A., 64n
Godelier, M., 92n
Godwin, W., 201
gold, 75, 82-4, 255, 269
  gold production, 27, 104, 182, 259
  gold rush, ix, xvi, 22, 81-6, 122, 126, 230, 256
Goldie, M., 44
González Prada, M., 49, 313
government, 235, 313, 316
  diffused government, 217-8, 223, 224, 227, 231, 234
  governance, x, 199, 202

indigenous government, 209
    in Africa, 201
    in Colombia, 203
    in North America, 204n
    minimal government, 210-14, 216, 218
    ritual, 214
    self-government, 200n, 204, 218, 220-1, 228, 233, 236, 241
    state relations, 61, 200-3
Gow, P., 182
Gramsci, A., 67
Grant Geophysical, 313; *see also* Mobil
Gray, A., 4, 14, 49, 51, 55n, 82, 83, 91, 123, 124, 125, 128, 164n, 167, 183, 197, 221, 222, 232, 238, 246n, 251n, 312
Gray, R., xv, 179
Grisel, E., 40
Grote, G., 201n
Grotius, H., 16, 42, 313
growth, 253; *see also* development, evolution
guardianship, 40
guerilla, 73
Guillen-Marroquin, J., 83

Hall, H.D., 200n
Halperin, M., 303
Hammergren, L., 69
Hanke, L., 203
Hannum, H., 292, 296n, 298
Hanson, F., 166
Harakmbut, 4, 5, 26, 94, 138, 141, 143, 303, 311; *see also* Amarakaeri, Arakmbut, Mashco
Harrod, R., 240
Hart, R., 180
Hawthorne, N., 242
health, 102, 173-4, 195, 196, 198, 234, 253
    ceremonies, 187-9
    see also Ametra, curing, shamanic practices
Hegel, F., 46, 63n, 201, 240n
Heinz, W., 40, 287n
Helberg, H., 7n, 27n, 148n
Held, D., 18n, 46, 60n, 63n, 64n, 200
Henley, P., 100n, 107
Henriksen, G., 245, 252, 271
Hettne, B., 237n, 238, 244, 245, 247
highlanders, 174, 230, 236-7, 262n; *see also* colonists

Hirsch, E., 105
history, xii, 47, 106, 126, 148n, 150, 309
Hitler, A., 288
Hobbes, T., 16, 43, 44, 63n, 237n, 241, 296
Hobsbawm, E, 158
Hocart, A., 121, 214, 216
Hoffman, J., 60, 63, 65, 89, 301, 302
holistic relationships, 106, 122, 157, 165
house, 191
household, 104, 112, 192, 210, 212, 213, 276, 309, 319
Huaypetue, 98, 123, 207, 247-51
Huallaga valley, 72, 73, 75
Huddleston, L., 42
Humboldt, A.von, 46
Hume, D., 19, 201, 214, 216, 241, 313
hunting, 26-7, 114, 115, 118, 270; *see also* production
Hvalkof, S., 183

identity, 145, 153, 154, 159, 162, 176, 227, 234, 235, 304, 309, 313, 316, 321
    Arakmbut identity, 136, 139, 147, 157, 161, 172, 173, 175, 196, 197, 198
    assimilation, 320
    self-identification, 159, 160
    two worlds, 195
    see also Arakmbut, persons, Peru
Incas, 4, 41, 64n, 119, 133, 136, 311; *see also* Manco
independence, 290, 295
Independent Commission on International Humanitarian Issues, 284
indigenous, 23
    definition, 8-9, 34, 36, 156
    legal systems, 18, 25, 28, 30-1, 53
    movement, 9-13, 50-1
    organisation, 80-1, 208-9, 223, 234
    relations with state, 54, 59, 81
indigenous peoples,
    Africa: 131, 132
    Asia, 10
    Australia, 11, 93
    North America, 10, 11
    Pacific, 10-11
    South America, 10

Index

Aguaruna, 10, 81, 88, 228
Amahuaca, 2, 230
Asháninka, 2, 73, 88, 228
Cocama, 2
Ese'eja, 2, 5, 21n, 137, 184, 226, 230
Huambisa, 10
Huitoto, 2
Iñapari, 2
Kayapó, 205
Mashco-Piro, 141, 229
Matsigenka, 2, 5, 86n, 137, 141, 174, 179, 183,216n, 226, 229, 311,
Panare, 107
Pemon, 203
Piaroa, 99
Santarosino (Quechua), 2, 230
Shipibo, 2, 81, 88, 183, 184, 185, 226, 228,230
Shuar, 10
Tukanoa, 108
Xavante, 205
Yagua, xvii
Yaminahua, 2
Yanesha, 79, 81
Yiné (Piro), 2, 140, 226, 230, 311
Yora (Nahua), 229
see also peoples, rights
informal sector, 71-2
initiation ceremony, 150, 169, 192
Inka Region, 81, 84, 232
integration, 50-2, 62, 87, 229, 230, 246, 319, 320
intellectual property rights, 105n
International Alliance of the Indigenous/Tribal Peoples of the Tropical Forest, 8, 205
International Indian Treaty Council, 10
International Labour Organisation (ILO), xviii, 14, 90, 93, 102n, 106n, 126, 128, 162, 251n
    Convention 107, 14, 15, 50, 51, 91, 128, 130
    Convention 169, 9, 14, 34, 36, 50, 106n, 127, 132, 200n, 320
International Monetary Fund (IMF), 80, 84, 238, 314
International Work Group for Indigenous Affairs (IWGIA), xv, 11, 21n, 75n, 79, 128, 204n, 272, 298n, 310, 312
Inuit Circumpolar Conference (ICC), 128
Ireyo (curer and myth-teller in San José), xvi, 169-171, 176, 177, 179, 281
Isaacs, R., 97
Isbell, B-J., 77
Ishiriwe river, 98, 106, 111, 114, 119, 172, 180, 186, 255
Iviche, A. (President of FENAMAD), 134, 208

Jackson, J., 107
jaguar, 28,
Jameson, A., 11
Jenkins, D., 97
Jipa, A., 21

Kamenka, 45, 46
Kant, E., 240n
Kaplan, J. *see under* Overing
Karene river, 95, 96, 98, 112, 197, 207, 210, 222, 224, 225n, 230, 255, 257, 259, 262, 266, 267, 277, 310-312
Kay, C., 242
Kedourie, E., 131n
Kelmm, G., 165
Kentehuari, E., xvi, 21, 22, 32, 36, 53, 277
Kickingbird, K., 295
Kingsbury, B., 9, 42, 286, 292, 299
Kipodneri, 98, 119
Kisambaeri (Amaiweri), 3, 5, 137, 141, 143, 311
knowledge, 32, 118, 172-6, 185, 191, 192, 193, 195, 308; *see also* culture, shamanic practices, women
Kroeber, A., 165

Lacaze, D., 184n
Lambery, C., xii
language, 118, 139, 171, 173, 174, 230-1
language families, 2
    Arawak, 2
    Harakmbut, 2, 137-8, 140
    Panoan, 2
    Tacana, 2, 137
Las Casas, B. de, 40-1, 42, 52, 203, 313
Lastarria, J., 47
law (Peruvian) *see under* Peruvian legislation

Index

Lawrence, T., 48
Leach, E., 26n, 131
League of Nations, 13, 287, 288,
    indigenous representation, 13-14, 288
    Mandates, 287n
    see also treaties
Lefeber, R., 294
Leguía, A. (Peruvian President), 50
Leinhardt, G., 146
Lenin. V., 65, 286, 288-9
Lewis, W., 241n
Leys, C., 244
Lindley, M., 40, 42, 48
Lloyd Thomas, D., 44
Locke, J., 16-17, 43, 44, 63n, 129n, 200, 237n, 241, 296
Lomasky, L., 16
Long, N., 243, 244n
López Albújar, E., 50
Lorimer, J., 48, 93
Lowie, R., 93
Lukes, S., 19n
Lyon, P., 5, 140
Lytle, C., 131n

Macpherson, C., 43, 44, 237n
Machiavelli, N., 64n
Madre de Dios (Eori), 2, 5, 8, 22, 98, 138, 225, 228, 231, 282, 265, 310
    population, 82-3
Maine, H., 48, 92, 93, 131n
Mair, L., 93, 130, 131, 201, 202, 216, 218
maloca (communal house), 98-9, 104, 149, 150, 181, 187, 196, 215, 223
maloca names,
    Apikmboteri, 98
    Kotsimberi, 94
    Wakutangeri, 169
Manco (Inca), 4, 103, 172
Manu National Park, 229, 230
Mariátegui, J-M, 49
market economy, 70, 125, 237, 238, 246, 270; *see also* neo-liberalism
marriage, 26, 27, 211, 212, 213, 223
Marshall, J., 48
Marshall Plan, 240
Marx, K., 49, 65, 103n, 240n
Marzal, M., 50
Mashco, viii, 140-1, 159; *see also* Amarakaeri, Arakmbut, Harakmbut

Matos Mar, J., 243
Maurtúa, V., 140
Mauss, M., 146
Mayer, D., 49
McGrane, B., 41, 45, 49, 51
McIver, R., 202, 216
medicine (western), 178, 189, 269; *see also* Ametra, curing, shamanic practices
Meek, R., 240
memory, 175
Mendoza Marsano, J., 4
Mexico, 203
Migdal, J., 62, 65, 66, 68, 69
Mill, J.S., 46, 47, 63, 129n, 130n
missionaries, 76, 82, 87, 181, 187, 193, 196, 197, 208, 219n, 227, 304
    Padre Busquets, 140
    Padre Elias, 142n
    Padre Rocamora, 140
mission, 5, 188, 220, 232, 266-8
    El Pilar (currently Shipibo community), 5, 208
    San Luis del Manu, 193
    San Miguel de Kaichihue, 94, 267n
    see also Shintuya
Mobil, 90, 101, 229, 310, 311, 313, 321, 322
Molina Enriques, A., 50
Montesinos, A. de., 40
Montesquieu, Baron de., 63n
moon, 104, 150
Moore, T., 7n, 82, 83, 140, 206, 224, 257n, 258, 261
Morales Bermúdez, F. (Peruvian President), 67, 77, 78, 89, 238n
morality, 25, 26, 32, 38; *see also* Christianity, relativity
Morgan, L.H., 48, 92-3, 130, 131n, 201, 240
Movimiento Revolucionario Tupac Amaru (MRTA), 73
Muñez, A., 247
municipality, 60n, 260; *see also* Boca Colorado
Myers, M., 295, 297
myths, xi, 26-33, 170, 176
    Aiwe and the Papa, ix, xiii, xvi, 26, 31, 32, 142, 195, 309
    Kumamin, 107, 109
    Marinke, ix, xiii, xvi, 26, 28, 101, 150, 309, 318

Wanamey, viii, xiii, xvi, 26, 94, 117, 142, 148n, 170, 172, 173, 180n, 309
mythology, viii, xii, xiii, 172, 309

name, 28, 145, 146, 172, 253
Nash, J., 12n, 102n
nation, 130-1n
native community, 6, 86; *see also* Barranco Chico, Boca Inambari, community, Peruvian legislation, Puerto Luz, San José, Shintuya
nature, 68, 116n
    natural law, 40, 42
Needham, R., 106, 214
neo-liberalism, 72, 89, 237, 238, 244; *see also* capitalism, Fujimori, market economy
Nettheim, G., 301n
New Laws, 40
Newing, H., 312
Nietzsche, F., 242
Nilsson, G., 253
Nisbet, R., 239, 240n, 241
NORAD (Norwegian Government Development Agency), 232
Nordenskjöld, E., 4
Nozick, R., 17

Ofautey-Kodjoe, W., 285n, 286, 290
O'Hanlon, M., 105n
oil, 75; *see also* Mobil
Olivera, J., 141
Olsen, J., 10
Organization of American States (OAS), 128
Ortiz, A., 102n
Osende, V., 187
'Other', the, 41, 51
Ots Cadequi, J., 39
Otzuka, L., 247-51
Overing, J., 99, 111

Pacuri, F., 83, 206, 225n, 232, 257n, 258
Pagden, A., 39, 40, 41, 43
Paine, T., 18n
Papal Bull Inter Caetera, 38-9, 40
Papal Bull Sublimis Deus, 40
Paredes Pando, O., 82
Parkin, C., 18n
Pauw, C. de, 42-3, 46
peach palm, 105, 109, 114, 191

Pennano, G., 5
peoples, x, 34, 36, 37, 159, 209, 228, 234-5, 302-5, 306, 313, 316, 317
    people versus peoples, 127, 129, 160, 161
    peoples versus populations, 35
person, 145n, 146, 149, 151, 153n, 157; *see also* identity
Peru, 285
    Amazon, 74-7
    government, 33, 34-7, 41, 49, 51, 129, 155, 238
    Indigenist Institute, 81, 204, 209, 221, 313
    individual identity as citizen, 73-4, 154, 156-7
    state, 24, 64, 66-74, 88-9, 158, 196, 292, 322
Peruvian Amazon Company, 49
Peruvian legislation
    Constitution, 67, 69, 77, 88, 79, 80, 204
    Land Law, 45, 73, 79, 80, 84, 204, 257
    Law of Native Communities, 6, 22, 23, 24, 33, 57, 61, 63, 64, 77, 78, 79, 80, 86, 87, 117, 122, 209, 210, 217, 220, 234, 249, 289, 293, 300, 322
    Mining Law, 24, 83, 84, 257, 258
    Municipal Law, 84
    see also citizenship, indigenous, territory
Pesha, M., 21n
Philip, M., 201
Pino Zambrano, V., 75
Pizarro, F., 40, 66
plagiarism, xvii *see also* Chaumeil, J-P, victim of
Plan Arakmbut (Karene), xvi, 216
Plant, Raymond, 46, 63n
Plant, Roger, 107n
politics, ix, 25, 28, 37, 199, 215, 224, 228, 308, 309
    boundaries, 220, 227, 308
    conflict resolution, 213-4
    decision-making, 199, 202, 210-13,
    encounters and meetings, 211, 212, 219, 224
    generosity, 182, 215, 308,
    leadership, 215
        community officers, 217

ohpu, 215, 216, 307
wairi, 215, 216
wantupa, 215, 216
resignation, 221, 227, 304
resistance, 214, 221, 223
see also government, Peru, Peruvian legislation, shamanic practices
political parties, 263
Pomerance, M., 302
Poole, D., 71, 72,
Pope Alejandro VI, 38, 39
Pope Paul III, 40
popular movement *see under* civil society
Posey, D., 105n, 164n
positivism, 36-7, 45-9, 52, 53,
possessive individualism, 43-4; *see also* Hobbes, Locke, Macpherson
potentiality, 120, 316-7; *see also* development, self-determination, spirit world
Prado, M (Peruvian President), 76
Prebisch R., 242
production, 26-7, 116, 122, 173, 210, 211, 269, 271, 308
property, 27, 109-110, 121, 213
Puerto Luz (Arakmbut community), 6, 7, 55-9, 133, 134, 136-8, 141, 143, 179, 190, 194, 205-7, 210, 222, 223, 225, 226, 257n, 266, 268, 271, 276-8, 281-4, 311
Puerto Maldonado, 1, 7, 74, 81, 84, 85, 119, 134-7, 153, 207, 222, 231, 233, 258, 270
Pukiri river, 94-8, 101, 106, 112, 117, 122, 222, 225, 249, 250, 255, 257, 268, 281
Pukirieri, 3, 5, 94, 137, 141

Quique, J., 96, 221, 222

race, 46-7, 132
racism, 52
Radcliffe-Brown, A.R., 26, 93
Rädda Barnen, 83
Raimondi, A., 5
Ramos, A., 12n
Ranger, T., 131n, 158
reciprocity, 27, 150, 182, 189, 223; *see also* marriage
relational pronouns, 147
relationship terminology, 26, 27, 148-9, 172

relativity, xvii, 17, 32, 53, 100, 132, 150
Rénique, G., 71, 72
requerimiento, 39
residence, ix, 26, 28; *see also* malocas, history
RESSOP (secular mission teaching network), 7
Reyna, E., 5
Ribeiro, D., 3, 100n
rights, xviii, 26n, 47, 196, 284, 314
  citizens rights, 159
  cultural rights, 171
  human rights, 12, 34, 83, 96, 135, 154, 156, 158, 233, 302, 313, 314, 315
  indigenous rights, xviii, x, xv, 12, 16-20, 18, 25, 28, 31, 33, 36, 52, 196, 198, 220, 313-19, 322
  individual rights, 43-5, 52
  justice and rights, 317, 321
  moral rights, 37, 47
  territorial rights, 125, 126
    ownership, 111, 120, 126
    possession, 110, 115-7, 126
    subsurface rights, 293
    use, 107, 109, 110, 112, 116, 126
  universal rights, 16-17, 37
  see also indigenous, peoples, territory
river, 101, 103-4, 118; *see also* barbasco, fishing, forest, spirits
road, 206, 247-52, 262, 264
Roberts, A., 42
Robertson, W., 42
Ronen, D., 286
Rorty, R., 18
Rosengren, D., 86n,
Rostow, W., 240, 254
Rousseau, J-J, 43, 44-5, 53, 63n, 129n, 200, 201, 241, 242, 313
Roxborough, I., 244n
rubber boom, 48, 75, 76, 82, 186, 228-9
Rummenhöller, K., 5, 7n, 82, 227
Rumrill, R., 72, 75
Russell, J., xii

Sachs, W., 240
Saint Augustine, 239n
Saint-Simon followers, 240
Sambo, D., 128, 272
San José (Arakmbut community), ix, xv, 1, 6, 7, 21, 22, 24, 31, 55-9, 86,

Index

90, 94-7, 108, 111, 112, 115-7, 122, 123, 133-7, 138, 141, 143, 144, 152, 169, 176, 180, 181n, 189, 190, 193, 194, 202, 205-10, 219-26, 230, 233, 236, 247-60, 266-8, 272, 276-84, 299, 311, 314, 319
Sapiteri, 3, 5, 94-8, 137, 140, 141, 181
Sarmiento, D., 47, 48
Satie, E., xi
Schapera, I, 93, 100n, 202
Scheffer, D., 303
Scholte, B., 167
school *see under* education
Schuurman, F., 244, 247
Sendero Luminoso, 67, 73
self-determination, ix, x, xviii, xix, 1, 8-9, 15, 23, 25, 31-7, 51, 53, 127, 129, 220n, 234, 235, 273-5, 284, 305-7, 316-22
    internal/external, 299-302,
    national determination theory, 286, 288
    national equality theory, 288
    origin of term, 285
    plebiscite theory, 286, 287
    territoriality, 292-5, 298
Sepúlveda, J. G. de, 40, 41, 42
Seri (traditional medicine consultants), 267
sexual relations, 26, 29-30, 150-1, 185
shamanic practices, ix, 25, 29-30, 32, 94, 118, 119, 170-1, 186, 202, 215, 308, 309, 319
    curing chants, 170, 183, 253
    wamenoka'eri (curer), 185, 186, 192, 216
    wayorokeri (dreamer), 185, 186, 192, 216
    see also Ametra, curing, medicines, sickness
Shenton, R, 240
Sherzer, J., 158
Shintuya (Arakmbut community and mission), ix, 5, 6, 7, 32, 94, 99, 100, 138, 183, 184, 186, 188, 194, 206, 207, 219n, 223, 231, 233, 304, 249, 257, 262, 266, 267, 271
Shivji, I., 298
sickness, 5, 188; *see also* Ametra, curing, medicines, shamanic practices
Simon, R., 67
Simpson, J., 72

SINAMOS, 70, 78
Skalnik, P., 60n
Skar, H., 70
Skar, S., 74
sky, 101; *see also* spirits, spirit world
Slater, D., 237n
slavery, 40, 122, 183
    natural slavery (Aristotle's theory), 39, 42
Smith, Adam, 240
Smith, Anthony, 144n
Smith, R., 76, 101
social movements, 12n
social organisation ix, 26; *see also* age, descent, gender, marriage, residence
Solórzano Pereira, J de, 39
songs, 212; *see also* shamanic practices – curing chants
sorcery, 29, 30, 185, 306
soul (nokiren), 26n, 28, 101, 119, 120, 146, 173, 227, 253, 308, 318
soul-matter, 29, 30, 102, 118, 139, 145, 306; *see also* spirits
South Africa, 93
Southall, A., 132
sovereignty, 201, 236, 295-8
Sowereri, 181
space, 149; *see also* history, maloca, residence
species, ix, 30, 118-9, 191; *see also* biodiversity, spirits, UN Convention of Biological Diversity
Spencer, H., 447, 48, 240n
spirits, 25, 29, 117, 121, 191
    beneficial spirits (ndakyorokeri), 29, 30, 118, 120
    chongpai (ayahuasca spirit), 29
    forest spirits, 103
    harmful spirits (toto), 29, 103, 174, 319
    river spirits, 32, 101, 104
    sky spirits, 101
    wachipai (otiose spirits), 29, 118
    wambetoeri (dead relatives), 119, 120
    wamawere (dispersed spirits), 29
    see also ayahuasca, potentiality, spirit world
spirit world, viii, xi, xii, xiii, xviii, xix, 28, 30, 102, 118, 120, 122, 126, 172-4, 185, 192, 197, 269, 307-9, 318, 319, 322

concentrated/dispersed, 227, 306-7
legitimacy of ownership, xviii, 119, 121
underworlds, 101
spirituality, 101, 174, 318
Stalin, J., 288-9
Starke, J., 42, 285
state, 60, 64n, 65-71, 76, 89, 237, 260-1, 294, 300
  boundaries, 158
  force and legitimacy, 63-5, 89
  government and state, 54-5
  market and state, 273
Stavenhagen R., 39, 40, 41, 46, 47, 50, 51, 128
Stefan, A., 68, 70
Steinzor, N., 17, 45
Steward, J., 131n
Stocking, G., 47
Suárez, F., 42
Suárez, N., 5
Sueyo, H., 21n, 197
sun, 150

Taka (non-Arakmbut), 99, 138
Tambopata-Candamo Reserved Zone, 310
Tambopata Reserve Society (TReeS), 310, 312
tapir, 32
Tayakome (Matsigenka community), 229, 231
territory, x, 18, 23, 24, 33, 34, 36, 37, 54, 89, 90-4, 98, 100, 120, 124, 144-5, 159, 176, 196, 228, 234-5, 246, 251, 257, 268, 271, 284, 300, 302, 306, 313, 316, 317, 321
  collective nature, 115, 122
  earth, 101-2, 125
  land, 102-4, 117, 125
  landscape, 104-6, 118, 126,
  terra nullius, 76-8
  see also rights
Thomas, D., 203
Thomas, N., 313
Thompson, J., 165n, 168n
Thornberry, P., 14, 18, 162, 163, 287n, 288n, 291
Tijé, F., 21n
Tijé, M., 21n
time, 149-50, 252-3; *see also* development, history, maloca, space

tobacco, 183, 196
Todaro, M., 240, 241n, 244n
Tonkin, E., 132
Torralba, A., 6, 140, 141
Touraine, A., 12n
Toyeri, 3, 5, 137, 141, 186
treaties, 287n, 294-5, 299n
Treaty Six (Canada), 295
Trend, J., 44, 45
Tres Islas (Shipibo community), 184
triadic structure, xi
tribe, 130-1n
trusteeship, 290
Turgot, Baron, 240
Tylor, E., 165,

Ucayali (region of Peru), 124
United Nations, xiv, xviii, 11, 14, 16, 17n, 18n, 21, 23, 24, 38, 49, 53, 91, 93, 106n, 126, 127, 128, 204n, 241, 285, 289, 290-2, 295, 298, 314
  Commission on Human Rights, xiv, 33, 34, 35, 129, 200, 291
  Conference on Environment and Development (UNCED – Agenda 21), 34, 36, 128, 163, 178
  Convention on Biological Diversity (CBD), 163, 164, 178, 312
  Covenant on Civil and Political Rights, 162-3, 307
  Declaration on Friendly Relations, 290-1, 297
  Declaration on the Right to Development, 272
  Decolonisation Committee, 299
  Draft Declaration on the Rights of Indigenous Peoples, xiv, 15, 24, 34, 35, 91, 126, 128, 129, 162, 163, 200, 220, 274, 291, 307, 314
  Indigenous Peoples, 13-15, 128
  NGO Conferences of 1977, & 1981, 10, 15, 275
  Subcommission on the Prevention of Discrimination and the Protection of Minorities, xiv, 15, 34, 275
  Working Group on Indigenous Populations, xiv, 9, 15, 20, 21,

34, 36, 66, 87, 90, 128, 138, 164, 274, 275, 291, 299, 301
UNESCO, 298n
USA, 10
Urban, G., 158
Utilitarians, 46-7

Valcarcel, L., 50
Vayussière, P., 46
Velasco, A (Peruvian President), 67, 70, 77, 89, 204, 237, 238n
Villa Santiago (Arasaeri community), 21n
Vincent, A., 17, 60n, 64n, 200, 202
Vincent, R., 17
Vitoria, F., 40, 41, 42, 45, 52, 203, 313

Wachipaeri, 5, 104, 137, 138, 140, 141, 142, 181, 230
Wagner, R., 167, 168
Wahl, L., 4, 7n, 82, 132, 180, 182, 225, 267
Wallerstein, I., 243
Walter, (Chino), 178-9
wambet (alliance-arranging category), 26, 27, 139, 148, 149, 211; *see also* cognatic relations
Wandakwe river, 106, 108, 111
Wandakweri Arakmbut, 98, 119, 169, 180
Watts, M., 239, 240
Weber, M., 65
Westlake, J., 48, 93
white-lipped peccary, 139-40
white people (Amiko), xi, 25, 174, 182, 195, 196, 198, 269, 309
  technology, 178-183
Whittaker, A., 83
Willemsen Diaz, A., 15
Williams, R., 121
Wilson, R., 10
Wilson, Woodrow, 287
Wise, M-R, 3
women, 211, 216; *see also* gender
woodpecker (mbegnko), 4, 118, 172
World Bank, 71, 238
World Commission on Environment and Development (Bruntland Commission), 245
World Council of Indigenous Peoples (WCIP), 10
world systems, 243

World War I, 287
World War II, 289

Yomibato, 229

Zieck, M., 294
Zulen, P., 49